Gary Spence

PROFESSIONAL BAKING

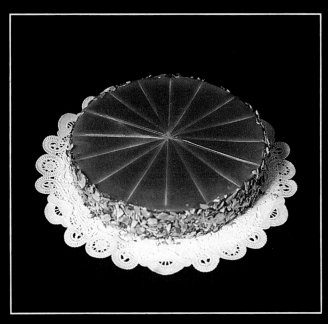

Dobos torte *(see page 238)*

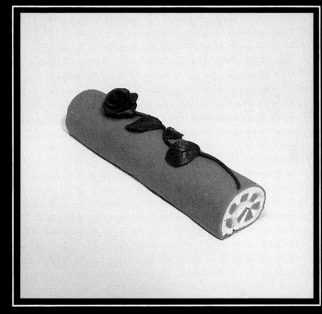

Harlequin roll *(see page 241)*

Fruit torte *(see page 237)*

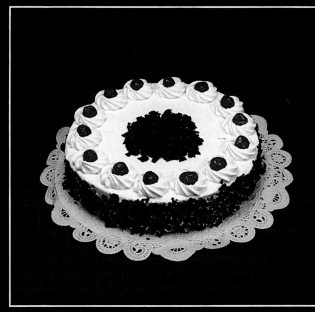

Black forest torte *(see page 236)*

Classic American birthday cake *(see page 234)*

Chocolate ganache torte *(see page 239)*

Pear almond tart *(see page 146)*

Bavarian cream torte *(see page 240)*

PROFESSIONAL BAKING

Wayne Gisslen

John Wiley & Sons
New York   Chichester   Brisbane   Toronto   Singapore

Library of Congress Cataloging in Publication Data:

Gisslen, Wayne, 1946–
    Professional baking.

    Includes index.
    1. Baking.   I. Title.
TX763.G47   1985b   664′.752   84-26988
ISBN 0-471-88668-8
ISBN 0-471-81444-X(pbk)

Printed in the United States of America

10 9 8 7 6 5 4

THIS BOOK IS DEDICATED TO MY PARENTS

PREFACE

The purpose of this book is to teach the fundamental principles and procedures for preparing baked goods, pastries, and desserts. With its attention to both theory and practice, it is designed as a primary text for use in colleges and vocational–technical schools, for baking courses within broader food service curricula, and for on-the-job training programs. It will also be valuable as a manual and handbook for cooks and bakers.

The methods and procedures covered in this book are primarily those of small bakeshops and food service organizations. The emphasis is on producing high-quality, handcrafted items. Development of manual skills is stressed. Such skills are a valuable asset even to those students who may eventually move on to more industrialized, automated production, as found in large commercial bakeries.

Bakeshops, restaurants, hotels, and institutional facilities that offer their customers high-quality, home-made baked goods and desserts have a distinct advantage over their competition. Premium-quality items draw repeat customers and contribute to the total profitability of an operation. In a restaurant, for example, the dinner rolls or bread may be the first foods a customer tastes, and the dessert puts the finishing touch on the meal. Thus, the impressions they create are very important. For this reason, a restaurant may choose to do its own baking rather than purchase such goods from an outside source, so that it can put its own distinctive stamp of quality on these parts of the meal.

In order to produce baked goods that will set an operation apart from the run-of-the-mill, careful attention must be paid to the selection of ingredients, to proper mixing and baking techniques, to careful makeup and assembly, and to the decoration and presentation of the finished goods. The goal of this book is to provide students with a solid theoretical and practical foundation in quality baking practices, so that, after sufficient practice and experience, their performance will meet these requirements.

The focus of this text is twofold: understanding and performing. To be successful in their careers, students must master a set of marketable skills. That is, they must be able to perform and produce. Thus, a major portion of the text is devoted to step-by-step procedures and production techniques. Makeup methods are explained and illustrated. A broad range of recipes and formulas reinforce the basic techniques.

At the same time, the text's practical material is supported by a systematic presentation of basic theory and ingredient information. In other words, students learn not only what techniques work but why they work.

THE ORGANIZATION OF THE TEXT

Two factors have strongly influenced the arrangement and organization of this book. The first is the dual emphasis already mentioned—the emphasis on both understanding and performing. It is not enough merely to present students with a collection of recipes. Nor is it enough to give them only a summary of baking theory and principles. They must be presented together, and the connections between them must be clear. Thus, when students practice preparing specific items, their study of theory helps them to understand what they are doing, why they are doing it, and how to get the best results. At the same time, each recipe they prepare helps to reinforce their understanding of the basic principles so that knowledge builds upon knowledge.

The second factor is that most of a baker's activities fall naturally into two categories: (1) mixing, baking, and/or cooking doughs, batters, fillings, creams, icings, and so on; (2) assembling these elements (for example, baked cake layers, fillings, and icings) into finished pieces. The first category of tasks requires careful selection of ingredients, accurate measurements, and close attention to mixing and baking procedures. Naturally, most of the detailed guidelines and procedures in this book are devoted to these kinds of tasks. The second category, assembly of pre-prepared components, is not so much a matter of scientific accuracy as it is of manual skills and artistic abilities.

This division of tasks is, of course, so well known to the practicing baker that it is usually taken for granted. Consequently, it is often neglected in written materials. As far as possible, the arrangement of subjects in this text reflects the working practices of bakeshops and kitchens. In a typical facility, operations such as mixing pie doughs, cooking fillings, preparing icings, and mixing and baking cake layers are done separately and in advance. Then, depending on demand, finished products can be quickly assembled. In this book, procedures for mixing and baking cakes, for example, are discussed separately from the procedures for assembling, icing, and decorating them. These are very different kinds of techniques, and it is helpful for students to approach them in a realistic context. Similarly, basic creams and icings are fundamental elements required for making a wide range of pastries, cakes, and other desserts; hence, they are treated fairly early in the text.

Although the arrangement of chapters represents a logical grouping of products and procedures, it is not intended to dictate the order in which each instructor should teach the units. Every curriculum has different requirements and constraints, so that the sequence of instruction varies from school to school and instructor to instructor. The arrangement of material in this text is designed to encourage maximum flexibility. Of course, baking techniques are highly interdependent; frequent cross-references help the students understand these connections.

An important element in the text is the participation of the instructor, whose ideas and professional experience are invaluable. There is no substitute for firsthand seeing and doing, under the guidance and supervision of experienced instructors. Baking is an art as much as a skill, and there are many points on which bakers and pastry chefs will differ in their preferences. The text frequently explains possible variations in theory and procedure, and students are encouraged to consult the instructor for the techniques he or she prefers. Throughout the book, the instructor's input is encouraged. Exposure to a variety of formulas and techniques can only enrich the students' education and enhance the flexibility of their skills.

The text is designed for readability and practicality. Discussions of baking theory are presented in easy-to-read, point-by-point explanations. Techniques and makeup methods are detailed in concise yet complete step-by-step procedures. The format emphasizes and highlights key points in bold type, italics, and numbered sequences, so that basic information can be located and reviewed at a glance.

THE RECIPES

Approximately 400 formulas and recipes are included for the most popular breads, cakes, pastries, and desserts. These recipes are not selected at random, merely for the sake of having recipes in the book. Rather they are carefully chosen and developed to teach and reinforce the techniques the students are learning, and to strengthen their understanding of basic principles. The goal is that the students will be able to understand and use not only the formulas in this book but any formula they may encounter.

The recipes in this book are instructional recipes. That is, their purpose is not merely to give directions for producing baked goods, but to provide an opportunity to practice, with specific ingredients, the general principles being studied. Directions within recipes are often abbreviated. For example, instead of spelling out the straight-dough method for breads in detail for each dough mixed in this way, the student is instead referred to the preceding discussion of the procedure. By making it necessary to think and review, the students derive a stronger learning experience from their lab work.

Many recipes are followed by variations. These are actually whole recipes, given in very abbreviated terms. This encourages students to see the similarities and differences among preparations. For example, there seems little point in giving a recipe for cream pie filling in the pie chapter, a recipe for custard filling for éclairs and napoleons in a pastry chapter, and separate recipes for each flavor of cream pudding in a pudding chapter, and never point out that these are all basically the same preparation. Skill as a baker depends on understanding and being able to exercise judgment, not just on following recipes. The ability to exercise judgment is essential in all branches of cookery, but especially in baking, where the smallest variation in procedures can produce significant changes in the baked product. The recipes in this text will help students develop judgment by requiring them to think about the relationships between general procedures and specific products.

Students are encouraged to study Chapter 1 before actually proceeding with any of the recipes. The first section of Chapter 1 explains the principles of measurement, the various formats used for the recipes in this book, the techniques for converting yield, and the usage of U.S. and metric measurements and baker's percentages.

ACKNOWLEDGMENTS

I wish to thank the many individuals who have contributed their thoughts and expertise to help make this book more useful and accurate. I am especially grateful to the following professionals who reviewed the manuscript and offered their criticism and suggestions: John R. Farris, Lansing Community College, Lansing, Michigan; Robert J. Galloway, Dunwoody Industrial Institute, Minneapolis, Minnesota; Jean Hassell, Youngstown State University, Youngstown, Ohio; Iris A. Helveston, State Department of Education, Tallahassee, Florida; Mike Jung, Hennepin Technical Centers, North Campus, Brooklyn Park, Minnesota; Fred Le-Meisz, St. Petersburg Vocational Technical Institute, St. Petersburg, Florida; Valeria S. Mason, State Department of Education, Gainesville, Florida; Philip Panzarino, New York City Technical College, Brooklyn, New York; Richard Petrello, Withlacoochee Vocational-Technical Center, Inverness, Florida; Patrick Sweeney, Johnson County Community College, Overland Park, Kansas; F. H. Waskey, University of Houston, Houston, Texas; J. William White, Pinellas County School System, St. Petersburg, Florida; and Ronald Zabkiewicz, South Technical Education Center, Boynton Beach, Florida.

Thanks are also due to Jim Smith for his fine photography, to Steve Jenkins for his excellent drawings, to Emanuel Darmanin and the staff of Vallette Pastry Corporation for providing some masterfully decorated cakes for this book's illustrations, to my wife Mary Ellen Griffin for her sharp, critical judgment and her moral support, and to my editor Judy Joseph and the rest of the staff at John Wiley for their creativity, patience, and hard work.

TABLE OF CONTENTS

RECIPE TABLE OF CONTENTS

PROFESSIONAL BAKING

CHAPTER 1

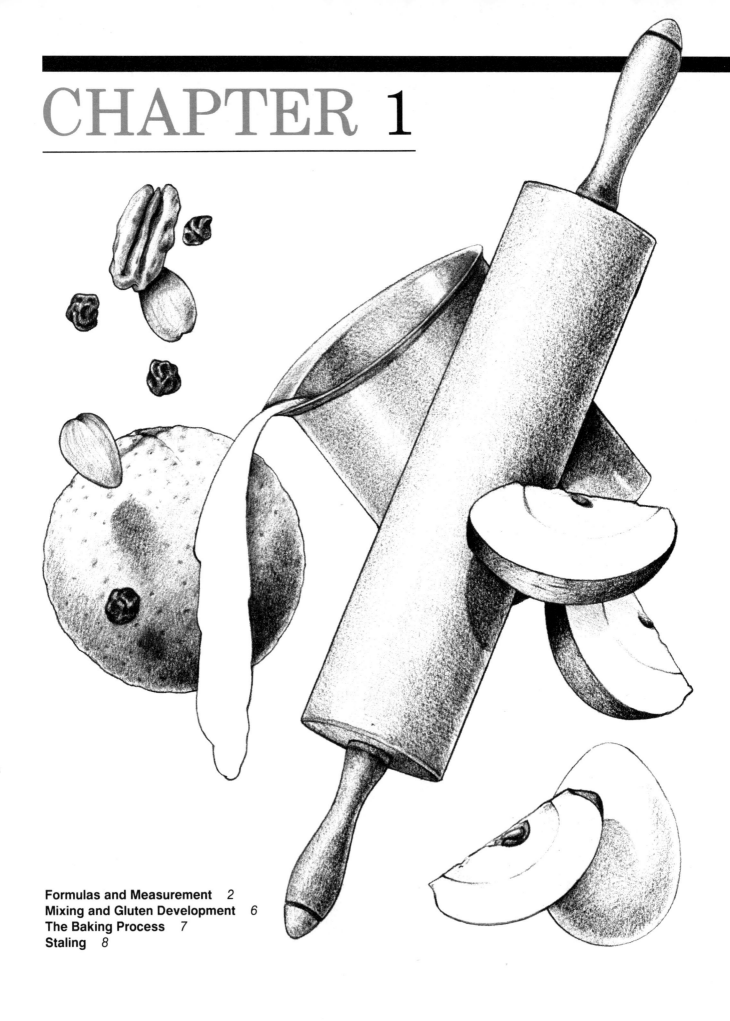

BASIC PRINCIPLES

After studying this chapter, you should be able to:
1. Explain the importance of weighing baking ingredients.
2. Use a baker's balance scale.
3. Use formulas based on baker's percentages.
4. Explain the factors that control the development of gluten in baked products.
5. Explain the changes that take place in a dough or batter as it bakes.
6. Prevent or retard the staling of baked items.

 hen you consider that most bakery products are made of the same few ingredients—flour, shortening, sugar, eggs, water or milk, and leavenings—then you should have no difficulty understanding the importance of accuracy in the bakeshop, since slight variations in proportions or procedures can mean great differences in the final product.

In this chapter you are introduced to bakeshop production through a discussion of the kinds of measurements and mathematical calculations necessary for baking and of the basic processes common to nearly all baked goods.

FORMULAS AND MEASUREMENT

Bakers generally talk about "formulas" rather than "recipes." If this sounds to you more like a chemistry lab than a food production facility, it is with good reason. The bakeshop is very much like a chemistry laboratory both in the scientific accuracy of the procedures and in the complex reactions that take place during mixing and baking.

Measurement

Ingredients are almost always weighed in the bakeshop, rather than measured by volume because measurement by weight is more accurate. Accuracy of measurement, as we have said, is essential in the bakeshop. Unlike homemakers' recipes, a professional baker's formula will not call for 6 cups of flour, for example.

To demonstrate to yourself the importance of weighing rather than measuring by volume, measure a cup of flour in two ways: a) Sift some flour and lightly spoon it into a dry measure. Level the top and weigh the flour. b) Scoop up some unsifted flour into the same measure and pack it lightly. Level the top and weigh the flour. Note the difference. No wonder home recipes can be so inconsistent!

The baker's term for weighing out ingredients is *scaling*.

The following ingredients, and only these ingredients, may sometimes be measured by volume, at the ratio of *one pint per pound* or *one liter per kilogram*:

Water

Milk

Eggs

Volume measure is often used when scaling water for small or medium-sized batches of bread. Results are generally good. However, whenever accuracy is critical, it is better to weigh. This is because a pint of water actually weighs slightly more than a pound, or approximately 16.7 ounces. (This figure varies with the temperature of the water.)

For convenience, volume measures of liquids are frequently used when products other than baked flour goods — such as sauces, syrups, puddings, and custards — are being made.

Units of Measure

The system of measurement used in the United States is very complicated. Even though we have used the system all our lives, we still sometimes have trouble remembering things like how many fluid ounces are in a quart or how many feet in a mile.

Table 1.1 lists equivalents among the units of measure used in the bakeshop and kitchen. You should memorize these thoroughly, so you don't have to lose time making simple calculations. Table 1.2 lists the abbreviations used in this book.

TABLE 1.1 **Units of Measure — U.S. System**

Weight	
1 pound	= 16 ounces
Volume	
1 gallon	= 4 quarts
1 quart	= 2 pints
	or
	4 cups
	or
	32 (fluid) ounces
1 pint	= 2 cups
	or
	16 (fluid) ounces
1 cup	= 8 (fluid) ounces
1 (fluid) ounce	= 2 tablespoons
1 tablespoon	= 3 teaspoons
Length	
1 foot	= 12 inches

Note: One fluid ounce (often simply called "ounce") of water weighs one ounce. One pint of water weighs approximately one pound.

TABLE 1.2 **Abbreviations of U.S. Units of Measure Used in This Book**

Pound	lb
Ounce	oz
Gallon	gal
Quart	qt
Pint	pt
Fluid ounce	fl oz
Tablespoon	tbsp
Teaspoon	tsp
Inch	in

The Metric System

The United States is the only major country that uses the complex system of measurement we have just described. Other countries use a much simpler system called the metric system. Someday we will be using the metric system in our bakeshops and kitchens, so it is important for us to become familiar with it.

Basic units

In the metric system, there is one basic unit for each type of measurement:

The *gram* is the basic unit of weight.

The *liter* is the basic unit of volume.

The *meter* is the basic unit of length.

The *degree Celsius* is the basic unit of temperature.

Larger or smaller units are simply made by multiplying or dividing by 10, 100, 1000, and so on. These divisions are expressed by *prefixes*. The ones you will need to know are:

kilo = 1000

deci = 1/10 or 0.1

centi = 1/100 or 0.01

milli = 1/1000 or 0.001

Once you know these basic units, there is no longer any need for complicated tables such as Table 1.1. Table 1.3 summarizes the metric units you will need to know in the bakeshop.

Converting to metric

Most people think that the metric system is much harder to learn than it really is. This is because they think about metric units in terms of U.S. units. They read that there are 28.35 grams in an ounce, and they are immediately convinced that they will never be able to learn metrics.

Do not worry about being able to convert U.S. units into metric units and vice versa. This is a very important point to remember, especially if you think that the metric system might be hard to learn.

The reason for this is very simple. You will usually be working in either one system or the other. You will rarely, if ever, have to convert from one to the other. (An exception might be if you have equipment based on one system, and you want to use a formula written in the other.) Many people today own imported cars and repair them with metric tools, without ever worrying about how many millimeters are in an inch. Similarly, when American bakeshops and kitchens change to the metric system, you will use scales that measure in grams and kilograms, volume measures that measure in liters and deciliters, and thermometers that measure in degrees Celsius. And you will use formulas that indicate these units. You will not have to worry about how many grams are in an ounce. All you will have to remember is the information in Table 1.3.

To become accustomed to working in metric units, it is helpful to have a feel for how large the units are. The following rough equivalents may be used to help you visualize metric units. They are not exact conversion factors. (When you need exact conversion factors, see Appendix One.)

A *kilogram* is slightly more than 2 pounds.

A *gram* is about 1/30 ounce. A half teaspoon of flour weighs a little less than a gram.

A *liter* is slightly more than a quart.

A *deciliter* is slightly less than a half cup.

A *centiliter* is about 2 teaspoons.

TABLE 1.3 **Metric Units**

Basic units

Quantity	Unit	Abbreviation
Weight	gram	g
Volume	liter	l
Length	meter	m
Temperature	degree Celsius	° C

Divisions and multiples

Prefix/Example	Meaning	Abbreviation
kilo-	1000	k
kilogram	1000 grams	kg
deci-	1/10	d
deciliter	0.1 liter	dl
centi-	1/100	c
centimeter	0.01 meter	cm
milli-	1/1000	m
millimeter	0.001 meter	mm

A *meter* is slightly more than 3 feet.

A *centimeter* is about ⅜ inch.

0° C is the freezing point of water (32° F).

100° C is the boiling point of water (212° F).

An increase or decrease of *one degree Celsius* is equivalent to about 2 degrees Fahrenheit.

Metric recipes

American industry will no doubt completely adopt the metric system someday. Many recipe writers are already eager to get a head start and are printing metric equivalents. As a result, you will see recipes calling for 454 grams of flour, 28.35 grams of butter, or a baking temperature of 191° C. No wonder people are afraid of the metric system!

Kitchens in metric countries do not work with such impractical numbers, any more than we normally use figures like 1 lb 1¼ oz flour, 2.19 oz butter, or a baking temperature of 348° F. That would defeat the whole purpose of the metric system, which is to be simple and practical. If you have a chance to look at a French cookbook, you will see nice, round numbers like 1 kg, 200 g, and 4 dl.

The metric measures in the formulas in this book are NOT equivalent to the U.S. measures given alongside them. You should think of the metric portion of the formulas as separate recipes with yields that are close to but not the same as the yields of the U.S. recipes. To have given exact equivalents would have required using awkward, impractical numbers. If you have metric equipment, use the metric units, and if you have U.S equipment, use the U.S. units. You should rarely have to worry about converting between the two.

Procedure for Using a Baker's Balance Scale

The principle of using a baker's scale is very simple: The scale must balance before setting the weights, and it must balance again after scaling. The following procedure applies to the commonly used type of scale shown in Figure 1.1.

1. Set the scale scoop or other container on the left side of the scale.

2. Balance the scale by placing counterweights on the right side and/or by adjusting the ounce weight on the horizontal bar.

3. Set the scale for the desired weight by placing weights on the right side and/or by moving the ounce weight.

   For example, to set the scale for 1 lb 8 oz, place a 1 pound weight on the right side, and move the ounce

FIGURE 1.1 A baker's balance scale.

weight to the right 8 ounces. If the ounce weight is already over 8 ounces, so that you cannot move it another 8, add 2 pounds to the right side of the scale, and subtract 8 ounces by moving the ounce weight 8 places to the left. The result is still 1 lb 8 oz.

4. Add the ingredient being scaled to the left side until the scale balances.

A good scale should be accurate to a quarter ounce (0.25 oz) or, if metric, to 5 grams. Dry ingredients weighing less than a quarter ounce can be scaled by physically dividing larger quantities into equal portions. For example, to scale one-sixteenth ounce (0.06 oz), first weigh out one-quarter ounce, then divide this into four equal piles using a small knife.

When very small quantities of items such as spices are required in formulas in this book, an approximate volume equivalent (usually in fractions of a teaspoon) are also included. However, remember that careful weighing on a good scale is more accurate. Approximate volume equivalents of selected ingredients are given in Appendix 3.

British bakers have a convenient method for measuring baking powder when small quantities are needed. They use a mixture called *scone flour*. To make a pound of scone flour, combine 15 ounces of flour and 1 ounce of baking powder; sift together three times. One ounce (one-sixteenth pound) of scone flour thus contains one-sixteenth ounce (0.06 oz) baking powder. For each sixteenth ounce of baking powder you need in a formula, substitute one ounce of scone flour for one ounce of the flour called for in the formula.

In order to make formula conversions and calculations easier, any fractions of ounces that appear in the ingredient tables of the formulas in this book are written as decimals. Thus, 1½ oz is written as 1.5 oz, and ¼ oz is written as 0.25 oz. For those who have trouble with decimals, a list of decimal equivalents is included in Appendix 2.

Baker's Percentages

Bakers use a simple but versatile system of percentages for expressing their formulas. Baker's percentages indicate the quantities of each item that would be required if 100 pounds of flour were used.

To put it differently, the percentage of each ingredient is its total weight divided by the weight of the flour, multiplied by 100%, or:

$$\frac{\text{total weight of ingredient}}{\text{total weight of flour}} \times 100\% = \% \text{ of ingredient}$$

Thus, flour is always 100%. If two kinds of flour are used, their total is 100%. Any ingredient that weighs the same as the flour is also given as 100%. The cake formula ingredients listed at the bottom of the page illustrate how these percentages are used. Check the figures with the above equation to make sure you understand them.

The advantages of using baker's percentages is that the formula is easily adapted for any yield, and single ingredients may be varied and other ingredients added without changing the whole formulation. For example, you can add raisins to a muffin mix formula, and the percentages of all the other ingredients can stay the same.

Procedure for Calculating the Weight of an Ingredient, When the Weight of Flour Is Known

1. Change the ingredient percentage to decimal form by moving the decimal point two places to the left.

2. Multiply the weight of the flour by this decimal figure to get the weight of the ingredient.

   Example: A formula calls for 20% sugar and you are using 10 pounds of flour. How much sugar do you need?

   20% = 0.20

   10 lb × 0.20 = 2 lb sugar

Note: In the U.S. system, weights must normally be expressed all in one unit, either ounces or pounds, in order for the calculations to work. Unless quantities are very large, it is usually easiest to express weights in ounces.

Example: 50% of 1 lb 8 oz = 0.50 × 24 oz = 12 oz

Procedure for Converting a Formula to a New Yield

1. Change the total percentage to decimal form by moving the decimal point two places to the left.

2. Divide the desired yield by this decimal figure to get the weight of flour.

3. If necessary, round off this number to the next highest figure. This will allow for losses in mixing, makeup, and panning, and it will make calculations easier.

4. Use the weight of flour and remaining ingredient percentages to calculate the weights of the other ingredients, as in the previous procedure.

   Example: In the sample cake formula above, how much flour is needed if you require 6 pounds of cake batter?

   377.5% = 3.775

   6 lb ÷ 3.775 = 96 oz ÷ 3.775 = 25.43 oz

   or, rounded off, 26 oz (1 lb 10 oz)

Clearly, a percentage system based on the weight of flour can be used only when flour is a major ingredient, as in breads, cakes, and cookies. However, this principle can be used in other formulas as well, by selecting a major ingredient and establishing it as 100%. In this book, *whenever an ingredient other than flour is used as the base of 100%, this fact is indicated at the top of the*

Ingredients	U.S. Weight	Metric Weight	%
cake flour	5 lb	2500 g	100
sugar	5 lb	2500 g	100
baking powder	4 oz	125 g	5
salt	2 oz	63 g	2.5
emulsified shortening	2 lb 8 oz	1250 g	50
skim milk	3 lb	1500 g	60
egg whites	3 lb	1500 g	60
Yield:	18 lb 14 oz	9438 g	377.5

formula above the percentage column. See, for example, the formulas for almond filling on p. 126. These recipes indicate "almond paste at 100%," and the weights of the sugar, eggs, and other ingredients are expressed as percentages of the weight of the almond paste. (In some of the formulas in this book, especially those without a predominant ingredient, percentages are not included.)

Formula Yields

Yields for the formulas in this book are indicated in one of two ways. In most cases, the yields are given as a total of the ingredient quantities. For example, in the sample formula on page 5, the yield tells us how much cake batter the formula makes. This is the figure we need to know for the purpose of scaling the batter into pans. The actual weight of baked cake will vary, depending on pan size and shape, oven temperature, and so on.

Other formulas of this type, in which the yield is the total weight of the ingredients, include formulas for bread doughs, coffee cake fillings, pastry doughs, and cookie doughs.

On the other hand, in some formulas the yield is not the same as the total weight of ingredients. For example, see the recipe for French buttercream, p. 126. When the sugar and water are boiled to make a syrup, about half of the water evaporates. Thus, the actual yield is less than the total weight of the ingredients.

In this book, when the yield is not the same as the total weight of the ingredients, the yield is indicated above the ingredients list rather than below it.

Also, please note that all yields, including percentage totals, are rounded off to the next lower whole number. This eliminates insignificant fractions and makes reading easier.

Selection of Ingredients

In addition to measuring, there is another basic rule of accuracy in the bakeshop: *Use the exact ingredients specified.*

As you will learn in the next chapter, different flours, shortenings, and other ingredients do not function alike. Baker's formulas are balanced for specific ingredients. For example, do not substitute bread flour for pastry flour, or regular shortening for emulsified shortening. They won't work the same way.

Occasionally a substitution may be made, such as active dry yeast for compressed yeast (see p. 23), but not without adjusting the quantities and rebalancing the formula.

MIXING AND GLUTEN DEVELOPMENT

Gluten is a substance made up of proteins present in wheat flour; it gives structure and strength to baked goods.

In order for gluten to be developed, the proteins must first absorb water. Then, as the dough or batter is mixed or kneaded, the gluten forms long, elastic strands. As the dough or batter is leavened, these strands capture the gases in tiny pockets or cells, and we say the product "rises."

When proteins are heated, they coagulate. This means they become firm or solidify. You are familiar with this process in the case of eggs, which are liquid when raw but firm when cooked.

This process is also important in baking. When dough or batter is baked, the gluten, like all proteins, coagulates or solidifies and gives structure to the product.

Controlling Gluten

Flour is mostly starch, as you know, but it is the protein or gluten content, not the starch, that concerns the baker most. Gluten proteins are needed to give structure to baked goods. The baker must be able to control the gluten, however. For example, we want French bread to be firm and chewy, which requires much gluten. On the other hand, we want cakes to be tender, which means we want very little gluten development.

Ingredient proportions and mixing methods are determined in part by how they affect the development of gluten. The baker has several methods for adjusting gluten development:

1. *Selection of flours*

   Wheat flours are classified as *strong* or *weak,* depending on their protein content.

   Strong flours come from *hard wheat* and have a high protein content.

   Weak flours come from *soft wheat* and have a low protein content.

   Thus we use strong flours for breads and weak flours for cakes. (The protein content of flours is discussed in greater detail in the next chapter.)

   Only wheat flour will develop enough gluten to make bread. To make bread from rye or other grains, the formula must be balanced with some high-gluten flour, or the bread will be heavy.

2. *Shortening*

Any fat used in baking is called a shortening because it shortens gluten strands. It does this by surrounding the particles and lubricating them so they do not stick together. Thus, *fats are tenderizers.* A cookie or pastry that is very crumbly, due to high fat content and little gluten development, is said to be "short."

You can see why French bread has little or no fat, while cakes contain a great deal.

3. *Liquid*

Since gluten proteins must absorb water before they can be developed, the amount of water in a formula can affect toughness or tenderness. Pie crusts and crisp cookies, for instance, are made with very little liquid, in order to keep them tender.

4. *Mixing methods*

In general, the more a dough or batter is mixed, the more the gluten develops. Thus, bread doughs are mixed or kneaded for a long time to develop the gluten. Pie crusts, muffins, and other products that must be tender are mixed for a short time.

It is possible to overmix bread dough, however. Gluten strands will stretch only so far. They will break if the dough is overmixed.

THE BAKING PROCESS

The changes undergone by a dough or batter as it bakes are basically the same in all baked products, from breads to cookies and cakes. You should know what these changes are so that you can learn how to control them.

The stages in the baking process are as follows:

1. *Formation and expansion of gases*

The gases primarily responsible for leavening baked goods are *carbon dioxide,* which is released by the action of yeast and by baking powder and baking soda; *air,* which is incorporated into doughs and batters during mixing; and *steam,* which is formed during baking.

Some gases — such as carbon dioxide in proofed bread dough and air in sponge cake batters — are already present in the dough. As they are heated, the gases expand and leaven the product.

Some gases are not formed until heat is applied. Yeast and baking powder form gases rapidly when first placed in the oven. Steam is also formed as the moisture of the dough is heated.

Leavening agents are discussed in greater detail in the next chapter.

2. *Trapping of the gases in air cells*

As the gases are formed and expand, they are trapped in a stretchable network formed by the proteins in the dough. These proteins are primarily gluten and sometimes egg protein.

Without gluten or egg protein, most of the gases would escape, and the product would be poorly leavened. Breads without enough gluten are heavy.

3. *Gelatinization of starches*

The starches absorb moisture, expand, and become firmer. This contributes to structure. Gelatinization of starches begins at about 150° F (65° C).

4. *Coagulation of proteins*

Like all proteins, gluten and egg proteins coagulate or solidify when they reach high enough temperatures. This process gives most of the structure to baked goods. Coagulation begins when the temperature of the dough reaches about 165° F (74° C).

Correct baking temperature is very important. If it is too high, coagulation will start too soon, before the expansion of gases has reached its peak. The resulting product will have poor volume or a split crust. If the temperature is too low, the proteins will not coagulate soon enough, and the product may collapse.

5. *Evaporation of some of the water*

This takes place throughout the baking process. If a baked product of a specific weight is required, allowance must be made for moisture loss when scaling the dough. For example, to get a 1-pound loaf of baked bread, it is necessary to scale about 18 ounces of dough.

6. *Melting of shortenings*

Different shortenings melt and release trapped gases at different temperatures, so the proper shortening should be selected for each product.

7. *Crust formation and browning*

A crust is formed as water evaporates from the surface and leaves it dry. Browning occurs when sugars caramelize and starches and sugars undergo certain chemical changes caused by heat. This contributes to flavor. Milk, sugar, and egg increase browning.

STALING

Staling is the change in texture and aroma of baked goods due to a change of structure and a loss of moisture by the starch granules. Stale baked goods have lost their "fresh baked" aroma and are firmer, drier, and more crumbly than fresh products. Prevention of staling is a major concern of the baker, because most baked goods lose quality rapidly.

Staling begins almost as soon as the baked items are taken from the oven. There are apparently two factors in staling. The first is loss of moisture or drying. This is apparent, for example, when a slice of fresh bread is left exposed to air. It soon becomes dry to the touch.

The second factor is a chemical change in the structure of the starch. This process, called starch retrogradation, occurs even when little or no moisture is lost. This means that even a well-wrapped loaf of bread will eventually become stale.

Chemical staling is very rapid at refrigerator temperatures, but it nearly stops at freezer temperatures. Thus, bread should not be stored in the refrigerator. It should be left at room temperature for short-term storage or frozen for long-term storage.

Chemical staling, if it is not too great, can be partially reversed by heating. Breads, muffins, and coffee cakes, for example, are frequently refreshed by placing them briefly in an oven. Remember, however, that this also results in more loss of moisture, so the items should be reheated only just before they are to be served.

Loss of crispness is caused by absorption of moisture, so in a sense it is the opposite of staling. The crusts of hard-crusted breads absorb moisture from the crumb and become soft and leathery. Reheating these products to refresh them will not only reverse chemical staling of the crumb but will also recrisp the crusts.

Loss of crispness is also a problem with low-moisture products such as cookies and pie crusts. The problem is usually solved by proper storage in airtight wraps or containers to protect the products from moisture in the air. Prebaked pie shells should be filled as close to service time as possible.

In addition to refreshing baked goods in the oven, there are three main techniques used to slow staling:

1. *Protecting the product from air*

   Two examples of protecting baked goods are wrapping bread in plastic and covering cakes with icing, especially icing that is thick and rich in fat.

   Hard-crusted breads, which stale very rapidly, should not be wrapped, or the crusts will quickly become soft and leathery. These bread products should always be served very fresh.

2. *Adding moisture retainers to the formula*

   Fats and sugars are good moisture retainers, so products high in these ingredients keep best.

   Some of the best French bread has no fat at all, so it must be served within hours of baking or it will begin to stale. For longer keeping, bakers often add a very small amount of fat and/or sugar to the formula.

3. *Freezing*

   Baked goods frozen before they become stale maintain quality for longer periods. They should be served very quickly after thawing. Frozen breads may be reheated with excellent results if they are to be served immediately.

   Refrigeration, on the other hand, speeds staling. Only baked goods that could become health hazards, such as those with cream fillings, are refrigerated.

TERMS FOR REVIEW

scaling
metric system
gram
liter
meter
degree Celsius
kilo-
deci-
centi-
milli-
gluten
coagulate
strong flour
weak flour
shortening
staling

QUESTIONS FOR DISCUSSION

1. Below are ingredients for a white cake. The weight of the flour is given, and the proportions of other ingredients are indicated by percentages. Calculate the weights required for each.

Cake flour	3 lb (100%)
Baking powder	4%
Shortening	50%
Sugar	100%
Salt	1%
Milk	75%
Egg whites	33%
Vanilla	2%

2. In the formula in question 1, how much of each ingredient is needed if you want a total yield of 4½ lb of batter?

3. Why are baking ingredients usually weighed rather than measured by volume?

4. Make the following conversions in the U.S. system of measurement:

    3½ pounds = _____ ounces
    6 cups = _____ pints
    8½ quarts = _____ fluid ounces
    ¾ cup = _____ tablespoons
    46 ounces = _____ pounds
    2½ gallons = _____ fluid ounces
    5 pounds 5 ounces divided by 2 = _____
    10 teaspoons = _____ fluid ounces

5. Make the following conversions in the metric system:

    1.4 kilograms = _____ grams
    53 deciliters = _____ liters
    15 centimeters = _____ millimeters
    2590 grams = _____ kilograms
    4.6 liters = _____ deciliters
    220 centiliters = _____ deciliters

6. Discuss four factors that affect the development of gluten in batters and doughs.

7. Why do some cakes fall if they are removed from the oven too soon?

8. Which kind of cake would you expect to have better keeping qualities, a sponge cake, which is low in fat, or a high-ratio cake, which is high in both fat and sugar?

CHAPTER 2

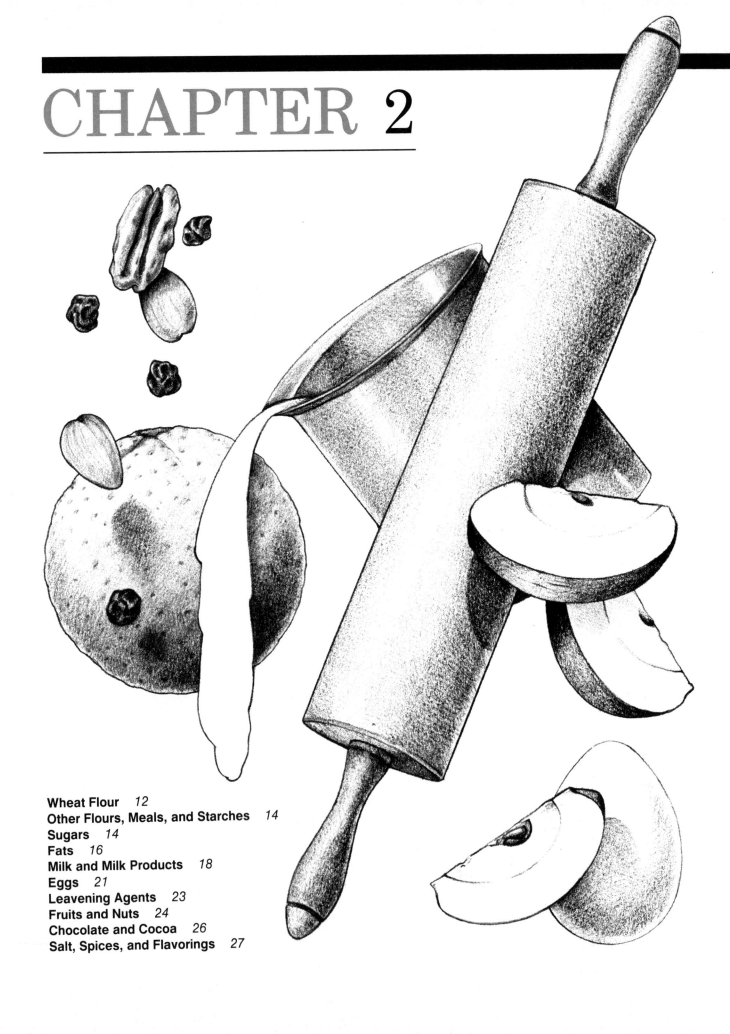

INGREDIENTS

After studying this chapter, you should be able to:
1. Understand the characteristics and functions of the major baking ingredients.
2. Make appropriate adjustments in formulas when substituting ingredients, such as dry milk for liquid milk or dry yeast for cake yeast.
3. Identify the main types of wheat flours by sight and feel.

he following introduction to baking ingredients is necessarily simplified. Hundreds of pages could be written—and have been—on wheat flour alone. Much of the available information, however, is very technical and is of concern primarily to large industrial bakers. In this chapter you will find the information you will need to produce a full range of baked items in a small bakeshop or a hotel or restaurant kitchen.

WHEAT FLOUR

Wheat flour is the most important ingredient in the bakeshop. It provides bulk and structure to most of the baker's products, including breads, cakes, cookies, and pastries. While the home cook depends almost exclusively on a product called "all-purpose flour," the professional baker has available a wide variety of flours with different qualities and characteristics. In order to select the proper flour for each product and to handle each correctly, you should understand the different types of flour and how they are milled.

Hard and Soft Wheats

The characteristics of flour depend on the variety of wheat from which it is milled, the location in which the wheat is grown, and the growing conditions. Types of wheat used in this country include Hard Red Spring, Hard Red Winter, Soft Red Winter, Durum, and White.

For our purposes, it is enough to know that some wheats are classified as "hard" and some as "soft." Hard wheats contain greater quantities of the proteins called *glutenin* and *gliadin,* which together form gluten when the flour is moistened and mixed.

You will recall from Chapter 1 that gluten development is one of the baker's major concerns when mixing doughs and batters. **Strong flours,** that is, flours from hard wheats with high protein content, are used primarily to make breads and other yeast products. **Weak flours,** that is, flours from soft wheats with low protein content, are important in the production of cakes, cookies, and pies.

The Milling of Hard Wheat

The wheat kernel consists of three main parts:

1. The *bran* is the hard outer covering of the kernel. It is present in whole wheat flour as tiny brown flakes, but it is removed in the milling of white flour.
2. The *germ* is the part of the kernel that will become the new wheat plant if the kernel is sprouted. It has a high fat content, which can quickly become rancid. Therefore, whole wheat flour containing the germ has poor keeping qualities.
3. The *endosperm* is the starchy part of the kernel that remains when the bran and germ are removed. It is the portion of the wheat kernel that is milled into white flour.

Depending on its source, the wheat endosperm contains about 63 to 73% starch and 7 to 15% protein, plus small amounts of moisture, fat, sugar, and minerals.

Modern milling of wheat into flour is accomplished by a fairly complex and highly refined system that uses grooved steel rollers. In what is called the "break system," the rollers are set so that the space between them is slightly smaller than the width of the kernels, and the rollers rotate at different speeds. When the wheat is fed between them, the rollers flake off the bran layers and germ and crack the endosperm into coarse pieces. Approximately 72% of the wheat kernel can be separated as endosperm, to be milled into flour. The remaining 28% consists of bran and other outer portions called "shorts."

The inner parts of the endosperm tend to break into smaller pieces than the outer parts. Therefore, by repeatedly sifting and breaking the wheat, different grades of flour can be extracted from one type of wheat. The term *extraction* means the portion of the endosperm that is separated into a particular grade of flour. For example, a flour with an extraction rate of 90% consists of all but 10% of the endosperm.

Straight flour

Straight flour is 100% extraction flour. In other words it is made from the entire wheat kernel after the bran and germ are removed. Straight flour from a hard wheat has a high protein content and can be used for making breads.

Patent flour

Patent flour is milled from the inner part of the endosperm, which breaks into finer particles than the part nearest the bran. Patent flour made from a hard wheat is a strong flour of excellent quality and is somewhat lighter in color than straight flour. When a formula calls for **bread flour,** patent flour is the flour of choice, although a strong straight flour could also be used.

The extraction rate of patent flour can be varied depending on specific needs and on the quality of the wheat. Fancy or extra short patent has an extraction rate of less than 60%. It comes from the innermost part of the kernel and is the whitest of all strong flours. Long patent may be as high as 90 or 95% extraction.

Clear flour

The portion of the endosperm that remains after the patent flour is removed is called clear flour. Since this portion of the wheat is closest to the bran, it is darker in color than patent flour. Clear flour may be separated into more than one grade, such as first clear (lighter in color) and second clear (darker, poorer grade).

Because of its color, clear flour is not suitable for making white breads. Its primary use is in making rye breads, where its color will not be noticed and its gluten content contributes strength. Clear flour can also be used in combination with whole wheat flour.

High-gluten flour

Flour that has an especially high protein content is sometimes used in hard-crusted breads and in such specialty products as pizza dough and bagels.

Aging and Bleaching

Freshly milled flour is not good for bread-making. The gluten is somewhat weak and inelastic, and the color may be yellowish. But if the flour is aged for several months, the oxygen in the air will mature the proteins so that they will be stonger and more elastic, and it will bleach the color.

Aging flour is costly and haphazard, however, so millers add small quantities of certain chemicals to flour to accomplish this quickly. Bromates, added to bread flours, mature the gluten but do not bleach the flour a great deal. Chlorine is added to cake flour because it is not only a maturing agent but it also bleaches the flour to pure white.

Enzymes in Flour

A small but important component of wheat flour is a group of enzymes called diastase. These enzymes break down some of the starch into sugars that can be acted on by yeast. If a particular flour is low in diastase, these enzymes can be added by the miller.

Soft Wheat Flours

In addition to bread flour (patent) and clear flour, both of which are strong, formulas in this book call for two types of weak flours.

Cake flour is a weak or low-gluten flour made from soft wheat. It has a very soft, smooth texture and a pure white color. Cake flour is used for cakes and other delicate baked goods that require low gluten content.

Pastry flour is also a weak or low-gluten flour, but it is slightly stronger than cake flour. It has the same creamy white color as bread flour, not the pure white of cake flour. Pastry flour is used for pie doughs and for some cookies, biscuits, and muffins.

Cake or pastry flour may be blended with bread flour in order to weaken it slightly for use in some rich, sweet yeast doughs.

Hand Test for Flour Strength

You should be able to identify bread flour, cake flour, and pastry flour by sight and touch, because sooner or later someone will dump a bag of flour into the wrong bin or label it incorrectly, and you will need to be able to recognize the problem.

Bread flour feels slightly coarse when rubbed between the fingers. If squeezed into a lump in the hand, it falls apart as soon as the hand is opened. Its color is creamy white.

Cake flour feels very smooth and fine. It stays in a lump when squeezed in the hand. Its color is pure white.

Pastry flour feels smooth and fine like cake flour and can also be squeezed into a lump. It has the creamy color of bread flour, not the pure white color of cake flour.

Other Wheat Flours

All-purpose flour, seen in retail markets, is not often found in bakeshops. This flour is formulated to be slightly weaker than bread flour so that it can be used for pastries as well. A professional baker, however, prefers to use flours that are formulated for specific purposes, because these give the best results.

Self-rising flour is a white flour to which baking powder and sometimes salt have been added. Its advantage is that the baking powder is blended in very uniformly. However, its use is limited by two facts. First, different formulas call for different proportions of baking powder. No single blend will be right for all purposes. Second, baking powder loses its aerating or leavening power with time, so the quality of baked goods made from this flour can fluctuate.

Whole wheat flour is made by grinding the entire wheat kernel, including the bran and germ. The germ, as you have learned, is high in fat, which can become rancid. So whole wheat flour does not keep as well as white flour.

Since it is made from wheat, whole wheat flour contains gluten, so it can be used alone in bread-making. However, a bread made with 100% whole wheat flour will be heavier than white bread, because the gluten strands are cut by the sharp edges of the bran flakes. Also, the fat from the wheat germ contributes to the shortening action. This is why most whole wheat breads are strengthened with white bread flour.

Bran flour is flour to which bran flakes have been added. The bran may be coarse or fine, depending on specifications.

OTHER FLOURS, MEALS, AND STARCHES

Rye Flour

Next to white and whole wheat, rye is the most popular flour for bread-making. Although rye flour contains some proteins, these proteins do not form gluten. Therefore, breads made with 100% rye flour will be heavy and dense. To make a lighter rye loaf, it is necessary to use a mixture of rye and hard wheat flours. Typical formulas call for 25 to 40% rye flour and 60 to 75% hard wheat flour.

Rye flour is milled much like wheat flour. The lightest rye flours, from the inner part of the kernel, have a low extraction rate, corresponding to patent flour. The following grades and types are generally available:

Light rye. The lightest is nearly white. It has a very fine texture and a high percentage of starch, with little protein.

Medium rye. This is a straight flour, milled from the whole rye grain after the bran has been removed. Thus, it is darker than light rye. It has a higher protein content.

Dark rye. Like clear flour milled from wheat, dark rye comes from that part of the rye grain closer to the bran. Thus, it is darker than other rye flours and has a lower percentage of fine starch particles.

Rye meal or **pumpernickel flour.** Rye meal is a dark, coarse meal made from the entire rye grain, including the bran. It looks somewhat like oatmeal. Rye meal is used for pumpernickel bread and similar specialty products.

Rye blend. This is a mixture of rye flour (generally about 25 to 40%) and a strong wheat flour such as clear flour.

Miscellaneous Flours and Meals

Products milled from other grains are occasionally used to add variety to baked goods. These include corn meal, rice flour, buckwheat flour, soy flour, potato flour, oat flour, and barley flour. The term *meal* is used for products that are not as finely ground as flour.

All of these products are normally used in combination with wheat flour, since they do not form gluten.

Starches

In addition to flours, some other starch products are also used in the bakeshop. Unlike flour, they are used primarily to thicken puddings, pie fillings, and similar products. The most important starches in dessert production are as follows:

1. *Cornstarch* has a special property that makes it valuable for certain purposes. Products thickened with cornstarch set up almost like gelatin when cooled. For this reason, it is used to thicken cream pies and other products that must hold their shape.

2. *Waxy maize* and other *modified starches* also have valuable properties. Since they do not break down when frozen, they are used for products that are to be frozen. Also, they are very clear when cooked and give a brilliant, clear appearance to fruit pie fillings.

    Waxy maize does not set up firm like cornstarch, but makes a soft paste, which has the same consistency hot and cold. Thus it is not suitable for cream pie fillings.

3. *Instant starches* have been precooked or pregelatinized, so they will thicken cold liquids without further cooking. They are useful when heat will damage the flavor of the product, as in fresh fruit glazes, such as strawberry.

SUGARS

Sugars or sweetening agents have the following purposes in baking:

- They add sweetness and flavor.
- They create tenderness and fineness of texture, partly by weakening the gluten structure.
- They give crust color.
- They increase keeping qualities by retaining moisture.
- They act as creaming agents with fats and as foaming agents with eggs.
- They provide food for yeast.

We customarily use the term "sugar" for regular refined sugars derived from sugar cane or beets. The chemical name for these sugars is sucrose. However, other sugars of different chemical structure are also used in the bakeshop.

Sugars belong to a group of substances called carbohydrates, a group that also includes starches. There are two basic groups of sugars: *simple sugars* (or *monosaccharides,* which means "single sugars") and *complex sugars* (or *disaccharides,* meaning "double sugars"). (Starches, or polysaccharides, are more complex chemical structures than sugars.) Sucrose is a disaccharide, as are maltose (malt sugar) and lactose (the sugar found in milk). Examples of simple sugars are glucose and fructose.

All these sugars have different degrees of sweetness. For example, lactose is much less sweet than regular table sugar (sucrose), while fructose (or fruit sugar, one of the sugars in honey) is much sweeter than sucrose.

Invert Sugar

When a sucrose solution is heated with an acid, some of the sucrose breaks down into equal parts of two simple sugars, dextrose and levulose. A mixture of equal parts of dextrose and levulose is called *invert sugar.* It is about 30% sweeter than regular sucrose.

Invert sugar has two properties that make it interesting to the baker. First, it holds moisture especially well and therefore helps keep cakes fresh and moist. Second, it resists crystallization. Thus, it promotes smoothness in candies, icings, and syrups. This is why an acid such as cream of tartar is often added to sugar syrups. The acids inverts some of the sugar when it is boiled, thus preventing graininess in the candy or icing.

Invert sugar is produced commercially, and it is also present in honey.

Regular Refined Sugars, or Sucrose

Refined sugars are classified by the size of the grains. However, there is no standardized system of labeling, so the names of the various granulations will vary, depending on the manufacturer.

Granulated Sugar

Regular granulated sugar, also called *fine granulated* or *table sugar,* is the most familiar and the most commonly used.

Very fine and *ultra-fine sugars* are finer than regular granulated sugar. They are prized for making cakes and cookies because they make a more uniform batter and can support higher quantities of fat.

Sanding sugars are coarser and are used for coating cookies, cakes, and other products.

In general, finer granulations are better for mixing into doughs and batters, because they dissolve more quickly. Coarse sugars are likely to leave undissolved grains, even after long mixing. These show up after baking as dark spots on crusts, irregular texture, and syrupy spots. Also, fine sugars are better for creaming with fats, because they create a finer, more uniform air cell structure and better volume.

Coarse sugar, on the other hand, can be used in syrups, where its mixing properties are not a factor. Even a very coarse sugar will dissolve readily when boiled with water. In fact, coarse crystalline sugar is often purer than fine sugar and makes a clearer syrup.

Confectioners' or Powdered Sugars

These sugars are ground to a fine powder and mixed with a small amount of starch (about 3%) to prevent caking. They are classified by coarseness or fineness.

10X is the finest sugar. It gives the smoothest textures in icings.

6X is the standard confectioners' sugar. It is used in icings, toppings, and cream fillings.

Coarser types (XXXX and XX) are used for dusting and for any purposes for which 6X and 10X are too fine.

Dehydrated Fondant

Dehydrated fondant is not a powdered sugar, though its appearance is similar. It is a dried form of fondant icing. During the manufacture of fondant, part of the sucrose is changed to invert sugar. This helps keep the sugar crystals very tiny, which makes for a very smooth, creamy icing with a good shine.

Fondant is discussed with other icings in Chapter 7.

Brown Sugar

Brown sugar is mostly sucrose (about 85 to 92%), but it also contains varying amounts of caramel, molasses, and other impurities, which give it its characteristic flavor. The darker grades contain more of these impurities. Basically, brown sugar is regular cane sugar that has not been completely refined. However, it can also be made by adding measured amounts of these impurities to refined white sugar.

Brown sugar was at one time available in fifteen grades, ranging from very dark to very light. Today, only two to four grades are generally available.

Because it contains a small amount of acid, brown sugar can be used with baking soda to provide some leavening (see p. 23). It is used in place of regular white sugar when its flavor is desired and its color would not be objectionable. Of course, it should not be used in white cakes.

Keep brown sugar in an airtight container to prevent it from drying out and hardening.

Syrups
Molasses

Molasses is concentrated sugar cane juice. *Sulfured molasses* is a by-product of sugar refining. It is the product that remains after most of the sugar has been extracted from cane juice. *Unsulfured molasses* is not a by-product but is a specially manufactured sugar product. It has a less bitter taste than sulfured molasses.

Molasses contains large amounts of sucrose and other sugars, including invert sugar. It also contains acids, moisture, and other constituents that give it its flavor and color. Darker grades are stronger in flavor and contain less sugar than lighter grades.

Molasses retains moisture in baked goods and therefore prolongs freshness. Crisp cookies made with molasses can become soft very quickly, because the invert sugars absorb moisture from the air.

Corn Syrup

Corn syrup or glucose syrup is a liquid sweetener consisting of water, a vegetable gum called dextrin, and various sugars, primarily *dextrose* (also called glucose). Corn syrup is made by converting cornstarch into simpler compounds through the use of enzymes.

Corn syrup aids in retaining moisture and is used in some icings and candies.

Honey

Honey is a natural sugar syrup consisting largely of the simple sugars glucose and fructose, in addition to other compounds that give it its flavor. Honeys vary considerably in flavor and color, depending on their source. Flavor is the major reason for using honey, especially since it can be expensive.

Because honey contains invert sugar, it helps retain moisture in baked goods. Like molasses, it contains acid, which enables it to be used with baking soda as a leavening.

Malt Syrup

Malt syrup, also called malt extract, is used primarily in yeast breads. It serves as food for the yeast and adds flavor and crust color to the breads. Malt is extracted from barley that has been sprouted (malted) and then dried and ground.

There are two basic types of malt syrup, *diastatic* and *non-diastatic*. Diastatic malt contains an enzyme called diastase, which breaks down starch into sugars that can be acted on by yeast. Thus, diastatic malt, when added to bread dough, is a powerful food for yeast. It is used when fermentation times are short. It should not be used when fermentation times are long, because too much starch will be broken down by the enzyme. This results in bread with a sticky crumb.

Diastatic malt is produced with high, medium, or low diastase content.

Non-diastatic malt is processed at high temperatures, which destroy the enzymes and also give the syrup a darker color and stronger flavor. It is used because it contains fermentable sugar and contributes flavor, crust color, and keeping qualities to breads.

Whenever malt syrup is called for in formulas in this book, non-diastatic malt should be used. There are no formulas requiring diastatic malt. If malt syrup is not available, you may substitute regular granulated sugar.

Malt is available in two other forms. *Dried malt extract* is simply malt syrup that has been dried. It must be kept in an airtight container to keep it from absorbing moisture from the air. *Malt flour* is the dried, ground, malted barley that has not had the malt extracted from it. It is obviously a much less concentrated form of malt. When used in bread-making, it is blended with the flour.

FATS

The major functions of fats in baked items are:

- To tenderize the product and soften the texture.
- To add moistness and richness.
- To increase keeping quality.
- To add flavor.
- To assist in leavening when used as creaming agents or when used to give flakiness to puff pastry, pie dough, and similar products.

Many different fats are available to the baker. These fats have different properties that make them suitable for different purposes. Among the properties a baker must consider when selecting a fat for a specific use are its melting point, its softness or hardness at different temperatures, its flavor, and its ability to form emulsions.

Fat Emulsions

Most bakery ingredients mix easily with water and other liquids and actually undergo a change in form. For example, salt and sugar dissolve in water; flour and starch absorb water and the water becomes bound up with the starch and protein molecules. Fat, on the other hand, does not change form when it is mixed with liquids or other bakery ingredients. Instead, the fat is merely broken down into smaller and smaller particles during mixing. These small fat particles then become more or less evenly distributed in the mix.

A uniform mixture of two unmixable substances, such as fat and water, is called an *emulsion.* Mayonnaise is a familiar example of an emulsion from outside the bakeshop—in this case, an emulsion of oil and vinegar. There are also emulsions of air and fat, such as that formed when shortening and sugar are creamed together in the production of cakes and other products (see p. 24).

Different fats have differing abilities to form emulsions. For example, if the wrong shortening is used in certain cakes, the emulsion may fail because the batter contains more water than the fat can hold. We then say that the batter "curdles" or "breaks."

Shortenings

Any fat acts as a shortening in baking, since it shortens gluten strands and tenderizes the product. However, we generally use the word shortening to mean any of a group of solid fats, usually white and tasteless, that have been especially formulated for baking. Shortenings generally consist of nearly 100% fat.

Shortenings may be made from vegetable oils, animal fats, or both. During manufacturing, the fats are *hydrogenated.* This process turns liquid oils into solid fats. Since shortenings are used for many purposes, manufacturers have formulated different kinds of fats with different properties. There are two main types: regular shortenings and emulsified shortenings.

Regular Shortenings

These shortenings have a fairly tough, waxy texture, and small particles of the fat tend to hold their shape in a dough or batter. They can be manufactured to be of varying degrees of hardness. Regular shortenings have a good creaming ability. This means that a good quantity of air can be mixed into them to give a batter lightness and leavening power (see p. 24). Also, this type of shortening melts only at a high temperature.

Because of their texture, regular shortenings are used for flaky products such as pie crusts and biscuits. They are also used in many other pastries, breads, and products mixed by creaming, such as certain pound cakes, cookies, and quick breads.

Unless another shortening is specified in a formula, regular shortening is generally used.

Emulsified Shortenings

These are soft shortenings that spread easily throughout a batter and quickly coat the particles of sugar and flour. Because they contain added emulsifying agents, they can hold a larger quantity of liquid and sugar than regular shortenings can. Thus, they give a smoother and finer texture to cakes and make them moister.

Emulsified shortening is often used when the weight of sugar in a cake batter is greater than the weight of flour. Because this shortening spreads so well, a simpler mixing method can be used, as explained in Chapter 10. Such cakes are referred to as *high-ratio cakes,* and emulsified shortening is sometimes called high-ratio shortening.

In addition, emulsified shortening is often used in icings because it can hold more sugar and liquid without curdling.

The term "emulsified shortenings" is not, strictly speaking, an accurate one. Pure fat cannot be emulsified, because an emulsion is a mixture of at least two substances. It would perhaps be more accurate to call them "emulsifier shortenings." However, the term "emulsified shortenings" is the more widely recognized and commonly used term.

Butter

Fresh butter consists of about 80% fat, about 15% water, and about 5% milk solids.

Butter is graded according to USDA standards, although grading is not mandatory. Grades are AA, A, B, and C. Most operations use grades AA and A because flavors of the lower grades may be off.

Butter is available *salted* and *unsalted.* Unsalted butter is more perishable, but it has a fresher, sweeter taste and is thus preferred in baking. If salted butter is used, the salt in the formula may have to be reduced.

Shortenings are manufactured to have certain textures and hardnesses so that they will be particularly suited to certain uses. Butter, on the other hand, is a natural product that doesn't have this advantage. It is hard and brittle when cold, very soft at room temperature, and it melts easily. Consequently, doughs made with butter are much harder to handle. Also, butter is more expensive than shortening.

On the other hand, butter has two major advantages:

1. *Flavor:* Shortenings are intentionally flavorless, but butter has a highly desirable flavor.

2. *Melting qualities:* Butter melts in the mouth. Shortenings do not. After eating pastries or icings made with shortening, one can be left with an unpleasant film of shortening coating the mouth.

For these reasons, many bakers and pastry chefs feel that the advantages of butter outweigh its disadvantages for many purposes. Frequently, you may blend 50% butter and 50% shortening to get both the flavor of butter and the handling qualities of shortening.

Margarine

Margarine is manufactured from various hydrogenated animal and vegetable fats, plus flavoring ingredients, emulsifiers, coloring agents, and other ingredients. It contains 80 to 85% fat, 10 to 15% moisture, and about 5% salt, milk solids, and other components. Thus, it may be considered a sort of imitation butter consisting of shortening, water, and flavorings.

Unlike the margarines sold by retail grocers, baker's margarines are formulated in different ways for different purposes. Following are the two major categories.

Cake Margarines or Baker's Margarines

These types of margarine are soft and have good creaming ability. They are used not only in cakes but in a wide variety of products.

Pastry Margarines

These margarines are tougher and more elastic and have a waxy texture. They are especially formulated for doughs that form layers, such as Danish dough and puff pastry.

Puff pastry margarine, the toughest of these fats, is sometimes called puff pastry shortening. However, like other margarines, it has a significant water content, which helps to give leavening power to the dough when it forms steam.

Puff pastry made with this margarine will generally rise higher than pastry made with butter. However, since the fat doesn't melt in the mouth like butter, many people find the pastry unpleasant to eat.

Oils

Oils are liquid fats. They are less often used as shortenings in baking, because they spread through a batter or dough too thoroughly and shorten too much. Some breads and a few cakes and quick breads use oil as a shortening. Beyond this, the usefulness of oil in the bakeshop is limited primarily to greasing pans, deep-frying doughnuts, and serving as a wash for some kinds of rolls.

Lard

Lard is the rendered fat of hogs. Because of its plastic quality, it was once highly valued for making flaky pie crusts. Since the development of modern shortenings, however, it is not often used in the bakeshop.

Storage of Fats

All fats will become rancid if exposed to the air too long. Also, they tend to absorb odors and flavors from other foods. Highly perishable fats, such as butter, should be stored well wrapped in the refrigerator. Other fats and oils should be kept in tightly closed containers in a cool, dry, dark place.

MILK AND MILK PRODUCTS

Next to water, milk is the most important liquid in the bakeshop. As we discussed in Chapter 1, water is essential for the development of gluten. Fresh milk, being 88 to 91% water fulfills this function. In addition, milk contributes to the texture, flavor, crust color, keeping quality, and nutritional value of baked products.

In this section, we discuss milk products in two parts: first, an explanation and definition of the various products available; second, guidelines for using milk products in baking.

Table 2.1 lists the water, fat, and milk solids content of the most important milk products. Milk solids include protein, lactose (milk sugar), and minerals.

TABLE 2.1 **Composition of Milk Products**

	Water (%)	Fat (%)	Milk Solids (%)
Fresh, whole	88	3.5	8.5
Fresh, skim	91	trace	9
Evaporated, whole	72	8	20
Evaporated, skim	72	trace	28
Condensed, whole[a]	31	8	20
Dried, whole	1.5	27.5	71
Dried, skim	2.5	trace	97.5

[a]Condensed milk also contains 41% sugar (sucrose).

Categories and Definitions

Fresh Liquid Milk

Whole milk is fresh milk as it comes from the cow, with nothing removed and nothing added (except when fortified with vitamin D). It contains 3½% fat (known as milk fat or butterfat), 8½% nonfat milk solids, and 88% water.

Fresh whole milk is available in several forms:

Pasteurized milk has been heated to kill disease-producing bacteria and then cooled. Most milk and cream products on the market have been pasteurized.

Raw milk is milk that has not been pasteurized. It is not often used and, in fact, is generally not allowed to be sold.

Certified milk is produced by disease-free herds under very strict sanitary conditions. It may be raw or pasteurized.

Homogenized milk has been processed so that the cream doesn't separate out. This is done by forcing the milk through very tiny holes, which break up the fat into particles so small that they stay distributed in the milk.

The above terms apply not only to whole milk but also to the following forms as well:

Skim or nonfat milk has had most or all fat removed. Its fat content is 0.5% or less.

Other forms available to food service and to retail outlets include low fat milk (0.5 to 3% milk fat), fortified non-fat or low fat milk, and flavored milk. However, these products are generally not used in bakeshops.

Cream

Various types of fresh cream, differing primarily in fat content, are available:

Whipping cream has a fat content of 30 to 40%. Within this category, you may find *light whipping cream* (30 to 35%) and *heavy whipping cream* (36 to 40%). Whipping cream labeled *ultrapasteurized* will keep longer than regular pasteurized cream, but it will not whip as well.

Light cream, also called table cream or coffee cream, contains 16 to 22% fat, usually about 18%.

Half-and-half has a fat content of 10 to 12%, too low for it to be called cream.

Fermented Milk Products

Buttermilk is fresh, liquid milk, usually skim milk, that has been cultured or soured by bacteria. It is usually called *cultured buttermilk* to distinguish it from the original buttermilk, which was the liquid left after buttermaking. Buttermilk is generally used in recipes calling for *sour milk*.

Sour cream has been cultured or fermented by adding lactic acid bacteria. This makes it thick and slightly tangy in flavor. It has about 18% fat.

Yogurt is milk (whole or low fat) cultured by special bacteria. It has a custardlike consistency. Most yogurt has additional milk solids added, and some of it is flavored and sweetened.

Evaporated and Condensed Milk

Evaporated milk is milk, either whole or skim, with about 60% of the water removed. It is then sterilized and canned. Evaporated milk has a somewhat "cooked" flavor.

Condensed milk is whole milk that has had about 60% of the water removed and is heavily sweetened with sugar. It is available canned and in bulk.

Dried Milk

Dried whole milk is whole milk that has been dried to powder. It has poor keeping qualities, because it still contains the original butterfat, which can become rancid. Therefore, it should be purchased in small quantities and always stored in a cool place.

Nonfat dry milk, also known as nonfat milk solids, is skim milk that has been dried to a powder. It is available in regular form and in instant form, which dissolves in water more easily.

Cheese

Two types of cheese are used in the bakeshop, primarily in the production of cheese fillings and cheesecakes.

Baker's cheese is a soft, unaged cheese with a very low fat content. It is dry and pliable and can be kneaded somewhat like a dough. Generally available in 30-lb and 50-lb packs, it can be frozen for longer storage.

Cream cheese is also a soft, unaged cheese, but it has a higher fat content, about 35%. It is used mainly in rich cheesecakes and in a few specialty products.

Guidelines for Using Milk Products in Baking

Fresh Liquid Milk

Whole milk contains fat, which must be calculated as part of the shortening in a dough. For this reason, whole and skim milk are not interchangeable in a formula, unless adjustments are made for the fat. Refer to Table 2.1 for the fat content of milk products.

Acid ingredients, such as lemon juice, cream of tartar, or baking powder, should normally not be added directly to milk, since they will curdle it.

Buttermilk

When buttermilk is produced, the lactose in the milk is converted to lactic acid. When buttermilk is used in place of regular milk in baked goods such as cakes or muffins, this acidity must, in most cases, be neutralized by adding baking soda to the formula. Then, because the soda and acid together release carbon dioxide, this extra leavening power must be compensated for by reducing the baking powder, as follows:

For each quart (2 lb) of buttermilk:	For each liter (1 kg) of buttermilk:
1. Add 0.5 oz baking soda	1. Add 15 g baking soda.
2. Subtract 1 oz baking powder.	2. Subtract 30 g baking powder.

Cream

Cream is not often used as a liquid in doughs and batters, except in a few specialty products. In these instances, because of its fat content, it functions as a shortening as well as a liquid.

Cream is more important in the production of fillings, toppings, dessert sauces, and cold desserts such as mousses and Bavarian creams. For detailed instructions on whipping heavy cream into a foam, see Chapter 7, p. 115.

Dried Milk

1. Dried milk is often used because of its convenience and low cost. In many formulas it is not necessary to reconstitute it. The milk powder is included with the dry ingredients, and water is used as the liquid. This practice is common in breadmaking and in no way reduces quality.

2. Proportions for reconstituting dry milk can be calculated from Table 2.1 For easy use, the equivalents in Table 2.2 can be used.

3. *Heat-treated* dry milk, not low-heat processed dry milk, should be purchased by the bakeshop. In the heat-treated product, certain enzymes that can break down gluten have been destroyed.

Storage of Milk Products

Fresh milk and cream, buttermilk and other fermented milk products, and cheese must be kept refrigerated at all times.

Evaporated milk in unopened cans may be kept in a cool storage area. After opening, store it in the refrigerator.

Condensed milk in large containers will keep for a week or more after opening if kept covered and in a cool place. The sugar acts as a preservative. Stir before using, because the sugar tends to settle to the bottom and sides.

Dried milk should be kept in a cool, dark place. It does not need refrigeration, though you should store it well away from ovens and other heat sources. Keep the container tightly closed to prevent the milk from absorbing moisture from the air.

TABLE 2.2 **Substituting Dry Milk for Liquid Milk**

To substitute for	Use
1 lb skim milk	14.5 oz water + 1.5 oz nonfat dry milk
1 lb whole milk	14 oz water + 2 oz dried whole milk
1 lb whole milk	14 oz water + 1.5 oz nonfat dried milk + 0.5 oz shortening *or* 0.7 oz butter
1 kg skim milk	910 g water + 90 g nonfat dry milk
1 kg whole milk	880 g water + 120 g dried whole milk
1 kg whole milk	880 g water + 90 g nonfat dry milk + 30 g shortening *or* 40 g butter

EGGS

Eggs should be well understood by the baker because they are used in large quantities in the bakeshop and are more expensive than many of the other high-volume ingredients like flour and sugar. For example, half or more of the ingredient cost of the average cake batter is for the eggs.

Composition

A whole egg consists primarily of a yolk, a white, and a shell. In addition, it contains a membrane that lines the shell and forms an air cell at the large end, and two white strands called chalazae that hold the yolk centered.

1. The yolk is high in both fat and protein, and it contains iron and several vitamins. Its color ranges from light to dark yellow, depending on the diet of the chicken.
2. The white is primarily albumin protein, which is clear and soluble when raw but white and firm when coagulated. The white also contains sulfur.
3. The shell is not the perfect package, in spite of what you may have heard. It is not only fragile but also very porous, allowing odors and flavors to be absorbed by the egg, and allowing the egg to lose moisture even if unbroken.

Table 2.3 lists the water, protein, and fat content of whole eggs, whites, and yolks.

Grades and Quality

Grades

Eggs are graded for quality by the U.S. Department of Agriculture. There are three grades: AA, A, and B. The best grade has a firm white and yolk that stand up high when broken onto a flat surface and do not spread over a large area. As eggs age, they become thinner and are graded lower.

As a baker, you will not be concerned so much with the firmness of the yolks and white. Rather, you will want eggs that are clean and fresh tasting, free of any bad odors or tastes caused by spoilage or absorption of foreign odors. One bad-smelling egg can ruin an entire batch of cakes.

Maintaining Quality

Proper storage is essential for maintaining quality. Eggs keep for weeks if held at 36° F (2° C) but lose quality quickly if held at room temperature. In fact, they can lose a full grade in one day at warm bakeshop temperatures. There's no point in paying for Grade AA eggs if they are Grade B by the time you use them.

Store eggs away from other foods that might pass on undesirable flavors or odors.

Size

Eggs are also graded by size. Table 2.4 gives the minimum weight per dozen (including shell) of each size category. Note that each size differs from the next by 3 ounces per dozen.

Large eggs are the standard size used in baking and in food service. Shelled large whole eggs, yolks, and whites have the following approximate weights.

Average Large Eggs, Approximate Weights without Shell

One whole egg	= 1.67 oz	47 g
One egg white	= 1 oz	28 g
One yolk	= 0.67 oz	19 g

9½ whole eggs	= 1 lb	21 whole eggs	= 1 kg
16 whites	= 1 lb	36 whites	= 1 kg
24 yolks	= 1 lb	53 yolks	= 1 kg

Market Forms

1. *Fresh eggs or shell eggs*
2. *Frozen eggs*

   Frozen eggs are usually made from high-quality fresh eggs and are excellent for use in baking. They

TABLE 2.3 **Average Composition of Fresh Liquid Eggs**

	Whole eggs (%)	Whites (%)	Yolks (%)
Water	73	86	49
Protein	13	12	17
Fat	12	—	32
Minerals and other components	2	2	2

TABLE 2.4 **Egg Size Classifications**

Size	Minimum Weight per Dozen	
	U.S.	Metric
Jumbo	30 oz	850 g
Extra large	27 oz	765 g
Large	24 oz	680 g
Medium	21 oz	595 g
Small	18 oz	510 g
Peewee	15 oz	425 g

are pasteurized and are usually purchased in 30-lb tins.

To thaw, place them unopened in refrigerator and hold for two days. Or place in a defrosting tank containing running water at 50 to 60° F (10 to 15° C) for about 6 hours. Do not defrost at room temperature or in warm water. Stir well before using.

    a. Whole eggs

    b. Whole eggs with extra yolks

    c. Whites

    d. Yolks

    Frozen yolks may contain a small amount of sugar (usually about 10%; check the label) to keep the components from separating while frozen.

    When these sugared yolks are used in products such as cakes, you should allow for this sugar content by reducing the sugar in the formula by the same amount. For example, if you are using 20 oz yolks with 10% sugar, subtract 2 oz (20 oz × .10) from the sugar in the formula.

3. *Dried eggs*

    a. Whole

    b. Yolks

    c. Whites

    Dried eggs are sometimes used in the bakeshop, though less often than frozen eggs. The whites are frequently used for making meringue powders. Dried egg products are also used by commercial manufacturers of cake mixes.

    Dried eggs are incorporated in baked goods in two ways: by reconstituting them with water to make liquid eggs, or by mixing them with the dry ingredients and adding the extra water to the liquid portion of the formula.

It is important to follow manufacturers' instructions for the ratio of egg to water, since egg products vary. After mixing, let the eggs stand to allow time for the water to be absorbed. This takes 1 hour for whole eggs and yolks, and sometimes 3 hours or more for whites. Mix again before using. The following are typical ratios for reconstituting eggs:

Product	**Ratio of egg to water, by weight**
Whole eggs	1:2½
Yolks	1:1 to 1:1½
Whites	1:5½ to 1:6

Unlike most dried products, dried eggs do not keep well. Keep refrigerated or frozen, tightly sealed.

Functions

Eggs perform the following functions in baking:

1. *Structure*

Like gluten protein, egg protein coagulates to give structure to baked products. This is especially important in high ratio cakes, in which the high content of sugar and fat weakens the gluten.

If used in large quantities, eggs give toughness or chewiness to baked products, unless balanced by fat and sugar, which are tenderizers.

2. *Emulsifying of fats and liquids*

Egg yolks contain natural emulsifiers, which help produce smooth batters. This contributes to volume and to texture.

3. *Leavening*

Beaten eggs incorporate air in tiny cells or bubbles. In a batter, this trapped air expands when heated and aids in leavening.

4. *Shortening action*

The fat in egg yolks acts as a shortening. This is an important function in products that are low in other fats.

5. *Moisture*

Eggs are mostly water (see Table 2.3.) This moisture must be calculated as part of the total liquid in a formula. If yolks are substituted for whole eggs, for example, or if dried eggs are used, adjust the liquid in the formula to allow for the different moisture content of these products.

6. *Flavor*

7. *Nutritional Value*

8. *Color*

Yolks impart a yellow color to doughs and batters. Also, eggs brown easily and contribute to crust color.

LEAVENING AGENTS

Leavening is the production or incorporation of gases in a baked product to increase volume and to produce shape and texture. These gases must be retained in the product until the structure is set enough (by the coagulation of gluten and egg products and the gelatinization of starches) to hold its shape.

Exact measurement of leavening agents is important, because small changes can produce major defects in baked products.

Yeast

Yeast is the leavening agent in breads, dinner rolls, Danish pastries, and similar products. This section discusses the characteristics of yeast. The handling of yeast and its use in yeast doughs are discussed in Chapter 3.

Fermentation is the process by which yeast acts on sugars and changes them into carbon dioxide gas and alcohol. This release of gas produces the leavening action in yeast products. The alcohol evaporates completely during and immediately after baking.

Fermentable sugar in bread dough comes from two sources:

1. It is added to the dough by the baker.

2. It is produced from flour by enzymes that break down the wheat starch into sugar. These enzymes

are present in the flour and/or are added by the baker in the form of diastatic malt (see p. 16).

Yeast is a microscopic plant that accomplishes this fermentation process by producing enzymes. Some of these enzymes change complex sugars (sucrose and maltose) into simple sugars. Other change the simple sugars into carbon dioxide gas and alcohol. The following formula describes this reaction in chemical terms:

$$C_6H_{12}O_6 \rightarrow 2CO_2 + 2C_2H_5OH$$
$$\text{simple sugar} \quad \text{carbon dioxide} \quad \text{alcohol}$$

Because yeast is a living organism, it is sensitive to temperatures.

34° F (1° C)	Inactive (Storage temperature)
60° to 70° F (15° to 20° C)	Slow action
70° to 90° F (20° to 32° C)	Best growth (Fermentation and proofing temperatures for bread doughs)
Above 100° F (38° C)	Reaction slows
140° F (60° C)	Yeast is killed

Yeast is available in two forms: compressed and active dry. The formulas in this book call for compressed yeast, which is prefered by professional bakers. *To convert recipes to use active dry yeast, use only 40% of the weight of compressed yeast specified.* In other words, in place of 1 pound of compressed yeast, use 6.5 oz dry yeast (.40 × 16 oz). Dry yeast must be dissolved in 4 times its weight of warm water (at about 110° F/43° C) before use.

Yeast also contributes flavor, in addition to leavening action.

Chemical Leaveners

Chemical leaveners are those that release gases produced by chemical reactions.

Baking Soda

Baking soda is the chemical sodium bicarbonate. If *moisture* and an *acid* are present, soda releases carbon dioxide gas, which leavens the product.

Heat is not necessary for the reaction (though the gas will be released faster at high temperatures). For this reason, products leavened with soda must be baked at once or gases will escape and leavening power will be lost.

Acids that react with soda in a batter include honey, molasses, buttermilk, fruit juices and purées, and chocolate. Sometimes cream of tartar is used for the acid. The amount of soda used in a formula is generally the amount needed to balance the acid. If more leavening power is needed, baking powder, not more soda, is used.

Baking Powder

Baking powders are mixtures of baking soda plus an acid to react with it. They also contain starch, which prevents lumping and brings the leavening power down to a standard level. Since baking powders do not depend for their leavening power on acid ingredients in a formula, they are more versatile.

Single-acting baking powders require only moisture to be able to release gas. Like baking soda, they can be used only if the product is to be baked immediately after mixing.

Double-acting baking powders release some gas when cold, but they require heat for complete reaction. Thus, cake batters made with these can incorporate the leavening agent early in the mixing period and can stand for some time before baked.

Do not include more baking powder than necessary in a formula, since undesirable flavors may be created. Also, excess leavening may create an undesirably light, crumbly texture. Cakes may rise too much and then fall before they become set.

Baking Ammonia

Baking ammonia is a mixture of ammonium carbonate, ammonium bicarbonate, and ammonium carbamate. It decomposes rapidly during baking to form carbon dioxide gas, ammonia gas, and water. Only heat and moisture are necessary for it to work. No acids are needed.

Since it decomposes completely, it leaves no residue that could affect flavor when it is properly used. However, it can be used only in small products that are baked until dry, such as cookies. Only in such products can the ammonia gas be completely driven off.

Because ammonia releases gases very quickly, it is sometimes used in products in which rapid leavening is desired, such as cream puffs. Use of ammonia enables the baker to lower the cost of such products by reducing the quantity of eggs. However, the quality of the resulting goods is lowered.

Storage of Chemical Leaveners

Baking soda, powder, and ammonia must always be kept tightly closed when not in use. If left open, they can absorb moisture from the air and lose part of their leavening power. Also, they must be stored in a cool place, because heat also causes them to deteriorate.

Air

Air is incorporated into a batter primarily by two methods, creaming and foaming. This air expands during baking and leavens the products.

1. *Creaming* is the process of beating fat and sugar together to incorporate air. It is an important technique in cake and cookie making. Some pound cakes and cookies are leavened almost entirely by this method.

2. *Foaming* is the process of beating eggs, with or without sugar, to incorporate air. Foams made with whole eggs are used to leaven sponge cakes, while angel food cakes, meringues, and soufflés are leavened with egg white foams.

Steam

When water turns to steam, it expands to 1100 times its original volume. Since all baked products contain some moisture, steam is an important leavening agent.

Puff pastry, cream puffs, popovers, and pie crusts use steam as their primary or only leavening agent. If the starting baking temperature for these products is high, steam will be produced rapidly and leavening will be greatest.

FRUITS AND NUTS

Fruit Products

Nearly any kind of fresh fruit can be used in the production of desserts. In addition, a wide variety of dried, frozen, canned, and processed fruit products are important ingredients in the bakeshop. The following is a list of some of the most important fruit products. Use of these products is covered in appropriate chapters throughout the book:

Fresh
    apples
    bananas
    oranges
    lemons
    limes
    berries

peaches
pears
apricots
plums
pineapple
grapes
rhubarb (actually not a fruit, but a stem)

Canned and frozen
apples, sliced
cherries, both sour and sweet
peaches, slices and halves
apricots, halves
blueberries
strawberries
pineapple, rings, chunks, nibs, crushed, juice

Dried
raisins, light and dark
currants (actually very small raisins)
prunes
dates
apricots
figs

Candied and glacé
cherries
lemon peel
orange peel
citron
pineapple
figs
fruitcake mix

Other processed fruits
prepared pie fillings
jams, jellies, and preserves
apricot glaze or coating

Nuts

Most nuts are available whole, halved, or broken or chopped. Because they are high in oil, all nuts can become rancid. Store them tightly closed in a cool, dark place.

Almonds
One of the most important nuts in the bakeshop. Available natural (skin on) and blanched (skin off) in many forms: whole, split, sliced, slivered, chopped, ground (almond flour).

Coconut
Sweetened coconut is used primarily for cake decoration.

Unsweetened coconut is used as an ingredient in a great variety of goods, such as cookies, macaroons, cakes, and fillings. Many types are available, based on the size of the individual grains, flakes, or shreds. The smallest types are *extra fine,* which is about the texture of granulated sugar, and *macaroon,* about the texture of cornmeal. Large sizes include *short and long shred, chip,* and *flake.*

Walnuts

Hazelnuts
Best if toasted before use.

Pecans
Expensive. Used in premium goods.

Peanuts

Brazil nuts

Cashews

Chestnuts
Must be cooked. Forms used in bakeshops are purée and glacée (in syrup).

Nut Products

Almond paste
An expensive but highly versatile nut paste used in a variety of cakes, pastries, cookies, and fillings. It is made from two parts finely ground almonds and one part sugar, plus enough moisture to bring it to the proper consistency.

Marzipan
Essentially a sweetened almond paste, used in decorative and confectionery work. This product can be purchased or made in the bakeshop from almond paste.

Kernel paste
A product similar to almond paste but less expensive. It is made from apricot kernels, which have a strong almondlike flavor.

Macaroon paste
This product stands between almond paste and kernel paste in that it is made from a blend of both almonds and apricot kernels.

Praline paste

A confectionery paste made from almonds and/or hazelnuts and caramelized sugar, all ground to a paste. It is used as a flavoring for icings, fillings, pastries, and creams.

CHOCOLATE AND COCOA

Chocolate and cocoa are derived from cocoa or cacao beans. When the beans are fermented, roasted, and ground, the resulting product is called *chocolate liquor*, which contains a white or yellowish fat called *cocoa butter.*

The following chocolate products are important in the bakeshop:

Cocoa

Cocoa is the dry powder that remains after part of the cocoa butter is removed from chocolate liquor. *Dutch process cocoa*, or *dutched cocoa*, is processed with an alkali. It is slightly darker, smoother in flavor, and more easily dissolved in liquids than is natural cocoa.

Natural cocoa is somewhat acidic. When it is used in such products as cakes, it is possible to use baking soda (which reacts with acid) as part of the leavening power. Dutched cocoa, on the other hand, is generally neutral or even slightly alkaline. Therefore, it will not react with baking soda (see Table 2.5). Instead, baking powder is used as the sole leavening agent. If you are substituting dutched for natural cocoa, you must increase the baking powder by 1 oz (30 g) for each ½ oz (15 g) of soda omitted.

If not enough soda is used in chocolate products, the color of the finished product may range from light tan to dark brown, depending on the quantity used. If too much is used, the color will be reddish-brown. This color is desired in devil's-food cakes, but it may not be wanted in other products. When switching from one kind of cocoa to another, you may have to adjust the soda in your recipes.

Bitter Chocolate

Bitter or unsweetened chocolate is straight chocolate liquor. It contains no sugar and has a strongly bitter taste. It is used to flavor items that have other sources of sweetness.

In some less expensive brands, some of the cocoa butter may be replaced by another fat.

Sweet Chocolate

Sweet chocolate is bitter chocolate with the addition of sugar in varying amounts. Normal proportions are equal parts sugar and chocolate liquor. If the percentage of sugar is low, sweet chocolate is sometimes called semi-sweet in the retail market. In this book and in most professional manuals, only the term "sweet chocolate" is used to refer to sweetened, dark chocolate.

Since sweet chocolate has only half the chocolate content of bitter chocolate, it is usually not economical to add it to products that are already highly sweetened, since twice as much will be needed. For example, it is better to use bitter chocolate when making chocolate fondant from plain white fondant.

When using pure sweet chocolate to coat candies, cookies, and other products, the chocolate must be prepared by a process called *tempering*. This involves carefully melting the chocolate without letting it get too warm, then bringing the temperature back down to a certain level. The process requires a fair amount of skill.

Less expensive chocolates, which have part of the cocoa butter replaced by other fats, are easier to handle and don't require tempering. However, they do not have the flavor and eating qualities of good chocolate. These products are sold under such names as "cookie coating" or "cake coating."

Milk Chocolate

Milk chocolate is sweet chocolate to which milk solids have been added. It is usually used as a coating chocolate and in various confections. It is seldom melted and then incorporated in batters, since it contains a relatively low proportion of chocolate liquor.

TABLE 2.5 **Baking Soda Needed To Balance the Acidity of Typical Cocoa Products**

	Amount of Baking Soda per lb	**Amount of Baking Soda per kg**
Natural cocoa	1.25 oz	80 g
Dutched cocoa	0	0
Bitter chocolate	0.8 oz	50 g
Sweet chocolate	0.4 oz	25 g

SALT, SPICES, AND FLAVORINGS **27**

Cocoa Butter

Cocoa butter is the fat that is pressed out of chocolate liquor when cocoa is processed. Its main use in the bakeshop is to thin melted coating chocolate to a proper consistency.

White Chocolate

White chocolate consists of cocoa butter, sugar, and milk solids. It is used primarily in confectionery. Some inexpensive brands, in which another fat is substituted for the cocoa butter, don't deserve the name chocolate at all, since they contain no chocolate or any of its components.

Substituting Cocoa and Chocolate

Since cocoa is the same as bitter chocolate, only with less cocoa butter, it is often possible to substitute the one product for the other. Shortening is usually used to take the place of the missing fat. However, various fats behave differently in baking. Regular shortening, for example, has about twice the shortening power of cocoa butter, so only half as much is needed in many products, such as cakes. The procedures below take this difference into account.

Because of these varying factors, as well as the different baking properties of cakes, cookies, and other products, it is recommended that you test-bake a small batch when making a substitution in a formula. You can then make additional adjustments, if necessary. *No single substitution ratio is adequate for all purposes.*

Procedure for Substituting Natural Cocoa in Place of Bitter Chocolate

1. Multiply the weight of the chocolate by ⅝. The result is the amount of cocoa to use.
2. Subtract the weight of the cocoa from the original weight of chocolate. Divide this difference by 2. The result is the amount of shortening to add to the formula.

   Example: Replace 1 lb chocolate with natural cocoa.

   $$⅝ \times 16 \text{ oz} = 10 \text{ oz cocoa}$$
   $$\frac{16 \text{ oz} - 10 \text{ oz}}{2} = \frac{6 \text{ oz}}{2} = 3 \text{ oz shortening}$$

Procedure for Substituting Bitter Chocolate for Natural Cocoa

1. Multiply the weight of the cocoa by ⅝. The result is the amount of chocolate to use.
2. Subtract the weight of cocoa from the weight of chocolate. Divide by 2. Reduce the weight of shortening in the mix by this amount.

   Example: Substitute bitter chocolate for 1 lb natural cocoa.

   $$⅝ \times 16 \text{ oz} = 26 \text{ oz chocolate (rounded off)}$$
   $$\frac{26 \text{ oz} - 16 \text{ oz}}{2} = \frac{10}{2} = 5 \text{ oz } less \text{ shortening}$$

Starch Content of Cocoa

Cocoa contains starch, which tends to absorb moisture in a batter. Consequently, when cocoa is added to a mix, for example, to change a yellow cake to a chocolate cake, the quantity of flour is reduced to compensate for this added starch. Exact adjustments will vary, depending on the product. However, the following may be used as a general rule of thumb:

Reduce the flour by ⅜ (37.5%) of the weight of cocoa added.

Thus, if 1 lb of cocoa is added, the flour is reduced by 6 oz. Or, if 400 g cocoa is added, reduce the flour by 150 g.

Chocolate, of course, also contains starch. When melted chocolate is added to the fondant, for example, the fondant gets stiffer because of this starch and usually requires thinning. Often, however, the drying effect of the starch is balanced by the tenderizing effect of the cocoa butter. Methods of incorporating both chocolate and cocoa in various products is discussed in appropriate chapters.

SALT, SPICES, AND FLAVORINGS

Salt

Salt plays a very important role in baking. It is more than just a seasoning or flavor enhancer. It also has these functions:

1. Salt strengthens gluten structure and makes it more stretchable. Thus it improves the texture of breads.

2. Salt inhibits yeast growth. It is therefore important for controlling fermentation in bread doughs and preventing the growth of undesirable wild yeasts.

For these reasons, the quantity of salt in a formula must be very carefully controlled. If too much salt is used, fermentation and proofing are slowed down. If not enough salt is used, fermentation proceeds too rapidly. The yeast uses up too much of the sugar in the dough and consequently the crust doesn't brown well. There are other results of over-fermentation, which are described in Chapter 3.

Because of the effect of salt on yeast, never add salt directly to the water in which yeast is softened.

Spices

Spices are plant or vegetable substances used to flavor foods. Plant parts used as spices include seeds, flower buds (e.g., cloves), roots (e.g., ginger), and bark (e.g., cinnamon). Spices are generally whole or ground. Ground spices lose their flavor rapidly, so it is important to have fresh spices always on hand. Keep them tightly sealed in a cool, dark, dry place.

Since a small amount of spices usually has a great deal of flavoring power, it is important to weigh spices carefully and accurately. A quarter ounce too much of nutmeg, for example, could make a product inedible. In most cases, it is better to use too little than too much.

The following are the most important spices and seeds in the bakeshop:

allspice
anise
caraway
cardamom
cinnamon
cloves
ginger
mace
nutmeg
poppy seeds
sesame seeds
zest of lemon and orange (the colored, outer part of the peel)

Extracts and Emulsions

Extracts are flavorful oils and other substances dissolved in alcohol. These include vanilla, lemon, and bitter almond.

Emulsions are flavorful oils mixed with water with the aid of emulsifiers such as vegetable gums. Lemon and orange are the most frequently used emulsions. Their flavor is strong. For example, it takes less lemon emulsion than lemon extract to give the same flavor.

Flavorings in general may be divided into two categories: natural and artificial. Natural flavorings are usually more expensive but have a superior flavor. Since flavorings and spices are used in small quantities, it is not much more expensive to use the best quality. Trying to save a few pennies on a cake by using inferior flavorings is false economy.

TERMS FOR REVIEW

hard wheat
soft wheat
strong flour
weak flour
bran
germ
endosperm
extraction rate
straight flour
patent flour
bread flour
clear flour
diastase
cake flour
pastry flour
whole wheat flour
bran flour
rye meal
rye blend
sucrose
invert sugar
granulated sugar
confectioners' sugar
brown sugar
molasses
corn syrup
malt syrup
emulsion
regular shortening
emulsified shortening
margarine
leavening
fermentation
chemical leavener
single and double acting baking powder
baking ammonia
creaming
foaming
almond paste
kernel paste
chocolate liquor
cocoa butter
cocoa
dutched cocoa
extract
emulsion

QUESTIONS FOR DISCUSSION

1. Why is white wheat flour used in rye breads? In whole wheat breads? Some bakeries in Europe produce a kind of pumpernickel bread with 100% rye flour. What would you expect its texture to be like?

2. Describe how to distinguish bread, pastry, and cake flours by touch and sight.

3. Why does white flour have better keeping qualities than whole wheat flour?

4. What is the importance of aging in the production of flour? How is this accomplished in modern flour milling?

5. What is clear flour? What products is it used for?

6. List four functions of sugars in baked foods.

7. What is invert sugar? What properties make it useful in baking?

8. True or false: 10X sugar is one of the purest forms of sucrose. Explain your answer.

9. What is the difference between regular and emulsified shortening? Between cake margarine and pastry margarine?

10. What are some advantages and disadvantages in using butter as the fat in pie dough?

11. List six functions of eggs in baked goods.

12. What is the difference between single-acting and double-acting baking powders? Which is most frequently used, and why?

CHAPTER 3

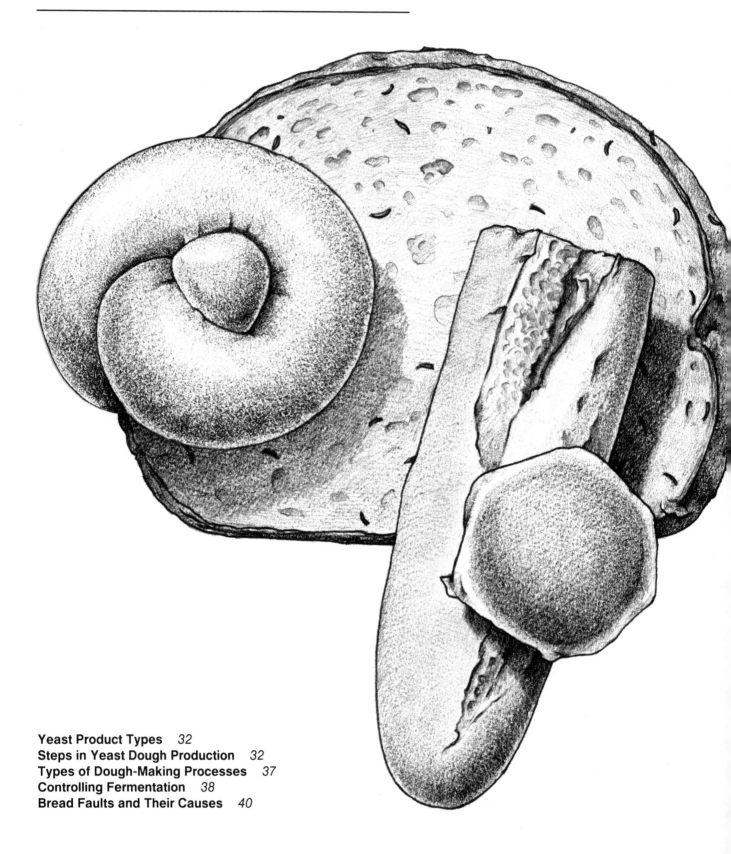

UNDERSTANDING YEAST DOUGHS

After studying this chapter, you should be able to:

1. List and describe the twelve basic steps in the production of yeast goods.
2. Explain the three basic mixing methods used for yeast doughs.
3. Understand and control the factors affecting dough fermentation.
4. Recognize and correct faults in yeast products.

In its simplest form, bread is nothing more than a baked dough made of flour and water, leavened by yeast. In fact, some hard-crusted French breads contain only these ingredients, plus salt. Other kinds of bread contain additional ingredients, including sugar, shortening, milk, eggs, and flavorings. But flour, water, and yeast are still the basic building blocks of all breads.

Yet, for something that seems so simple, bread can be one of the most exacting and complex products to make. Success in bread-making depends largely on your understanding of two basic principles: gluten development, which was discussed in Chapter 1, and yeast fermentation, which has already been touched on and which will be described in greater detail here.

This chapter focuses on the basic procedures in the production of many kinds of yeast products. Special attention is given to mixing methods and to control of fermentation. In Chapter 4, these procedures will be applied to specific formulas.

YEAST PRODUCT TYPES

Though all yeast doughs are made according to essentially the same basic principles, it is useful to divide yeast products into categories such as the following:

Lean Dough Products

A lean dough is one that is low in fat and sugar.

1. Hard-crusted breads and rolls, including French and Italian breads, kaiser rolls and other hard rolls, and pizza: These are the leanest of all bread products.
2. Other white and whole wheat breads and dinner rolls: These have a higher fat and sugar content and sometimes also contain eggs and milk solids. Because they are slightly richer, they generally have soft crusts.
3. Breads made with other grains: Rye breads are the most common. Many varieties of rye breads are produced, with light or dark flours or with pumpernickel flour, and with various flavorings, especially molasses and caraway seeds.

Rich Dough Products

There is no exact dividing line between rich and lean doughs, but in general rich doughs are those that contain higher proportions of fat, sugar, and sometimes eggs.

1. Non-sweet breads and rolls, including rich dinner rolls and brioche: These have a high fat content, but their sugar content is low enough to allow them to be served as dinner breads. Brioche dough, made with a high proportion of butter and eggs, is especially rich.
2. Sweet rolls, including coffee cakes and many breakfast and tea rolls: These have high fat and sugar content and usually contain eggs. They generally have a sweet filling or topping.

Rolled-in Yeast Dough Products

Rolled-in doughs are those in which a fat is incorporated into the dough in many layers by using a rolling and folding procedure. The alternating layers of fat and dough give the baked product a flaky texture.

1. Non-sweet rolled-in dough: croissants.
2. Sweet rolled-in doughs: Danish pastry.

STEPS IN YEAST DOUGH PRODUCTION

There are twelve basic steps in the production of yeast breads. These steps are generally applied to all yeast products, with some variations depending on the particular product.

1. Scaling ingredients
2. Mixing
3. Fermentation
4. Punching
5. Scaling
6. Rounding
7. Benching
8. Make-up and panning
9. Proofing
10. Baking
11. Cooling
12. Storing

As you can see, mixing of ingredients into a dough is only one part of a complex procedure.

This section describes each of these twelve steps, including the basic procedures. In the next sections, dough-making and fermentation are discussed in greater detail. Specific makeup procedures are included with the formulas in the next chapter.

Scaling Ingredients

All ingredients must be weighed accurately.

Water, milk, and eggs may be measured by volume. They are scaled at one pint per pound, or one kilogram per liter. However, if quantities are large, it is more accurate to weigh these liquids (see p. 2).

Special care must be taken when measuring spices and other ingredients used in very small quantities. This is particularly important with salt, which affects the rate of fermentation (see p. 27).

Mixing

Mixing yeast doughs has three main purposes:

- To combine all ingredients into a uniform, smooth dough.
- To distribute the yeast evenly throughout the dough.
- To develop the gluten.

Three principle mixing methods are used for yeast doughs: the straight dough method, the modified straight dough method, and the sponge method (also called the sponge-and-dough method).

Straight Dough Method

In its simplest form, the straight dough method consists of only one step: Combine all ingredients in the mixing bowl and mix. Many bakers make good quality products by using this procedure. However, there is the possibility that the yeast may not be evenly distributed in the dough. It is therefore safer to mix the yeast separately with a little of the water.

Procedure: Straight Dough Mixing Method for Yeast Products

1. Soften the yeast in a little of the water.
   Fresh yeast: Mix with about twice its weight in water, or more.
   Ideal water temperature: 100° F (38° C).
   Active dry yeast: Mix with about four times its weight in water.
   Ideal water temperature: 110° F (43° C).
2. Combine the remaining ingredients, including the rest of the water, in the mixing bowl. Add the dissolved yeast, taking care not to let it come in contact with the salt.
3. Mix to a smooth, developed dough.

Modified Straight Dough Method

For rich sweet doughs, the straight dough method is modified to ensure even distribution of the fat and sugar.

Procedure: Modified Straight Dough Method

1. Soften the yeast in part of the liquid, using a separate container.
2. Combine the fat, sugar, salt, milk solids, and flavorings and mix until well combined, but do not whip until light.
3. Add the eggs gradually, as fast as they are absorbed.
4. Add the liquid and mix briefly.
5. Add the flour and yeast. Mix to a smooth dough.

Sponge Method

Sponge doughs are prepared in two stages. This procedure gives the yeast action a head start.

Procedure: Sponge Method

1. Combine the liquid, the yeast, and part of the flour (and sometimes part of the sugar). Mix into a thick batter or soft dough. Let ferment until double in bulk.
2. Punch down and add the rest of the flour and the remaining ingredients. Mix to a uniform, smooth dough.

There are many variations of this procedure. Part of the liquid is occasionally reserved for step 2. The sponge sometimes incorporates a sour starter, which is essentially an older sponge. Frequently, the sponge is fermented longer, until it has expanded as much as possible and falls back upon itself.

Mixing Times

The first two purposes of mixing — combining the ingredients into a dough and distributing the yeast — are accomplished during the first part of mixing. The remaining time is necessary to develop the gluten. Overmixed and undermixed doughs have poor volume and texture (Review Gluten Development, p. 6).

Mixing times given in formulas in this book are *only guidelines*. You must learn to tell by sight and feel when a dough is thoroughly mixed. This can be done only through experience. A properly developed dough should feel smooth and elastic. A lean dough should not be sticky.

Rich doughs are generally undermixed slightly, because a greater tenderness is desired for these products. Rye breads are also mixed less because of their weaker gluten, which tears easily.

Overmixing is a common error in bread-making. Gluten that is developed too long has stretched nearly as far as it can and loses its elasticity. Then it tears instead of stretching, and molding is more difficult. The texture and volume of the overmixed products are less desirable.

Salt, used in proper quantities, helps alleviate this problem because it makes gluten stronger and more elastic.

Fermentation

Fermentation is the process by which yeast acts on the sugars and starches in the dough to produce carbon dioxide gas (CO_2) and alcohol. The action of the yeast is described in Chapter 2 (p. 23).

Procedure for Fermenting Yeast Dough

Place the dough in a container large enough to allow for expansion of the dough. Cover the container and let the dough rise at a temperature of about 80° F (27° C), or at the temperature indicated in the specific formula. Ideally, the fermentation temperature should be the same as the temperature of the dough when it is taken from the mixer.

If proper containers are not available, or if humidity is too low to prevent a crust from forming on the dough, you may oil the surface of the dough lightly.

Fermentation is complete when the dough has doubled in volume. A dent will remain or fill very slowly after the fingers are pressed lightly into the top of the dough if fermentation is complete. If the dough springs back, fermentation is not complete.

Gluten becomes smoother and more elastic during fermentation, so that it can stretch farther and hold more gas. An underfermented dough will not develop proper volume and the texture will be coarse. A dough that ferments too long or at too high a temperature will become sticky, hard to work, and slightly sour. An underfermented dough is called a *young dough*. An overfermented dough is called an *old dough*.

Doughs with weak gluten, such as rye doughs and rich doughs, are usually underfermented, or "taken to the bench young."

Yeast action continues until the yeast cells are killed when the temperature of the dough reaches 140° F (60° C) in the oven. It is important to be aware that fermentation continues during the next steps in yeast dough production—punching, scaling, rounding, benching, and makeup or molding. Failure to allow for this time may result in overfermented doughs. Doughs that are to be made into rolls and loaves requiring a great deal of makeup time should be slightly underfermented to prevent the dough from being too old by the time makeup is completed.

More detailed information on dough-making and on controlling fermentation is given in the sections beginning on p. 37.

Punching

Punching is *not* hitting the dough with your fist. It is a method of deflating the dough that *expels carbon dioxide, redistributes the yeast* for further growth, *relaxes the gluten,* and *equalizes the temperature* throughout the dough.

Procedure for Punching Dough

Pull up the dough on all sides, fold it over the center, and press down. Then turn the dough upside-down in the container.

Additional fermentation and punching may or may not be necessary, depending on the product.

Scaling

Using a baker's scale, divide the dough into pieces of the same weight, according to the product being made.

During scaling, allowance is made for weight loss due to evaporation of moisture in the oven. This weight loss is approximately 10 to 13% of the weight of the dough. Allow an extra 1½ to 2 ounces of dough for each 1 pound of baked bread, or 50 to 65 grams per 500 grams.

Actual baking loss depends on baking time, size of the unit, and whether it is baked in a pan or free standing.

Scaling should be done rapidly and efficiently to avoid overfermenting the dough.

If a dough divider is used to make rolls, the dough is scaled into "presses," which are then divided into 36 equal pieces (see p. 66). For example, if 1⅓-ounce rolls are desired, the presses should be scaled at 3 lb (36 × 1⅓ oz), plus 6 oz to allow for baking loss. Presses are rounded, relaxed, and divided; the divided units may or may not be rounded again, depending on the product.

Rounding

After scaling, the pieces of dough are shaped into smooth, round balls. This procedure forms a kind of skin by stretching the gluten on the outside of the dough into a smooth layer. Rounding simplifies the later shaping of the dough and also helps retain gases produced by the yeast.

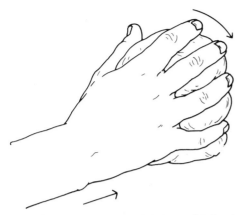

FIGURE 3.1 **To round a piece of dough, roll the dough on the bench with the palm of your hand. As you rotate the dough, the edge of your hand should pinch the dough against the bench. This movement stretches the surface of the dough so that it is completely smooth except for a seam at the bottom where it was pinched together.**

Your instructor will demonstrate rounding techniques. Machines are also available that divide and round portions of dough automatically. Figure 3.1 illustrates a piece of dough being rounded.

Benching, Bench Proofing, or Intermediate Proofing

Rounded portions of dough are allowed to rest for 10 to 20 minutes. This relaxes the gluten to make shaping the dough easier. Also, fermentation continues during this time.

In large operations, the rounded dough is placed in special proofers for this rest. Smaller operations place the dough in boxes that are stacked on one another to keep the dough covered. Or the dough may simply be placed on the work bench and covered — hence the term benching.

Makeup and Panning

The dough is shaped into loaves or rolls and then placed in pans or on baking sheets. In large commercial bakeries this is done by machine, but the baker in a small operation does most of the makeup by hand.

Proper makeup or molding is of critical importance to the finished, baked product. All gas bubbles should be expelled during molding. Bubbles left in the dough will result in large air holes in the baked product.

For both pan breads and hearth breads, the seam must be centered on the bottom to avoid splitting during baking. For units baked in pans, the pan size must be matched to the weight of the dough. Too little or too much dough will result in a poorly shaped loaf.

Breads and rolls take a great many forms. Many shapes and techniques are presented in the next chapter

Proofing

Proofing is a continuation of the process of yeast fermentation, which increases the volume of the shaped dough. Bakers use two different terms so they can distinguish between fermentation of the mixed dough and proofing of the made-up product before baking. Proofing temperatures are generally higher than fermentation temperatures.

Procedure for Proofing Yeast Dough Items

1. Place the panned products in a proof box at 90 to 100° F (32 to 38° C) and about 85% humidity. Proof until double in bulk.

   Avoid using too much steam. This weakens the surface of the dough and causes uneven proofing.

   If a proof box is not available, come as close to these conditions as you can by covering the products to retain moisture and setting them in a warm place.

2. Test proof by sight (the unit doubles in bulk) and by touch. When touched *lightly,* properly proofed dough springs back slowly. If it is still firm and elastic, it needs more proofing. If the dent remains in the dough, the dough is probably overproofed.

Underproofing results in poor volume and dense texture. Overproofing results in coarse texture and some loss of flavor.

French bread is generally given a long proof to create its characteristic open texture. Its strong gluten will withstand the extra stretching of a long proof.

Rich doughs are slightly underproofed, because their weaker gluten structure will not withstand too much stretching.

Baking

As you recall from Chapter 1, many changes take place in the dough during baking. The most important changes are:

1. *Oven spring,* which is the rapid rising in the oven due to production and expansion of trapped gases as a result of the oven heat. The yeast is very active at first but is killed when the temperature inside the dough reaches 140° F (60° C).

2. Coagulation of proteins and gelatinization of starches. In other words, the product becomes firm and holds its shape.

3. Formation and browning of the crust.

In order to control the baking process, the following factors should be considered.

Oven Temperature and Baking Time

Temperatures must be adjusted for the product being baked. At the proper temperature, the inside of the unit becomes completely baked at the same time that the crust achieves the desired color. Therefore:

Large units are baked at a lower temperature and for a longer time than small rolls spaced apart.

Rich doughs and sweet doughs are baked at a lower temperature because their fat, sugar, and milk content makes them brown faster.

French breads made with no added sugar and a long fermentation require very high temperatures to achieve the desired crust color.

Popular American lean breads are baked at 400 to 425° F (205 to 220° C).

Some French breads are baked at 425 to 475° F (220 to 245° C).

Rich products are baked at 350 to 400° F (175 to 205° C).

A golden-brown crust color is the normal indication of doneness. Loaves that are done sound hollow when thumped.

Washes

Many if not most yeast products are brushed with a liquid, called a wash, just before baking. The most common washes are as follows:

1. *Water* is used primarily for hard-crusted products, such as French bread. Like steam in the oven (p. 37), the water helps keep the crust from drying too quickly and thus becoming too thick.

2. *Starch paste* is used primarily for rye breads. In addition to keeping the crust from drying too quickly, the starch paste helps give a shine to the crust.

   To make a starch paste, mix an ounce of light rye flour with one quart of water (60 g rye per 500 ml water). Bring to a boil while stirring. Cool. If necessary, thin with water to the consistency of cream.

3. *Egg wash* is used to give a shiny brown crust to soft breads and rolls and to rich doughs and Danish. It is made by mixing beaten eggs with water or sometimes with milk. Proportions may vary greatly depending on how strong a wash is desired.

Cutting

A break on the side of the loaf is caused by continued rising after the crust is formed. To allow for this expansion, the tops of hard crusted breads are cut before baking. Slashes are made on the top of the loaf with a sharp knife or razor immediately before it is put into the oven. The pattern created by the cuts also contributes to the appearance of the bread.

Small rolls often bake completely without a break, so they are usually cut only for the sake of appearance.

Note: The term "docking" is often used for this procedure. However, many bakers object that the term docking should be reserved for a different process, namely, piercing or perforating of pastry and pie doughs. To avoid this confusion, this book uses only the term "cutting" for the slashing of bread crusts; but you should be aware of the other term, since you will hear it used.

Loading the Ovens

Proofed doughs are fragile until they become set by baking. They should be handled carefully when being loaded into the ovens. And they should not be disturbed during the first part of baking.

Breads and rolls are baked either directly on the bottom of the oven (hearth breads) or in pans.

1. *Hearth breads*

   To load ovens, place the proofed units on peels that have been well dusted with cornmeal. Slide the peel into the oven. Then, with a quick snap, remove the peel, leaving the loaves or rolls in place. To remove baked items, quickly slide the peel under them and pull them out.

2. *Pan breads and rolls*

   Freestanding items may be baked on sheet pans instead of on the hearth. Bakers generally refer to such breads and rolls as "hearth breads," even if they are not baked directly on the bottom of the oven. Sprinkle the pans with cornmeal to keep the units from sticking and to simulate the appearance of hearth-baked items. Pans may also be lined with silicone paper. Perforated sheet pans or screens are also available. These allow better air circulation and therefore permit more even browning.

Sandwich loaves and other pan breads are, of course, baked in loaf pans or other appropriate pans. Details are given in the make-up section of Chapter 4.

Steam

Hard-crusted breads are baked with steam injected into the ovens during the first part of the baking period. Rye breads also benefit from baking with steam for the first 10 minutes.

The effect of the steam can be described as follows: The steam helps keep the crust soft during the first part of baking so that the bread can expand rapidly and evenly. The steam also helps to distribute the heat in the oven, further aiding oven spring. When the moisture of the steam reacts with the starches on the surface, some of the starches form dextrins. Then, when the steam is withdrawn, these dextrins, along with sugars in the dough, caramelize and turn brown. The result is a thin, crisp, glazed crust.

Rich doughs, those with higher fat and/or sugar content, do not form crisp crusts and are usually baked without steam.

Cooling

After baking, bread must be removed from pans and cooled on racks to allow the escape of the excess moisture and alcohol created during fermentation.

Small rolls spaced out and baked on sheets may be left on them, since they will get adequate air circulation.

If soft crusts are desired, breads may be brushed with melted shortening before cooling.

Do not cool in a draft, since the crusts may crack.

Storing

Breads to be served within 8 hours may be left on racks. For longer storage, wrap cooled breads in moisture-proof bags to retard staling. Bread must be thoroughly cool before wrapping, or moisture will collect inside the bags.

Wrapping and freezing maintains quality for longer periods. Refrigeration, on the other hand, increases staling.

Hard-crusted breads should not be wrapped (unless frozen), since the crusts will soften and become leathery.

TYPES OF DOUGH-MAKING PROCESSES

Straight Dough

In the typical small retail shop, most breads are mixed by the straight dough method — that is, all ingredients are mixed in one operation, as described on p. 33. The dough is then given a bulk fermentation time (that is, up until molding and proofing) of 1 to 2½ hours. This is called a *short fermentation straight dough.*

A *no-time dough* is made with a large quantity of yeast, taken from the mixer at a higher temperature (up to 90° F/32° C), and given only a few minutes rest before being scaled and made up. It is also given a shorter proof. This process should be used only in emergencies, since the final product does not have as good a texture and flavor.

Long-fermentation doughs are fermented for 5 or 6 hours or longer, sometimes overnight, at a temperature of 75° F (24° C) or lower. The advantage of this method is that the long, slow fermentation greatly enhances the flavor of the product. Some of the best European breads have been made this way.

The major disadvantage — beside being harder on the work schedule — is that the fermentation is harder to control because of fluctuations in temperature and other factors. Doughs often become overfermented. Therefore, this process is used much less today than in past decades.

To avoid the problems of a long-fermentation straight dough but achieve the flavor created by a long fermentation, one can use the sponge method.

Sponge Processes

Sponge processes involve a two-stage mixing method, as described on p. 33. First a sponge is made of water, flour, and yeast and is allowed to ferment. Then the dough is made by mixing in the remaining ingredients. The finished dough may be given a short fermentation, or if the sponge has had a long fermentation, it may be scaled immediately, like a no-time dough.

Advantages of the Sponge Method

1. Shorter fermentation time for the finished dough.

2. Scheduling flexibility. Sponges can usually be held longer than finished dough.

3. Increased flavor, developed by the long fermentation of the sponge.

4. Stronger fermentation of rich doughs. High sugar and fat content inhibits yeast growth. When the sponge method is used, most of the fermentation is completed before the fat and sugar are incorporated.

5. Less yeast is needed, because it multiplies greatly during the sponge fermentation.

Sourdoughs

Before commercially prepared yeast was widely available, bread was often started by mixing flour and water and letting this mixture stand until wild airborne yeasts settled on it and began to ferment it. This "starter" was then used to leaven bread. A portion of the starter was saved, mixed with more flour and water, and set aside to leaven the next day's bread.

This process is still used today, though the sours are generally started with commercial yeast. Rye breads made with sours are the most popular, though wheat-flour sours are also used.

The sour is actually a kind of sponge, except that it is allowed to ferment until it becomes strongly acidic. It may be used in two ways:

1. The sour is "built" by mixing in more flour and water and allowing it to ferment. The amounts of flour and water added are determined by how much bread is to be produced. This building process may be repeated more than once in a production day, if a large quantity is needed. The completed sour is then used like a *sponge* in the production of the bread dough, except that a portion is saved for the next day's production. Additional yeast may or may not be added to the bread dough, depending on the desired fermentation time and the proportion of sour used.

2. A small portion of sour may be added to a straight dough. In this case, it contributes little leavening power. Its purpose is primarily flavoring.

Commerical sour cultures are available for bakers who do not wish to maintain sour cultures. While these cultures do not add the same flavor as a naturally fermented sour, they have the advantage of convenience. They may be added as a flavoring ingredient to straight doughs, or they may be used in place of, or in addition to, yeast to leaven a sponge. This sponge is then used like a fermented sour.

Still another process used by many bakers is to simply save a small piece of dough from the day's production and mix it into the next day's dough. While this, of course, is not a sour, it does contribute to the flavor of the bread by incorporating a piece of dough that has had long fermentation.

CONTROLLING FERMENTATION

Proper fermentation—that is, fermentation that produces a dough that is neither underripe (young) nor overripe (old)—requires a balance of time, temperature, and yeast quantity.

Time

Fermentation times vary, so the time to punch the dough is indicated not by the clock but by the appearance and feel of the dough. Fermentation times given in the formulas in this book are only guidelines.

To vary the fermentation time, you must control the dough temperature and the amount of yeast.

Temperature

Ideally, dough is fermented at the temperature at which it is taken from the mixer. Large bakeries have special fermentation rooms for controlling temperature and humidity, but small bakeshops or restaurant kitchens seldom have this luxury. If a short-fermentation process is used, however, the fermentation is completed before the dough is greatly affected by changes in shop temperature.

Water Temperature

Dough must be at the proper temperature, usually 78 to 80° F (25.5 to 26.7° C), in order to ferment at the desired rate. The temperature of the dough is affected by several factors:

1. Shop temperature

2. Flour temperature

3. Water temperature

Of these, the water temperature is the easiest to control in the small bakeshop. Therefore, when the water is scaled, it should be brought to the required temperature. On cold days, it may have to be warmed, while on hot days, it may be necessary to use a mixture of crushed ice and water. Also, if a long fermentation is used, the dough temperature must be reduced in order to avoid overfermenting.

Procedure for Determining Water Temperature

1. Multiply the desired dough temperature by three.
2. Add together the flour temperature and room temperature, plus 20° F (11° C) to allow for the friction caused by mixing (see note).
3. Subtract the result of step 2 from that of step 1. The difference is the required water temperature.

Example: Dough temperature needed = 80° F
Flour temperature = 68° F
Room temperature = 72° F
Machine friction = 20° F
Water temperature = ?

1. 80° × 3 = 240°
2. 68° + 72° + 20° = 160°
3. 240° − 160° = 80°

Therefore, the water temperature should be 80° F.

Note: This procedure is precise enough for most purposes in the small bakeshop. However, there are other complications, such as variations in machine friction, that you may want to consider if you wish to be even more exact. To make these calculations, see Appendix 4.

Yeast Quantity

If other conditions are constant, the fermentation time may be increased or decreased by decreasing or increasing the quantity of yeast.

Procedure for Modifying Yeast Quantities

1. Determine a factor by dividing the old fermentation time by the fermentation time desired.
2. Multiply this factor by the original quantity of yeast to determine the new quantity.

$$\frac{\text{old fermentation time}}{\text{new fermentation time}} \times \text{old yeast quantity}$$
$$= \text{new yeast quantity}$$

Example: A formula requiring 12 oz yeast has a fermentation time of 2 hours at 80° F. How much yeast is needed to reduce the fermentation time to 1½ hours?

$$\frac{2 \text{ hours}}{1.5 \text{ hours}} \times 12 \text{ oz yeast} = 16 \text{ oz yeast}$$

Caution: This procedure should be used only within narrow limits. An excessive increase or decrease in yeast quantities introduces many other problems and results in inferior products

Small Batches

When very small quantities of dough—only a few pounds—are made, the dough is more likely to be affected by shop temperature. Thus, it may be necessary to slightly increase the yeast quantity in cool weather and slightly decrease it in hot weather.

Other Factors

The salt in the formula, the minerals in the water, and the use of dough conditioners or improvers affect the rate of fermentation. See p. 28, for a discussion of salt and its affect on fermentation.

Water that is excessively soft lacks the minerals that ensure proper gluten development and dough fermentation. On the other hand, water that is very hard—that is, has high mineral content and, as a result, is alkaline—also inhibits the development of the dough. These conditions are more of a problem for lean doughs than for rich doughs. In most localities, small bakeshops can overcome these problems with the proper use of salt or, in areas with alkaline water, by adding a very small amount of a mild acid to the water. Various dough conditioners, buffers, and improvers that can correct these conditions are available from bakers' suppliers. Their use should be determined by local water conditions.

The richness of the dough must also be considered. Doughs high in fat/or sugar ferment more slowly than lean doughs. This problem can be avoided by using a sponge instead of a straight dough.

Retarding

Retarding means slowing down the fermentation or proof of yeast doughs by refrigeration. This may be done in regular refrigerators or in special retarders that maintain a high humidity. If regular refrigerators are used, the product must be covered to prevent drying and the formation of a skin.

Retarded Fermentation

Dough to be retarded in bulk is usually given partial fermentation. It is then flattened out on sheet pans, covered with plastic wrap, and placed in the retarder. The layer of dough must not be too thick, since the inside will take too long to chill and will overferment. When needed, the dough is allowed to warm up before molding. Some doughs high in fat are made up while chilled so that they do not become too soft.

Retarded Proof

Made-up units to be retarded are made from young dough. After makeup, they are immediately placed in the retarder. When needed, they are allowed to warm up and finish their proof, if necessary. They are then baked.

BREAD FAULTS AND THEIR CAUSES

Because of the complexity of bread production, many things can go wrong. To remedy common bread faults, check the following trouble-shooting guide for possible causes and correct your procedures.

Fault	Causes
Shape	
Poor volume	Too much salt
	Too little yeast
	Too little liquid
	Weak flour
	Under- or overmixing
	Oven too hot
Too much volume	Too little salt
	Too much yeast
	Too much dough scaled
	Overproofed
Poor shape	Too much liquid
	Flour too weak
	Improper molding or makeup
	Improper fermentation or proofing
	Too much oven steam
Split or burst crust	Overmixing
	Underfermented dough
	Improper molding— seam not on bottom
	Uneven heat in oven
	Oven too hot
	Insufficient steam
Texture and crumb	
Too dense or close-grained	Too much salt
	Too little liquid
	Too little yeast
	Underfermented
	Underproofed
Too coarse or open	Too much yeast
	Too much liquid
	Incorrect mixing time
	Improper fermentation
	Overproofed
	Pan too large
Streaked crumb	Improper mixing procedure
	Poor molding or makeup techniques
	Too much flour used for dusting
Poor texture or crumbly	Flour too weak
	Too little salt
	Fermentation time too long or too short
	Overproofed
	Baking temperature too low
Gray crumb	Fermentation time or temperature too high
Crust	
Too dark	Too much sugar or milk
	Underfermented ("young dough")
	Oven temperature too high
	Baking time too long
	Insufficient steam at beginning of baking

Too pale	Too little sugar or milk Overfermented ("old dough") Overproofed Oven temperature too low Baking time too short Too much steam in oven	Blisters on crust	Too much liquid Improper fermentation Improper shaping of loaf

Flavor

Flat taste	Too little salt
Poor flavor	Inferior, spoiled, or rancid ingredients Poor bakeshop sanitation Under- or overfermented

Too thick	Too little sugar or fat Improper fermentation Baked too long and/or at wrong temperature Too little steam

TERMS FOR REVIEW

lean dough
rich dough
rolled-in dough
straight dough method
sponge method
fermentation
young dough
old dough
punching
rounding
oven spring
wash
hearth bread
no-time dough
sourdough
retarding

QUESTIONS FOR DISCUSSION

1. What are the main differences in ingredients between French bread and white sandwich bread?
2. Why is Danish pastry dough flaky?
3. What are the twelve steps in the production of yeast products? Explain each briefly.
4. What are the three major purposes of mixing yeast doughs?
5. Explain the differences in procedure between the straight dough method and the sponge method. How is the straight dough method sometimes modified for sweet doughs, and why is this necessary?
6. What are the purposes of punching a fermented dough?
7. How much French bread dough will you need if you want to make sixteen loaves that weigh 12 oz each after baking?
8. List four advantages of the sponge method for mixing bread doughs.
9. What is the importance of water temperature in mixing yeast doughs?

CHAPTER 4

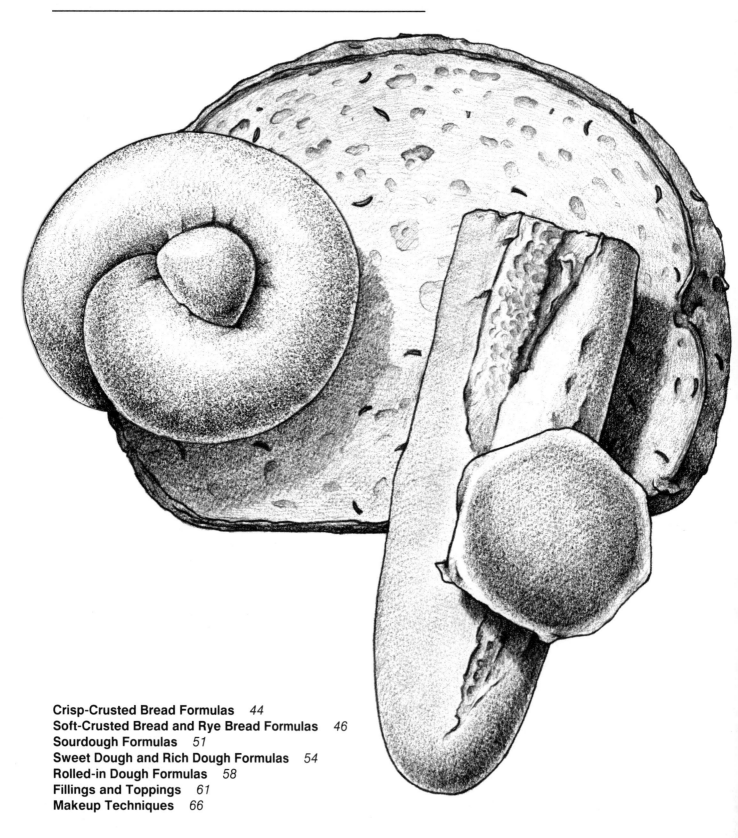

YEAST DOUGH FORMULAS AND TECHNIQUES

The basic yeast dough production methods discussed in Chapter 3 apply to the formulas presented in this chapter. Therefore, the methods are not repeated in detail for each formula. The basic procedures are indicated, and you should refer to the preceding chapter if you need to refresh your memory of the details.

Makeup techniques for loaves, rolls, and other items are described and illustrated beginning on page 66. Makeup procedures are given in a separate section rather than repeated after each formula in order to avoid excessive repetition. Each dough may be made into many types of loaves and rolls, and each makeup technique may be applied to many different formulas.

Large bakeries have machinery that automatically forms loaves and rolls of many types. In a small bakeshop, however, the baker still makes up most products by hand. Learning how to shape loaves, rolls, and pastries is an important part of the art and craft of fine baking.

After studying this chapter, you should be able to:
1. Produce breads and dinner rolls.
2. Produce sweet dough products.
3. Produce Danish pastry and croissants.

CRISP-CRUSTED BREAD FORMULAS

The crisp, thin crusts of French, Italian, and Vienna breads and of hard rolls are achieved by using formulas with little or no sugar and fat and by baking with steam. Because the crust is part of the attraction of these items, they are often made in long thin shapes that increase the proportion of crust.

These breads are usually baked freestanding, either directly on the hearth or on sheet pans. The water content must be low enough so that the units will hold their shape in the oven.

There is no clear difference between French bread dough and Italian bread dough. Some sources say that French bread contains a little fat and sugar, while Ital-ian bread does not. Other sources give Italian bread formulas that contain fat and sugar. Furthermore, breads containing neither of these ingredients are common in both France and Italy. Also, both Italy and France produce breads in many shapes, not only in the long, thin loaf shape familiar here.

In practice, French and Italian bread formulas in the United States are widely interchangeable. The best practice is to follow regional preferences and to produce good quality products that are appealing to your customers.

To create the open cell structure characteristic of French bread, give the loaves a very full proof before baking.

	Hard Rolls			**Vienna Bread**			
Ingredients	U.S.	Metric	%	U.S.		Metric	%
Water	3 lb	1400	55	3 lb		1400	55
Yeast	3 oz	90 g	3.5	3	oz	90 g	3.5
Bread flour	5 lb 8 oz	2500 g	100	5 lb 8	oz	2500 g	100
Salt	2 oz	55 g	2.25	2	oz	55 g	2.25
Sugar	2 oz	55 g	2.25	2.5 oz		75	3
Malt	—	—	—	1	oz	25 g	1
Shortening	2 oz	55 g	2.25	—		—	—
Oil	—	—	—	2.5 oz		75 g	3
Egg whites	2 oz	55 g	2.25	—		—	—
Whole eggs	—	—	—	3.5 oz		100 g	4
Yield:	9 lb 3 oz	4210 g	167	9 lb 6	oz	4320 g	171

Mixing: Straight dough method
10 minutes at second speed

Fermentation: About 1 hour at 80° F (27° C)

Makeup: See pp. 66–69.

Baking: 425° F (218° C) for loaves; 450° F (230° C) for rolls. Steam for first 10 minutes.

Ingredients	Italian Bread				French Bread			
	U.S.		*Metric*	*%*	*U.S.*		*Metric*	*%*
Water	4 lb		1700 g	57	4 lb		1700 g	57
Yeast	3	oz	80 g	2.75	3	oz	80 g	2.75
Bread flour	7 lb		3000 g	100	7 lb		3000 g	100
Salt	2	oz	50 g	1.75	2	oz	50 g	1.75
Malt syrup	0.5 oz		15 g	0.5	0.5 oz		15 g	0.5
Sugar	—		—	—	2	oz	50 g	1.75
Shortening	—		—	—	2	oz	50 g	1.75
Yield:	11 lb 5	oz	4845 g	162	11 lb 9	oz	4945 g	165

Mixing: Straight dough method
8 – 10 minutes at second speed.

Fermentation: 1½ hours at 80° F (27° C) or 2 hours at 75° F (24° C)

Makeup: See pp. 66 – 69.

Baking: 425° F (218° C) for loaves; 450° F (230° C) for rolls. Steam for first 10 minutes.

Variations

Whole Wheat French and Italian Breads:

Use the following proportions of flour in the above formulas:

Whole Wheat flour	3 lb	1300 g	43%
Bread Flour	4 lb	1700 g	57%

Increase the water to 59 – 60% to allow for the extra absorption by the bran. Mix 8 minutes.

Pizza:

Add 2.5% vegetable oil or olive oil (2.5 oz/75 g) to Italian Bread formula. For dough to be retarded, also add 1% sugar (1 oz/30 g). Ferment, scale (see Table 4.1), and round. After bench rest, sheet or roll out, and apply tomato sauce, cheese, and toppings. Bake without proofing. Baking temperature: 550° F (290° C).

TABLE 4.1 **Scaling Guidelines for Pizza**

	12-inch	14-inch	16-inch
Dough	10 – 12 oz	13 – 15 oz	18 – 20 oz
Tomato sauce	3 oz	4½ oz	5½ oz
Cheese	4 oz	5½ oz	7½ oz

French Bread (Sponge)

Ingredients	U.S.		Metric	%
Sponge				
Bread flour	2 lb		1000 g	33
Water	2 lb		1000 g	33
Yeast	2	oz	60 g	2
Malt syrup	1	oz	30 g	1
Dough				
Bread flour	4 lb		2000 g	67
Water	1 lb 10	oz	810 g	27
Salt	1.75	oz	52 g	1.75
Yield:	9 lb 14	oz	4952 g	164

Mixing: Sponge method

Fermentation: Sponge: 4 hours at 75° F (24° C), or overnight at 65° F (18° C)
Dough: 30 minutes at 80° F (27° C)

Makeup: See p. 69.

Baking: 425° F (218° C)

Variation

Country-style French Bread:

Use the following proportions of flour and water in the dough stage of the above formula:

Clear or bread flour	1 lb 10 oz	800 g	27%
Whole wheat flour	2 lb 6 oz	1200 g	40%
Water	1 lb 13 oz	900 g	30%

Make up the dough into round loaves.

SOFT-CRUSTED BREAD AND RYE BREAD FORMULAS

This category includes sandwich-type breads baked in loaf pans, soft rolls, braided breads, and straight-dough rye (sour rye breads are in the next section). Many of these formulas incorporate milk, eggs, and higher percentages of sugar and fat.

Formulas for water bagels and English muffins are also included here because there is great interest in them. These items are normally produced in specialty bakeries having specialized equipment, rather than in general retail bakeshops. Production methods for them are unusual: Bagels are boiled in a malt solution before being baked, and English muffins are baked on a griddle rather than in an oven. Methods presented here are modified for the general-purpose bakeshop.

White Pan Bread

Ingredients	U.S.		Metric	%
Water	3 lb		1200 g	60
Yeast		3 oz	75 g	3.75
Bread flour	5 lb		2000 g	100
Salt		2 oz	50 g	2.5
Sugar		3 oz	75 g	3.75
Nonfat milk solids		4 oz	100 g	5
Shortening		3 oz	75 g	3.75
Yield:	8 lb 15 oz		3575 g	178

Mixing: Straight dough method
10 minutes at second speed

Fermentation: 1½ hours at 80° F (27° C)

Makeup: See p. 72.

Baking: 400° F (200° C)

Variation

Whole Wheat Bread:

Use the following proportions of flour in the above formula:

Bread flour	2 lb	800 g	40%
Whole wheat flour	3 lb	1200 g	60%

White Bread (Sponge)

Ingredients	U.S.		Metric	%
Sponge				
Flour	4 lb		2000 g	67
Water	2 lb 12	oz	1350 g	45
Yeast		2.5 oz	75 g	2.5
Malt syrup		0.5 oz	15 g	0.5
Dough				
Flour	2 lb		1000 g	33
Water		14 oz	450 g	15
Salt		2 oz	60 g	2
Nonfat milk solids		3 oz	90 g	3
Sugar		5 oz	150 g	5
Shortening		3 oz	90 g	3
Yield:	10 lb 10	oz	5280 g	176

Mixing: Sponge method

Fermentation: Sponge—about 4 hours at 75° F (24° C)
Dough—about 15 minutes at 80° F (27° C)

Makeup: See p. 72. Especially suitable for pullman loaf.

Baking: 400° F (200° C)

	Soft Rolls				Egg Rolls and Bread				
Ingredients	U.S.			Metric	%	U.S.			Metric	%
Water	3 lb			1425 g	57	2 lb 10	oz	1250 g	50
Yeast		3	oz	90 g	3.5	3	oz	90 g	3.5
Bread flour	5 lb	4	oz	2500 g	100	5 lb 4	oz	2500	100
Salt		1.5 oz		45 g	1.75	1.5 oz		45 g	1.75
Sugar		8	oz	240 g	9.5	8	oz	240 g	9.5
Nonfat milk solids		4	oz	120 g	4.75	4	oz	120 g	4.75
Shortening		4	oz	120 g	4.75	4	oz	120 g	4.75
Butter		4	oz	120 g	4.75	4	oz	120 g	4.75
Eggs	—			—	—	8	oz	240 g	9.5
Yield:	9 lb 12		oz	4660 g	186	9 lb 14	oz	4725 g	188

Mixing: Straight dough method
10–12 minutes at second speed

Fermentation: 1½ hours at 80° F (27° C)

Makeup: See pp. 69–75.

Baking: 400° F (200° C)

Variations

Raisin Bread:

Scale 75% raisins (4 lb/1875 g). Soak in warm water to soften; drain and dry. Add to Soft Roll Dough 1–2 minutes before end of mixing.

Cinnamon Bread:

Make up Soft Roll Dough as for pan bread (p. 72), but after flattening out each unit (see Figure 4.14), brush with melted butter and sprinkle with cinnamon sugar. After baking, while still hot, brush tops of loaves with melted butter or shortening and sprinkle with cinnamon sugar (p. 61).

100% Whole Wheat Bread

Ingredients	U.S.	Metric	%
Water	4 lb	1860 g	62
Yeast	3 oz	90 g	3
Whole wheat flour	6 lb 8 oz	3000 g	100
Sugar	2 oz	60 g	2
Malt syrup	2 oz	60 g	2
Nonfat milk solids	3 oz	90 g	3
Shortening	4 oz	120 g	4
Salt	2 oz	60 g	2
Yield:	11 lb 7 oz	5340 g	178

Mixing: Straight dough method
10 minutes at second speed

Fermentation: 1½ hours at 80° F (27° C)

Makeup: See pp. 69–75.

Baking: 400° F (200° C)

Challah

Ingredients	U.S.		Metric	%
Water	2 lb		800 g	40
Yeast	3	oz	80 g	3.75
Bread flour	5 lb		2000 g	100
Egg yolks	1 lb		400 g	20
Sugar	6	oz	150 g	7.5
Malt syrup	0.5 oz		10 g	0.6
Salt	1.5 oz		38 g	1.9
Vegetable oil	8	oz	250 g	10
Yield:	9 lb 3	oz	3728 g	183

Mixing: Straight dough method
10 minutes at second speed

Fermentation: 1½ hours at 80° F (27° C)

Makeup: See pp. 73–75.

Baking: 400° F (200° C)

English Muffins

Ingredients	U.S.		Metric	%
Water (see mixing instructions)	3 lb		1500 g	75
Yeast	1	oz	30 g	1.5
Bread flour	4 lb		2000 g	100
Salt	1	oz	30 g	1.5
Sugar	1	oz	30 g	1.5
Nonfat milk solids	1.5 oz		45 g	2.3
Shortening	1	oz	30 g	1.5
Yield:	7 lb 5	oz	3665 g	183

Mixing: Straight dough method
20–25 minutes at second speed
This dough is intentionally overmixed to develop its characteristic coarse texture. Because of this long mixing time, use twice your normal machine friction factor (see p. 39) when calculating water temperature. For this reason, and because of the low fermentation temperature, it is usually necessary to use very cold water or part crushed ice.

Fermentation: Dough temperature: 70° F (21° C). Ferment 2½ to 3 hours.

Scaling and makeup: Because this dough is very soft and sticky, you must use plenty of dusting flour. Scale at 1.5 oz (45 g) per unit. Round and relax the units, then flatten with the palms of the hands. Place on cornmeal-covered trays to proof.

Baking: Bake on both sides on a griddle at low heat.

Light American Rye Bread and Rolls

Ingredients	U.S.		Metric	%
Water	3 lb		1400 g	60
Yeast		3 oz	90 g	3.75
Light rye flour	2 lb		1000 g	40
Bread or clear flour	3 lb		1400 g	60
Salt		1.5 oz	45 g	2
Shortening		2 oz	60 g	2.5
Molasses (or malt syrup)		2 oz	60 g	2.5
Caraway seeds (optional)		1 oz	30 g	1.25
Rye flavor		1 oz	30 g	1.25
Yield:	8 lb 10 oz		4105 g	173

Mixing: Straight dough method
5–6 minutes at second speed

Fermentation: 1½ hours at 80° F (27° C)

Makeup: See pp. 66–72.

Baking: 400° F (200° C). Steam for first 10 minutes.

Water Bagels

Ingredients	U.S.		Metric	%
Water	2 lb		1000 g	50
Yeast		2 oz	60 g	3
High-gluten flour	4 lb		2000 g	100
Malt syrup		4 oz	120 g	6
Salt		1 oz	30 g	1.5
Oil		0.5 oz	16 g	0.8
Yield:	6 lb 7 oz		3226 g	161

Mixing: Straight dough method
8–10 minutes at low speed

Fermentation: 1 hour at 80° F (27° C)

Makeup and baking:

1. Scale at 1.75 to 2 oz (50 to 55 g) per unit.

2. Roll with the palms of the hands into ropes (as for knotted or tied rolls). Loop around palms into doughnut shape. Seal the ends together well by rolling under the palms on the bench.

3. Give half proof.

4. Boil in a malt solution (⅓ qt malt syrup per 4 gallons of water, or 3 dl malt per 15 l water) about 1 minute.

5. Place on sheet pans about 1 inch apart. Bake at 450° F (230° C) until golden brown, turning them over when they are half baked.

Total baking time is about 20 minutes.
If desired, bagels may be sprinkled with sesame seeds, poppy seeds, diced onion, or coarse salt before baking.

Onion Rye

Ingredients	U.S.		Metric	%
Water	3 lb		1200 g	60
Yeast	3	oz	75 g	3.75
Light rye flour	1 lb 12	oz	700 g	35
Clear flour	3 lb 4	oz	1300 g	65
Dried onions, scaled, soaked in water, and well drained	4	oz	100 g	5
Salt	1.5	oz	40 g	1.9
Caraway seeds	1	oz	25 g	1.25
Rye flavor	1	oz	25 g	1.25
Malt syrup	2	oz	50 g	2.5
Yield:	8 lb 12	oz	3515 g	172

Mixing: Straight dough method
5 minutes at second speed

Fermentation: 1½ hours at 76° F (24° C), punch down, then 1 more hour.

Makeup: See pp. 66–72.

Baking: 400° F (200° C). Steam for first 10 minutes.

Variation

Onion Pumpernickel (Non-sour):

Use the following proportions of flour in the above formula:

Pumpernickel flour (rye meal)	1 lb	400 g	20%
Medium rye flour	12 oz	300 g	15%
Clear flour	3 lb 4 oz	1300 g	65%

Dough may be colored with caramel color or cocoa powder.

SOURDOUGH FORMULAS

The purposes of a sour are to provide *flavor* and *leavening power*. If a large proportion of active sour is used, it can provide all the leavening, so that little or no additional yeast is needed. If a small percentage of sour is used, it functions primarily as a flavoring ingredient, and additional yeast is generally required for the dough.

Sours are used primarily for rye breads in this country. Two formulas for rye sours are given here. The first is adequate for small or moderate production requirements. If large quantities are being made, the second is more useful. Either sour can be used in the bread formulas given here.

Sour rye doughs are stickier than regular doughs, so handling of the dough and makeup of loaves requires more skill and practice. Also, care should be taken not to overmix the dough. Use low speed to avoid damaging the gluten.

Underproof sourdough breads, especially if a high percentage of sour is used. Proofed units are very fragile. Steam should be used in baking to allow the crust to expand without breaking.

Sours may also be used for white breads, although this is not as common in the United States, with the well-known exception of the San Francisco area. Unique sour cultures thrive in that environment, and the sourdough breads baked there are prized for their flavor. Unfortunately, those cultures apparently cannot be easily duplicated or maintained in other areas.

To make a white sour, substitute bread flour for rye flour in either of the two sour formulas.

Sour I

Ingredients	U.S.	Metric	%
Rye flour	5 lb	2000 g	100
Water	3 lb 12 oz	1500 g	75
Yeast	4 oz	100 g	5
1 onion, cut in half (optional)			
Yield:	9 lb	3600 g	180

Procedure:

1. Dissolve yeast in water.
2. Add rye flour and mix until smooth.
3. Bury the onion in the mix.
4. Let stand 24 hours. Desired temperature: 70° F (21° C).
5. Remove onion.

To use:

1. Add to doughs as needed.
2. Save some of the sour as starter for next batch of starter. Add flour and water in same proportions as formula (75% water to 100% flour) and let ferment until next day. Additional yeast will not be needed as long as the sour is active.

Sour II

Ingredients	U.S.	Metric	%
Starter			
Light rye flour	1 lb	500 g	100
Water	12 oz	375 g	75
Yeast	2 oz	60 g	12.5
First build			
Light rye flour	4 lb	2000 g	100
Water	3 lb	1500 g	75
Second build			
Light rye flour	4 lb	2000 g	100
Water	3 lb	1500 g	75
Third build			
Light rye flour	up to 24 lb	up to 10,000 g	100
Water	up to 18 lb	up to 7500 g	75
Yield:	up to 57 lb	25,000 g	

Mixing

1. Mix starter ingredients. Let stand at shop temperature 24 hours.
2. Add first build ingredients. Ferment at 80° F (27° C) until it falls back, about 3 hours.
3. Repeat with remaining builds. Second build may be omitted if schedule does not permit. Amounts added in last build depend upon production requirements.
4. Save about 2 lb (1 kg) sour as starter for next day's production.

Sour Rye

Ingredients	U.S.		Metric	%
Water	3 lb		1200 g	50
Yeast		1 oz	25 g	1
Fermented sour	3 lb	8 oz	1440 g	60
Clear flour	6 lb		2400 g	100
Salt		2 oz	50 g	2
Yield:	12 lb	11 oz	5115 g	213

Optional ingredients:

Caraway seeds	up to 1.5 oz	up to 35 g	up to 1.5
Molasses or malt	up to 3 oz	up to 70 g	up to 3
Caramel color	up to 1.5 oz	up to 35 g	up to 1.5

Mixing:

1. Dissolve yeast in water.

2. Add the sour and mix to break up the sour.

3. Add the clear flour, salt, and optional flavoring ingredients.
Develop the dough 5 minutes at low speed. Do not overmix.

Fermentation: Rest 15 minutes, then scale.

Makeup: See pp. 66–72.
Give only ¾ proof.

Baking: 425° F (218° C) with steam for first 10 minutes.

Pumpernickel

Ingredients	U.S.		Metric	%
Water	3 lb		1500 g	50
Yeast		1 oz	30 g	1
Fermented sour	2 lb	8 oz	1260 g	42
Rye meal (pumpernickel)	1 lb	4 oz	600 g	20
Clear flour	4 lb	12 oz	2400 g	80
Salt		2 oz	60 g	2
Malt syrup		1 oz	30 g	1
Molasses		2 oz	60 g	2
Caramel color (optional)		1.5 oz	45 g	1.5
Yield:	11 lb	15 oz	5985 g	199

Mixing:

1. Dissolve the yeast in water.

2. Add the sour and mix to break up the sour.

3. Add the rye meal, clear flour, salt, malt, molasses, and color. Develop the
dough: 5 minutes at low speed. Do not overdevelop the dough.

Fermentation: Rest 15 minutes, then scale.

Makeup: See pp. 66–72.
Give only ¾ proof.

Baking: 425° F (218° C) with steam for first 10 minutes.

American Rye II

Add up to 10% sour to Light American Rye formula (p. 50) as a flavoring ingredient. Do not reduce the yeast in the formula.

SWEET DOUGH AND RICH DOUGH FORMULAS

It must be remembered that high percentages of fat and sugar in a yeast dough inhibit fermentation. For this reason, most of the doughs in this section are mixed by the sponge method, so that most of the fermentation can take place before the sugar and fat are added. The one exception here is the regular sweet dough or bun dough, which is low enough in fat and sugar so that it can be mixed by the modified straight dough method. The quantity of yeast is also increased.

High levels of fat and eggs make rich doughs very soft. The amount of liquid is reduced to compensate for this.

Because they are so tender, rich doughs are generally underfermented and underproofed. About three-quarters proof is best for rich doughs. Overproofed units may collapse in baking.

Bun pans should be lined with silicone paper whenever there is danger of sticking. This is especially true in items with fruit fillings or other sugary fillings or toppings.

Note that the recipes exemplify two ways of mixing rich sponge doughs. Rich sweet dough and kugelhopf dough are high in sugar. To ensure even distribution in the dough, the sugar is creamed with the fat, just as in the modified straight dough method. In brioche and baba doughs, there is little sugar, so this method is not used. The fat is mixed into the dough last.

Sweet Roll Dough

Ingredients	U.S.		Metric	%
Water	2 lb		800 g	40
Yeast		6 oz	150 g	7.5
Butter/margarine/ shortening (see note)	1 lb		400 g	20
Sugar	1 lb		400 g	20
Salt		1 oz	25 g	1.25
Nonfat milk solids		4 oz	100 g	5
Eggs		12 oz	300 g	15
Bread flour	4 lb		1600 g	80
Cake flour	1 lb		400 g	20
Yield:	10 lb	7 oz	4075 g	208

Note: Any of the fats listed may be used alone or in combination.

Mixing: Modified straight dough method
Develop the dough 4 minutes at second speed.

Fermentation: 1½ hours at 80° F (27° C)

Makeup: See pp. 77–82.

Baking: 375° F (190° C)

Rich Sweet Dough

Ingredients	U.S.	Metric	%
Milk, scalded and cooled	2 lb	800 g	40
Yeast	4 oz	100 g	5
Bread flour	2 lb 8 oz	1000 g	50
Butter	2 lb	800 g	40
Sugar	1 lb	400 g	20
Salt	1 oz	25 g	1.25
Eggs	1 lb 4 oz	500 g	25
Bread flour	2 lb 8 oz	1000 g	50
Yield:	11 lb 9 oz	4625 g	231.25

Mixing: Sponge method

1. Make a sponge with the first three ingredients. Ferment until double.

2. Cream butter, sugar, and salt until well blended. Blend in eggs.

3. Add the sponge. Mix to break up the sponge.

4. Add the flour and develop the dough. Mixing time: about 3 minutes.

Fermentation: 30 – 40 minutes, or retard immediately. Retarding will make it easier to handle the dough, which is very soft.

Variations

Stollen:

Add to butter and sugar during blending stage:

Almond extract	0.5 oz	10 g	0.5%
Lemon rind, grated	0.5 oz	10 g	0.5%
Vanilla	0.5 oz	10 g	0.5%

Knead into the dough:

Raisins (light, dark, or a mixture)	1 lb 8 oz	600 g	30%
Mixed glacéed fruit	1 lb 12 oz	700 g	35%

Makeup:

1. Scale, round, and let rest. Scaling weights may range from 12 oz to 2 lb (350 g to 1 kg), depending on individual needs.

2. With hands or a rolling pin, flatten out slightly into an oval shape.

3. Wash the top with butter.

4. Make a crease down the length of the oval about ½ inch (1 cm) off center. Fold one side (the smaller side) over the other, as though you are making a large, wide Parker House roll (see Figure 4.12).

5. Give three-quarters proof. Wash the tops with melted butter.

6. Bake at 375° F (190° C).

7. Cool. Dredge heavily with 4X or 6X sugar.

(Continues)

Rich Sweet Dough Variations *(Continued)*

Babka:

Add to butter during blending stage:

Vanilla	0.5 oz	10 g	0.5%
Cardamom	0.25 oz	5 g	0.25%

Knead into dough:

Raisins	1 lb	400 g	20%

Makeup: Loaf-type coffee cake (p. 81). May be topped with streusel.

Baking: 350° F (175° C). Be sure to bake thoroughly; underbaked units will have sticky crumb and may collapse.

Kugelhopf

Ingredients	U.S.		Metric	%
Milk, scalded and cooled	12	oz	375 g	30
Yeast	2	oz	60 g	5
Bread flour	12	oz	375 g	30
Butter	1 lb		500 g	40
Sugar	8	oz	250 g	20
Salt	0.5	oz	15 g	1.25
Eggs	14	oz	440 g	35
Bread flour	1 lb 12	oz	875 g	70
Raisins	5	oz	150 g	12.5
Yield:	6 lb 1	oz	3040 g	243

Mixing: Sponge method

1. Make a sponge with the first three ingredients. Ferment until double.
2. Cream the butter, sugar, and salt until well blended. Blend in the eggs.
3. Add the sponge. Mix to break up the sponge.
4. Add the flour and develop the dough. Mixing time: about 3 minutes. Dough will be very soft and sticky.
5. Carefully blend in the raisins.

Fermentation: Needs only 15–20 minutes bench rest before scaling and panning. Or retard immediately.

Makeup: Heavily butter kugelhopf molds or tube pans. Line with sliced almonds (which will stick to the buttered sides). Fill molds halfway with dough (each quart of volume will require about 1 lb of dough, or each liter will require about 500 g). Give three-quarters proof.

Baking: 375° F (190° C)
Unmold and cool completely. Dust with confectioners' sugar.

Baba/Savarin Dough

Ingredients	U.S.			Metric	%
Milk	1 lb			500 g	40
Yeast		2	oz	60 g	5
Bread flour		10	oz	300 g	25
Eggs	1 lb	4	oz	600 g	50
Bread flour	1 lb	14	oz	900 g	75
Sugar		1	oz	30 g	2.5
Salt		0.5	oz	15 g	1.25
Butter, melted	1 lb			500 g	40
Yield:	5 lb	15	oz	2905 g	238

Mixing: Sponge method

1. Scald milk and cool to lukewarm. Dissolve yeast. Add flour and mix to make a sponge. Let rise until double.

2. Gradually mix in eggs and then dry ingredients (using the paddle attachment) to make a soft dough.

3. Beat in butter a little at a time until it is completely absorbed and the dough is smooth. Dough will be very soft and sticky.

Makeup and baking:

1. Fill greased molds half full. Average baba molds require about 2 oz (60 g). For savarin molds (ring molds), the following are averages:

       5-inch ring: 5–6 oz   13-cm ring: 140–170 g
       7-inch ring: 10–12 oz   18-cm ring: 280–340 g
       8-inch ring: 14–16 oz   20-cm ring: 400–450 g
       10-inch ring: 20–24 oz   25-cm ring: 575–675 g

1. Proof until dough is level with top of mold.

3. Bake at 400° F (200° C).

4. While still warm, soak in dessert syrup (p. 115) flavored with rum or kirsch. Drain.

5. Glaze with apricot glaze. If desired, decorate with candied fruits.

Variation

Add 25% raisins (10 oz/300 g) to baba dough.

Brioche

Ingredients	U.S.			Metric	%
Milk		8	oz	250 g	20
Yeast		2	oz	60 g	5
Bread flour		8	oz	250 g	20
Eggs	1 lb	4	oz	600 g	50
Bread flour	2 lb			950 g	80
Sugar		2	oz	60 g	5
Salt		0.5	oz	15 g	1.25
Butter, softened	1 lb 12		oz	850 g	70
Yield:	6 lb	4	oz	3035 g	251

Mixing: Sponge method

1. Scald milk and cool to lukewarm. Dissolve yeast. Add flour and mix to make a sponge. Let rise until double.

2. Gradually mix in eggs and then dry ingredients (using the paddle attachment) to make a soft dough.

3. Beat in butter a little at a time until it is completely absorbed and the dough is smooth. Dough will be very soft and sticky.

Note: To make dough less sticky and less difficult to handle, the butter may be reduced to 50% (1 lb 4 oz/600 g). However, the product will not be as rich and delicate.

Fermentation:

1. If the dough will require much handling in makeup, as for small brioche rolls, it is easiest to retard the dough overnight. It can then be made up while chilled in order to reduce stickiness.

2. If the dough is to be simply deposited in pans, the stickiness and softness of the dough is not a problem, so the dough need not be retarded. Ferment 20 minutes, then scale and pan.

Makeup: See p. 76. Egg wash before baking.

Baking: 400° F (200° C) for small rolls; 375° F (190° C) for large units

ROLLED-IN DOUGH FORMULAS

Rolled-in doughs contain many layers of fat sandwiched between layers of dough. These layers create the flakiness that you are familiar with in Danish pastry.

Two basic kinds of rolled-in yeast dough are made in the bakeshop: sweet (Danish pastry) and non-sweet croissants). Rolled-in doughs are mixed only slightly, because the rolling-in procedure continues to develop the gluten.

Butter is the preferred fat because of its flavor and melt-in-the-mouth qualities in rolled-in doughs. The best-quality products utilize butter for at least part of the rolled-in fat. However, butter is difficult to work because it is very hard when cold and very soft when a little too warm. Specially formulated shortenings and margarines can be used when lower cost and greater ease of handling are important considerations.

Rolling-in Procedure for Danish and Croissant Dough

The rolling-in procedure has two parts:

1. *Enclosing the fat in the dough.*

   In the method illustrated in Figure 4.1, the fat is spotted on two-thirds of the dough and the dough is folded in thirds like a business letter. This results in five layers: three layers of dough and two layers of fat.

2. *Rolling out and folding the dough to increase the number of layers.*

In these doughs, we use a *simple fold*, or *three-fold*, which means that we fold the dough in thirds. Each complete rolling and folding step is called a turn. We give Danish four turns, creating over 300 layers of dough and fat.

FIGURE 4.1 Rolling-in Procedure for Danish and Croissant Dough.
(*a*) Roll out the dough ½ to ¾ inch (1 to 2 cm) thick into a rectangle about three times as long as it is wide.

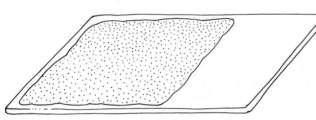

(*b*) Spot the butter over two-thirds of the length of the dough as shown, leaving a 1-inch (2½ cm) margin at the edges.

(*c*) Fold the third without fat over the center third.

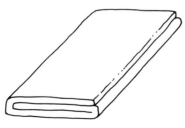

(*d*) Fold the remaining third on top. Rest the dough in the retarder (under refrigeration) 20 to 30 minutes to allow the gluten to relax.

(*e*) Place the dough on the bench at right angles to its position in step *d*. This step must be taken before each rolling-out of the dough, so that the gluten is stretched in all directions, not just lengthwise.

(*f*) Roll out the dough into a rectangle.

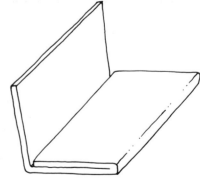

(*g*) Fold again into thirds. Be sure to brush off excess dusting flour from between the folds. You have now completed the first turn or fold; incorporating the butter doesn't count as a turn. Press one finger into the dough near the end to make one indentation. This indicates "1 turn" to anyone who may have to take up where you left off, or to you if you have several batches going. Refrigerate the dough 20 to 30 minutes to relax the gluten. Repeat the above rolling and folding procedures for a second and third turn, resting the dough in between turns. Mark the number of turns in the dough with two or three fingers. After the third turn, rest the dough in the retarder for several hours or overnight. Cover it with plastic film to prevent crusting. The dough is then ready for makeup.

Croissants

Ingredients	U.S	Metric	%
Milk	2 lb	900 g	57
Yeast	2 oz	60 g	4
Sugar	2 oz	60 g	4
Salt	1 oz	30 g	2
Butter, soft	6 oz	160 g	10
Bread flour	3 lb 8 oz	1600 g	100
Butter	2 lb	900 g	57
Yield:	8 lb 3 oz	3710 g	234

Mixing: Straight dough method. Scald milk, cool to lukewarm, and dissolve yeast. Add remaining ingredients except last 2 lb (900 g) butter. Mix into a smooth dough, but do not develop the gluten. Gluten development will take place during rolling in procedure.

Fermentation: 1 hour at 80° F (27° C)
Punch down, spread out on a flat pan, and rest in retarder 30 minutes.

Roll in last amount of butter and give three 3-folds (Figure 4.1). Rest in retarder overnight.

Makeup: See Figure 4.20.
Proof at 80° F (27° C). Egg wash after proofing.

Baking: 400° F (200° C)

Danish Pastry

Ingredients	U.S.			Metric	%
Water	2 lb			800 g	40
Yeast		5	oz	125 g	6.25
Butter		10	oz	250 g	12.5
Sugar		12	oz	300 g	15
Nonfat milk solids		4	oz	100 g	5
Salt		1	oz	25 g	1.25
Cardamom or mace (optional)		0.16 oz (2 tsp)		4 g	0.2
Eggs	1 lb			400 g	20
Egg yolks		4	oz	100 g	5
Bread flour	4 lb			1600 g	80
Cake flour	1 lb			400 g	20
Butter (for rolling in)	2 lb 8		oz	1000 g	50
Yield:	12 lb 12		oz	5104 g	255

Mixing: Modified straight dough method
Develop dough 3–4 minutes at 2nd speed.
Rest in retarder 30 minutes.
Roll in last quantity of butter. Give four 3-folds (Figure 4.1).

Makeup: See pp. 77–82.
Proof at 90° F (32° C) with little steam. Egg wash after proofing.

Baking: 375° F (190° C)

FILLINGS AND TOPPINGS

The formulas in this section include many of the most popular fillings and toppings for Danish pastry, coffee cakes, and other sweet yeast products. Several of these items, such as cinnamon sugar, streusel topping, almond filling, and clear glaze, are used for many other bakery products, including cakes, cookies, puff pastries, pies and tarts. However, their primary use is in the production of yeast goods.

Many of these and similar fillings are available ready-made from bakery supply houses. For example, good-quality prune, poppy, apricot, and other fruit and nut fillings can be purchased in No. 10 cans.

Cinnamon Sugar

Ingredients	U.S.	Metric	Sugar at 100% %
Sugar	2 lb	1000 g	100
Cinnamon	1 oz	30 g	3
Yield:	2 lb 1 oz	1030 g	103

Procedure: Stir together thoroughly.

Streusel or Crumb Topping

Ingredients	U.S.	Metric	%
Butter and/or shortening	1 lb	500 g	50
Sugar, granulated	10 oz	300 g	30
Sugar, brown	8 oz	250 g	25
Salt	0.16 oz (1 tsp)	5 g	0.5
Cinnamon or mace	0.08–0.16 oz (1–2 tsp)	2.5–5 g	0.25–0.5
Pastry flour	2 lb	1000 g	100
Yield:	4 lb 2 oz	2060 g	206

Procedure: Rub all ingredients together until crumbly.

Variation

Nut Streusel:

Add 25% chopped nuts (8 oz/250 g).

Clear Glaze

Ingredients	U.S.	Corn syrup at 100% Metric	%
Water	8 oz	250 g	50
Light corn syrup	1 lb	500 g	100
Granulated sugar	8 oz	250 g	50
Yield:	2 lb	1000 g	200

Procedure:

1. Mix ingredients together and bring to a boil. Stir to ensure that sugar is completely dissolved.

2. Apply while hot, or reheat before use.

Date, Prune, or Apricot Filling
Yield: about 6 lb (3000 g)

Ingredients	U.S.	Metric	Fruit at 100% %
Dates, prunes (pitted), or dried apricots	4 lb	2000 g	100
Sugar	12 oz	400 g	20
Water	2 lb	1000 g	50

Procedure:

1. Pass the fruit through a grinder.

2. Combine all ingredients in a saucepan. Bring to a boil. Simmer and stir until thick and smooth, about 10 minutes.

3. Cool before using.

Variations

1. Date or prune filling may be flavored with lemon and/or cinnamon.

2. Add 12.5% (8 oz/250 g) chopped walnuts to date or prune filling.

Almond Filling I (Frangipane)

Ingredients	U.S.	Metric	Almond paste at 100% %
Almond paste	2 lb	1000 g	100
Sugar	2 lb	1000 g	100
Butter and/or shortening	1 lb	500 g	50
Pastry or cake four	8 oz	250 g	25
Eggs	8 oz	250 g	25
Yield:	6 lb	3000 g	300

Procedure:

1. With paddle attachment, mix almond paste and sugar at low speed until evenly mixed.

2. Mix in fat and flour until smooth.

4. Beat in eggs, a little at a time, until smooth.

Almond Filling II (Frangipane)

Ingredients	U.S.		Almond paste at 100% Metric	%
Almond paste	1 lb		500 g	100
Sugar	1 lb		500 g	100
Eggs	4 oz		125 g	25
Cake crumbs	1 lb 8 oz		750 g	150
Milk	8 oz	or as needed	250 g	50
Yield:	4 lb 4 oz		2125 g	425

Procedure:

1. With paddle attachment, mix almond paste and sugar at low speed until evenly blended.
2. Blend in eggs until smooth.
3. Slowly blend in cake crumbs.
4. Add just enough milk to give a soft, spreadable consistency.

Almond Filling III (Frangipane)

Ingredients	U.S.	Almond paste at 100% Metric	%
Almond paste	1 lb	400 g	100
Sugar	2 oz	50 g	12.5
Butter	8 oz	200 g	50
Cake flour	2 oz	50 g	12.5
Eggs	8 oz	200 g	50
Yield:	2 lb 4 oz	900 g	225

Procedure:

1. With the paddle attachment, mix almond paste and sugar at low speed until evenly blended.
2. Blend in the butter.
3. Blend in the cake flour.
4. Blend in the eggs until smooth.

Lemon Filling

Ingredients	U.S.	Pie filling at 100% Metric	%
Lemon pie filling (p. 185)	2 lb	1000 g	100
Cake crumbs	1 lb	500 g	50
Lemon juice	4 oz	125 g	12.5
Yield:	3 lb 4 oz	1625 g	162

Procedure: Mix ingredients together until smooth.

Cheese Filling

Ingredients	U.S.		Metric	Cheese at 100% %
Baker's cheese	2 lb		1000 g	100
Sugar	10	oz	300 g	30
Salt	0.25	oz	7 g	0.7
Eggs	6	oz	200 g	20
Butter and/or shortening, soft	6	oz	200 g	20
Vanilla	0.5	oz	15 g	1.5
Grated lemon zest (optional)	0.25	oz	7 g	0.7
Cake flour	3	oz	100 g	10
Milk	6–10	oz	200–300 g	20–30
Raisins (optional)	8	oz	250 g	25
Yield:	4 lb		2030 g	203
	to		to	to
	4 lb 12	oz	2280 g	228

Procedure:

1. Using the paddle attachment, cream the cheese, sugar, and salt until smooth.
2. Add the eggs, butter, vanilla, and lemon zest. Blend in.
3. Add the cake flour. Blend just until absorbed. Add the milk a little at a time, adding just enough to bring the mixture to a smooth, spreadable consistency.
4. Stir in the raisins, if desired.

Hazelnut Filling

Ingredients	U.S.		Metric	Nuts at 100% %
Hazelnuts, toasted and ground	1 lb		500 g	100
Sugar	2 lb		1000 g	200
Cinnamon	0.5	oz	15 g	3
Eggs	6	oz	190 g	37.5
Cake crumbs	2 lb		1000 g	200
Milk	1–2 lb		500–1000 g	100–200
Yield:	6 lb 6	oz	3205 g	640
	to		to	to
	7 lb 6	oz	3705 g	740

Procedure:

1. Blend together all ingredients except milk.
2. Mix in enough milk to bring the mixture to a spreadable consistency.

Poppy Seed Filling

Ingredients	U.S.			Poppy seeds at 100% Metric	%
Poppy seeds	1 lb			400 g	100
Water		8	oz	200 g	50
Butter, soft		6	oz	150 g	38
Honey		4	oz	100 g	25
Sugar		6	oz	150 g	38
Cake crumbs	1 lb			400 g	100
Eggs		3	oz	75 g	19
Lemon rind, grated		0.25	oz	6 g	1.5
Cinnamon		0.125 oz	(1½ tsp)	3 g	0.75
Water (as needed)					
Yield:	3 lb 11		oz	1484 g	372
	or more, depending on amount of water added				

Procedure:

1. Soak the seeds overnight. Grind to a paste.

2. Add remaining ingredients and blend until smooth.

3. Add water as needed to bring to a spreadable consistency.

Chocolate Filling

Ingredients	U.S.		Cake crumbs at 100% Metric	%
Sugar	1 lb		400 g	33
Cocoa		6 oz	150 g	12
Cake crumbs	3 lb		1200 g	100
Eggs		4 oz	100 g	8
Butter, melted		6 oz	150 g	12
Vanilla		1 oz	25 g	2
Water (as needed)		12 oz	300 g	25
Yield:	5 lb 13 oz		2425 g	192

Procedure:

1. Sift together the sugar and cocoa.

2. Mix in the cake crumbs.

3. Add the egg, melted butter, vanilla, and a little of the water. Blend in. Add enough additional water to bring to a smooth, spreadable consistency.

Variation

Mix 50% (1 lb 8 oz/600 g) miniature chocolate chips into the filling.

Honey Pan Glaze (for Caramel Rolls)

Ingredients	U.S.		Brown sugar at 100%	
			Metric	%
Brown sugar	2 lb	8 oz	1000 g	100
Butter, margarine, or shortening	1 lb		400 g	40
Honey		10 oz	250 g	25
Corn syrup (or malt syrup)		10 oz	250 g	25
Water (variable)		4 oz	100 g	10
Yield:	5 lb		2000 g	200

Procedure:

1. Cream together the brown sugar, fat, honey, and corn syrup.

2. Add enough water to bring the mixture to a spreadable consistency.

MAKEUP TECHNIQUES

The object of yeast dough makeup is to shape the dough into rolls or loaves that bake properly and have an attractive appearance. When you shape a roll or loaf correctly, you stretch the gluten strands on the surface into a kind of smooth skin. This tight gluten surface holds the item in shape. This is especially important for loaves and rolls that are baked freestanding, not in pans. Units that are not made up correctly will develop irregular shapes and splits and may flatten out.

Use of Dusting Flour

In most cases, the bench and the dough must be dusted lightly with flour to prevent the dough from sticking to the bench and to the hands. Some bakers use light rye flour for dusting. Others prefer bread flour.

Whichever flour you use, one rule is very important: *Use as little dusting flour as possible.* Excessive flour makes seams difficult to seal and shows up as streaks in the baked product.

Procedure for Scaling and Dividing Dough for Rolls

This procedure involves the use of a dough divider. A dough divider cuts a large unit of dough, called a *press*, into small units of equal weight. If this equipment is not available, you must scale individual roll units.

1. Scale the dough into "presses" of desired weight. One press makes 36 rolls.

2. Round the presses and allow them to relax.

3. Divide the dough using a dough divider. Separate the pieces, using a little dusting flour to prevent sticking.

4. Make up the rolls as desired. In some cases, the pieces are rounded first. In other cases, the rolls are made up without rounding, just as they come from the divider.

Crisp-Crusted Products and Rye Products

Round Rolls

1. Scale the dough as required, such as 3½ lb (1600 g) per press or 1½ oz (45 g) per roll. Divide presses into rolls.

2. Round each unit (see Figure 4.2).

3. Place rolls 2 inches (5 cm) apart on sheet pans sprinkled with cornmeal.

4. Proof, wash with water, and bake with steam.

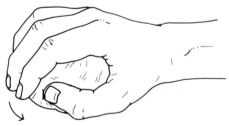

FIGURE 4.2 Rounding small rolls is nearly the same as rounding large loaves (Figure 3.1), except that the whole ball fits under the hand. Roll the piece of dough vigorously in a tight circle on the bench until it forms a ball with a smooth surface, except for a slight pucker on the bottom.

Oval Rolls

1. Scale and round the rolls as indicated above for round rolls.

2. Roll the rounded units back and forth under the palms of the hands so that they become slightly elongated and tapered.

3. Proof and wash with water. Slash with one lengthwise cut or three diagonal cuts.

4. Bake with steam.

Split Rolls

1. Round up the rolls as for round rolls. Let them rest a few minutes.

2. Dust the tops lightly with rye flour. Using a lightly oiled ¾-inch (2 cm) thick wooden pin, press a crease in the center of each roll.

3. Proof upside-down in boxes or on canvas dusted with flour. Turn right side up and place on pans or peels dusted with cornmeal. Do not slash. Bake as for other hard rolls.

Club Rolls

1. Make up as shown in Figure 4.3. Rather than being rounded, these units are molded as they come from the divider.

2. Place units 2 inches (5 cm) apart on sheet pans sprinkled with cornmeal.

3. Proof, wash with water, and slash with one cut lengthwise. Bake with steam.

Crescent Rolls

1. Scale the dough into 16- to 20-oz (450 to 575 g) units. Round and relax the units.

2. Flatten the dough and roll out into 12-inch (30 cm) circles.

3. With a pastry wheel, cut each dough circle into 12 equal wedges or triangles. (Alternative method: For large quantities of dough, roll out into a rectangle and cut like croissant dough, Figure 4.20).

4. Roll the triangles into crescents using the same technique as for croissants, Figure 4.20. The rolls may be either left as straight sticks or bent into crescents.

5. Proof. Wash with water and, if desired, sprinkle with poppy seeds, caraway seeds, sesame seeds, or coarse salt. Bake with steam.

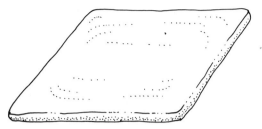

FIGURE 4.3 Making Club Rolls.
(*a*) Flatten the piece of dough roughly into a rectangle.

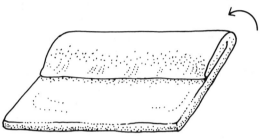

(*b*) Begin to roll up the dough by folding over the back edge of the rectangle. Press the seam firmly with the fingertips.

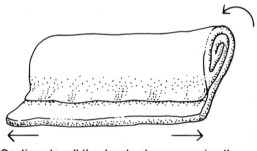

(*c*) Continue to roll the dough, always pressing the seam firmly after each turn. As you roll up the dough, the front edge will appear to shrink. Stretch the front corners as shown by the arrows, to keep the width uniform.

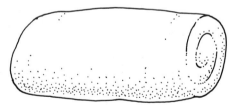

(*d*) When the roll is finished, seal the seam well, so that you have a tight roll.

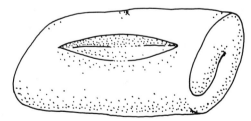

(*e*) Docking the proofed roll with a single slash gives the baked roll this appearance.

Onion Rolls (for Rye or Hard Roll Dough)

1. Prepare onion mixture:

    a. Cover 1 lb (500 g) dried onions with water and soak until soft. Drain.

    b. Mix with 2 oz (60 g) oil and ½ oz (15 g) salt.

    c. Place on a flat pan. Keep covered until ready to use.

2. Divide and round the dough for rolls. Let rest 10 minutes.

3. Place the rolls face down on top of the onions and flatten well with the hands. Place the flattened rolls onion side up on paper-lined pans.

4. Proof. Press the center of each roll with two fingers to make an indentation. Bake with steam.

Kaiser Rolls

Kaiser rolls are popular hard rolls often used for sandwiches. They may be shaped by using a folding technique (the original method) or by stamping a rounded roll with a specially designed cutter. Vienna dough (p. 44) is most commonly used for these rolls.

Method 1

1. Scale the dough to produce rolls of desired size. 5-lb (2300 g) presses will yield baked rolls of 2 oz (60 g), large enough for sandwiches.

2. Press the dough in the divider and separate the pieces, dusting them with light rye flour.

3. Round the units and let them rest. With a rolling pin, roll out units into circles.

4. Fold the pieces as shown in Figure 4.4.

5. Place the rolls upside-down on boxes or trays sprinkled generously with poppy seeds or lined with canvas cloth. Proof.

6. Place right-side up on cornmeal-dusted baking sheets or peels. Place in oven and bake with steam.

Method 2

1. Scale, divide, round, and rest the dough as in Method 1.

2. Flatten the pieces lightly with the hands.

3. Stamp each roll with a kaiser roll tool (Figure 4.5). The cuts should go about halfway through the rolls. Do not cut all the way through.

4. Proof and bake as in Method 1.

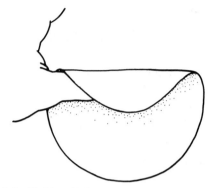

FIGURE 4.4 Making Kaiser Rolls.
(a) Flatten the dough into a circle. Place the thumb of the left hand on the edge of the circle. Fold part of the dough (about one-fifth of the circle) over the thumb to the center of the circle, as shown. Keeping the thumb under the dough, press this flap of dough down firmly in the center with the edge of the right hand.

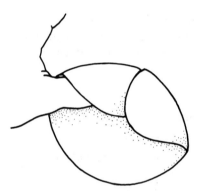

(b) Make a second fold the same way, one-fifth of the way around the circle clockwise.

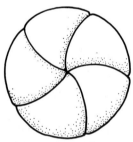

(c) Continue, making a total of five folds. Tuck the end of the fifth fold under the first fold in the space left by the thumb. Proof the roll upside down to preserve the pattern of folds.

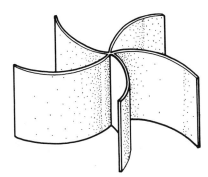

FIGURE 4.5 Kaiser Roll Tool.

French, Italian, and Vienna Loaves

These loaves vary in shape from thick, elongated ovals to long, thin French baguettes (Figure 4.6).

1. Flatten the rounded, relaxed dough with the hands. Roll up tightly, sealing the seam well after each turn, as in making club rolls (Fig. 4.3). Roll the loaf on the bench under the palms of the hands to even out the shape. This will produce an elongated, oval-shaped loaf. The ends should be tapered and rounded, not pointed.

2. If a longer, thinner loaf is desired, relax these units again for a few minutes. Flatten them with the palms of the hands and stretch the dough lightly to increase its length. Once again, roll up tightly and seal the seam well. Roll on the bench under the palms of the hands to even it out and to stretch it to the desired shape and length.

3. Place seam side down on pans dusted with cornmeal. Proof. Wash with water, slash with diagonal cuts or one lengthwise cut. Bake with steam for first 10 minutes.

FIGURE 4.6 Various Shapes of French, Italian, and Vienna Loaves.

Round Loaves

1. Flatten the rounded, relaxed dough into a circle. Fold the four sides over the center, then round again.

2. Place on pans sprinkled with cornmeal. Proof, wash with water, slash the tops, and bake with steam.

Soft Roll Doughs, Pan Loaves, and Braided Breads

Tied or Knotted Rolls

1. Scale the dough into presses of desired size. Divide the presses.

2. With the palms of the hands, roll each unit on the workbench into a strip or rope of dough.

3. Tie the rolls as shown:

   Single-knot rolls: Figure 4.7
   Double-knot rolls: Figure 4.8
   Braided rolls: Figure 4.9
   Figure-eight rolls: Figure 4.10

4. Place rolls 2 inches (5 cm) apart on greased or paper-lined baking sheets.

5. Proof, egg wash, and bake without steam.

Crescent Rolls

1. Make up as for hard crescent rolls, except brush the triangles with melted butter before rolling up.

2. Proof, egg wash, and sprinkle with poppy seeds. Bake without steam.

Pan Rolls

1. Scale dough into presses of desired size. Divide.

2. Make up as for round hard rolls.

3. Place on greased pans ½ in (1 cm) apart.

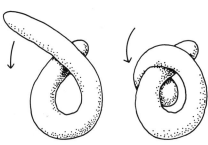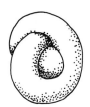

FIGURE 4.7 Tying a Single-Knot Roll.

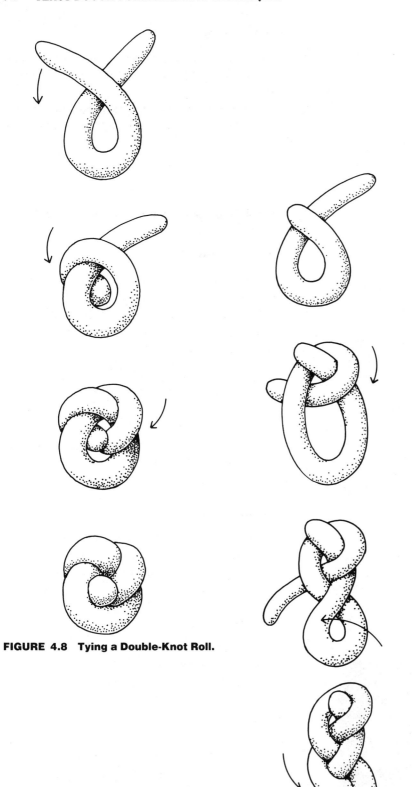

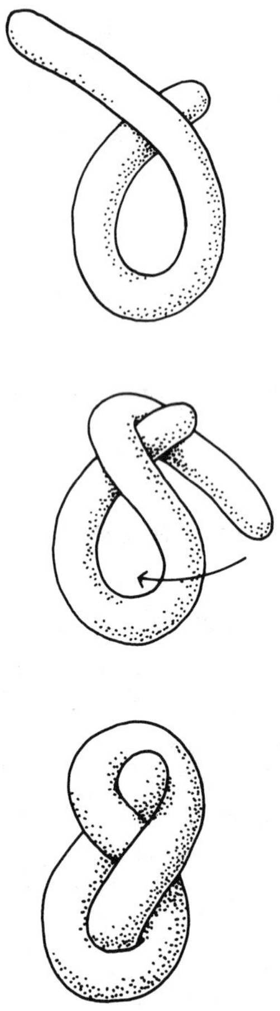

FIGURE 4.10 Tying a Figure-Eight Roll.

FIGURE 4.8 Tying a Double-Knot Roll.

FIGURE 4.9 Tying a Braided Roll.

Cloverleaf Rolls

1. Scale dough into presses of desired size. Divide.
2. Make up and pan as shown in Figure 4.11.

Parker House Rolls

1. Scale dough into presses of desired size. Divide.
2. Make up as shown in Figure 4.12.
3. Place on greased baking sheet ½ in (1 cm) apart.

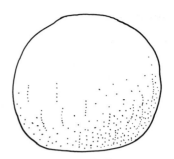

FIGURE 4.12 Parker House Rolls.
(*a*) Round the scaled piece of dough.

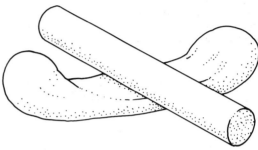

(*b*) Flatten the *center* of the dough with a narrow rolling pin as shown.

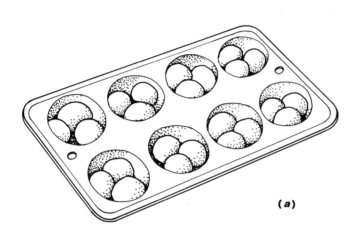

(*a*)

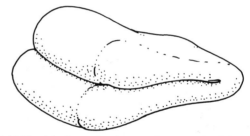

(*c*) Fold the dough over and press down on the folded edge to make a crease.

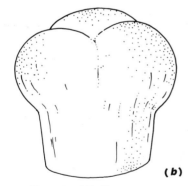

(*b*)

FIGURE 4.11 Cloverleaf Rolls.
(*a*) Divide each piece of dough into three equal parts and shape them into balls. Place three balls in the bottom of each greased muffin tin. (*b*) The baked roll has this appearance.

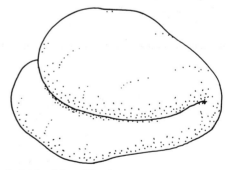

(*d*) The baked roll has this shape.

Butterflake Rolls

Make up as shown in Figure 4.13.

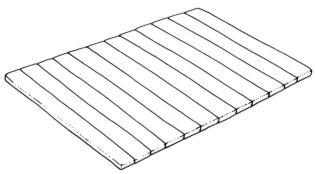

FIGURE 4.13 Butterflake Rolls.
(*a*) Roll the dough out into a very thin rectangular shape. Brush it with melted butter. Cut it into strips 1 inch (2.5 cm) wide.

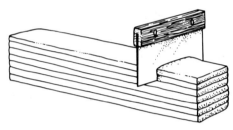

(*b*) Stack up six strips. Cut into 1½ inch (3½ cm) pieces.

(*c*) Place the pieces on end in greased muffin tins. Proof.

(*d*) The baked rolls have this appearance.

Pan Loaves

The shaping of dough into loaves to be baked in loaf pans is illustrated in Figure 4.14.

For split-top loaves, make one cut from end to end in top of loaf after proofing.

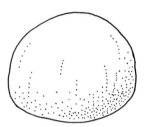

FIGURE 4.14 Pan Loaves.
(*a*) Start with the rounded, benched dough.

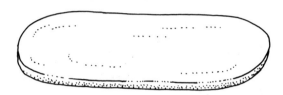

(*b*) Stretch it out into a long rectangle.

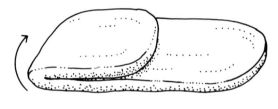

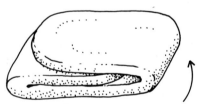

(*c,d*) Fold into thirds.

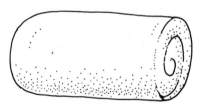

(*e*) Roll the dough up into a tight roll that has the same length as the pan it is to be baked in. Seal the seam very well and place the dough seam side down in the greased pan.

Pullman Loaf

Pullman loaves are baked in loaf pans with sliding lids, so that slices from the loaf are square, ideal for sandwiches. Pans are usually of standard sizes to make 1-lb (450 g), 1½-lb (675 g), 2-lb (900 g), and 3-lb (1350 g) loaves.

1. Scale the dough to fit the loaf pans. Add an extra 2 oz (50 g) of dough per pound (450 g) to allow for baking loss.

2. Make up loaves in one of two ways:

   a. Make up as for standard pan loaves as in the preceding technique.

   b. Or divide each scaled unit into two pieces. Roll out into strips and twist the two strips together. Seal the ends well. This method is preferred by many bakers because it gives extra strength to the loaf structure. The sides of the loaf are less likely to collapse.

3. Place the made-up loaves in lightly greased pans. Put on the lids (greased on the underside), but leave them open about an inch (2.5 cm).

4. Proof until the dough has risen almost to the lids.

5. Close the lids. Bake at 400 to 425° F (200 to 218° C) without steam.

6. Remove the lids after 30 minutes. The bread should be taking on color by this time. If the lid sticks, it may be because the bread requires a few more minutes of baking with the lid. Try again after a few minutes.

7. Complete baking with lid off to allow moisture to escape.

Braided Loaves

Egg-enriched soft roll dough and challah dough are the most appropriate for braided loaves. The dough should be relatively stiff so that the braids hold their shape.

Braids of one to six strands are commonly made. More complicated braids of seven or more strands are not presented here because they are rarely made.

Braided breads are egg-washed after proofing. If desired, they may also be sprinkled with poppy seeds after washing.

One-Strand Braid

1. Roll the dough into a smooth, straight strip with the palms of the hands. The strip should be of uniform thickness from end to end.

2. Tie or braid the strip the same way as for a braided roll (Figure 4.9).

Two-, Three-, Four-, Five-, and Six-Strand Braids

1. Divide the dough into equal pieces, depending on how many strips are required.

   For a double three-strand braid (Figure 4.16), divide the dough into 4 equal pieces. Then divide one of these pieces into three smaller pieces, so that you will have three large and three small pieces.

2. Roll the pieces with the palms of the hands into long, smooth strips. The pieces should be thickest in the middle and gradually tapered toward the ends.

3. Braid the strips as shown in the illustrations. Please note that the numbers used in these descriptions refer to the *positions* of the strands (numbered from left to right). At each stage in the braiding, number 1 always indicates the first strand on the left.

   2-strand: Figure 4.15
   3-strand: Figure 4.16
   4-strand: Figure 4.17
   5-strand: Figure 4.18
   6-strand: Figure 4.19

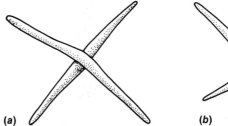

(a)   (b)

FIGURE 4.15 Two-Strand Braid.
(a) Cross the two strands in the middle.
(b) Fold the two ends of the bottom strand over the other one.

(c)   (d)

(c) Now fold the ends of the other strand over in the same way.
(d) Repeat steps *b* and *c* until the braid is finished.

(a)   (b)

FIGURE 4.16 Three-Strand Braid.
(a) Lay the three strands side by side. Starting in the center, fold the left strand over the center one (1 over 2).
(b) Now fold the right strand over the center (3 over 2).

(a)   (b)

FIGURE 4.17 Four-Strand Braid.
(a) Start with four strands, fastened at the end. The sequence is as follows.
(b) 4 over 2.

(c)   (d)

(c) Repeat the sequence (1 over 2, 3 over 2).
(d) When you reach the end of the strands, turn the braid over.

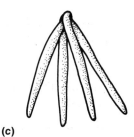

(c)   (d)

(c) 1 over 3.
(d) 2 over 3.

(e)   (f)

(e) Braid the other half.
(f) If desired, a smaller three-strand braid can be placed on top.

(e)

(e) Repeat, 4 over 2, etc.

(f)

(f) The finished braid.

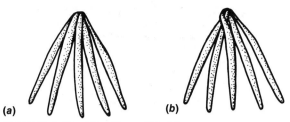

(a)   **(b)**

FIGURE 4.18   Five-Strand Braid.
(a) Start with five strands, fastened at the end. The sequence is as follows.
(b) 1 over 3.

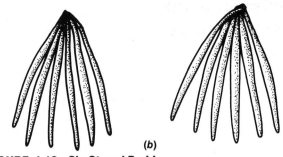

(a)   **(b)**

FIGURE 4.19   Six-Strand Braid.
(a) Start with 6 strands, fastened at the end.
(b) The first step, 6 over 1, is *not* part of the repeated sequence.

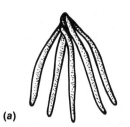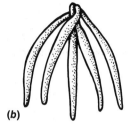

(a)   **(b)**

(c) 2 over 3.
(d) 5 over 2.

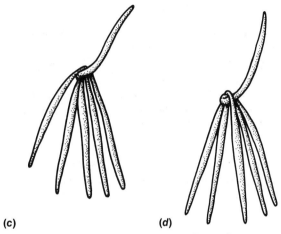

(c)   **(d)**

(c) The repeated sequence begins with 2 over 6.
(d) 1 over 3.

(e) Repeat, 1 over 3, etc.

(f) The finished braid.

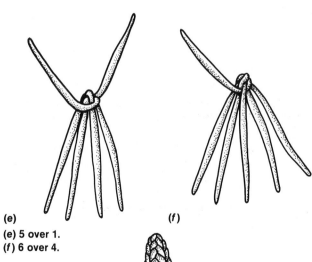

(e)   **(f)**

(e) 5 over 1.
(f) 6 over 4.

(g) The finished braid.

Croissant Dough

Plain Croissants

Make up as shown in Figure 4.20.

FIGURE 4.20   Making Croissants.
(*a*) Roll the dough out into a rectangle 10 inches (25 cm) wide and about ⅛ inch (3 mm) thick. The length depends on the amount of dough used.

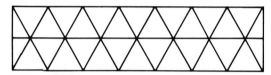

(*b*) Cut the rectangle into triangles as shown. Special roller cutters that do this very quickly are available.

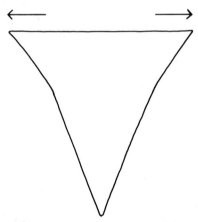

(*c*) Place one of the triangles on the bench in front of you. Stretch the back corners outward slightly, as shown by the arrows.

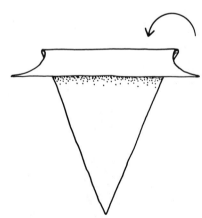

(*d*) Begin to roll up the dough toward the point.

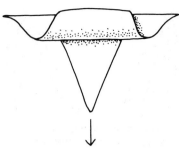

(*e*) Stretch out the point of the triangle slightly as you roll it up.

(*f*) Finish rolling up the dough.

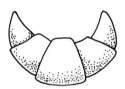

(*g*) Bend the roll into a crescent shape. The point of the triangle must face the inside of the crescent and be tucked under the roll so that it won't pop up during baking.

Filled Croissants

Make up as for plain croissants, except place a small amount of desired filling on the base of each triangle before rolling up.

Petits Pains au Chocolate (Chocolate Rolls)

1. Roll out croissant dough into a sheet as for croissants.

2. Cut into rectangles 6 inches by 4 inches (15 by 10 cm).

3. Arrange a row of chocolate chips about 1½ inches (4 cm) from the narrow end of each rectangle. Use ⅓ oz (10 g) chocolate per roll.

4. Egg wash the opposite end of each rectangle, so that the rolls will seal.

5. Roll up the dough tightly around the chocolate.

6. Proof, egg wash, and bake as for croissants.

Brioches

The traditional brioche shape is shown in Figure 4.21. Brioches may also be baked as pan loaves in many sizes and shapes.

FIGURE 4.21 Making Brioches.
(*a*) For a small brioche, roll the dough into a round piece.

(*b*) Using the edge of the hand, pinch off about one-fourth of the dough without detaching it. Roll the dough on the bench so that both parts are round.

(*c*) Place the dough in the tin large-end first. With the fingertips, press the small ball into the larger one as shown.

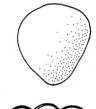

(*d*) For a large brioche, separate the two parts of the dough. Place the large ball in the tin and make a hole in the center. Form the smaller ball into a pear shape and fit it into the hole.

(*e*) A baked large brioche.

Sweet Rolls and Danish Rolls

Note: Many sweet dough products, including most Danish products, are glazed with clear glaze (p. 61) after baking, while still hot. After cooling, they may also be decorated with flat icing (p. 131). Flat icing is drizzled over the products, so that it doesn't cover them completely.

Crumb Buns

1. With a rolling pin, roll out sweet dough about ½ inch (12 mm) thick.
2. Cut into 2-inch (5 cm) squares.
3. Arrange the squares in rows on paper-lined sheet pans so that they touch each other.
4. Wash with egg wash or milk.
5. Sprinkle the tops heavily with streusel topping.
6. Proof. Bake at 400° F (200° C).
7. When the buns are cool, they may be dusted lightly with 6X sugar.

Filled Buns

1. Scale the sweet dough into presses of desired size. Suggested size: 3 lb (1400 g) for 36 rolls. Round the presses, relax, and divide.
2. Round up the units and place them on paper-lined sheet pans in one of two ways:
   a. Place them 2 inches (5 cm) apart so that they bake without touching.
   b. Place them in rows so that they are just touching each other. Rolls baked in this way will rise higher and must be broken apart before being served.
3. Give the rolls a half proof.
4. Using either the fingers or a small, round object, press a round 1-inch (2.5 cm) indentation in the center of each roll.
5. Egg wash the tops of the rolls.
6. Fill the centers with desired filling, using about ½ oz (15 g) per roll.
7. Continue proofing to about three-quarters proof. Bake at 400° F (200° C).
8. When cool, drizzle flat icing over the rolls.

Cinnamon Rolls (Figure 4.22)

1. Scale the dough into 20-oz (570 g) units, or as desired. On a floured bench, roll each piece of dough into a 9 × 12-inch rectangle about ¼ inch thick (23 × 30 × 0.5 cm). Brush off excess flour.
2. Brush with butter and sprinkle with 2 oz (60 g) cinnamon sugar.
3. Roll up like a jelly roll 12 inches (30 cm) long, as shown in the illustration.
4. Cut into 1-inch (2.5 cm) rolls.
5. Place cut side down in greased muffin tins or on greased sheet pans. One full-size 18 × 26-inch (46 × 66 cm) pan holds 48 rolls arranged in 6 rows of 8.

Cinnamon Raisin Rolls

Prepare like cinnamon rolls, but add 2 oz (60 g) raisins to the filling.

Caramel Rolls

1. Prepare like cinnamon rolls.
2. Before panning, spread the bottoms of the pans with honey pan glaze (p. 66). Use about 1 oz (30 g) per roll.

Caramel Nut Rolls or Pecan Rolls

Prepare like caramel rolls, but sprinkle the pan glaze with chopped nuts or pecan halves before placing the rolls in the pans.

Danish Spirals or Snecken

1. Roll out the Danish dough into a rectangle as for cinnamon rolls. The width of the roll may vary, depending on the desired size of the finished units. A wider rectangle will produce a thicker roll and, therefore, larger finished units.
2. Spread or sprinkle the rectangle with the desired filling. For example:

   Butter, cinnamon sugar, chopped nuts, and cake crumbs

   Butter, cinnamon sugar, and raisins

   Almond filling

   Prune filling

   Chocolate filling

   Loose fillings such as chopped nuts should be pressed on gently with a rolling pin.
3. Roll up like a jelly roll.

4. Slice to desired size.
5. Place the rolls on paper-lined pans and tuck the loose ends underneath.
6. Proof, egg wash, and bake at 400° F (200° C).

Variations Made from Filled Dough Roll or Danish Spiral

1. *Filled Spirals*

   Make up like Danish Spirals, above. Give half proof, then press an indentation in the center and fill with desired filling. Complete the proof and bake as above.

See Figure 4.22 for the following variations:

2. *Combs and Bear Claws*
3. *Figure Eight Rolls*
4. *Three-Leaf Rolls*
5. *Butterfly Rolls*

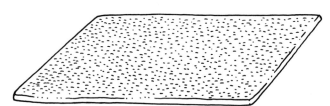

FIGURE 4.22 The Filled Dough Roll is the Starting Point for a Variety of Sweet Dough and Danish Products.
(*a*) Roll the dough out into a rectangle. Brush with butter and sprinkle with cinnamon sugar, or spread with desired filling.

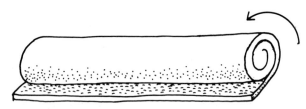

(*b*) Roll up like a jelly roll.

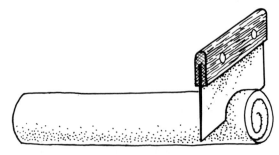

(*c*) For cinnamon rolls and similar products, cut off 1-inch (2.5-cm) pieces.

(*d*) For butterfly rolls, cut off slightly larger pieces. Crease them by pressing the center firmly with a wooden rod, as shown.

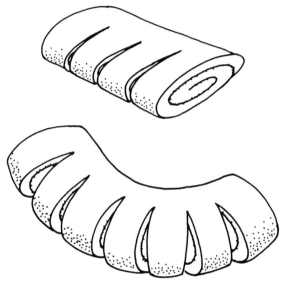

(*e*) For combs or bear claws, make the roll thinner and cut it into longer pieces. Flatten the pieces slightly and cut part way through each in three to five places, as shown. Leave straight, or bend into a curve to open up the cuts.

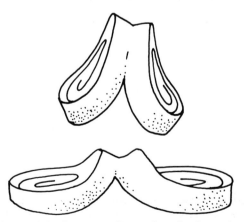

(*f*) For figure-eight cinnamon rolls, cut the rolls almost through as shown. Open them up and lay them flat on the baking sheet.

(*g*) For three-leaf rolls, cut the pieces in two places, and spread the three segments as shown.

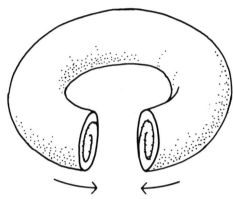

(*h*) To make a wreath-shaped coffee cake, join the ends of the dough roll to make a circle.

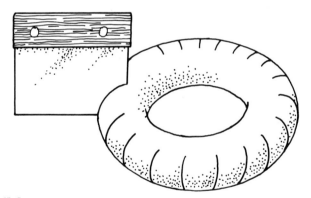

(*i*) Cut part way through the dough at 1-inch (2.5-cm) intervals as shown.

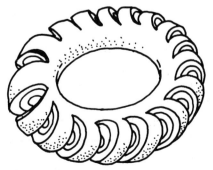

(*j*) Twist each segment outward to open the cuts.

Filled Danish Crescents

Make up like filled croissants (p. 76).

Danish Twists or Snails

Make up as shown in Figure 4.23.

Danish Pockets

Make up as shown in Figure 4.24.

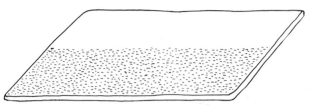

FIGURE 4.23 Danish Twists or Snails.
(*a*) Roll out the dough into a rectangle 16 inches (40 cm) wide and less than ¼ inch (5 mm) thick. (The length of the rectangle depends on the quantity of dough.) Brush the dough with melted butter. Sprinkle half of it with cinnamon sugar as shown.

Coffee Cakes

Coffee cakes can be made up into many different sizes and shapes. The weight of the dough required and the size of the cake can be varied greatly according to the needs of the bakeshop. Except when a specific dough is indicated, the following can be made with either a sweet dough or Danish dough.

(*b*) Fold the unsugared half over the sugared half. You now have a rectangle 8 inches (20 cm) wide. Roll the dough very gently with a rolling pin to press the layers together.

Wreath Coffee Cake

1. Using a sweet dough or Danish dough, make a filled dough roll as for cinnamon rolls (Figure 4.22), but do not cut into separate pieces. Other fillings, such as prune or date, may be used instead of butter and cinnamon sugar.
2. Shape the roll into a circle as shown in Figure 4.22(h). Place on a greased baking sheet. Cut and shape as shown in the illustration.
3. Egg wash after proofing.

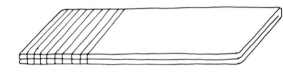

(*c*) Cut the dough into strips ½ inch (1 cm) wide.

(*d*) Place one strip crosswide in front of you on the bench.

(*e*) With the palms of your hands on the ends of the strip, roll one end toward you and the other end away from you, so that the strip twists. Stretch the strip slightly as you twist it.

Filled Coffee Cake

1. Scale sweet dough or Danish dough into 12-oz (340 g) units.
2. Roll each unit into a rectangle 9 × 18 inches (23 × 46 cm).
3. Spread half of each rectangle with desired filling, using about 6 oz (170 g) filling.
4. Fold the unspread half over the spread half to make a 9-inch (23 cm) square.
5. Place in greased 9-inch (23 cm) square pan.
6. Sprinkle with streusel topping, about 4 oz (110 g) per pan.
7. Proof. Bake at 375° F (190° C).

(*f*) Curl the strip into a spiral shape on the baking sheet. Tuck the end underneath and pinch it against the roll to seal it in place. If desired, press a hollow in the center of the roll and place a spoonful of filling in the center.

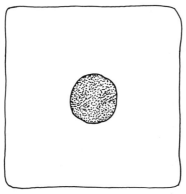

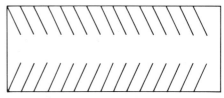

FIGURE 4.25 Braided Coffee Cake.
(*a*) Roll out the dough into a rectangle 8 inches (20 cm) wide, 12 to 18 inches (30 to 46 cm) long, and less than ½ inch (5 mm) thick. Make diagonal cuts from the outer edges 1 inch (2.5 cm) apart and 3 inches (7.5 cm) long, as shown.

FIGURE 4.24 Danish Pockets.
(*a*) Roll out the dough less than ¼ inch (5 mm) thick. Cut it into 5-inch (13-cm) squares. Place desired filling in the center of each square. Brush the four corners lightly with water to help them seal when pressed together.

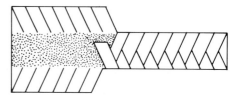

(*b*) Spread the filling down the center and fold alternate strips of dough over the filling.

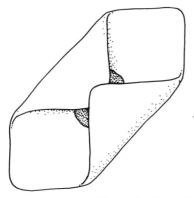

Braided Coffee Cake

Make up sweet dough or Danish dough as shown in Figure 4.25. Egg wash after proofing. Bake at 375° F (190° C).

(*b*) Fold two opposite corners over the center. Press down firmly to seal them together. (If desired, rolls may be left in this shape.)

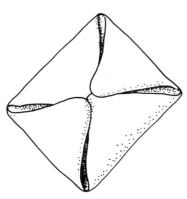

Loaf Coffee Cake

1. Using babka dough, make a filled dough roll as for cinnamon rolls, using desired filling.

2. Fold the roll in half and then twist it up.

3. Place the twisted roll in a greased loaf pan. Or coil the twist up like a snail and place in a round pan.

4. Proof, wash with melted butter, and bake at 350° F (175° C).

(c) Fold the other two corners over the center and, again, press them firmly together.

FIGURE 4.26 Danish Pretzel, Before Proofing.

Danish Pretzel

1. Using almond filling, make up Danish dough into a long, thin dough roll as for cinnamon rolls.
2. Twist the roll into a pretzel shape as shown in Figure 4.26. Place on a sheet pan.
3. Proof, egg wash, and bake at 375° F (190° C).

Strip Coffee Cake or Danish Strip

1. Roll the Danish dough out about ¼ inch (6 mm) thick into a rectangle the length of the desired strip and about twice as wide.
2. Spread the desired filling lengthwise down the center of the dough, leaving a ½-inch (1 cm) margin at both ends.
3. Brush both ends and one edge of the rectangle with egg wash (in order to seal the seams).
4. Fold the side of the rectangle without the egg wash over the center of the filling. Fold the other side over the center, overlapping the first side by ½ inch (1 cm).
5. Turn the strip over and place it seam-side down on a paper-lined pan. Make five or six diagonal slashes in the top of the dough; cut through to the filling but not to the bottom layer of dough.
6. Proof, egg wash, and bake at 375° F (190° C).

Danish Ring

1. Using desired filling, make up Danish dough into a filled dough roll as for cinnamon rolls, but make it longer and thinner.
2. Flatten the roll slightly with a rolling pin. Make two parallel cuts lengthwise through the dough; cut through the bottom layer, but leave about 1 inch (2.5 cm) uncut at both ends.
3. Twist the strip as in Figure 4.27. Form the twist into a ring and seal the ends together.
4. Proof and egg wash. Ring may also be sprinkled with chopped or sliced nuts. Bake at 375° F (190° C).

FIGURE 4.27 Danish Ring.
(*a*) Flatten the dough roll slightly. Make two cuts lengthwise through the dough, leaving the ends uncut.

(*b*) Twist the strip.

(*c*) Shape the strip into a ring and seal the ends together. Turn the ring over so that the ends are on the bottom.

TERMS FOR REVIEW

French bread
bagel
English muffin
sour
pumpernickel
brioche
baba
croissant
simple fold
pullman loaf
press

QUESTIONS FOR DISCUSSION

1. How would the baked loaves be different if you increased the shortening in the French bread formula (p. 45) to 7%?

2. Why is the baking temperature for Italian bread (p. 45) higher than that for challah (p. 49)?

3. How could you modify the formula for Vienna bread (p. 44) if you didn't have any malt?

4. There are no formulas for white sourdough bread in this book. If you were asked to improvise a formula for white sourdough French bread based on formulas in this book, how might you begin?

5. What mixing method is used for kugelhopf dough and brioche dough? Why?

6. As you know, butter is very hard when cold and melts quickly at warm temperatures. What precautions do you think are necessary when using butter as the rolling-in fat for Danish pastry?

7. Why is it important not to use too much dusting flour when making up breads and rolls?

CHAPTER 5

QUICK BREADS

Quick breads are the perfect solution for food service operations that want to offer their patrons fresh, homemade bread products but can't justify the labor cost of making yeast breads. Retail bakeries, too, have discovered a great demand for such items as fresh muffins. Also, quick breads have the advantage of being easily made in almost unlimited varieties, using such ingredients as whole wheat flour, rye flour, cornmeal, bran, oatmeal, and many kinds of fruits, nuts, and spices. Even breads made with vegetables have become popular.

As their name implies, quick breads are quick to make. Since they are leavened by chemical leaveners and steam, not by yeast, no fermentation time is necessary. And since they are usually tender products with little gluten development, mixing them takes just a few minutes.

Although prepared biscuit and muffin mixes are available, the only extra work that making these products "from scratch" requires is the time to scale a few extra ingredients. With a careful and imaginative selection of ingredients and an understanding of basic mixing methods, you can create superior products.

After studying this chapter, you should be able to:
1. Prepare baking powder biscuits and variations of them.
2. Prepare muffins, loaf breads, coffee cakes, and corn breads.
3. Prepare popovers.

MIXING AND PRODUCTION METHODS

Dough mixtures for quick breads are generally of two types:

1. *Soft doughs* are used for biscuits. They are, with a few exceptions, rolled out and cut into desired shapes.

2. *Batters* may be either *pour batters,* which are liquid enough to be poured, or *drop batters,* which are thick enough to be dropped from a spoon in lumps.

Gluten Development in Quick Breads

Only slight gluten development is desirable in most quick breads. Tenderness is a desirable quality, rather than the chewy quality of many yeast breads.

In addition, chemical leavening agents do not create the same kind of texture that yeast does, and they are not strong enough to create a light, tender product if the gluten is too strong.

Muffin, loaf bread, and pancake batters are mixed as little as possible, only until the dry ingredients are moistened. This, plus the presence of fat and sugar, keeps gluten development low. Overmixing muffin batter produces not only toughness, but also irregular shapes and large, elongated holes inside the muffins. This last condition is called tunneling.

Biscuit dough is often lightly kneaded, enough to help develop some flakiness, but not enough to toughen the product.

Popovers are the exception among quick breads. They are made with a thin batter and leavened only by steam. Very large holes develop inside the product during baking, and the structure must be strong enough to hold up without collapsing. Thus, bread flour is used, and the batter is mixed well to develop the gluten. The high percentage of egg in popovers also helps build structure.

Mixing Methods

Most quick-bread doughs and batters are mixed by one of three mixing methods.

1. The *biscuit method* is used for biscuits, scones, and similar products. It is sometimes called the pastry method because it is like that used for mixing pie pastry.

2. The *muffin method* is used for muffins, pancakes, waffles, and many loaf-type or sheet-type quick breads. This method is fast and easy. However, the danger is that the dough can very quickly become overmixed, resulting in toughness. *Muffin batter should be mixed only until the dry ingredients are just moistened.* Do not attempt to achieve a smooth batter. Some loaf breads and coffee cakes are higher in fat and sugar than muffins, so they can withstand a little more mixing without becoming tough.

3. The *creaming method* is a cake mixing method that is sometimes applied to muffins and loaf breads. Actually, there is no exact dividing line between muffin products and cakes, and if they are rich enough, muffin products may be considered cakes rather than breads.

The creaming method is a more time-consuming procedure than the muffin method. However, it produces fine-textured goods, and there is less danger of overmixing. The creaming method is especially useful for products with a high fat and sugar content because it helps mix the ingredients more uniformly.

Some biscuits are also mixed by the creaming method. These have a texture that is more cakelike and less flaky than that produced by the biscuit method.

The Biscuit Method

Procedure

1. Scale all ingredients accurately.
2. Sift the dry ingredients together into a mixing bowl.
3. Cut in the shortening, using the paddle attachment or the pastry knife attachment. Or, if you prefer, cut in the fat by hand, using a pastry blender or your fingers. Continue until the mixture resembles a coarse cornmeal.
4. Combine the liquid ingredients.
5. Add the liquid to the dry ingredients. Mix just until the ingredients are combined and a soft dough is formed. Do not overmix.
6. Bring the dough to the bench and knead it lightly by pressing it out and folding it in half. Rotate the dough 90 degrees between folds.
7. Repeat this procedure about 10 to 20 times, or for about 30 seconds. The dough should be soft and slightly elastic, but not sticky. Overkneading toughens the biscuits.

The dough is now ready for makeup.

Variations

Changes in the basic procedure produce different characteristics in the finished product:

1. Using slightly more shortening and cutting it in less — only until the pieces are the size of peas — produces a flakier biscuit.

2. Omitting the kneading step produces very tender, crustier biscuits, but with less volume.

Makeup of Biscuits

1. Roll the biscuit dough out into a sheet about ½ inch (1 cm) thick, being careful to roll it evenly and to a uniform thickness.

   Biscuits will approximately double in height during baking.

2. Cut into desired shapes.

   When using round hand cutters, cut straight down. Do not twist the cutter. Space the cuts as closely as possible to minimize scraps. Reworked scrap dough produces tougher biscuits.

   Cutting into squares or triangles with a pastry cutter or knife eliminates scraps that would have to be rerolled. Roller cutters also eliminate or reduce scraps.

3. Place the biscuits ½ inch (1 cm) apart on greased or paper-lined baking sheets. Or, for softer biscuits without crusty sides, arrange the units so that they touch each other; these will have to be broken apart after baking.

4. If desired, brush the tops with egg wash or milk to aid browning.

5. Bake as soon as possible.

The Muffin Method

Procedure

1. Sift together the dry ingredients.

2. Combine all liquid ingredients, including melted fat or oil.

3. Add the liquids to the dry ingredients and mix just until all the flour is moistened. The batter will look lumpy. Do not overmix.

4. Pan and bake immediately. The dry and liquid mixtures may be prepared in advance. But once the mixtures are combined, the batter should be baked without delay, or loss of volume may result.

The Creaming Method

Procedure for Biscuits

1. Combine the fat, sugar, salt, and milk powder (if used) in the bowl of a mixer fitted with the paddle attachment.

2. Blend to a smooth paste.

3. Add the eggs and blend in thoroughly.

4. Add the water or milk (liquid) and mix in.

5. Sift together the flour and baking powder. Add to the bowl and mix to a smooth dough.

Procedure for Muffins, Loaves, and Coffee Cakes

1. Combine the fat, sugar, salt, spices, and milk powder (if used) in the bowl of a mixer fitted with the paddle attachment.

2. Cream the ingredients together until light.

3. Add the eggs in two or three stages. Cream well after each addition before adding more eggs.

4. Add the liquid ingredients and stir lightly.

5. Sift together the flour and baking powder. Add and mix just until smooth.

Panning Muffin Products

Muffin tins and loaf pans should be greased with shortening and dusted with flour or greased with a commercial pan grease preparation. Sheet pans for corn breads and other sheet products may be lined with silicone paper.

Paper liners may be used for muffin tins. However, because the muffins do not stick to greased tins, they rise more freely and take a better shape without paper liners.

When portioning batter into muffin tins, be careful

not to stir the mix and toughen it. Scoop the batter from the outside edge for best results.

Batters for muffins and quick loaf breads are generally interchangeable. In other words, formulas for banana bread or date-nut bread, for example, may be baked as muffins instead of as loaves. Similarly, standard muffin batters may also be baked as loaves or sheets.

FORMULAS

Biscuits

Ingredients	U.S.			Metric	%
Bread flour	1 lb	4	oz	600 g	50
Pastry flour	1 lb	4	oz	600 g	50
Salt		0.75	oz	24 g	2
Sugar		2	oz	60 g	5
Baking powder		2.5	oz	72 g	6
Shortening (regular) and/or butter		14	oz	420 g	35
Milk	1 lb	10	oz	800 g	65
Yield:	5 lb	5	oz	2576 g	213

Mixing: Biscuit method

Scaling: Approximately 1 lb (450 g) per dozen 2-inch (5 cm) biscuits

Baking: 425° F (218° C), about 15–20 minutes

Variations

Buttermilk Biscuits:

Use buttermilk in place of regular milk.

Cheese Biscuits:

Add to dry ingredients:

Grated cheddar cheese	12 oz	360 g	30%

Currant Biscuits:

Increase sugar to:

Sugar	4 oz	120 g	10%

Add to dry ingredients:

Dried currants	6 oz	180 g	15%

Sprinkle tops with cinnamon sugar before baking.

Herb Biscuits:

Add to dry ingredients:

Fresh chopped parsley	2 oz	60 g	5%

Biscuits

Ingredients	U.S.			Metric		%
Shortening (see variation)		6	oz	150	g	15
Sugar		4	oz	100	g	10
Salt		0.5	oz	12.5	g	1.25
Nonfat milk solids		2	oz	50		5
Eggs		3	oz	75	g	7.5
Water	1 lb	8	oz	600	g	60
Bread flour	1 lb	12	oz	700	g	70
Cake flour		12	oz	300	g	30
Baking powder		2	oz	50	g	5
Yield:	5 lb	1	oz	2037	g	203

Mixing: Creaming method

Baking: 425° F (218° C)

Variation

Substitute the following for the shortening:

Butter 7.5 oz 190 g 19%

Corn Bread, Muffins, or Sticks

Ingredients	U.S.			Metric	%
Pastry flour	1 lb	4	oz	600 g	50
Cornmeal	1 lb	4	oz	600 g	50
Sugar		6	oz	180 g	15
Baking powder		2	oz	60 g	5
Nonfat milk solids		3	oz	90 g	7.5
Salt		0.75	oz	24 g	2
Eggs, beaten		8	oz	240 g	20
Water	2 lb	2	oz	1000 g	85
Corn syrup		2	oz	60 g	5
Melted butter or shortening		12	oz	360 g	30
Yield:	6 lb	11	oz	3214 g	269

Mixing: Muffin method

Scaling: 60 oz (1700 g) per half-size sheet pan (13 × 18 in/33 × 46 cm)
24 oz (680 g) per 9-inch (23 cm) square pan or per dozen muffins
10 oz (280 g) per dozen corn sticks

Baking: 400° F (200° C) for corn bread, 25–30 minutes
425° F (218° C) for muffins or sticks, 15–20 minutes

Variation

Use buttermilk instead of water and omit nonfat milk solids. Reduce baking powder to 2.5% (1 oz/30 g) and add 1.25% (0.5 oz/15 g) baking soda.

Plain Muffins

Ingredients	U.S.			Metric	%
Pastry flour	2 lb	8	oz	1200 g	100
Sugar		12	oz	360 g	30
Baking powder		2.5	oz	72 g	6
Salt		0.5	oz	15 g	1.25
Eggs, beaten		8	oz	240 g	20
Milk	2 lb			950 g	80
Melted butter or shortening		12	oz	360 g	30
Yield:	6 lb	7	oz	3197 g	267

Mixing: Muffin method

Panning: Grease and flour muffin tins. Fill tins half full. Exact weight depends on pan size. Average-size muffins require about 2 oz (60 g) per unit.

Baking: 400° F (200° C), about 20 minutes

Variations

Raisin Spice Muffins:

Add to dry ingredients:

Raisins	8	oz	240	g	20%
Cinnamon	0.17 oz (2½ tsp)		5	g	0.4%
Nutmeg	0.08 oz (1 tsp)		2.5	g	0.2%

Blueberry Muffins:

Fold into finished batter:

Blueberries (well drained)	1 lb	480 g	40%

Whole Wheat Muffins:

Adjust the flour and leavening to the following:

Pastry flour	1 lb 12	oz	840	g	70%
Whole wheat flour	12	oz	360	g	30%
Baking powder	1.5	oz	50	g	4%
Baking soda	0.3	oz (2 tsp)	10	g	0.75%

Add to liquid ingredients:

Molasses	4	oz	120	g	10%

Corn Muffins:

Adjust the flour as follows:

Pastry flour	1 lb 10	oz	800	g	65%
Cornmeal	14	oz	400	g	35%

(See also the Corn Bread formula on p. 89.)

Corn Cheese Muffins:

Add to the dry ingredients in the above Corn Muffin formula:

Grated cheddar cheese	1 lb	4	oz	600	g	50%

Use half the amount of sugar.

Bran Muffins:

Adjust the flour to the following:

Pastry flour		12	oz	360	g	30%
Bread flour	1 lb			480	g	40%
Bran		12	oz	360	g	30%

Increase the eggs to the following:

Eggs	12	oz	360	g	30%

Add to dry ingredients:

Raisins	6	oz	180	g	15%

Add to liquid ingredients:

Molasses	6	oz	180	g	15%

Crumb Coffee Cake:

Increase sugar and fat to:

Sugar	1 lb	4	oz	600	g	50%
Butter or shortening	1 lb	4	oz	600	g	50%

Pour into greased, paper-lined sheet pan and spread smooth. Top with:

Streusel (p. 61)	2 lb	1000	g	80%

Bake at 360° F (182° C), about 30 minutes.

Muffins

Ingredients	U.S.		Metric		%
Shortening and/or					
butter	1 lb		400	g	40
Sugar	1 lb 4	oz	500	g	50
Salt	0.5	oz	12	g	1.25
Nonfat milk solids	3	oz	70	g	7
Eggs	12	oz	300	g	30
Water	1 lb 14	oz	750	g	75
Cake flour	2 lb 8	oz	1000	g	100
Baking powder	2	oz	50	g	5
Yield:	7 lb 11	oz	3082	g	308

Mixing: Creaming method

Scaling: Fill tins half full

Baking: 400° F (200° C), about 20 minutes

Variations

Chocolate Chip Muffins:

Adjust the sugar as follows:

White granulated					
sugar	1 lb		400	g	40%
Brown sugar	4	oz	100	g	10%

Add to formula:

Vanilla	0.5	oz	12.5	g	1.25%
Chocolate chips	12	oz	300	g	30%

Top with cinnamon sugar before baking.

Blueberry Muffins:

Fold into finished batter:

Blueberries					
(well drained)	1 lb 4	oz	500	g	50%

Raisin Spice Muffins:

Add to dry ingredients:

Raisins	10	oz	250	g	25%
Cinnamon	0.2 oz (3½ tsp)		5	g	0.5 %
Nutmeg	0.1 oz (1¼ tsp)		2.5	g	0.25%

Scones

Ingredients	U.S.			Metric	%
Bread flour	1 lb	8	oz	600 g	50
Pastry flour	1 lb	8	oz	600 g	50
Sugar		6	oz	150 g	12.5
Salt		0.5	oz	12 g	1
Baking powder		3	oz	72 g	6
Shortening and/or butter	1 lb			400 g	33
Egg		10	oz	240 g	20
Milk	1 lb	10	oz	650 g	54
Yield:	6 lb	13	oz	2724 g	226

Mixing: Biscuit method

Makeup variations:

1. Scale at 1 lb (450 g), round up, and flatten to ½ inch (12 mm) thick. Cut into eight wedges.

2. Roll out into a rectangle ½ inch (12 mm) thick and cut into triangles as for croissants (Figure 4.20).

3. Roll out into a rectangle ½ inch (12 mm) thick and cut out with cutters like biscuits.

Place on greased or paper-lined sheet pans. Egg wash tops.

Baking: 425° F (218° C), about 15–20 minutes

Variation

Add the following to the dry ingredients after cutting in fat:

Raisins or currants   12 oz   300 g   25%

Steamed Brown Bread

Ingredients	U.S.			Metric	%
Bread flour		8	oz	250 g	28.5
Whole wheat flour		4	oz	125 g	14
Light rye flour		8	oz	250 g	28.5
Cornmeal		8	oz	250 g	28.5
Salt		0.75	oz	10 g	1
Baking soda		1.25		20 g	2
Raisins		8	oz	250 g	28.5
Buttermilk	2 lb			1000 g	114
Molasses		15	oz	475 g	54
Yield:	5 lb	5	oz	2630 g	299

Mixing: Muffin method

Scaling and cooking: Fill well-greased molds half full, about 16 oz for each quart of capacity (500 g per liter). Cover molds and steam for 3 hours.

Orange Nut Bread

Ingredients	U.S.			Metric	%
Sugar		12	oz	350 g	50
Grated orange zest		1	oz	30 g	4
Pastry flour	1 lb	8	oz	700 g	100
Nonfat milk solids		2	oz	60 g	8
Baking powder		1	oz	30 g	4
Baking soda			0.3 oz (2 tsp)	10 g	1.4
Salt			0.3 oz (2 tsp)	10 g	1.4
Chopped walnuts		12	oz	350 g	50
Eggs		5	oz	140 g	20
Orange juice		6	oz	175 g	25
Water	1 lb			450 g	65
Oil or melted butter or shortening			2.5 oz	70 g	10
Yield:	5 lb	2	oz	2375 g	329

Mixing: Muffin method. Blend the sugar and orange zest thoroughly before adding remaining ingredients, to ensure even distribution.

Scaling: 1 lb 4 oz (575 g) per 7⅜ × 3⅝-inch (19 × 9 cm) loaf pan
1 lb 10 oz (750 g) per 8½ × 4½-inch (22 × 11 cm) loaf pan

Baking: 375° F (190° C), about 50 minutes

Variation

Lemon Nut Bread

Substitute grated lemon zest for the orange zest. Omit the orange juice and add 8% (2 oz/60 g) lemon juice. Increase the water to 83% (1 lb 4 oz/580 g).

Banana Bread

Ingredients	U.S.			Metric	%
Pastry flour	1 lb	8	oz	700 g	100
Sugar		10	oz	280 g	40
Baking powder		1.25	oz	35 g	5
Baking soda			0.14 oz (1 tsp)	4 g	0.6
Salt			0.33 oz (2 tsp)	9 g	1.25
Chopped walnuts		6	oz	175 g	25
Eggs		10	oz	280 g	40
Ripe banana pulp, puréed	1 lb	8	oz	700 g	100
Oil or melted shortening or butter		8	oz	230 g	33
Yield:	5 lb	4	oz	2413 g	344

Mixing: Muffin method

Scaling: 1 lb 4 oz (575 g) per 7⅜ × 3⅝-inch (19 × 9 cm) loaf pan
1 lb 10 oz (750 g) per 8½ × 4½-inch (22 × 11 cm) loaf pan

Baking: 375° F (190° C), about 50 minutes

Variation

For a more delicate, cake-like product, make the following adjustments:

Fat: Increase to 40% (10 oz/280 g). Use shortening and/or butter, not oil.
Sugar: Increase to 60% (15 oz/420 g).
Flour: Use cake flour.
Mixing: Mix by the *creaming method.*

Date Nut Bread

Ingredients	U.S.		Metric		%
Shortening and/or butter	1 lb		400	g	40
Brown sugar	1 lb		400	g	40
Salt		0.5 oz	12.5	g	1.25
Nonfat milk solids		3 oz	70	g	7
Eggs		12 oz	300	g	30
Water	1 lb 14	oz	750	g	75
Cake flour	2 lb		800	g	80
Whole wheat flour		8 oz	200	g	20
Baking powder		1.5 oz	38	g	3.75
Baking soda		0.5 oz	12.5	g	1.25
Dates (see note)	1 lb 4	oz	500	g	50
Chopped walnuts		12 oz	300	g	30
Yield:	9 lb 7	oz	3783	g	378

Note: After scaling the dates, soak them in water until very soft. Drain and chop.

Mixing: Creaming method. Fold dates and nuts into finished batter.

Scaling: 1 lb 4 oz (575 g) per 7⅜ × 3⅝ inch (19 × 9 cm) loaf pan
1 lb 10 oz (750 g) per 8½ × 4½ inch (22 × 11 cm) loaf pan

Baking: 375° F (190° C), about 50 minutes

Variations

Substitute other nuts, or a mixture, for the walnuts. For example:

pecans
hazelnuts, toasted
almonds, toasted

Substitute other dried fruits for the dates. For example:

prunes
raisins
dried apricots
dried apples
dried figs

Soda Bread

Ingredients	U.S.			Metric	%
Pastry flour	2 lb	8	oz	1200 g	100
Baking powder		2	oz	60 g	5
Baking soda		0.5	oz	15 g	1.25
Salt		0.5	oz	15 g	1.25
Sugar		2	oz	60 g	5
Shortening or butter		4	oz	120 g	10
Currants		8	oz	240 g	20
Buttermilk	2 lb	4	oz	1080 g	90
Yield:	5 lb	13	oz	2790 g	232

Mixing: Biscuit method. Stir in currants after cutting in fat.

Scaling: 1 lb (450 g) per unit

Makeup: Round into a ball-shaped loaf. Place on sheet pan. Cut a deep cross into the top.

Baking: 400° F (200° C), about 40–50 minutes

Variation

Add 1.25% (0.5 oz/15 g) caraway seeds. Omit currants or leave them in, as desired.

Popovers

Ingredients	U.S.			Metric	%
Eggs	1 lb 4		oz	625 g	125
Milk	2 lb			1000 g	200
Salt		0.5	oz	15 g	3
Melted butter or shortening		2	oz	60 g	12.5
Bread flour	1 lb			500 g	100
Yield:	4 lb 6		oz	2200 g	440

Mixing:

1.   Beat eggs, milk, and salt together with whip attachment until well blended. Add melted fat.

2.   Replace whip with paddle. Mix in flour until completely smooth.

Scaling and panning: Grease every other cup of muffin tins (to allow room for expansion). Fill cups about half full, about 1½ oz (45 g) batter per unit.

Baking: 425° F (218° C) for 30–40 minutes. Before removing them from the oven, be sure popovers are dry and firm enough to avoid collapsing. Remove from pans immediately.

Ingredients	Old-Fashioned Gingerbread U.S.			Metric	%	Pain d'Epices (French Gingerbread) U.S.			Metric		%
Pastry flour	2 lb	8	oz	1100 g	100	1 lb	4	oz	550	g	50
Rye flour	—			—	—	1 lb	4	oz	550	g	50
Salt		0.25	oz	7 g	0.6		0.25	oz	7	g	0.6
Baking soda		1.25	oz	33 g	3		1.25	oz	33	g	3
Baking powder		0.6	oz	16 g	1.5		0.6	oz	16	g	1.5
Ginger		0.5	oz	14 g	1.25		0.5	oz	14	g	1.25
Cinnamon	—			—	—		0.25	oz	7	g	0.6
Cloves, ground	—			—	—		0.12	oz	3.5	g	0.3
Anise, ground	—			—	—		0.5	oz	14	oz	1.25
Orange rind, grated	—			—	—		0.5	oz	14	oz	1.25
Currants	—			—	—		8	oz	220	g	20
Molasses	2 lb	8	oz	1100 g	100	—			—		—
Honey	—			—	—	1 lb	14	oz	825	g	75
Hot water	1 lb	4	oz	550 g	50	1 lb	4	oz	550	g	50
Melted butter or shorten- ing		10	oz	275 g	25		10	oz	275	g	25
Yield:	7 lb	1	oz	3095 g	281	6 lb	15	oz	3078	g	279

Mixing: Muffin method

Panning: Old-fashioned gingerbread: greased, paper-lined sheet pans, about 6.5 to 7 lb per sheet (one recipe per sheet).
Pain d'epices (pronounced "pan day peece"): greased loaf pans. Fill about half full of batter.

Baking: 375° F (190° C)

TERMS FOR REVIEW

pour batter
drop batter
tunneling
biscuit method
muffin method
creaming method

QUESTIONS FOR DISCUSSION

1. If you made a batch of muffins that came out of the oven with strange, knobby shapes, what would you expect to be the reason?

2. What is the most important difference between the biscuit method and the muffin method?

3. Why do popovers require more mixing than other quick breads?

CHAPTER 6

DOUGHNUTS, FRITTERS, PANCAKES, AND WAFFLES

nlike the products we have discussed so far, those included in this chapter are cooked not by baking in ovens but by deep-frying, by cooking in greased fry-pans or on griddles, or, in the case of waffles, by cooking in specially designed griddles that heat the product from both sides at once.

There are several types of doughs or batters for these products. To produce the two most popular types of doughnuts, you will need to understand the principles of yeast dough production (Chapters 3 and 4) and the creaming method used for mixing some quick breads (Chapter 5). French doughnuts are a fried version of the same pastry used to make cream puffs and éclairs (Chapter 10). American pancakes are made from chemically leavened batters mixed by the muffin method, while French pancakes or crêpes are made from thin, unleavened batters made of milk, eggs, and flour.

After studying this chapter, you should be able to:
1. Prepare doughnuts and other deep-fried desserts and pastries.
2. Prepare pancakes and waffles.
3. Prepare crêpes and crêpe desserts.

DOUGHNUTS

Yeast-Raised Doughnuts

The mixing method used to prepare yeast-raised doughnuts is the modified straight dough method (p. 33). Review this procedure before beginning doughnut production. In addition, the following points will help you understand and produce high-quality doughnuts. Makeup and finishing procedures follow the formula.

1. The dough used for yeast doughnuts is similar to regular sweet dough or bun dough, except that it is often not as rich—that is, doughnuts are made with less fat, sugar, and eggs (compare the formulas on pp. 54 and 101). Doughs that are too rich will brown too fast and will absorb too much frying fat. The finished products will be greasy and either too dark on the outside or insufficiently cooked inside. Also, a leaner dough has stronger gluten, which can better withstand the handling involved in proofing and frying.

2. Punch the dough and bring it to the bench in sufficient time to allow for makeup. Remember that fermentation continues during makeup. If the dough gets too old, the doughnuts will require longer frying to become browned and will thus be greasier. When you are preparing a large quantity of doughnuts, it may be necessary to place some of the dough in the retarder so that it doesn't become old.

3. Watch the dough temperature carefully, especially in warm weather. If the dough is much above 80° F (24° C), it will become old more quickly.

4. Proof the doughnuts at a lower temperature and humidity than those used for breads. Some bakers proof them at room temperature. Doughnuts proofed this way are less likely to be deformed or dented when handled or brought to the fryer.

5. Handle fully proofed units very carefully, since they are soft and easily dented. Many bakers give doughnuts only three-quarters proof. This makes a denser doughnut, but one that is more easily handled.

6. Heat the frying fat to the proper temperature. Fat temperature for raised doughnuts varies from 365 to 385° F (185 to 195° C), depending on the formula. Richer formulas require a lower temperature to avoid excessive browning. The formulas in this book require a frying temperature of 375 to 380° F (190 to 193° C).

7. Arrange the proofed units on screens on which they can be lowered into fat. (For small quantities, you can place them by hand in the fryer, but be careful not to burn yourself.) Frying time is about 2½ minutes. The doughnuts must be turned over when they are half done in order to brown evenly on both sides.

Cake-type Doughnuts

Operations that produce cake doughnuts in volume use equipment that forms the dough and drops it directly into the hot fat. This equipment is usually automatic, although small hand-operated depositors are also available. Automatic depositors use a relatively slack dough that is generally made from prepared mixes. To use these mixes and depositors, follow two important guidelines:

1. Follow manufacturers' directions closely when preparing the mix.

2. Keep the depositor head 1½ in (4 cm) above the fat. If the doughnut must drop much farther than this into the fat, poor shapes may result.

Operations that make cake doughnuts by hand use a stiffer mix that is rolled out and cut with cutters. Two formulas for this type of mix are included in this chapter. Follow these guidelines when preparing cake doughnuts:

1. Scale ingredients very carefully. Even small errors can result in products with unsatisfactory texture or appearance.

2. Mix the dough until smooth, but do not overmix. Undermixed doughs result in a rough appearance and excessive fat absorption. Overmixed doughs result in tough, dense doughnuts.

3. Dough temperature should be about 70 to 75° F (21 to 24° C) when the units are fried. Be especially careful of dough temperature during hot weather.

4. Let the cutout units rest about 15 minutes before frying in order to relax the gluten. Failure to relax the dough results in toughness and poor expansion.

5. Fry at proper temperature. Normal fat temperature for cake doughnuts is 375 to 385° F (190 to 195° C). Frying time is about 1½ to 2 minutes. Doughnuts must be turned over when half done.

Preparation and Care of Frying Fat

Properly fried doughnuts absorb about 2 oz of fat per dozen. Therefore, frying fat should be of good quality and be properly maintained; otherwise the quality of the doughnuts will suffer. Observe the following guidelines for care of frying fat:

1. Use good-quality, flavorless fat. The best fat for frying has a high smoke point (the temperature at which the fat begins to smoke and to break down rapidly).

   Solid shortenings are popular for frying because they are stable, and because they congeal when the doughnuts cool, making them *appear* less greasy. However, such doughnuts can have an unpleasant eating quality, since the fat does not melt in the mouth.

2. Fry at the proper temperature. Using too low a temperature extends frying time, causing excessive greasiness.

If you do not have automatic equipment with thermostatic temperature controls, keep a fat thermometer clipped to the side of the frying kettle.

3. Maintain the fat at the proper level in the fryer. When additional fat must be added, allow time for it to heat up.

4. Do not fry too many doughnuts at a time. Overloading will lower the fat temperature, will not allow room for expansion of the doughnuts, and will make it difficult to turn them over.

5. Keep fat clean. Skim out food particles as necessary. After each day's use, cool the fat until it is warm, strain it, and clean the equipment.

6. Discard spent fat. Old fat loses frying ability, browns excessively, and imparts a bad flavor.

7. Keep fat covered when not in use. Try to aerate the fat as little as possible when filtering.

Yeast-Raised Doughnuts

Ingredients	U.S.			Metric	%
Water	2 lb			825 g	55
Yeast		3	oz	75 g	5
Shortening		6	oz	150 g	10
Sugar		8	oz	210 g	14
Salt		1	oz	26 g	1.75
Mace		0.17	oz (1 tsp)	5 g	0.3
Nonfat milk solids		3	oz	75 g	5
Eggs		8	oz	210 g	14
Bread flour	3 lb 10		oz	1500 g	100
Yield:	7 lb 7		oz	3075 g	205

Mixing: Modified straight dough method
Develop the dough completely, about 6–8 minutes at second speed.

Fermentation: About 1½ hours at 80° F (24° C)

Scaling: 1.5 oz (45 g) per unit
See below for makeup.

Frying: 375° F (190° C)
When fried, lift doughnuts from fat and let excess fat drip off. Place doughnuts in one layer on absorbent paper. Cool.

(Continues)

Yeast-Raised Doughnuts *(Continued)*

Makeup of Yeast-Raised Doughnuts

Ring Doughnuts:

1. Roll out dough ½ inch (12 mm) thick. Make sure dough is of even thickness. Let the dough relax.

2. Cut out doughnuts with a doughnut cutter. Cut as close together as possible to minimize the quantity of scrap.

3. Combine the scrap dough and let it relax. Roll out and let it relax again. Continue cutting doughnuts.

Jelly-filled Doughnuts or Bismarcks:

Method 1:

1. Scale the dough into 3½ lb (1600 g) presses. Let them relax for 10 minutes.

2. Divide the dough. Round the small units.

3. Let them relax a few minutes, then flatten lightly.

Method 2:

1. Roll out the dough ½ inch (12 mm) thick as for ring doughnuts.

2. Cut out with round cutters (biscuit cutters, or doughnut cutters with the ''hole'' removed).

After frying and cooling, use a doughnut pump or jelly pump to fill the doughnuts. Using a sharp, straight nozzle, pierce the side of the doughnut and inject the jelly into the *center*.

Other fillings besides jelly may be used, such as lemon, custard (see pastry cream, p. 120), and cream. If a filling containing egg, milk, or cream is used, the doughnuts must be kept refrigerated.

Long Johns:

1. Roll out the dough ½ inch (12 mm) thick as for ring doughnuts.

2. With a pastry wheel, cut into strips 1½ inches (4 cm) wide and 3½ inches (9 cm) long.

Fried Cinnamon Rolls:

1. Make up like baked cinnamon rolls (p. 78), except omit the butter in the filling. Make sure the edges are well sealed so the rolls don't unwind during frying.

Twists:

1. Scale into presses, divide the dough, and round the units as for filled doughnuts.

2. Roll each unit on the bench with the palms of the hands to a strip about 8 inches (20 cm) long.

3. Place one hand over each end of the strip. Roll one end toward you and the other away from you to twist the strip.

4. Holding it by the ends, lift the strip off the bench and bring the two ends together. The strip will twist around itself.

5. Seal the ends together.

Ingredients	Cake Doughnuts					Chocolate Cake Doughnuts				
	U.S.		Metric	%		U.S.		Metric	%
Shortening		6 oz	180 g	9		6 oz	180 g	9
Sugar	14	oz	440 g	22	1 lb			500 g	25
Salt		0.5 oz	15 g	0.8		0.5 oz	15 g	0.8
Nonfat milk solids		3 oz	90 g	4.7		3 oz	90 g	4.7
Mace		0.25 oz	8 g	0.4	—		—	—
Vanilla		1 oz	30 g	1.5		1 oz	30 g	1.5
Eggs, whole		6 oz	180 g	9		6 oz	180 g	9
Egg yolks		2 oz	60 g	3		2 oz	60 g	3
Water	2 lb		1000 g	50	2 lb	2 oz	1060 g	53
Cake flour	2 lb	8 oz	1500 g	62.5	2 lb	8 oz	1500 g	62.5
Bread flour	1 lb	8 oz	500 g	37.5	1 lb	8 oz	500 g	37.5
Cocoa powder	—		—	—		5 oz	155 g	7.8
Baking powder		2.5 oz	80 g	4		2 oz	60 g	3
Baking soda	—		—	—		0.4 oz	13 g	0.63
						(1 tbsp)		
Yield:	8 lb	3 oz	4088 g	204	8 lb	11 oz	4198 g	217

Mixing: Creaming method (p. 87)

Mix the dough until it is smooth, but do not overmix.

Makeup

1. Place the dough on the bench and form into a smooth rectangular shape with the hands; let rest 15 minutes.

2. Roll out to about ⅜ inch (1 cm) thick. Make sure the dough is of even thickness and is not sticking to the bench.

3. Cut out doughnuts with cutters.

4. Collect the scrap dough and let it relax. Roll it out again and continue cutting doughnuts.

5. Place the doughnuts on lightly floured pans and let them relax 15 minutes.

Frying: 380° F (193° C)

Caution: Watch chocolate doughnuts carefully because it is harder to tell doneness by their color.

Lift doughnuts from fat, let excess fat drip off, and place them in one layer on absorbent paper. Cool.

Finishing Doughnuts

Doughnuts should be well drained and cooled before finishing with sugar or other coatings. If they are hot, steam from the doughnuts will soak the coating. The following are some popular coatings and finishes for doughnuts:

1. To glaze, dip in *warm* doughnut glaze (recipe follows) or in a warmed, thinned simple icing or fondant. Place on screens until glaze sets.

2. After glazing, while glaze is still moist, doughnuts may be rolled in coconut or chopped nuts.

3. Roll in cinnamon sugar.

4. Roll in 4X sugar. (To keep sugar from lumping and absorbing moisture, it may be sifted with cornstarch. Use about 2 to 3 ounces of starch per pound of sugar, or about 150 grams per kilogram.)

5. Ice the tops of the doughnuts with a fondant or fudge icing (see Chapter 7).

Doughnut Glaze

Ingredients	U.S.		Metric	Sugar at 100% %
Gelatin	0.25 oz		6 g	0.3
Water	1 lb		400 g	20
Corn syrup	4	oz	100 g	5
Vanilla	0.5	oz	12 g	0.6
4X or 6X sugar	5 lb		2000 g	100
Yield:	6 lb 4	oz	2518 g	125

Procedure:

1. Soften the gelatin in the water.

2. Heat the water until the gelatin dissolves.

3. Add the remaining ingredients and mix until smooth.

4. Dip doughnuts into warm glaze, or rewarm the glaze as necessary.

Variation

Honey Glaze:

Substitute honey for the corn syrup.

French Doughnuts

French doughnuts are made from éclair paste (p. 157) that has been piped into ring shapes and deep fried.

Procedure

1. Cut heavy brown paper into pieces that will fit in the doughnut fryer. Grease the paper thoroughly with shortening.

2. Fit a pastry bag with a star tube about ½ inch (12 mm) in diameter. Fill the bag with freshly made, warm éclair paste.

3. Bag out rings of desired size on the greased paper. For 1-ounce doughnuts, make 2-inch (5 cm) rings. Space the rings evenly, about 1 inch (2.5 cm) apart.

4. Carefully lower one sheet of the paper into the hot fat (375° F/190° C). When all the rings float free, remove the paper.

5. Fry until golden brown on one side. Turn them over and brown on the second side.

6. French doughnuts must be completely fried or they may collapse when cooling. Therefore it is a good idea to turn them over again and fry the first side for another 30 to 60 seconds.

7. Remove doughnuts from fryer, let excess fat drip back into the fryer, and place them ridged-side up on absorbent paper to drain and cool.

8. When cool, ice with fondant or dust with confectioners' sugar.

FRITTERS

The term *fritter* is used for a great variety of fried items, including both sweet and savory foods including many kinds made with vegetables, meats, or fish. In the pastry shop, we are especially concerned with two popular varieties of fritters:

Fruit fritters: Pieces of fresh, cooked, or canned fruit dipped in batter, fried, and served warm.

Beignets soufflés: Small pieces of éclair paste, fried and served warm, usually with sugar and a sauce. (Beignets is pronounced "ben yay.")

Procedure for Preparing Fruit Fritters

1. Prepare batter (see formulas that follow).

2. Prepare the desired fruit. Popular fruits for fritters are:

Apples: Peel, core and slice into rings ¼ inch (6 mm) thick.

Bananas: Peel, cut in half lengthwise, and then cut crosswise to make four quarters.

Pineapple: Use fresh or canned rings.

Apricots and plums: Split in half and remove the stones.

For extra flavor, fruits may be sprinkled heavily with sugar and rum or kirsch and marinated 1 to 2 hours.

3. Drain the fruit pieces well and dip them in batter to coat completely. Dip only as much as can be fried in one batch.

4. Drop into hot fat (375° F/190° C). Fry until golden brown on all sides.

5. Remove from fat and drain well.

6. Serve warm, sprinkled with cinnamon sugar. Vanilla sauce or fruit sauce (p. 132) may be served on the side.

Fritter Batter I

Ingredients	U.S.			Metric	%
Pastry flour	2 lb	4	oz	1000 g	100
Sugar		2	oz	60 g	6
Salt		0.5	oz	15 g	1.5
Baking powder		0.5	oz	15 g	1.5
Eggs, beaten	1 lb	2	oz	500 g	50
Milk	2 lb			900 g	90
Oil		2	oz	60 g	6
Vanilla		0.33 oz (1 tsp)		10 g	1
Yield:	5 lb	11	oz	2560 g	256

Mixing: Muffin method (p. 87)

1. Sift together the dry ingredients.
2. Combine the liquid ingredients.
3. Gradually stir the liquid into the dry ingredients. Mix until nearly smooth, but do not overmix.
4. Let stand at least 30 minutes before using.

Procedure for Preparing Beignets Soufflés

1. Prepare éclair paste (p. 157) using only 42% butter or shortening.

2. Using a pastry bag with a large plain tube, pipe small mounds (about ¾ oz/20 g, or as desired) onto greased brown paper. Lower the paper into fat heated to 360° F (180° C).

   Alternative method: Bag directly into the hot fat, cutting the lumps of paste from the tube with a knife as it is forced out.

3. Fry until puffed and golden brown on all sides.

4. Drain well. Serve warm, dusted with confectioners' sugar. Serve a fruit sauce or vanilla sauce on the side.

PANCAKES AND WAFFLES

While pancakes and waffles are rarely produced in the retail bakeshop, they are essential items on the breakfast, brunch, and dessert menus in food service operations. In addition, a French waffle formula, especially well suited for dessert, is included here. This batter is actually an éclair paste that is thinned out with cream or milk. French pancakes, or crêpes, and various desserts made from them are also presented.

American-style Pancakes and Waffles

American-style pancakes and waffles are made from pourable batters mixed by the muffin method, which is presented in the preceding chapter. As with muffins, it is important to avoid overmixing the batters for these products in order to prevent excessive gluten development.

Pancakes and waffles can be made in almost unlimited varieties by substituting other types of flour, such as buckwheat flour, whole wheat flour, and cornmeal, for part of the pastry flour. Since some of these absorb more water than others, additional liquid may be needed to thin out the batter.

Compare the formulas for pancakes and waffles. In particular, you should notice these differences:

1. Waffle batter contains more fat. This makes the waffles richer and crisper and aids in their release from the waffle iron.

2. Waffle batter contains less liquid, so it is slightly thicker. This, too, makes waffles crisp, since crispness depends on low moisture content.

3. Whipping the egg whites separately and folding them into the batter gives waffles added lightness.

Fritter Batter II

Ingredients	U.S.		Metric	%
Bread flour	1 lb 8	oz	750 g	75
Cake flour	8	oz	250 g	25
Salt	0.5	oz	15	1.5
Sugar	1	oz	30 g	3
Milk	2 lb 4	oz	1250 g	125
Egg yolks, beaten	4	oz	125 g	12.5
Oil	4	oz	125 g	12.5
Egg whites	8	oz	250 g	25
Yield:	5 lb 5	oz	2795 g	279

Mixing:

1. Sift together the dry ingredients.
2. Combine the milk, egg yolks, and oil.
3. Stir the liquid into the dry ingredients. Mix until smooth.
4. Let rest until ready to use, at least 30 minutes.
5. Whip the egg whites until stiff but not dry.
6. Fold the egg whites into the batter. Use immediately.

Ingredients	Pancakes				Waffles			
Yield: about 2 qt (2 l)								
	U.S.		Metric	%	U.S.		Metric	%
Pastry flour	1 lb		450 g	100	1 lb		450 g	100
Sugar	2	oz	60 g	12.5	—		—	—
Salt	0.33 oz (2 tsp)		10 g	2	0.33 oz (2 tsp)		10 g	2
Baking powder	1	oz (2 tbsp)	30 g	6	1	oz (2 tbsp)	30 g	6
Whole eggs, beaten	7	oz (4 large)	200 g	44	—		—	—
Egg yolks, beaten	—		—	—	4	oz (6 large)	110 g	25
Milk	2 lb		900 g	200	1 lb 8	oz	675 g	150
Melted butter or oil	4	oz	110 g	25	8	oz	225 g	50
Egg whites	—		—	—	6	oz (6 large)	170 g	38
Sugar	—		—	—	2	oz	60 g	12.5

Mixing: Muffin method (p. 87)

1. Sift together the dry ingredients.
2. Combine the eggs or egg yolks, milk, and fat.
3. Add the liquid ingredients to the dry ingredients. Mix until just combined. Do not overmix.
4. For waffles: Just before they are to be cooked, whip the egg whites until they form soft peaks, then beat in the sugar until the meringue is stiff. Fold into the batter.

Cooking pancakes:

1. Using a 2-ounce (60 ml) ladle, measure portions of batter onto a greased, preheated griddle (375° F/190° C), allowing space for spreading.
2. Fry the pancakes until the tops are full of bubbles and begin to look dry, and the bottoms are golden brown.
3. Turn and brown the other side.
4. Serve hot, accompanied by butter, maple syrup, fruit syrup, jams or preserves, applesauce, or fresh berries.

Cooking waffles:

1. Pour enough batter onto a lightly greased, preheated waffle iron to almost cover the surface. Close the iron.
2. Cook the waffles until the signal light indicates they are done, or until steam is no longer emitted. The waffles should be brown and crisp.
3. Serve warm, with confectioners' sugar, syrup, jam, or fresh fruit.

(Continues)

Pancakes and Waffles *(Continued)*

Variation

Buttermilk Pancakes and Waffles:

Use buttermilk instead of milk. Reduce baking powder to 2% (0.33 oz or 2 tsp/10 g) and add 2 tsp (10 g) baking soda. If the batter is too thick, thin it with a little milk or water.

Pre-Preparation for Volume Service

1. Pancake and waffle batters leavened *only by baking powder* may be mixed the night before and stored in the cooler. Some rising power may be lost, so baking powder may have to be increased.

2. Batters leavened by *baking soda* should not be made too far ahead, because the soda will lose its power. Mix dry ingredients and liquid ingredients ahead, and combine just before service.

3. Batters using beaten egg whites and baking powder may be partially made ahead, but *incorporate the egg whites just before service.*

Gaufres (French Waffles)

Ingredients	U.S.		Metric	%
Milk	2 lb		1000 g	200
Salt		0.5 oz	15 g	3
Butter		6 oz	190 g	37.5
Bread flour	1 lb		500 g	100
Eggs	1 lb 10 oz		800 g	162.5
	(about 16 large eggs)			
Cream	1 lb		500 g	100
Milk		8 oz	250 g	50
Yield:	6 lb 8 oz		3255 g	653

Procedure:

1. Combine the milk, salt, and butter in a saucepan or kettle. Carefully bring to a boil.

2. Add the flour all at once and stir vigorously. Continue to stir until the mixture forms a ball and pulls away from the sides of the kettle.

3. Remove from the heat and transfer to the bowl of a mixer. Let cool 5 minutes.

4. With the mixer on low speed, add the eggs a little at a time. Wait until each addition is absorbed before adding more.

5. With the mixer continuing to run, sowly pour in the cream, then the milk. Don't worry if the batter is slightly lumpy even after all the milk is added; this is normal. The batter should be slightly thicker than regular waffle batter. If it is much thicker, add a little more milk.

6. Bake as you would regular waffles.

Crêpes

Crêpes are thin, unleavened pancakes. They are rarely served plain but are instead used to construct a great variety of desserts by being rolled around various fillings, layered with fillings, or served with sweet sauces. Unsweetened crêpes are used in similar ways, but filled with various meat, fish, and vegetable preparations.

Unlike leavened pancakes, crêpes may be made in advance, covered and refrigerated, and used as needed. When the crêpes are filled and rolled or folded, the side that was browned first, which is the most attractive side, should be on the outside.

Crêpes

Ingredients	U.S.		Metric	%
Bread flour	8	oz	250 g	50
Cake flour	8	oz	250 g	50
Sugar	2	oz	60 g	12.5
Salt	0.5	oz	15 g	3
Eggs (7 large eggs)	12	oz	375 g	75
Milk	2 lb		1000 g	200
Oil or clarified butter	5	oz	150 g	30
Yield:	4 lb 3	oz	2100 g	421
	enough for about 50 crêpes			

Mixing:

1. Sift the flour, sugar, and salt into a bowl.

2. Add the eggs and just enough of the milk to make a soft paste with the flour. Mix until smooth and lump-free.

3. Gradually mix in the rest of the milk and the oil. The batter should be about the consistency of heavy cream. If it is too thick, mix in a little water. If it has lumps, pour it through a strainer.

4. Let the batter rest 2 hours before frying.

Frying:

1. Rub a 6- or 7-inch (15–18 cm) crêpe pan or skillet lightly with oil. Heat over moderately high heat until it is very hot.

2. Remove from heat and pour in about 3–4 tablespoons (45–60 ml) of the batter. Very quickly tilt the pan to cover the bottom with a thin layer. Immediately dump out any excess batter, since the crêpe must be very thin.

3. Return to the heat for about 1 to 1½ minutes, until the bottom is lightly browned. Flip the crêpe over and brown the second side. The second side will brown only in a few spots and will not be as attractive as the first side. The first side should always be the visible side when the crêpe is served.

4. Slide the crêpe onto a plate. Continue making crêpes and stacking them up as they are finished. Grease the pan *lightly* when necessary.

5. Cover the finished crêpes and refrigerate until needed.

Crêpe Desserts

The following are only a few of many possible suggestions. The variety of crêpe desserts you can prepare is limited only by your imagination.

Crêpes Normande. Sauté fresh sliced apples in butter and sprinkle with sugar and a dash of cinnamon. Roll up the apples in crêpes and dust with confectioners' sugar.

Banana Crêpes. Sauté sliced bananas quickly in butter and sprinkle with brown sugar and a dash of rum. Roll up the filling in the crêpes. Serve with apricot sauce (p. 132).

Crêpes with Jam. Spread apricot jam on crêpes and roll them up. Sprinkle with sugar and run under the broiler quickly to glaze the sugar.

Glazed Crêpes. Fill crêpes with vanilla pastry cream (p. 120) and roll them up. Sprinkle with sugar and run under the broiler to glaze the sugar.

Crêpes Frangipane. Spread the crêpes with frangipane filling (p. 63) and roll them up or fold them in quarters. Brush with butter and sprinkle with sugar. Place in a buttered baking dish and bake in a hot oven about 10 minutes to heat through. Serve with chocolate sauce or vanilla sauce.

Crêpes Suzette. This most famous of all crêpe desserts is generally prepared at tableside by the waiter, according to the procedure in the following recipe. The crêpes, fruit, sugar, and butter are supplied by the kitchen. It can also be prepared in the kitchen or pastry department by modifying the procedure as in the variation following the recipe.

Crêpes Suzette
Yield: 4 servings

Ingredients	U.S.	Metric
Sugar	3 oz	85 g
Orange	1	1
Lemon	½	½
Butter	2 oz	60 g
Orange-flavored liqueur	1 oz	30 ml
Cognac	2 oz	60 ml
Crêpes	12	12

Procedure for dining room preparation:

1. In a flambé pan, heat the sugar until it melts and begins to caramelize.

2. Cut several strips of rind from the orange and one from the lemon; add them to the pan.

3. Add the butter and squeeze the juice from the orange and lemon into the pan. Cook and stir until the sugar is dissolved and the mixture is a little syrupy.

4. Add the orange liqueur. One by one, dip the crêpes in the sauce to coat them, then fold them into quarters in the pan.

5. Add the cognac and allow it to heat for a few seconds. Flame by *carefully* tipping the pan towards the burner flame until the cognac ignites.

6. Shake the pan gently and spoon the sauce over the crêpes until the flame dies down.

7. Serve three crêpes per portion. Spoon a little of the remaining sauce over each serving.

Variation

Kitchen Preparation:

1. Cream the butter and half the sugar together until light.

2. Add some grated orange and lemon rind, the orange juice, and the lemon juice. Mix well. (The mixture may separate, but it will work just as well.)

3. Spread this mixture over the crêpes and fold them in quarters. Arrange them in a buttered pan and sprinkle with the remaining sugar.

4. Place the pan in a hot oven until the crêpes are bubbling.

5. Combine the orange liqueur and cognac in a small saucepan. Heat the mixture, ignite it, and pour it over the crêpes.

TERMS FOR REVIEW

modified straight dough method
glaze
French doughnut
fritter
beignet soufflé
gaufre
crêpe
Crêpes Suzette

QUESTIONS FOR DISCUSSION

1. Two yeast doughnut formulas have the same quantities of fat and milk, but one has more sugar than the other. Which one do you expect would require a higher frying temperature? Why?

2. Why is it important to carefully control the mixing time when making cake doughnuts?

3. List five rules for maintaining frying fat to produce good-quality fried foods.

4. What type of leavening is used in crêpes (French pancakes)? In French doughnuts?

5. Why does waffle batter often contain less liquid (water or milk) than pancake batter?

6. Which mixing method is used to make American-style pancakes? What are the steps in this method?

CHAPTER 7

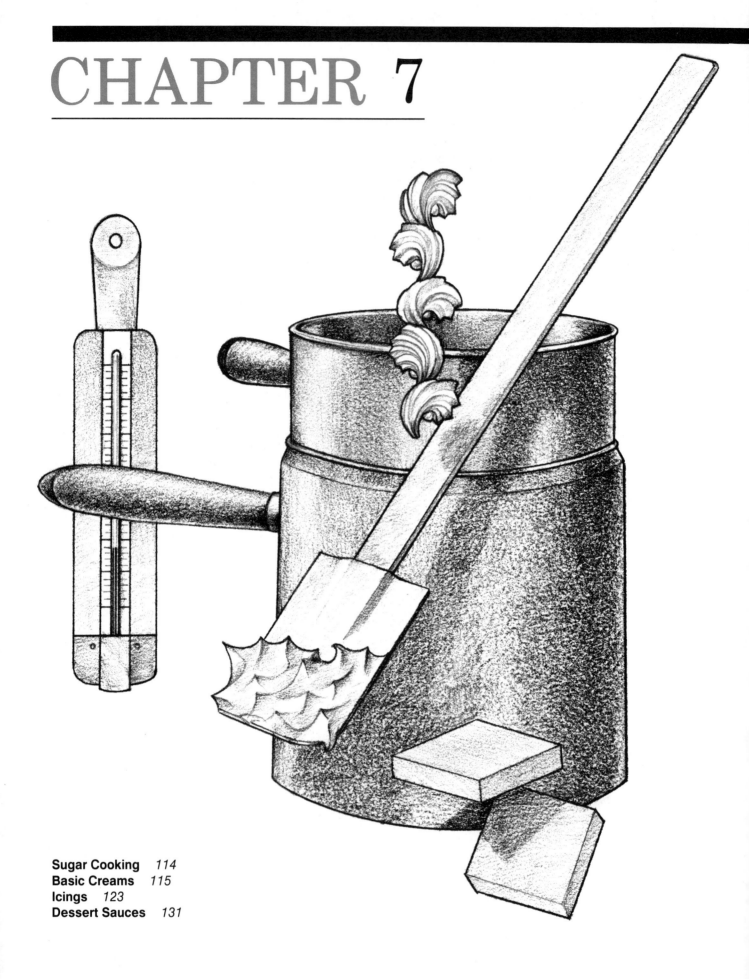

BASIC SYRUPS, CREAMS, ICINGS, AND SAUCES

uch of the baker's craft consists of mixing and baking flour goods, such as breads, cakes, and pastries. However, the baker also must be able to make a variety of other products sometimes known as "adjuncts," such as toppings, fillings, icings, and sauces. These are not baked goods in themselves, but they are essential in the preparation of many baked goods and desserts.

Several of the procedures you learn in this chapter are used in many ways. For example, crème anglaise or custard sauce is used not only as a dessert sauce but is also the basis for such items as Bavarian creams and ice creams. Pastry cream, with a variety of flavorings, is also used for pie fillings, puddings, and soufflés.

After studying this chapter, you should be able to:
1. Cook sugar syrups to various stages of hardness.
2. Prepare whipped cream, meringues, custard sauces, and pastry cream variations.
3. Prepare icings.
4. Prepare dessert sauces.

SUGAR COOKING

Understanding sugar cooking is important in the preparation of desserts and confections, because sugar syrups of various strengths are often required (see, for example, Italian meringue, p. 118).

Syrup Strength

The principle of sugar cooking is fairly simple: A solution or syrup of sugar and water is boiled to evaporate part of the water. As the water is boiled off, the temperature of the syrup gradually rises. When all the water has evaporated, you are left with melted sugar. The sugar will then begin to *caramelize,* or turn brown and change flavor. If heating continues, the sugar will continue to darken and then burn.

A syrup cooked to a high temperature will be harder when it is cooled than will a syrup cooked to a lower temperature. For example, a syrup cooked to 240° F (115° C) will form a soft ball when cooled. A syrup cooked to 300° F (150° C) will be hard and brittle when cooled.

One pint (one pound) of water is enough to dissolve up to 3 or 4 pounds of sugar. There is no point in adding more water than you need for a particular purpose, since you will just have to boil it off again.

Pure, clean granulated sugar is used to make syrups. Impurities will cloud the syrup and form a scum or foam on the syrup as it is being boiled. Any scum should be carefully skimmed off.

Crystallization and Inversion

Graininess is a common fault in many candies and desserts. Graininess results when cooked sugar crystallizes, that is, turns to tiny sugar crystals rather than staying dissolved in the syrup. If even one sugar crystal comes in contact with a cooked syrup, it can start a chain reaction that turns the whole thing into a mass of sugar crystals.

To avoid crystallization during the first stages of boiling sugar syrups, use one of the following techniques:

1. As you boil the sugar, wash down the sides of the saucepan with a brush dipped in water. Do not let the brush touch the syrup, but let water from the brush run down the sides of the pan. This will remove crystals that may "seed" the whole batch.

2. When first bringing the syrup to a boil, cover the pan and boil for several minutes. Condensed steam will wash down the sides of the pan. Uncover and finish cooking without stirring.

Syrups cooked until they have a high concentration of sugar are liable to crystallize after they have been cooled. This can be controlled by a process called *inversion.* As explained in Chapter 2 (p. 15), inversion is a chemical change of regular sugar (sucrose) into another form of sugar that resists crystallizing.

If an acid, such as cream of tartar or lemon juice, is added to a syrup before or during cooking, some of the sugar is inverted. The type and amount of acid used affect the amount of sugar that is inverted. Therefore, specific formulas should be followed carefully whenever acids are required in sugar boiling.

Glucose or corn syrup may also be added to control crystallization in boiling syrups. It is convenient to use and produces good results.

Stages of Sugar Cooking

Testing the temperature with a candy thermometer is the most accurate way to determine the doneness of a syrup.

In the old days, a syrup was tested by dropping a little of it into a bowl of cold water and then checking the hardness of the cooled sugar. The stages of doneness were given names that described their hardness.

Table 7.1 lists these stages of sugar cooking. Please note that the names for the various stages are not absolute; different sources may use slightly different names. In fact, all such tables are misleading, because they suggest that the syrup jumps from one stage to the next. Actually, of course, it changes *gradually* as the water is boiled off. For this reason, it is best to simply rely on the thermometer and not worry too much about the names.

Basic Syrups for the Bakeshop

Two basic syrups are kept in stock in the bakeshop and used in a variety of ways. *Simple syrup,* also known as stock syrup, is a solution of equal weights of sugar and water. It is used for such purposes as diluting fondant (p. 124) and for preparing a variety of dessert syrups. *Dessert syrup* is simply a flavored simple syrup. It is used to moisten and flavor sponge cakes and various desserts, such as babas au rum (p. 57).

The concentration of both these syrups may be varied to taste. Some chefs prefer a sweeter syrup for some purposes, such as 1 part water to 1½ parts sugar. Others use a less sweet syrup, such as 2 parts water to one part sugar.

TABLE 7.1 **Stages of Doneness in Sugar Cooking**

| | Temperature | |
Stage	° F	° C
Thread	230	110
Soft ball	240	115
Firm ball	245	118
Hard ball	250–260	122–127
Small crack	265–270	130–132
Crack	275–280	135–138
Hard crack	290–310	143–155
Caramel	320–340	160–170

Procedure for Preparing Simple Syrup

1. Combine the following ingredients in a saucepan:

    water   1 pt   5 dl
    sugar   1 lb   500 g

2. Stir and bring to a boil over moderate heat. Cook and stir until the sugar is dissolved.

3. Remove any scum. Cool syrup and store in a covered container.

Procedure for Preparing Dessert Syrup

Method 1:

Prepare and cool a simple syrup. Add any desired flavoring according to taste. Extracts such as vanilla or liquors such as rum or kirsch may serve as flavorings. A flavoring should be added after the syrup has cooled, since some of the flavor may evaporate if it is added to hot syrup.

Method 2:

Prepare a simple syrup, but add the rind of one orange and/or one lemon to the sugar and water before bringing it to a boil. Let the syrup simmer for 5 minutes before cooling. Remove the rind from the cooled syrup.

BASIC CREAMS

Many of the preparations discussed in this section are among the most important and useful preparations in the bakeshop or pastry shop. They find their way into a great variety of desserts — as fillings or components of

cakes and pastries, as ingredients of such desserts as Bavarian creams and mousses, and as sauces or toppings. Learn these techniques well because you will use them over and over again in other parts of this book.

Whipped Cream

Whipped cream is not only one of the most useful dessert toppings and fillings, but it is also an ingredient in many desserts. Cream with a fat content of 30% or more, but preferably over 35%, can be whipped into a foam. One quart of cream will produce about 2 to 2½ quarts of whipped cream.

For best results, follow the guidelines outlined in the following procedure.

Procedure for Making Whipped Cream

Basic ratios:

Heavy cream	1 qt	1 l
Sugar, confectioners' or extra fine granulated	2–4 oz	60–120 g
Flavorings (choice of one):		
Vanilla	½ oz	15 ml
Liquors (rum, kirsch, etc.)	2–4 oz	60–120 g

1. Cream for whipping should be at least one day old. Very fresh cream doesn't whip well.

2. Chill well the cream and all equipment, especially in hot weather. Cream that is too warm is hard to whip and will curdle easily.

3. Use a wire whip for beating by hand. For machine whipping, use the whip attachment, and run the machine at medium speed.

4. If the cream is to be sweetened, do not add sugar until the cream is three-fourths whipped, that is, not until you are able to see marks of the whip in the cream. Sugar decreases stability and makes the cream harder to whip. Use extra fine granulated sugar or, for best stability, sifted confectioners' sugar.

5. Do not overwhip. Stop beating when the cream forms peaks that hold their shape. If the cream is whipped longer, it first becomes grainy in appearance and then separates into butter and whey.

6. Cream to be folded into other ingredients should be slightly underbeaten, since the action of folding whips it more and may overbeat it.

7. Fold in flavoring ingredients last, after the cream is whipped.

8. If the cream is not to be used immediately, store it, covered, in the refrigerator.

Procedure for Stabilizing Whipped Cream

During warm weather, it is sometimes helpful to add gelatin or a commercial stabilizer to whipped cream so that it will hold up. This is especially true of whipped-cream-topped items displayed on a buffet.

1. To use a commercial stabilizer, sift it with the sugar used to sweeten the cream. Use about ¼ oz stabilizer per quart of cream (7 grams per liter). Add the sugar as in the basic procedure.

2. To use gelatin, use the following proportions:

Heavy cream	1 qt	1 l
Gelatin	⅓ oz	10 g
Cold water	2 oz	60 ml

Soften the gelatin in the cold water, then warm it until the gelatin dissolves. Cool it, but do not let it set. Beat it into the cream just as the cream begins to thicken.

Procedure for Making Chocolate Whipped Cream

1. Use the following proportions:

Heavy cream	1 qt	1 l
Sweet chocolate	12 oz	375 g

2. Whip the cream as in the basic procedure, but underwhip it slightly.

3. Grate or chop the chocolate into small pieces and place in a saucepan. Set over warm water and stir until the chocolate is melted. Let it cool to lukewarm. It must not cool too much or it will solidify before it can be mixed evenly with the cream.

4. Stir about one-fourth of the whipped cream into the chocolate until it is well mixed.

5. Fold the chocolate mixture into the rest of the cream carefully but thoroughly. Be careful not to overwhip the cream.

Meringue

Meringues are whipped egg whites sweetened with sugar. They are most frequently used in this country for pie toppings and cake icings. They are also used to give volume and lightness to buttercream icings and to such preparations as mousses and dessert soufflés.

Another excellent use for meringues is to bake them in a slow oven until crisp. In this form, they can be used as cake layers or pastry shells to make very light, elegant desserts. To add flavor, chopped nuts may be folded into meringues before forming and baking. Pastries and cakes incorporating crisp meringues are discussed in Chapters 8 and 11.

Basic Meringue Types

Meringues may be whipped to various degrees of stiffness, as long as they are not overbeaten until they are too stiff and dry. For most purposes, they are beaten until they form stiff or nearly stiff, moist peaks.

1. **Common meringue** is made from egg whites at room temperature, beaten with sugar. It is the easiest to make, and it is reasonably stable due to the high percentage of sugar.

2. **Swiss meringue** is made from egg whites and sugar that are warmed over a hot water bath while they are being beaten. This warming gives the meringue better volume and stability.

3. **Italian meringue** is made by beating a hot sugar syrup into the egg whites. This meringue is the most stable of the three because the egg whites are cooked by the heat of the syrup. When flavored with vanilla, it is also known as boiled icing. It is also used in meringue-type buttercream icings.

The amount of sugar used in meringues may vary. *Soft meringues,* those used for pie toppings, may be made with as little as one pound of sugar per pound of egg whites. *Hard meringues,* those baked until crisp, are made with up to twice as much sugar as egg whites.

Guidelines for Making Meringues

1. *Fats prevent whites from foaming properly.*

   This is very important. Make sure that all equipment is free of any trace of fat or grease, and that the egg whites have no trace of yolks in them.

2. *Egg whites foam better if they are at room temperature than if they are cold.*

   Remove them from the cooler an hour before whipping.

3. *Do not overbeat.*

   Beaten egg whites should look moist and shiny. Overbeaten meringues look dry and curdled; they are difficult to fold into other ingredients and have lost much of their ability to leaven cakes and souflés.

4. *Sugar makes egg white foams more stable.*

   Meringues are thicker and heavier than unsweetened egg white foams, and they are more stable. However, egg whites can hold only a limited amount of sugar without sacrificing some volume. For this reason, when making common meringues, many cooks prefer to whip the egg whites with no more than an equal weight of sugar. Additional sugar can be folded in after the meringue is whipped.

5. *Mild acids help foaming.*

   A small amount of cream of tartar or lemon juice is sometimes added to egg whites for whipping, in order to give them more volume and stability. This is especially helpful when the whipped whites are folded into other ingredients to provide lightness or leavening, as in the case of angel food cakes. Use about 2 teaspoons cream of tartar per pound of egg whites (15 g per kg).

Common Meringue

Ingredients	U.S.	Egg whites at 100% Metric	%
Egg whites	1 lb	500 g	100
Sugar, fine granulated	1 lb	500 g	100
Sugar, fine granulated or sifted 4X or 6X	1 lb	500 g	100
Yield:	3 lb	1500 g	300

Procedure:

1. With the whip attachment, beat the egg whites first at medium speed, then at high speed, until they form soft peaks.

2. Add the first quantity of sugar, a little at a time, with the machine running. Whip until stiff.

3. Stop the machine. Fold in the remaining sugar with a spatula.

Note: For soft meringue pie toppings, the second quantity of sugar may be omitted.

Variation

Chocolate Meringue:

Use the 4X or 6X sugar in step 3 of the above formula. Sift the sugar twice with the following:

Cocoa powder   4 oz   125 g   25%

Swiss Meringue

Ingredients	U.S.	Metric	Egg whites at 100% %
Egg whites	1 lb	500 g	100
Sugar	2 lb	1000 g	200
Yield:	3 lb	1500 g	300

Procedure:

1. Place the egg whites and sugar in a stainless steel bowl or in the top of a double boiler. Beat with a wire whip over hot water until the mixture is warm (about 120° F/50° C).

2. Transfer the mixture to the bowl of a mixing machine. Whip it at high speed until stiff peaks form.

Italian Meringue
Yield: about 1 gal (4 l)

Ingredients	U.S.	Metric	Egg whites at 100% %
Sugar	2 lb	1000 g	200
Water	8 oz	250 ml	50
Egg whites	1 lb	500 g	100

Procedure:

1. Heat the sugar and water in a saucepan until the sugar dissolves and the mixture boils. Boil until a candy thermometer placed in the syrup registers 240° F (115° C).

2. While the syrup is cooking, beat the egg whites in a mixing machine until they form soft peaks.

3. With the machine running, very slowly beat in the hot syrup.

4. Continue beating until the meringue is cool and forms firm peaks.

Vanilla Custard Sauce

Vanilla custard sauce, also known as *crème anglaise* (pronounced "krem awng glezz"), is a stirred custard. It consists of milk, sugar, and egg yolks stirred over very low heat until slightly thickened, and flavored with vanilla.

The recipe that follows gives the method for preparing custard sauce. Special care is necessary in preparing this sauce, because the eggs can curdle very easily if overcooked. The following guidelines will help you be successful:

1. Use clean, sanitized equipment, and follow strict sanitation procedures. Egg mixtures are good breeding grounds for bacteria that cause food poisoning.

2. Heat the milk to scalding (just below simmering) in a double boiler before combining with the egg yolks. This makes the final cooking much shorter.

3. *Slowly* beat the hot milk into the beaten eggs and sugar. This raises the temperature of the eggs gradually and helps prevent curdling.

4. Heat the mixture slowly in a double boiler, stirring constantly, in order to prevent curdling.

5. To test for doneness, two methods are available. Keep in mind that this is a very light sauce, so you can't expect a lot of thickening.

    a. Check the temperature with a thermometer. When it reaches 185° F (85° C), the sauce is cooked. Never let the temperature go above 190° F (87° C).

    b. When the mixture lightly coats the back of a spoon, instead of running off it like milk, the sauce is cooked.

6. Immediately cool the sauce by setting the pan or bowl in ice water. Stir occasionally to cool it evenly.

7. If the sauce accidentally curdles, it is sometimes possible to save it. Immediately stir in 1 to 2 ounces of cold milk, transfer the sauce to a blender, and blend at high speed.

Vanilla Custard Sauce (Crème Anglaise)
Yield: about 2½ pt (1¼ l)

Ingredients	U.S.		Metric	Milk at 100% %
Egg yolks (12 yolks)	8	oz	250 g	25
Sugar	8	oz	250 g	25
Milk	2 lb (1 qt)		1 l	100
Vanilla	0.5 oz (1 tbsp)		15 ml	1.5

Procedure:

1. Review the guidelines for preparing custard sauce preceding this recipe.

2. Combine the egg yolks and sugar in the bowl of a mixer. Beat with the whip attachment until thick and light.

3. Scald the milk in a double boiler.

4. With the mixer running at low speed, very gradually pour the scalded milk into the egg yolk mixture.

5. Pour the mixture back into the double boiler. Heat it slowly, stirring constantly, until it thickens enough to coat the back of a spoon (or until it reaches 185° F/85° C).

6. Immediately remove the top part of the double boiler from the heat and set it in a pan of cold water. Stir in the vanilla. Stir the sauce occasionally as it cools.

Variations

Chocolate Custard Sauce:

Melt 6 oz (180 g/18%) sweet chocolate. Stir it into the vanilla custard sauce while it is still warm (not hot).

Coffee Custard Sauce:

Add 2 tbsp (8 g) instant coffee to the warm custard sauce.

Pastry Cream

Although it requires more ingredients and steps, pastry cream is easier to make than vanilla custard sauce, because it is less likely to curdle. Pastry cream contains a starch thickening agent, which stabilizes the eggs. It can actually be boiled without curdling. In fact, it must be brought to a boil, or the starch will not cook completely, and the cream will have a raw, starchy taste.

Strict observance of all sanitation rules is essential when preparing pastry cream because of the danger of bacterial contamination. Use clean, sanitized equipment. Do not put your fingers in the cream, and do not taste except with a clean spoon. Chill the finished cream rapidly in shallow pans. Keep the cream and all cream-filled products refrigerated at all times.

The procedure for preparing pastry cream is given in the recipe that follows. Note that the basic steps are similar to those for custard sauce. In this case, however, a starch is mixed with the eggs and half the sugar to make a smooth paste. (In some recipes with lower egg content, it is necessary to add a little cold milk to provide enough liquid to make a paste.) Meanwhile, the milk is scalded with the other half of the sugar. The egg mixture is then tempered with some of the hot milk and then returned to the kettle and brought to a boil. Some chefs prefer to add the cold paste gradually to the hot milk, but the tempering procedure described here seems to give better protection against lumping.

Pastry Cream Variations

Pastry cream has many applications in the bakeshop, so it is important to master the basic technique. Pastry cream and its variations are used as fillings for cakes and pastries, as fillings for cream pies (p. 183), and as puddings (p. 282). With more liquid added, it can also be used as a custard sauce.

Cornstarch should be used as the thickening agent when the cream is to be used as a pie filling, so that the cut slices will hold their shape. For other uses, either cornstarch or flour may be used. Remember that twice as much flour is needed to provide the same thickening power as cornstarch.

Other variations are possible, as you will see in the recipes. Sometimes whipped cream is folded into pastry cream to lighten it and make it creamier. Adding meringue makes a cream called crème St. Honoré (pronounced "krem sant oh no ray").

Vanilla Pastry Cream
Yield: about 2¼ qt (2¼ l)

Ingredients	U.S.	Metric	Milk at 100% %
Milk	4 lb (2 qt)	2 l	100
Sugar	8 oz	250 g	12.5
Egg yolks (8)	5 oz	150 g	8
Whole eggs (4)	7 oz	220 g	11
Cornstarch	5 oz	150 g	8
Sugar	8 oz	250 g	12.5
Butter	4 oz	125 g	6
Vanilla	1 oz (2 tbsp)	30 ml	1.5

Procedure:

1. In a heavy saucepan or kettle, dissolve the sugar in the milk and bring just to a boil.
2. With a whip, beat the egg yolks and whole eggs in a stainless steel bowl.
3. Sift the starch and sugar into the eggs. Beat with the whip until perfectly smooth.
4. Temper the egg mixture by slowly beating in the hot milk in a thin stream.
5. Return the mixture to the heat and bring to a boil, stirring constantly.
6. When the mixture comes to a boil and thickens, remove from the heat.
7. Stir in the butter and vanilla. Mix until the butter is melted and completely blended in.
8. Pour out into a clean, sanitized hotel pan or other shallow pan. Dust lightly with sugar and cover with waxed paper to prevent a crust from forming. Cool and chill as quickly as possible.
9. For filling pastries such as éclairs and napoleons, whip the chilled pastry cream until smooth before using.

Variations

Deluxe Pastry Cream:

Omit the whole eggs in the basic recipe and use 16–20 egg yolks (10–13 oz/ 300–400 g/15–20%).

Pastry Cream Mousseline:

For a lighter pastry cream filling, fold whipped heavy cream into the chilled pastry cream. Quantities may be varied to taste. In general, for every 2 qt (2 l) pastry cream, use 1–2 cups (2.5–5 dl) heavy cream.

Chocolate Pastry Cream:

Melt together 4 oz (125 g) sweet chocolate and 4 oz (125 g) unsweetened chocolate. Stir into the hot pastry cream.

Coffee Pastry Cream:

Add 4 tbsp (15 g) instant coffee powder to the milk in step 1.

Crème St. Honoré:

This cream is pastry cream with the addition of beaten egg whites. The cream does not keep well, so if it is not to be used immediately, it can be stabilized with gelatin. For the basic pastry cream recipe, assemble the following ingredients:

Egg whites (24)	1 lb 8 oz	750 g	38 %
Optional:			
Gelatin	1 oz	30 g	1.5%
Cold water	8 oz	250 ml	12.5%

Whip the egg whites until they form soft peaks. Soften the gelatin in the cold water. As soon as the pastry cream is made, stir in the softened gelatin until it dissolves. Immediately fold in the whipped egg whites.

Chocolate Creams

Ganache (pronounced "gah nahsh") is a rich chocolate cream used as a filling for cakes, tortes, and meringue pastries. It can also be used as an icing, somewhat like fondant. While it is still warm (after step 3 in the rec-ipe), pour it over the product to be iced. It will set into a soft icing when it cools.

The chocolate mousse included here is well suited for fillings and pastries. It can also be served by itself as a dessert. A rather different chocolate mousse recipe is included with the puddings in Chapter 13.

Ganache (Chocolate Cream Filling)

Ingredients	U.S.	Chocolate at 100% Metric	%
Sweet chocolate	2 lb 8 oz	1250 g	100
Heavy cream	2 lb (1 qt)	1000 g (1 l)	80
Yield:	4 lb 8 oz	2250 g	180

Procedure:

1. Chop the chocolate into small pieces.

2. Bring the cream just to a boil, stirring to prevent scorching. (Use very fresh cream; old cream is more likely to curdle when it is boiled.)

3. Add the chocolate. Remove from the heat, stir, and let stand for a few minutes. Stir again until the chocolate is completely melted and the mixture is smooth. If necessary, warm gently over low heat to completely melt the chocolate.

4. Cool the mixture. This can be done by setting the bowl in crushed ice and stirring constantly, or by placing the bowl in the refrigerator and stirring it from time to time. The mixture must be cooled until it is very thick and smooth, but not firm. If it is not cooled enough, it won't whip up properly. If it is too cold, it will be lumpy.

5. With a wire whip or the whip attachment on the mixer, whip the ganache until it is light, thick, and creamy. Chill until needed.

Note: The proportions of chocolate and cream may be varied. For a firmer filling, or if the weather is warm, increase the chocolate. For a softer filling, or if the weather is cold, increase the cream.

Chocolate Mousse

Ingredients	U.S.		Metric	Chocolate at 100% %
Sweet chocolate	2 lb		1000 g	100
Butter	1 lb	2 oz	560 g	56
Egg yolks		10 oz	310 g	31
Egg whites	1 lb	8 oz	750 g	75
Sugar		5 oz	160 g	16
Yield:	5 lb	9 oz	2780 g	278

Procedure:

1. Melt the chocolate over hot water.

2. Remove from the heat and add the butter. Stir until the butter is melted and completely mixed in.

3. Add the egg yolks one at a time. Mix in each egg yolk completely before adding the next.

4. Beat the egg whites until they form soft peaks. Add the sugar and beat until the egg whites form stiff but moist peaks. Do not overbeat.

5. Fold the egg whites into the chocolate mixture.

ICINGS

Icings, also called frostings, are sweet coatings for cakes and other baked goods. Icings have three main functions:

- They contribute flavor and richness.
- They improve appearance.
- They improve keeping qualities by forming protective coatings around cakes.

There are six basic types of icings:

Fondant

Buttercreams

Foam-type icings

Fudge-type icings

Flat-type icings

Royal or decorator's icing

In addition, we will consider another type of coating for cakes and pastries: glazes.

Use top-quality flavorings for icings, so that they will enhance the cake rather than detract from it. Use moderation when adding flavors and colors. Flavors should be light and delicate. Colors should be delicate pastel shades—except chocolate, of course.

Fondant

Fondant is a sugar syrup that is crystallized to a smooth, creamy white mass. It is familiar as the icing for napoleons, eclairs, petits fours, and some cakes. When applied, it sets up into a shiny, nonsticky coating.

Because it is difficult to make in the bakeshop, fondant is almost always purchased already prepared, either in the ready-to-use moist form or in the dry form, which requires only the addition of water. In an emergency (for instance, if you run out of fondant, and there is no time to get more from your supplier), flat icing can be substituted for fondant, though it will not perform as well.

For those who wish to try making fondant in the bakeshop, a recipe is included here. The purpose of the glucose or the cream of tartar in the recipe is to invert some of the sugar in order to get the right amount of crystallization. If none is used, the syrup will set up to be too unworkable, and it will not be smooth and white. When an excess of glucose or cream of tartar is added, not enough crystallization will take place, and the fondant will be too soft and syrupy. Also, if the hot syrup is disturbed before it cools sufficiently (step 6 in the procedure), large crystals will form, and the fondant will not be smooth and shiny.

Procedure and Guidelines for Using Fondant

1. Heat fondant over a warm water bath, stirring constantly, to thin out the icing and make it pourable. *Do not heat it over 100° F (38° C) or it will lose its shine.*

2. If it is still too thick, thin it out with a little simple sugar syrup or water.

3. Flavorings and colorings may be added as desired.

4. To make *chocolate fondant,* stir melted bitter chocolate into warm fondant until the desired color and flavor are reached (up to about 3 oz bitter chocolate per lb of fondant, or 190 g per kg). Chocolate will thicken the fondant, so the icing may require more thinning with sugar syrup.

5. Apply the warm fondant by pouring it over the item or by dipping items into it.

Fondant
Yield: 6–7 lb (3–3.5 kg)

Ingredients	U.S.		Metric	Sugar at 100% %
Sugar	6 lb		3000 g	100
Water	1 lb 8	oz	750 g	25
Glucose	1 lb 2	oz	570 g	19
OR				
Cream of tartar	0.5 oz		15 g	0.5

Procedure:

1. Clean a marble slab well and moisten it with water. Set four steel bars on the slab in the shape of a square to hold the hot syrup when it is poured onto the marble.

2. Combine the sugar and water in a heavy kettle and heat to dissolve the sugar. Boil until the temperature reaches 225° F (105° C).

3. If glucose is used, warm it. If cream of tartar is used, disperse it in a little warm water. Add the glucose or the cream of tartar to the boiling syrup.

4. Continue to boil the syrup until it reaches 240° F (115° C).

5. Pour the boiling syrup onto the marble slab and sprinkle it with a little cold water to prevent crystallization.

6. Let the syrup cool undisturbed to about 110° F (43° C).

7. Remove the steel bars and work the sugar with a steel scraper, turning it from the outside to the center. It will turn white and begin to solidify.

8. Continue to work the fondant, either by hand or by putting it in a mixing bowl and working it slowly with the paddle attachment, until it is smooth and creamy.

9. Keep the fondant in a tightly covered container.

Buttercreams

Buttercream icings are light, smooth mixtures of fat and sugar. They may also contain eggs to increase their smoothness or lightness. These popular icings for many kinds of cakes are easily flavored and colored to suit a variety of purposes.

There are many variations of buttercream recipes. We cover four basic kinds in this chapter:

1. *Simple buttercreams* are made by creaming together fat and confectioners' sugar to the desired consistency and lightness. A small quantity of egg whites, yolks, or whole eggs may be whipped in. Some formulas also include nonfat milk solids.

   Decorator's buttercream (sometimes called rose paste) is used for making flowers and other cake decorations. It is creamed only a little, since too much air beaten into it would make it unable to hold delicate shapes.

2. *Meringue-type buttercreams* are a mixture of butter and meringue. These are very light icings.

3. *French buttercreams* are prepared by beating a boiling syrup into beaten egg yolks and whipping to a light foam. Soft butter is then whipped in. These are very rich, light icings.

4. *Quick or emergency buttercreams* are quickly made with only one or two ingredients on hand. No recipe is needed for the following two types, since they are so simple:

   Fondant type: Cream together equal parts butter and fondant.

   Pastry-cream type: Cream together equal parts butter and thick pastry cream. If more sweetness is desired, add sifted 10X sugar.

Butter, especially sweet unsalted butter, is the preferred fat for buttercreams because of its flavor and melt-in-the-mouth quality. Icings made only with shortening can be unpleasant because the fat congeals and coats the inside of the mouth, where it does not melt. However, butter makes a less stable icing because it melts so easily. There are two ways around this problem:

- Use buttercreams only in cool weather.
- Blend a small quantity of emulsifier shortening with the butter to stabilize it.

Buttercreams may be stored, covered, in the refrigerator for several days. However, they should always be used at room temperature in order to have the right consistency. Before using, remove buttercream from the refrigerator at least an hour ahead of time and let it come to room temperature. If it must be warmed quickly, or if it curdles, warm it gently over warm water and beat it well until smooth.

Flavoring Buttercreams

Because buttercreams may be combined with many different flavorings, they are versatile and adaptable to many kinds of cakes and desserts.

The quantities given in the following variations are *suggested* amounts for each pound (or 500 g) of buttercream. In practice, flavorings may be increased or decreased to taste, but avoid flavoring icings too strongly.

Unless the instructions say otherwise, simply blend the flavoring into the buttercream.

1. *Chocolate:* Use 3 oz (90 g) sweet chocolate.

   Melt chocolate and cool slightly (chocolate must not be too cool, or it will solidify before completely blending with the buttercream). Blend with about one quarter of the buttercream, then blend this mixture into the rest.

   For very sweet buttercreams, use 1½ oz (45 g) unsweetened chocolate instead of the sweet chocolate.

2. *Coffee:* Use 1½ tbsp (5 g) instant coffee dissolved in ½ oz (15 ml) water.

3. *Marron* (chestnut): Use 8 oz (250 g) chestnut purée.

   Blend with a little of the buttercream until soft and smooth, then blend this mixture into remaining buttercream. Flavor with a little rum or brandy, if desired.

4. *Praline:* Use 2 to 3 oz (60 to 90 g) praline paste.

   Blend with a little of the buttercream until soft and smooth, then blend this mixture into remaining buttercream.

5. *Almond:* Use 6 oz (180 g) almond paste.

   Soften almond paste with a few drops of water. Blend in a little of the buttercream until soft and smooth, then blend this mixture into remaining buttercream.

6. *Extracts and emulsions (orange, lemon, etc.):* Add according to taste.

7. *Spirits and liqueurs:* Add according to taste. For example: kirsch, orange liqueur, rum, and brandy.

French Buttercream
Yield: 5 lb 8 oz (2750 g)

Ingredients	U.S.			Metric	Sugar at 100% %
Sugar	2 lb			1000 g	100
Water		8	oz	250 ml	25
Egg yolks		12	oz	375 g	37.5
Butter, soft	2 lb	8	oz	1250 g	125
Vanilla		0.5	oz	15 ml	1.5

Procedure:

1. Combine the sugar and water in a saucepan. Bring to a boil, while stirring to dissolve the sugar.

2. Continue to boil until the syrup reaches a temperature of 240° F (115° C).

3. While the syrup is boiling, beat the yolks with the whip attachment until they are thick and light.

4. As soon as the syrup reaches 240° F, pour it *very slowly* into the beaten yolks while the mixer is running at second speed.

5. Continue to beat until the mixture is *completely cool* and the yolks are very thick and light.

6. With the mixer still running, add the butter a little at a time. Add it just as fast as it can be absorbed by the mixture.

7. Beat in the vanilla. If the icing is too soft, refrigerate it until it is firm enough to spread.

Simple Buttercream

Ingredients	U.S.			Metric	Sugar at 100% %
Butter	2 lb			1000 g	50
Emulsified shortening	1 lb			500 g	25
10X sugar	4 lb			2000 g	100
Egg whites		5	oz	150 g	7.5
Lemon juice		0.33	oz (2 tsp)	10 g	0.5
Vanilla		0.5	oz	15 g	0.8
Water (optional)		4	oz	125 g	6.25
Yield:	7 lb	9	oz	3800 g	190

Procedure:

1. Using the paddle attachment, cream together the butter, shortening, and sugar until well blended.

2. Add the egg whites, lemon juice, and vanilla. Blend in at medium speed. Then mix at high speed until light and fluffy.

3. For a softer buttercream, blend in the water.

Simple Buttercream

Variations

Simple Buttercream with Egg Yolks or Whole Eggs:

Instead of the egg whites in the above recipe, substitute an equal weight of egg yolks or whole eggs. These substitutions make slightly richer icings. Also, the egg yolks help make a better emulsion.

Decorator's Buttercream or Rose Paste:

Use 2 lb 4 oz (1125 g) regular shortening instead of butter (or use part butter and part shortening for better flavor). Omit emulsifier shortening, lemon juice, and vanilla. Add 3 oz (90 ml) of either water or egg whites. Blend at low speed until smooth; do not whip.

Cream Cheese Icing:

Substitute cream cheese for the butter and shortening. Omit egg whites. If necessary, thin the icing with cream or milk. If desired, flavor with grated lemon or orange zest instead of vanilla, and use orange juice and/or lemon juice instead of milk for thinning the icing.

Meringue-type Buttercream
Yield: 5 lb 12 oz (2900 g)

Ingredients	U.S.		Metric	Sugar at 100% %
Italian meringue:				
Sugar	2 lb		1000 g	100
Water	8	oz	250 ml	25
Egg whites	1 lb		500 g	50
Butter	2 lb		1000 g	100
Emulsified shortening	8	oz	250 g	25
Lemon juice	0.33 oz (2 tsp)		10 ml	1
Vanilla	0.5 oz		15 ml	1.5

Procedure:

1. Make the meringue (procedure on p. 118). Whip until *completely cool.*

2. Cream the butter, shortening, lemon juice, and vanilla until soft and light.

3. Add the meringue, a little at a time, blending it in well.

Foam-type Icings

Foam icings, sometimes called boiled icings, are simply meringues made with a boiling syrup. Some also contain stabilizing ingredients like gelatin.

Foam icings should be applied thickly to cakes and left in peaks and swirls.

These icings are not stable. Regular boiled icing should be used the day it is prepared. Marshmallow icing should be made just before using and applied while still warm, before it sets.

Plain Boiled Icing

Follow the recipe for Italian meringue (p. 118), but include 4 oz (125 g) corn syrup with the sugar and water for the boiled syrup. Flavor the icing to taste with vanilla.

Marshmallow Icing

Soak ½ oz (15 g) gelatin in 3 oz (90 ml) cold water. Warm the water to dissolve the gelatin. Prepare plain boiled icing. Add the dissolved gelatin to the icing after adding the hot syrup. Scrape down the sides of the bowl to make sure that the gelatin is evenly mixed in. Use while still warm.

Chocolate Foam Icing and Filling

Prepare boiled icing. After the syrup has been added, blend in 10 oz (300 g) melted, unsweetened chocolate.

Fudge-type Icings

Fudge-type icings are rich, heavy icings. Many of them are made somewhat like candy. They may be flavored with a variety of ingredients and are used on cupcakes, layer cakes, loaf cakes, and sheet cakes.

Fudge icings are stable and hold up well on cakes and in storage. Stored icings must be covered tightly to prevent drying and crusting.

To use stored fudge icing, warm it in a double boiler until it is soft enough to spread.

Cocoa Fudge Icing
Yield: 4 lb 12 oz (2375 g)

Ingredients	U.S.		Granulated sugar at 100% Metric	%
Granulated sugar	2 lb		1000 g	100
Corn syrup	10	oz	300 g	30
Water	8	oz	250 ml	25
Salt	0.2 oz (1 tsp)		5 g	0.5
Butter, or part butter and part emulsified shortening	8	oz	250 g	25
Confectioners' sugar (10X or 6X)	1 lb		500 g	50
Cocoa	6	oz	180 g	18
Vanilla	0.5 oz		15 ml	1.5
Hot water	as needed		as needed	

Procedure:

1. Combine the sugar, syrup, water, and salt in a saucepan. Bring to a boil, stirring to dissolve the sugar. Boil the mixture until it reaches 240° F (115° C).

2. While the sugar is cooking, mix the fat, sugar, and cocoa until evenly combined, using the paddle attachment of the mixer.

3. With the machine running at low speed, very slowly pour in the hot syrup.

4. Mix in the vanilla. Continue to beat until the icing is smooth, creamy, and spreadable. If necessary, thin out with a little hot water.

5. Use while still warm, or rewarm in a double boiler.

Variation

Vanilla Fudge Icing:

Use evaporated milk or light cream instead of water for the syrup. Omit cocoa. Adjust consistency with additional confectioners' sugar (to thicken) or water (to thin out). Other flavorings, such as almond, maple, peppermint, or coffee, may be used in place of vanilla.

Caramel Fudge Icing
Yield: 4 lb (2 kg)

Ingredients	U.S.		Metric	Sugar at 100% %
Brown sugar	3 lb		1500 g	100
Milk	1 lb 8	oz	750 g	50

Butter, or part
  butter and part
  shortening
	12	oz	375 g	25

Salt	0.2 oz (1 tsp)		5 g	0.4
Vanilla	0.5 oz		15 ml	1

Procedure:

1. Combine the sugar and milk in a saucepan. Bring to a boil, stirring to dissolve the sugar. Boil the mixture until it reaches 240° F (115° C).

2. Pour the mixture into the bowl of a mixer. Let it cool to 110° F (43° C).

3. Turn on the machine and mix at low speed with the paddle attachment.

4. Add the butter, salt, and vanilla and continue to mix at low speed until cool. Beat the icing until it is smooth and creamy in texture. If it is too thick, thin it with a little water.

Quick White Fudge Icing I

Ingredients	U.S.		Metric	Confectioners' sugar at 100% %
Water	8	oz	250 ml	12.5
Butter	4	oz	125 g	6
Emulsified shortening	4	oz	125 g	6
Corn syrup	3	oz	90 g	4.5
Salt	0.2 oz (1 tsp)		5 g	0.25
Confectioners' sugar (10X or 6X)	4 lb		2000 g	100
Vanilla	0.5 oz		15 ml	0.75
Yield:	5 lb 3	oz	2610 g	129

Procedure:

1. Place the water, butter, shortening, syrup, and salt in a saucepan. Bring to a boil.

2. Sift the sugar into the bowl of a mixer.

3. Using the paddle attachment and with the machine running on low speed, add the boiling water mixture. Blend until smooth. The more the icing is mixed, the lighter it will become.

4. Blend in the vanilla.

5. Use while still warm, or rewarm in a double boiler. If necessary, thin out with hot water.

Variation

Quick Chocolate Fudge Icing:

Omit the butter in the basic recipe. After step 3, blend in 12 oz (375 g) melted unsweetened chocolate. Thin the icing out with hot water as needed.

Quick Fudge Icing II

Ingredients	U.S.		Metric	Fondant at 100% %
Fondant	2 lb 8	oz	1000 g	100
Corn syrup	4	oz	100 g	10
Butter, soft	4	oz	100 g	10
Emulsified shortening	6	oz	150 g	15
Salt	0.25	oz	6 g	0.6
Flavoring (see below)				
Liquid, to thin (see below)				
Yield:	3 lb 6	oz or more	1356 g or more	135 or more

Procedure:

1. Warm the fondant to 95° F (35° C).

2. Combine the fondant, corn syrup, butter, shortening, and salt in the bowl of a mixer. Blend with the paddle attachment until smooth.

3. Blend in the desired flavoring (see below).

4. Thin out to spreading consistency with appropriate liquid (see below).

Flavoring variations: Add desired flavoring to taste, such as vanilla, almond, maple, lemon or orange (extract, emulsion, or grated zest), or instant coffee dissolved in water. Crushed fruit, such as pineapple, strawberries, or ground maraschino cherries, may be used.

For *chocolate icing,* add 12 oz (375 g) melted unsweetened chocolate.

Liquids for adjusting consistency: With fruit flavorings such as orange or lemon, use lemon juice and/or orange juice. With other flavors, use simple syrup or evaporated milk.

Flat Icings

Flat icings, also called water icings, are simply mixtures of 10X sugar and water, sometimes with corn syrup and flavoring added. They are used mostly for coffee cakes, Danish pastry, and sweet rolls.

Flat icings are warmed to 100° F (38° C) for application and are handled like fondant.

Flat Icing

Ingredients	U.S.		Metric	Sugar at 100% %
Confectioners' sugar (10X or 6X)	4 lb		2000 g	100
Water, hot	12	oz	375 ml	19
Corn syrup	4	oz	125 g	6
Vanilla	0.5	oz	15 g	0.8
Yield:	5 lb		2500 g	125

Procedure:

1. Mix all ingredients together until smooth.

2. To use, place the desired amount in a double boiler. Warm to 100° F (38° C) and then apply to the product to be iced.

Royal Icing

This icing, also called decorating or decorator's icing, is similar to flat icings except that it is much thicker and is made with egg whites, which make it hard and brittle when dry. It is used almost exclusively for decorative work.

To prepare royal icing:

1. Place desired amount of 10X sugar in a mixing bowl. Add a small quantity of cream of tartar (for whiteness), about ⅛ teaspoon per pound of sugar (1 gram per kilogram).

2. Beat in egg whites a little at a time, until the sugar forms a smooth paste. You will need 2 to 3 ounces of egg whites per pound of sugar (125 grams per kilogram).

3. Keep unused icing covered with a damp cloth at all times to prevent hardening.

Glazes

Glazes are thin, glossy, transparent coatings that give a shine to baked products and also help prevent drying.

The simplest glaze is a sugar syrup or diluted corn syrup brushed onto coffee cakes or Danish pastries while it is hot (see p. 61 for recipe). Syrup glazes may also contain gelatin or waxy maize starch.

Fruit glazes, the most popular of which are apricot and red currant, are available commercially prepared. They are melted, thinned out with a little water, syrup, or liquor, and brushed on while hot. Fruit glazes may also be made by melting apricot or other preserves and forcing them through a strainer. It helps to add some melted, strained preserves to commercial glazes, since the commercial products usually have little flavor.

DESSERT SAUCES

In addition to the recipes presented in this section, the following types of dessert sauces are discussed elsewhere in this book or can be made easily without recipes.

1. *Custard Sauces*

   Vanilla custard sauce, or crème anglaise, is presented earlier in this chapter (p. 119). It is one of the most basic preparations in dessert cookery. Chocolate or other flavors may be added to create variations.

   Pastry cream (p. 120) can be thinned out with heavy cream or milk to make another type of custard sauce.

2. *Chocolate Sauce*

   In addition to the two recipes that follow, chocolate sauce may be made in several other ways. For example:

   - Flavor vanilla custard sauce with chocolate (see p. 119).
   - Prepare ganache (p. 122) through step 3 in the procedure. Then thin out to desired consistency with cream, milk, or simple syrup.

3. *Lemon Sauce*

    Prepare lemon filling (p. 185), but use only 1½ oz (45 g) cornstarch, or use 1 oz (30 g) waxy maize.

4. *Fruit Sauces*

    Some of the best fruit sauces are also the simplest. These are of two types:

    *   Purées of fresh or cooked fruits, sweetened with sugar.
    *   Heated, strained fruit jams and preserves, diluted with simple syrup, water, or liquor.

    More economical fruit sauces can be "stretched" by diluting them with water, adding more sugar, and thickening them with starch. These may also be flavored with spices and/or lemon juice.

Procedures for Preparing Fruit Sauces

These procedures can be used to make apricot sauce, raspberry sauce, strawberry sauce, and other fruit sauces.

Method 1

1. Using fresh, canned, or frozen fruit, rub the fruit through a sieve or purée it in a blender.
2. Mix fruit with sugar to taste. Bring to a boil, and let it simmer until thickened to desired consistency.

Method 2

1. Melt jam or preserves, diluted with a little water, syrup, or appropriate liquor such as kirsch.
2. Rub through a sieve. Adjust consistency by adding more liquid to it (to thin out) or by cooking it down (to thicken).

Chocolate Sauce I

Yield: 1 qt (1 l)

Ingredients	U.S.	Metric
Sweet chocolate	1 lb	500 g
Water	1 pt	500 ml
Butter	6 oz	190 g

Procedure:

1. Chop the chocolate into small pieces.
2. Place the chocolate and water in a saucepan. Heat over low heat or over hot water until the chocolate is melted. Stir while cooking to make a smooth mixture.
3. Remove from the heat and add the butter. Stir until the butter is melted and mixed in.
4. Set the pan in a bowl of ice water and stir the sauce until it is cool.

Chocolate Sauce II

Yield: 2 qt (2 l)

Ingredients	U.S.	Metric
Water	1 qt	1 l
Sugar	4 lb	2 kg
Corn syrup	12 oz	750 g
Unsweetened chocolate	1 lb	500 g
Butter	4 oz	125 g

Procedure:

1. Combine the water, sugar, and syrup and bring to a boil, stirring to dissolve the sugar.
2. Boil 1 minute and remove from the heat. Let cool a few minutes.
3. Melt the chocolate and butter together over low heat. Stir until smooth.
4. Very slowly stir the hot syrup into the chocolate.
5. Place over moderate heat and bring to a boil. Boil for 4 minutes.
6. Remove from the heat and cool.

Melba Sauce

Yield: about 1 pt (400 ml)

Ingredients	U.S.	Metric
Frozen, sweetened raspberries	1 lb 8 oz	600 g
Red currant jelly	8 oz	200 g

Procedure:

1. Thaw the raspberries and force them through a sieve to purée them and remove the seeds.
2. Combine with the jelly in a saucepan. Bring to a boil, stirring until the jelly is melted and completely blended with the fruit purée.

Variation

Melba sauce may be made with only raspberries (sweetened), without the currant jelly.

Caramel Sauce

Yield: 1½ qt (1½ l)

Ingredients	U.S.	Metric
Sugar	2 lb	1 kg
Water	8 oz	250 ml
Lemon juice	1 tbsp	30 ml
Heavy cream	1½ pt	750 ml
Milk	1 pt	500 ml

Procedure:

1. Combine the sugar, water, and lemon juice in a heavy saucepan. Bring to a boil, stirring to dissolve the sugar. Cook the syrup to the caramel stage (see p. 114). Toward the end of the cooking time, turn the heat to very low to avoid burning the sugar or letting it get too dark. It should be a golden color.
2. Remove from the heat and cool 5 minutes.
3. Bring the heavy cream to a boil. Add a few ounces of it to the caramel.
4. Stir and continue to add the cream slowly. Return to the heat and stir until all the caramel is dissolved.
5. Let cool completely.
6. Stir the milk into the cooled caramel to thin it out.

Variations

Hot Caramel Sauce:

Proceed as directed through step 4. Omit the milk.

Clear Caramel Sauce:

Substitute 10–12 oz (300–350 ml) water for the heavy cream and omit the milk. If the sauce is too thick when cool, add more water.

Butterscotch Sauce:

Use brown sugar instead of white granulated sugar in the basic recipe. Omit the lemon juice. In step 1, cook the syrup only to 240° F (115° C). Add 8 oz (250 g) butter before adding the heavy cream.

Hard Sauce

Yield: about 1 qt (1 l)

Ingredients	U.S.	Metric
Butter	1 lb	500 g
Confectioners' sugar	2 lb	1000 g
Brandy or rum	2 oz	60 ml

Procedure:

1. Cream the butter and sugar until light and fluffy, as for simple buttercream.
2. Beat in the brandy or rum.
3. Serve with steamed puddings, such as English Christmas pudding.

Sabayon

Yield: about 1 qt (900 ml)

Ingredients	U.S.	Metric
Egg yolks (6 yolks)	4 oz	115 g
Sugar	8 oz	225 g
Dry white wine	8 oz	225 ml

Procedure:

1. In a stainless steel bowl, beat the yolks until foamy.

2. Beat in the sugar and wine. Place over a hot water bath and continue beating until thick and hot.

3. Serve hot as a dessert or as a sauce for fruit or fritters.

Variations

Cold Sabayon:

Dissolve 0.08 oz (1 tsp/2 g) gelatin in the wine. Proceed as in the basic recipe. When the sauce is done, place the bowl over ice and whip the sauce until it is cool.

Zabaglione:

This is the Italian sauce and dessert that is the origin of sabayon. Use sweet Marsala wine instead of the dry white wine, and use only half the sugar.

Other wines or spirits may be used, such as port or sherry. Adjust the sugar according to the sweetness of the wine.

TERMS FOR REVIEW

caramelize
simple syrup
dessert syrup
crystallize
common meringue
Swiss meringue
Italian meringue
crème anglaise
pastry cream
crème St. Honoré
ganache
fondant
buttercream
boiled icing
marshmallow icing
flat icing
royal icing

QUESTIONS FOR DISCUSSION

1. How can you avoid unwanted crystallization when cooking sugar syrups?

2. Why is cream of tartar or lemon juice sometimes added to a sugar syrup before or during cooking?

3. Vanilla custard sauce and pastry cream both contain eggs. Why is it possible to boil pastry cream but not custard sauce?

4. Explain the importance of sanitation in the production of pastry cream. What specific steps should you take to ensure a safe product?

5. Explain the effects of fat, sugar, and temperature on the whipping of egg whites into foams.

6. What is the most important rule to consider when using fondant?

7. What are the advantages and disadvantages of using butter and using shortening in buttercream icings?

8. Describe two simple ways of preparing fruit syrups.

CHAPTER 8

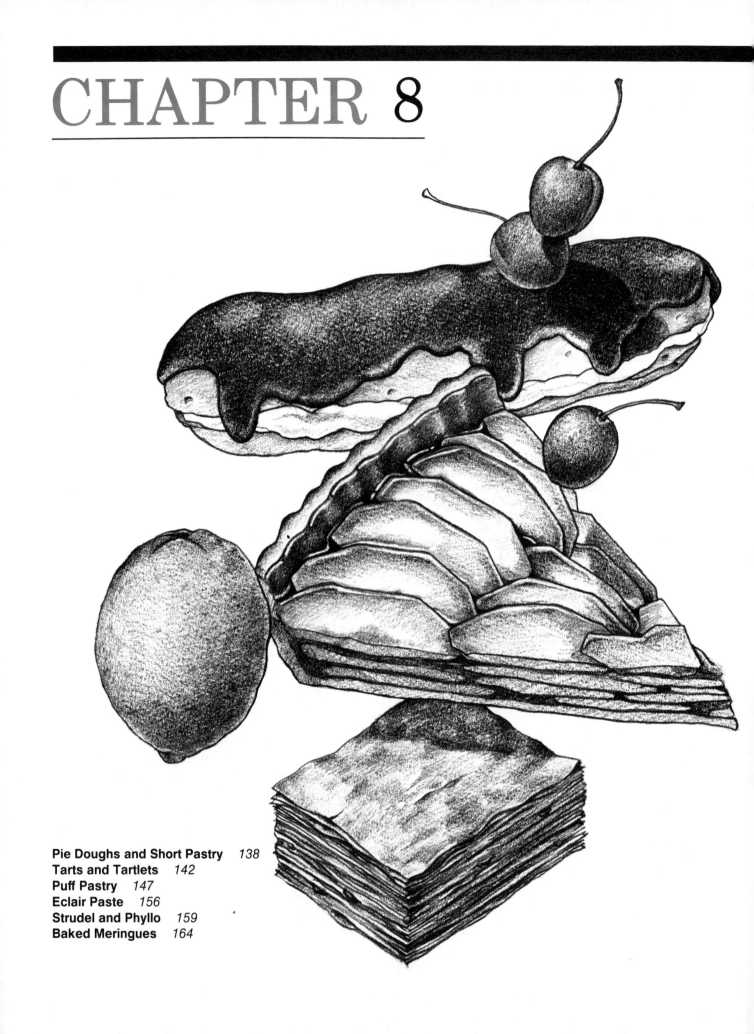

PASTRIES

The term "pastry" comes from the word "paste," meaning in this case a mixture of flour, liquid, and fat. In the bakeshop, pastry refers both to various pastes or doughs and to the many products made from these doughs.

Besides Danish pastry, a yeast dough that we discussed in Chapters 3 and 4, the most important pastry doughs in American bakeshops are pie doughs of various sorts, puff paste, and éclair paste, all of which are treated in this chapter. We also take a look at strudel and phyllo doughs, which are important for some specialty items. Finally, we look at crisp meringues, which are not pastries in the original sense of the word, because they are not made from a flour paste. Nevertheless, they are used like flour pastries in combination with creams, fillings, fruits, and icings to create a wide range of desserts.

Pies are undoubtedly America's favorite type of pastry. Although they resemble somewhat the more delicate European pastries called tarts and tartlets, American-style pies are different in character from most of the pastries considered in this chapter. The subjects of pie fillings and of assembling and baking pies are covered in the next chapter.

After studying this chapter, you should be able to:
1. Prepare pie doughs and short pastry.
2. Prepare baked and unbaked fruit tarts.
3. Prepare puff pastry dough, blitz puff dough, and baked goods made from these doughs.
4. Prepare éclair paste and baked goods made from éclair paste.
5. Prepare strudel dough, handle commercial phyllo (strudel) dough, and prepare strudels using either homemade or commercial dough.
6. Bake meringues and japonaise meringues, and assemble various desserts with these meringues.

PIE DOUGHS AND SHORT PASTRY

Before you begin studying this section, it would be a good idea for you to review the section on gluten development in Chapter 1. Pie pastry is a very simple product in terms of its ingredients: flour, shortening, water, and salt. Yet success or failure depends on how the shortening and flour are mixed and how the gluten is developed. The key to making pie dough is proper technique, and you will remember the techniques better if you understand why they work.

Ingredients

1. *Flour*

   Pastry flour is the best choice for pie doughs. It has enough gluten to produce the desired structure and flakiness, yet is low enough in gluten to yield a tender product, if handled properly. If stronger flours are used, the percentage of shortening should be increased slightly to provide more tenderness.

2. *Fat*

   Regular hydrogenated shortening is the most popular fat for pie crusts because it has the right plastic consistency to produce a flaky crust. It is firm and moldable enough to make an easily workable dough. Emulsified shortening should not be used, since it blends too quickly with the flour and makes it difficult to achieve a flaky pastry.

   Butter contributes excellent flavor to pie pastry, but it is frequently avoided in volume production for two reasons: it is expensive, and it melts very easily, making the dough difficult to work.

   It is desirable, if costs permit, to blend a quantity of butter into the shortening used for pie crusts in order to improve flavor. The large quantity of pie crust that is dumped into the garbage after customers have eaten out the filling is evidence that many people are not satisfied with the taste of shortening pie crusts.

   If butter is used to replace all the shortening for pie doughs, the percentage of fat in the formula should be increased by about one-fourth. (If 1 lb shortening is called for, use 1 lb 4 oz butter.) The liquid can be reduced slightly, since butter contains moisture.

   In the case of richer pastries and short doughs, butter is specified as the primary fat in the formulas here. These doughs are used primarily for European-style tarts and pastries, in which the flavor of the butter is an important part of the dessert.

   Lard is an excellent shortening for pies because it is firm and plastic. However, it is not widely used in food service.

3. *Liquid*

   Water is necessary to develop some gluten in the flour and to give structure and flakiness to the dough. If too much water is used, the crust will become tough because of too much gluten development. If not enough water is used, the crust will fall apart.

   Milk makes a richer dough that browns more quickly. However, the crust is less crisp and the production cost is higher. If dry milk is used, it should be dissolved in the water to ensure even distribution in the dough.

   Whether water or milk is used, it must be added cold (40° F/4° C or colder) to maintain proper dough temperature.

4. *Salt*

   Salt has some tenderizing and conditioning effect on the gluten. However, it contributes mainly to flavor. Salt must be dissolved in the liquid before being added to the mix in order to ensure even distribution.

Temperature

Pie dough should be kept cool, about 60° F (15° C), during mixing and makeup, for two reasons.

1. Shortening has the best consistency when cool. If it is warm, it blends too quickly with the flour. If it is very cold, it is too firm to be easily worked.

2. Gluten develops more slowly at cool temperatures than at warm temperatures.

Pie Dough Types

There are two basic types of pie dough:

Flaky pie dough

Mealy pie dough

The difference between the two is in how the fat is blended with the flour. Complete mixing procedures are given in the formulas that follow. First, it is important to understand the basic distinction between the two types.

Flaky Pie Dough

For flaky dough, the fat is cut or rubbed into the flour until the particles of shortening are about the size of peas or hazelnuts. That is, the flour is not completely blended with the fat, and the fat is left in pieces. (Many bakers distinguish between this crust, which they call *short-flake,* and *long-flake* crusts, in which the fat is left in pieces the size of walnuts, and the flour is coated even less with shortening. Blitz puff paste, introduced in the next section, is actually a long-flake pie dough that is rolled and folded like puff paste.)

When water is added, the flour absorbs it and develops some gluten. When the dough is rolled out, the lumps of fat and moistened flour are flattened and become flakes of dough separated by layers of fat.

Mealy Pie Dough

For mealy dough, the fat is blended into the flour more thoroughly, until the mixture looks like coarse cornmeal. The more complete coating of the flour with fat has several results:

- The crust is very "short" and tender because less gluten can develop.
- Less water is needed in the mix because the flour won't absorb as much as in flaky dough.
- The baked dough is less likely to absorb moisture from the filling and become soggy.

Mealy dough is used for bottom crusts, especially in baked fruit pies and soft or custard-type pies, because it resists sogginess. Flaky doughs are used for top crusts and sometimes for prebaked shells.

To produce mealy doughs with even more resistance to soaking, the flour and fat can be blended together completely to make a smooth paste. Such a dough is very short when baked. It is especially appropriate for custard pies.

The formula called Enriched Pie Pastry included in this section is essentially a mealy dough, except that it contains more sugar, is enriched with egg yolks, and works especially well with butter as the only fat. Its delicate, rich flavor makes it suited for European-style tarts.

Trimmings

Reworked scraps or trimmings will be tougher than freshly made dough. They may be combined with mealy dough and used for bottom crusts only.

Mixing

Hand mixing is best for small quantities of dough, especially flaky dough, because you have more control over the mixing. Quantities up to 10 pounds can be mixed almost as quickly by hand as by machine.

For machine mixing, use a pastry knife or paddle attachment. Blend at low speed.

Other Pie and Tart Pastries and Crusts

Short Doughs

Short pastry is actually a kind of cookie dough. It is richer than regular pie pastry and contains butter, sugar, and eggs. Because it is more difficult to handle than pie dough, it is used primarily for small fruit tarts.

Short doughs are mixed by a cookie mixing method called creaming (see p. 249). Like the creaming method used for cakes and quick breads, this procedure begins by blending together the fat and sugar.

As you will recall from the discussion of leavening agents in Chapter 2, creaming fat and sugar together provides leavening because air is incorporated into the mixture. In the case of short dough for tart shells, very little leavening is desired. Therefore, the mixture should be blended just enough to combine the ingredients. Do not cream until light.

Two formulas for short doughs are given here, a basic short dough or sugar dough and an almond short dough. The spiced hazelnut variation of the almond dough, Linzer dough, is used in the popular Linzertorte, which is actually a type of fruit tart made with raspberry jam.

Crumb Crusts

Graham cracker crusts are popular because they have an appealing flavor and are much easier to make than pastry crusts. For variations, vanilla or chocolate wafer crumbs, gingersnap crumbs, or zwieback crumbs may be used instead of graham cracker crumbs. Ground nuts may be added for special desserts.

Crumb crusts are used primarily for unbaked pies, such as cream pies and chiffon pies. They can also be used for such desserts as cheesecake. Be sure that the flavor of the crust is compatible with the filling. A lime chiffon pie with a chocolate crumb crust is not an appealing combination. Some cream fillings are so delicate in flavor that they would be overwhelmed by a crust that is too flavorful.

Baking a crumb crust before filling it makes it firmer and less crumbly, and gives it an attractive toasted flavor.

Ingredients	Flaky Pie Dough					Mealy Pie Dough				
	U.S.			Metric	%	U.S.			Metric	%
Pastry flour	5 lb			2000 g	100	5 lb			2000 g	100
Shortening, regular	3 lb 8		oz	1400 g	70	3 lb 4		oz	1300 g	65
Water, cold	1 lb 8		oz	600 g	30	1 lb 4		oz	500 g	25
Salt		1.5	oz	40 g	2		1.5	oz	40 g	2
Sugar (optional)		4	oz	100 g	5		4	oz	100 g	5
Yield:	10 lb 5		oz	4140 g	207	9 lb 13		oz	3940 g	197

Procedure:

1. Sift flour into a mixing bowl. Add shortening.
2. Rub or cut shortening into flour to the proper degree:

   For flaky dough, until fat particles are the size of peas or hazelnuts.

   For mealy dough, until mixture resembles cornmeal.
3. Dissolve salt and sugar (if used) in cold water.
4. Add water to flour mixture. Mix very gently, just until water is absorbed. Do not overwork the dough.
5. Place dough in pans, cover with plastic film, and place in refrigerator or retarder for at least 4 hours.
6. Scale portions of dough as needed.

Enriched Pie Pastry

Ingredients	U.S.			Metric	%
Pastry flour	3 lb			1500 g	100
Sugar		8	oz	250 g	17
Butter	1 lb	8	oz	750 g	50
Egg yolks		4	oz	120 g	8
Water, cold		12	oz	375 g	25
Salt		0.5	oz	15 g	1
Yield:	6 lb			3010 g	201

Procedure:

This pastry is mixed somewhat like mealy pie dough, except that the quantity of sugar is too large to dissolve easily in the water.

1. Sift the flour and sugar into a mixing bowl.
2. Add the butter and rub it in until it is well combined and no lumps remain.
3. Beat the egg yolks with the water and salt until the salt is dissolved.
4. Add the liquid to the flour mixture. Mix gently until it is completely absorbed.
5. Place the dough in pans, cover with plastic film, and place in refrigerator for at least 4 hours.
6. Scale portions as needed.

Variation

For quiches and other savory pies and tarts, omit the sugar.

Short Dough (Sugar Dough)

Ingredients	U.S.		Metric	%
Butter, or part butter and part shortening	2 lb		1000 g	67
Sugar	12	oz	375 g	25
Salt	0.25	oz	8 g	0.5
Eggs	9	oz	280 g	19
Pastry flour, sifted	3 lb		1500 g	100
Yield:	6 lb 5	oz	3163 g	211

Procedure:

1. Using the paddle attachment, mix the butter, sugar, and salt at low speed until smooth and evenly blended.
2. Add the eggs and mix just until absorbed.
3. Add the flour. Mix just until evenly blended.
4. Chill several hours before using.

Almond Short Dough

Ingredients	U.S.		Metric	%
Butter	2 lb		800 g	80
Sugar	1 lb 8	oz	600 g	60
Salt	0.4 oz (2½ tsp)		10 g	1
Almonds, ground fine	1 lb 4	oz	500 g	50
Eggs	6.5 oz		165 g	16.5
Vanilla extract	0.2 oz (1¼ tsp)		5 g	0.5
Pastry flour, sifted	2 lb 8	oz	1000 g	100
Yield:	7 lb 11	oz	3080 g	308

Procedure:

1. Using the paddle attachment, blend the butter, sugar, and salt at low speed until smooth and well mixed. Do not cream until light.
2. Add the nuts and blend in.
3. Add the eggs and vanilla. Mix just until absorbed.
4. Add the flour. Mix just until evenly blended.
5. Chill several hours before using.

Variation

Linzer Dough:

Use ground hazelnuts, ground almonds, or a mixture of the two. Mix in the following spices with the salt in the first step:

Cinnamon	0.25 oz (4½ tsp)	6 g	0.6%
Nutmeg	0.04 oz (½ tsp)	1 g	0.1%

Graham Cracker Crust

Ingredients	U.S.	Metric	Crumbs at 100% %
Graham cracker crumbs	1 lb	450 g	100
Sugar	8 oz	225 g	50
Butter, melted	8 oz	225 g	50
Yield:	2 lb	900 g	200

Enough for four 9-inch pies, or five 8-inch pies

Procedure:

1. Mix crumbs and sugar in a mixing bowl.

2. Add melted butter and mix until evenly blended; crumbs should be completely moistened by the butter.

3. Scale the mixture into pie pans:

   8 oz (225 g) for 9-inch pans

   6 oz (180 g) for 8-inch pans

4. Spread the mixture evenly on bottom and sides of pan. Press another pan on top to pack crumbs evenly.

5. Bake at 350° F (175° C) for 10 minutes.

5. Cool thoroughly before filling.

Variation

Substitute chocolate or vanilla wafer crumbs, gingersnap crumbs, or zwieback crumbs for the graham cracker crumbs.

TARTS AND TARTLETS

A tart is not just a pie without a top crust. Although they may resemble pies, tarts are actually more closely related to the other European-style pastries in this chapter. They are light, usually less than an inch (2.5 cm) thick, and often very colorful. Their appearance usually depends on a pattern of carefully arranged fruit. Tartlets are basically the same as tarts but are made in small, individual-portion sizes.

Unlike pie pans, tart pans are shallow and straight-sided. Often the sides are fluted. Since tarts are usually removed from the pans before serving, false-bottom pans are easiest to use. To remove a tart from a false-bottom pan, first remove the outside ring, then slide the tart from the flat base onto a cardboard circle or onto a serving dish. A flan ring, which is a simple metal hoop, is another form of tart pan. When a flan ring is placed on a baking sheet it forms the side of the pan, and the baking sheet serves as the bottom.

Small tartlet pans are not false-bottomed. Since the tartlets are quite small, it is easy to remove them from their tins. The tins may have straight or sloping sides, which may or may not be fluted.

Tarts need not be round. Square and rectangular tarts are also made, especially when puff pastry is used instead of short dough or pie pastry (see p. 156).

Since tarts contain less filling than pies do, the flavor of the dough is very important. Although regular pie dough can be used, the richer, buttery flavor of enriched pie pastry (p. 140) and short dough (p. 141) make them better choices. Since short dough is a little harder to handle than enriched pie pastry, it is used most often for individual tartlets. Almond short dough can also be used for tartlets.

Procedure for Making Tart Shells

This procedure is for making large tart shells. For individual tartlet shells, see the following variation.

1. Remove short dough or enriched pie dough from refrigerator. Scale the dough as required.

    10–12 oz (300–340 g) for 10-inch (25-cm) tarts

    8–10 oz (225–300 g) for 9-inch (23-cm) tarts

    6–8 oz (175–225 g) for 8-inch (20-cm) tarts

    4–5 oz (115–140 g) for 6-inch (15-cm) tarts

2. Let the dough stand a few minutes, or work it briefly with the hands to make it pliable. Dough should be cold, but if it is too cold and hard, it is difficult to roll out without cracking.

3. Roll out the dough on a floured surface or floured canvas. Enriched pie dough should be rolled to about ⅛ inch (3 mm) thick. Short dough can be a little thicker, slightly less than ¼ inch (5 mm).

4. Place the dough in the tart pan. To lift the dough without breaking it, roll it loosely around the rolling pin. Allow the dough to drop into the pan and then press it into the corners without stretching it. Stretched dough will shrink during baking.

5. Flute edges if desired and trim off excess dough. At this point, the dough is ready to be filled with the fillings that are to be baked in the shell. For tart shells that are to be baked empty, continue with step 6.

6. Prick the bottom of the dough all over with a fork (this is called *docking*). Line the shell with parchment and fill it with dried beans. These two steps keep the crust from puffing and blistering during baking.

7. Bake at 400° F (200° C) until shells are fully baked and lightly browned, about 20 minutes. Remove the paper liners and beans. If the centers of the shells are still slightly underbaked, return them to the oven and bake for a few minutes more.

8. Cool the shells completely.

Procedure Variation: Small Tartlet Shells

Individual tartlet molds come in many shapes, including plain round, fluted round, rectangular, and barquette (boat-shaped).

Method 1

1. Arrange the tartlet shells close together on the work surface, so that there is as little space as possible between them. Different shapes may be used at the same time, as long as they are the same height.

2. Roll out the dough as in the basic procedure.

3. Lift the dough by rolling it loosely around the rolling pin. Drape it over the tartlet shells. Let the dough settle into the tins.

4. Run the rolling pin over the top of the dough. This will cut the dough off at the edges of the tins.

5. Using a small ball of scrap dough, press the pastry firmly into the shells.

6. Continue as in the basic procedure (step 5).

Method 2: for round shells only

1. Roll out the dough as in the basic procedure.

2. With a round cutter about ½ inch (1 cm) larger than the top diameter of the tartlet shells, cut the dough into circles.

3. For each shell, fit a circle of dough into a tin and press it well against the bottom and sides. If you are using fluted tins, make sure the dough is thick enough on the sides so that it won't break apart at the ridges.

4. Continue as in the basic procedure.

Procedure for Making Unbaked Fruit Tarts and Tartlets

1. Assemble the following ingredients:

    Baked tart shells

    Pastry cream (p. 120)

    Choice of fruits (poached, canned or fresh)

    Apricot glaze or red currant glaze (p. 131)

2. Prepare fruit as necessary. Trim and wash fresh fruits. Cut large fruits, such as peaches, into even slices. Poach hard fruits, such as apples or pears (see p. 278 for poaching methods). Drain all fruits well.

3. Spread a layer of pastry cream in the shells. Fill them about half full.

4. Arrange the fruits on the pastry cream in an attractive pattern. Concentric circles are most commonly used for round tarts.

5. Brush the tops of the fruits with the desired glaze. Apricot glaze is appropriate for most fruits, especially light-colored fruits. Red currant glaze is best for red fruits, such as strawberries, or for dark-colored fruits, such as black grapes.

6. Keep refrigerated until sold or served.

Note: Baked tart shells may also be made of puff pastry (p. 156), in addition to short dough and enriched pie dough.

Baked Tarts

In its simplest form, a baked fruit tart is nothing more than an unbaked tart shell filled with a layer of fresh fruit and a little sugar and then baked. Many types of fruits may be used, the most popular being apples, pears, peaches, plums, apricots, and cherries.

A number of variations on this theme are possible, allowing you to create a wide variety of tarts. Among the more popular varieties are as follows:

1. When using juicy fruits, sprinkle the bottom of the tart shell with a thin layer of cake crumbs, cookie crumbs, or even bread crumbs. These absorb some of the excess juices during baking and also contribute to the texture and flavor of the filling.

2. Chopped nuts may also be sprinkled in the bottom of the tart shell.

3. Frangipane cream (p. 63) may be spread on the bottom of the shell. This creates a rich, luxuriously almond-flavored fruit tart.

4. Pastry cream may be used in place of frangipane cream, especially for small, individual tartlets. Arrange the fruit so that it covers the cream completely.

5. If the raw fruit is very hard (some apples, pears, and plums, for example), it may not cook to tenderness in the time it takes to bake the pastry. This is especially true if frangipane or pastry cream is used under the fruit. In such cases, precook the fruit by poaching it in syrup (p. 278) or sautéing it in butter and sugar.

6. Before serving or displaying fruit tarts for sale, dress them up by brushing them with a glaze or by dusting them lightly with confectioners' sugar.

FIGURE 8.1   Apple tart.

Quantity Notice

Ingredient quantities in the following recipes may need to be adjusted. For example, especially sour fruit may need more sugar. Also, fruit may yield more or less than average quantities after trimming (peeling, pitting, etc.).

The following recipes are for 10-inch (25-cm) tarts. For smaller tarts, *multiply or divide each ingredient quantity by the factors indicated below* to get the approximate quantities needed.

Tart size:	Factor:
9-inch (23-cm)	multiply by 0.8 (or ⅘)
8-inch (20-cm)	multiply by 0.66 (or ⅔)
7-inch (18-cm)	divide by 2
6-inch (15-cm)	divide by 3
5-inch (13-cm)	divide by 4
4-inch (10-cm)	divide by 6
3-inch (7.5 cm)	divide by 10

Apple Tart

Yield: one 10-inch (25-cm) tart

Ingredients	U.S.	Metric
Firm, flavorful cooking apples	1 lb 12 oz	750 g
10-inch (25-cm) unbaked tart shell	1	1
Sugar	3 oz	90 g
Apricot glaze	as needed	as needed

Procedure:

1. Peel, core, and cut the apples into thin slices. You should have about 1 lb 6 oz (600 g) apple slices.

2. Arrange the apple slices in the tart shell. Save the best, most uniform slices for the top, and arrange them shingle-fashion in concentric rings (see Figure 8.1).

3. Sprinkle the sugar evenly over the apples.

4. Bake at 400° F (200° C) about 45 minutes, or until the pastry is browned and the apples are tender.

5. Cool. Brush with apricot glaze.

Variations

Saving enough of the best slices for a top layer, chop the rest of the apples and cook them with 2 oz (60 g) of the sugar and ½ oz (15 g) butter until they make a thick applesauce. Cool and spread in the bottom of the tart shell. Arrange apple slices on top. Sprinkle with remaining sugar and bake.

If apple slices are very hard, sauté them lightly in 1 to 2 oz (30 to 60 g) butter and 1 oz (30 g) sugar, until they begin to get soft and lightly browned. Turn them carefully to avoid breaking them. Proceed as in the basic recipe.

Apple Custard Tart:

Reduce the apples to 1 lb 4 oz/560 g (or 1 lb/450 g after peeling and coring). Reduce the sugar to 1.5 oz (45 g). Assemble and bake as in the basic recipe. When about half done, carefully pour in a custard mixture made by mixing the following ingredients:

Milk	4 oz	120 ml
Cream, heavy	4 oz	120 ml
Sugar	2 oz	60 g
Egg, whole	1	1
Egg yolk	1	1
Vanilla extract	1 tsp	5 ml

Continue baking until set. Cool and dust with confectioners' sugar.

Plum, Apricot, Cherry, or Peach Tart:

Follow the basic recipe, but sprinkle a thin layer (0.5 to 1 oz/15 to 30 g) of cake crumbs, cookie crumbs, or bread crumbs in the unbaked shell before adding fruit. Adjust sugar according to the sweetness of the fruit.

Appropriate spices, such as cinnamon for plums or apples, may be added in small quantities.

Pear Almond Tart

Yield: one 10-inch (25-cm) tart

Ingredients	U.S.	Metric
10-inch (25-cm) tart shell	1	1
Frangipane filling (p. 63)	12 oz	350 g
Pear halves, canned or poached	8	8
Apricot glaze	as needed	as needed

Procedure:

1. Spread the frangipane filling evenly in the tart shell.

2. Drain the pears well. Cut them crosswise into thin slices, but keep the slices together in the shape of pear halves.

3. Arrange the sliced pear halves in a star pattern (Figure 8.2) on top of the frangipane filling. Push them gently into the cream.

4. Bake at 425° F (220° C) about 30 minutes.

5. Cool. Brush the top with apricot glaze.

Variations

Cooked or canned peaches, apples, apricots, plums, or cherries may be used instead of pears. For small fruits such as apricots, plums, and cherries, reduce the quantity of frangipane filling and use enough fruit to cover the top completely.

Fruit Tart with Pastry Cream:

Omit the frangipane and, instead, cover the bottom of the tart shell with a ½-inch (1-cm) layer of pastry cream. Or use a mixture of 2 or 3 parts pastry cream blended smooth with 1 part almond paste. Cover the cream with a layer of fruit, arranged attractively.

Frangipane Tart:

Omit the fruit. Spread the bottom of the tart shell with a thin layer of apricot jam. Fill with frangipane filling. Bake and cool. Instead of glazing, dust lightly with confectioners' sugar. This recipe is especially appropriate for small, individual tartlets.

FIGURE 8.2 Pear almond tart.

Linzertorte

This famous Austrian pastry is called a torte, but it is actually a tart, filled with raspberry jam.

Yield: one 10-inch (25-cm) tart

Ingredients	U.S.	Metric
Linzer dough	1 lb 8 oz	700 g
Raspberry jam	14 oz (1¼ cups)	400 g

Procedure:

1. Roll out about two-thirds of the dough to about ⅓ to ¼ inch (6 to 8 mm) thick.

2. Line a greased 10-inch (25-cm) tart pan with the dough.

3. Spread the jam evenly in the shell.

4. Roll out the remaining dough and cut it into strips about ⅜ inch (1 cm) wide. Arrange the strips in a lattice pattern on top of the tarts. The strips should be at an angle so that they form diamond shapes rather than squares (Figure 8.3).

5. Turn down the sides of the dough shell to make a border and to cover the ends of the lattice strips.

6. Bake at 375° F (190° C) for 35–40 minutes.

FIGURE 8.3 Linzertorte.

PUFF PASTRY

Puff pastry is one of the most remarkable products of the bakeshop. Although it includes no added leavening agent, it can rise to eight times its original thickness when baked.

Puff pastry is a rolled-in dough, like Danish and croissant doughs. This means that it is made up of many layers of fat sandwiched between layers of dough.

Unlike Danish dough, however, puff pastry contains no yeast. Steam, created when the moisture in the dough is heated, is responsible for the spectacular rising power of puff pastry.

Puff pastry, or puff dough, is one of the most difficult bakery products to make. Because it consists of over 1000 layers, many more than in Danish dough, the rolling-in procedure requires a great deal of time and care.

Like so many other products, there are nearly as many versions of puff pastry as there are bakers. Both formulas and rolling-in techniques vary. The formula provided here contains no eggs, for example, although some bakers add them.

The rolling-in technique described here differs somewhat from that used by European pastry chefs, but it is widely used by American bakers.

Butter is the preferred fat for rolling in because of its flavor and melt-in-the-mouth quality. Special puff pastry shortening is also available. This shortening is easier to work because it is not as hard when refrigerated and because it doesn't soften and melt at warm temperatures as easily as butter does. It is also less expensive than butter. However, it can be unpleasant to eat because it tends to congeal and coat the inside of the mouth.

The quantity of rolled-in fat may vary from 50 to 100% of the weight of the flour, or 8 oz to 1 lb fat per pound of flour. If the lower quantity of fat is used, the dough should be left slightly thicker when rolled out.

Puff pastry that is low in fat will not rise as high and may rise unevenly. This is because there is less fat between the dough layers, so that the layers are more likely to stick together.

Puff Pastry

Ingredients	U.S.	Metric	%
Bread flour	3 lb	1500 g	75
Cake flour	1 lb	500 g	25
Butter, soft	8 oz	250 g	12.5
Salt	1 oz	30 g	1.5
Cold water	2 lb 4 oz	1125 g	56
Butter	4 lb	2000 g	100
Bread flour (see note)	8 oz	250 g	12.5
Yield:	11 lb 5 oz	5655 g	282

Note: The purpose of the 8 oz (250 g) bread flour is to absorb some of the moisture of the butter and help make the dough more manageable. Omit this flour if shop temperature is cool or if puff paste shortening is used instead of butter.

Mixing procedure:

1. Place the first quantities of flour and butter in a mixing bowl. With the paddle attachment, mix at low speed until well blended.

2. Dissolve the salt in the cold water.

3. Add the salted water to the flour mixture and mix at low speed until a soft dough is formed. Do not overmix.

4. Remove the dough from the mixer and let it rest in the refrigerator or retarder for 20 minutes.

5. Blend the last quantities of butter and flour at low speed in the mixer until the mixture is the same consistency as the dough, neither too soft nor too hard.

6. Roll the butter into the dough following the procedure shown in Figure 8.4. Give the dough *four 4-folds* or *six 3-folds*.

FIGURE 8.4 Rolling-in procedure for puff pastry.
(*a*) Dust the bench lightly with flour. Roll out the dough into a rectangle about three times as long as it is wide and about ½ inch (1 to 1.5 cm) thick. Make the corners as square as possible.

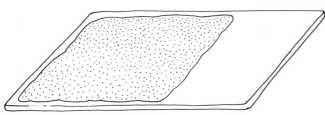

(*b*) Spot the butter *evenly* over two-thirds the length of the dough as shown, leaving a 1-inch (2.5-cm) margin at the edges. The butter should be about the same consistency as the dough. If the butter is too hard, it will puncture the dough and not spread evenly. If it is too soft, it will ooze out when rolled.

(*c*) Fold the unbuttered third over the center third.

(*d*) Fold the remaining third on top. All ends and corners should be folded evenly and squarely. This procedure, enclosing the butter in the dough, does not count as one of the folds. The folding procedure starts with the next step.

(*e*) Turn the dough 90 degrees on the bench so that the length becomes the width. This step must be taken before each rolling-out of the dough so that the gluten is stretched in all directions, not just lengthwise. Failure to do this will result in products that deform or shrink unevenly when they bake.

(*f*) Roll the dough out lengthwise into a rectangle. Make sure the corners are square. Roll smoothly and evenly. Do not press down when rolling, or the layers may stick together and the product will not rise properly.

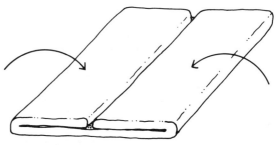

(*g*) Brush excess flour from the top of the dough. Fold the two ends to the center. Make sure the corners are square and even. Again brush off excess flour.

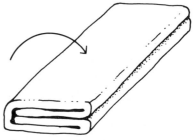

(*h*) Fold the dough in half like a closed book. You have now given the dough *one 4-fold*. Refrigerate the dough for 15 to 20 minutes to relax the gluten. Do not refrigerate it too long or the butter will become too hard. (If it does, let it soften a few minutes at room temperature.) Give the dough another *three 4-folds*, as in steps *f-h* above. After another rest, the dough is now ready to be rolled out and made up into the desired products.
Alternative method: Instead of giving the dough four 4-folds, you may give it *six 3-folds*. See Danish pastry, p. 59, for the 3-fold method.

Blitz Puff Pastry

This product is much easier and quicker to make than classic puff dough. ("Blitz" is the German word for "lightning.") It does not rise as high as true puff pastry, so it is not suitable for patty shells and other products in which a high, light pastry is desirable. However, it bakes up very crisp and flaky and is perfectly suitable for napoleons and similar desserts that are layered with cream fillings.

Blitz puff paste, as you will see, is actually a very flaky pie dough that is rolled and folded like regular puff dough.

Blitz Puff Pastry

Ingredients	U.S.	Metric	%
Bread flour	1 lb	500 g	50
Pastry flour	1 lb	500 g	50
Butter, slightly softened	2 lb	1000 g	100
Salt	½ oz	15 g	
Cold water	1 lb	500 g	50
Yield:	5 lb	2515 g	250

Mixing Procedure:

1. Sift the two flours together into a mixing bowl.
2. Cut the butter into the flour as for pie dough, but leave the fat in very large lumps, 1 inch (2½ cm) across.
3. Dissolved the salt in the water.
4. Add the water to the flour/butter mixture. Mix until the water is absorbed.
5. Let the dough rest 15 minutes. Refrigerate it if the bakeshop is warm.
6. Dust the bench with flour and roll out the dough into a rectangle. Give the dough *three 4-folds*.

General Guidelines for Makeup and Baking of Puff Dough Products

1. Dough should be cool and firm when it is rolled and cut. If it is too soft, layers may stick together at the cuts, preventing proper rising.
2. Cut with straight, firm, even cuts. Use a sharp cutting tool.
3. Avoid touching the cut edges with the fingers, or layers may stick together.
4. For best rising, place units upside-down on baking sheets. Even sharp cutting tools may press the top layers of dough together. Baking upside-down puts the stuck-together layers at the bottom.
5. Avoid letting egg wash run down the edges. Egg wash can cause the layers to stick together at the edges.
6. Rest made-up products for 30 minutes or more in a cool place or in the refrigerator before baking. This relaxes the gluten and reduces shrinkage.
7. Trimmings may be pressed together, keeping the layers in the same direction. After being rolled out and given a 3-fold, they may be used again, although they will not rise as high.
8. Baking temperatures of 400 to 425° F (200 to 220° C) are best for most puff dough products. Cooler temperatures will not create enough steam in the products to leaven them well. Higher temperatures will set the crust too quickly.
9. Larger products such as Pithiviers (p. 156) are harder to bake through than small ones. To avoid underbaked, soggy interiors, start large items at a high temperature and bake until they are well risen. Then turn the temperature down to about 350° F (175° C) and finish baking until crisp.

Procedures for Making Puff Pastry Desserts

The following procedures include instructions for most popular puff dough products. If any of your products do not turn out well, consult the trouble-shooting guide in Table 8.1.

TABLE 8.1 **Puff Pastry Faults and Their Causes**

Faults	Possible Causes
Shrinkage during baking	Dough not relaxed before baking
Poor lift or rising	Too little or too much fat used Dough rolled out too thin or given too many turns Oven too hot or too cold
Uneven lift or irregular shapes	Improper rolling-in procedure Uneven distribution of fat before rolling Dough not relaxed before baking Uneven heat in oven
Fat running out during baking	Too much fat used Not enough turns given Oven too cool (Note: Some fat running out is normal, but it should not be excessive.)

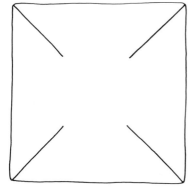

FIGURE 8.5 Makeup of pinwheels.
(a) Cut the dough into 5-inch (12-cm) squares. Wash the centers with water. Cut the squares diagonally from corners to 1 inch (2.5 cm) from center.

Pinwheels (see Figure 8.5)

1. Roll out puff dough ⅛ inch (3 mm) thick.
2. Cut into 5-inch (12 cm) squares.
3. Wash centers with water.
4. Cut diagonally from the corners to about 1 inch (2.5 cm) from center.
5. Fold every other corner into the center and press in place.
6. Bake at 400° F (200° C).
7. Let cool. Spoon desired fruit filling into centers. Dust lightly with confectioners' sugar. (Pinwheels may also be filled before baking if the filling is thick and not likely to run out and burn.)

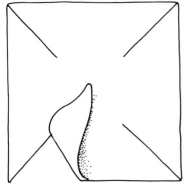 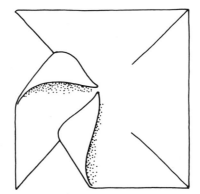 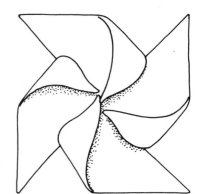

(b-d) Fold every other corner to center and press down. Fill centers with fruit filling before or after baking.

Patty Shells (see Figure 8.6)

1. Roll out puff dough ⅛ inch (3 mm) thick.

2. Roll out a second piece of dough ¼ inch (6 mm) thick.

3. Cut the same number of circles from each piece of dough with a round 3-inch (7.5 cm) cutter.

4. With a 2-inch (5 cm) cutter, cut out the centers of the *thick* circles.

5. Wash the thin circles with water or egg wash and place one of the rings on top of each. Wash the top carefully with egg wash (do not drip wash down the edges). Let them rest 30 minutes.

6. Place a sheet of greased parchment over the tops of the shells to prevent their toppling over while baking.

7. Bake at 400° F (200° C) until brown and crisp.

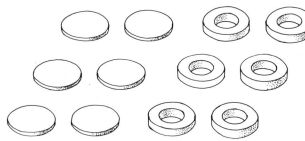

FIGURE 8.6 Makeup of patty shells.
(a) Roll out one sheet of puff dough ⅛ inch (3 mm) thick, and another sheet ¼ inch (6 mm) thick. Cut out an equal number of 2- to 3-inch (5- to 7.5-cm) circles from each. Cut out the centers of the thick circles with smaller cutters.

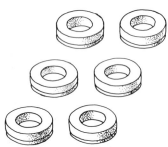

(b) Wash the thin circles with water or egg wash and place the thick circles on top.

Cream Horns (see Figure 8.7)

1. Roll out puff dough into a sheet ⅛ inch (3 mm) thick and about 15 inches (38 cm) wide.

2. Cut out strips 1¼ inches (3 cm) wide by 15 inches (38 cm) long.

3. Wash the strips with water.

4. With the washed side facing outward, roll the strips diagonally onto cream horn tubes, making spirals. Overlap the edges by about ⅜ inch (1 cm). If you are using conical tubes, start at the small end.

5. Roll horns in granulated sugar and lay them on baking sheets. The end of the dough strip should be on the bottom so that it will not pop up during baking.

6. Bake at 400° F (200° C) until brown and crisp.

7. Slip out tubes while still warm.

8. Just before service, fill the horns from both ends with whipped cream or pastry cream, using a pastry bag with a star tip. Dust with confectioners' sugar.

Sacristains

1. Roll out puff dough ⅛ inch (3 mm) thick. Cut into long strips 4 inches (10 cm) wide.

2. Brush the dough with egg wash and sprinkle with coarse granulated sugar or a mixture of sugar and chopped almonds. Lightly press the sugar and nuts into the dough with a rolling pin.

3. Turn the strips over and coat the other side with egg wash, sugar, and almonds in the same way.

4. Cut the strips crosswise into small strips ¾ inch (2 cm) wide and 4 inches (10 cm) long.

5. Twist each strip to make a shape like a corkscrew. Place on paper-lined baking sheets and press down the ends lightly so that the twists do not unwind during baking.

6. Bake at 425° F (220° C) until brown and crisp.

Palmiers

1. Roll out puff pastry dough into a long strip about 10 to 12 inches (25 to 30 cm) wide and ⅛ inch (3 mm) thick. Trim the sides of the strip so that they are straight.

2. Sprinkle the surface evenly with granulated sugar.

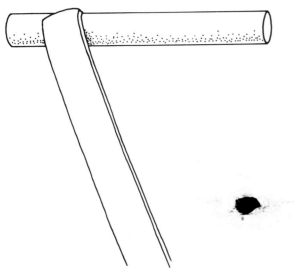

FIGURE 8.7 Makeup of cream horns.
(*a*) Roll out puff dough ⅛ inch (3 mm) thick and cut into strips 1¼ inch (3 cm) wide and 15 inches (38 cm) long. Wash the strips with water and press one end (washed side out) onto one end of cream horn tube as shown.

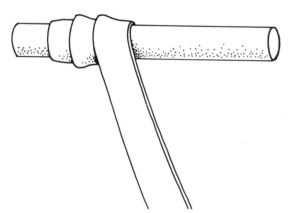

(*b*) Roll up the dough strip in a spiral by turning the tube. Overlap the edges by about ⅜ inch (1 cm). Do not stretch the dough.

(*c*) Roll up completely and press the end in place to seal.

3. Determine the center of the strip. Then fold each long side into the center in thirds (see Figure 8.8), so that the two halves are each three layers thick and meet exactly in the center.

4. Fold one half over the other to make a strip six layers thick.

5. Refrigerate until firm.

6. Cut the strip into ¼-inch (6-mm) slices with a sharp knife.

7. Place the pieces cut side up on parchment-lined baking sheets. Leave several inches between pieces to allow for spreading. Spread the open ends of each piece apart slightly.

8. Bake at 425° F (220° C) until the bottoms are browned. Turn the palmiers over with a bowl knife and continue baking until the other sides are browned.

Variation

For smaller palmiers, roll the puff pastry into a strip 5 inches (13 cm) wide. Fold the edges into the center and then fold in half, making the strip four layers thick instead of six.

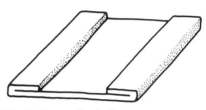

FIGURE 8.8 Makeup of palmiers.
(*a*) Fold the sides of the dough to the center in thirds. To do this, first fold the sides half-way to the center.

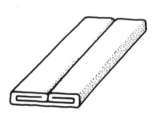

(*b*) Then fold again as shown.

(*c*) Fold in half.

(*d*) After placing the cut pieces on the baking sheet, spread the ends open slightly.

Allumettes

1. Roll out puff pastry dough ⅛ inch (3 mm) thick. Cut into long strips 3 inches (7.5 cm) wide.

2. Place the strips on baking sheets. Spread the top of each with a thin layer of royal icing (p. 131). Let the icing dry for a few minutes.

3. Cut the strips crosswise into pieces ¾ inch (2 cm) wide, but do not separate them.

4. Set 1-inch-high (2.5-cm) blocks (or any other objects the same height, such as cutters) at the corners of the baking sheet. Set an icing rack over the pan so that it is supported on the blocks. This will keep the pastry at a uniform height when it rises.

5. Bake at 400° F (200° C) until browned.

6. Remove allumettes from the oven and immediately check if any of the strips have stuck together. If so, cut them apart with a knife. Also, make sure that the insides are crisp. If they are still soft and moist, lower the oven heat to 350° F (175° C) and continue baking until they are crisp.

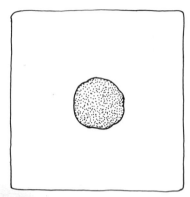

FIGURE 8.9 Makeup of turnovers.
(a) Cut the dough into 4-inch (10-cm) squares. Wash the edges with water and place filling in the center of each square.

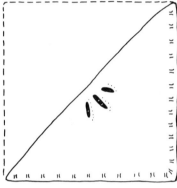

(b) Fold over the squares diagonally and press the edges together. Puncture two or three steam holes on top.

Turnovers (see Figure 8.9)

1. Roll out puff pastry dough ⅛ inch (3 mm) thick.

2. Cut into 4-inch (10-cm) squares. Wash the edges of each with water.

3. Place a portion of the desired filling into the center of each square.

4. Fold the squares diagonally and press the edges together. With a knife, puncture the tops in two or three places to allow steam to escape. Let them rest 30 minutes.

5. Brush the tops with egg wash, if desired, or brush with milk or water and sprinkle with sugar.

6. Bake at 400° F (200° C) until crisp and brown.

Napoleons

1. Roll puff dough into a very thin sheet about the size of a sheet pan. Blitz puff paste or rerolled trimmings may be used.

2. Place on sheet pan and let rest 30 minutes.

3. Dock with a fork to prevent blistering.

4. Bake at 400° F (200° C) until brown and crisp.

5. Trim the edges of the pastry sheet and cut with a serrated knife into equal strips 3 to 4 inches (7.5 to 10 cm) wide. Set the best strip aside for the top layer. If one of the strips breaks, it can be used as the middle layer.

6. Spread one rectangle with pastry cream (p. 120) or with a mixture of pastry cream and whipped cream.

7. Top with a second sheet of pastry.

8. Spread with another layer of pastry cream.

9. Place third pastry rectangle on top, with flattest side up.

10. Ice top with fondant (p. 123).

11. To decorate, pipe four stripes of chocolate fondant lengthwise on the white fondant. Draw a spatula or the back of a knife across the top in opposite directions, 1 inch (2.5 cm) apart, as shown in Figure 8.10.

12. Cut into strips 1½ to 2 inches (4 to 5 cm) wide.

FIGURE 8.10 Decorating napoleons.
(a) Spread the top of the assembled napoleon with white fondant. With a paper cone, pipe on four strips of chocolate fondant.

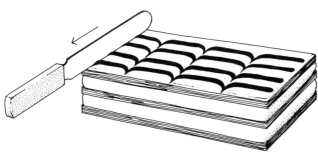

(b) Draw a spatula or the back of a knife across the icing at 2-inch (5-cm) intervals.

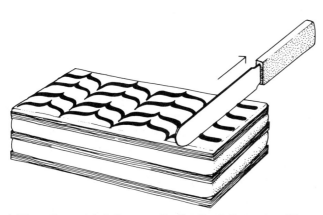

(c) Draw the spatula in the opposite direction in the center of these 2-inch intervals, as shown.

(d) Cut the napoleon into 2-inch (5-cm) wide strips.

Baked Apple Dumplings

1. Peel and core as many small, tart baking apples as desired.

2. Roll out puff pastry dough ⅛ inch (3 mm) thick. Cut out squares large enough to cover an apple completely when the points of the square are overlapped at the top of the apple. The dough must not be stretched over the apple or it will pull away during baking. Caution: Cut out one square and test it to be sure it is large enough to cover the apple. Then cut out the remaining squares.

3. If the dough becomes soft, refrigerate it for 15 to 30 minutes before continuing.

4. Place a teaspoonful of cake crumbs in the center of each pastry square. Then place an apple on top of the crumbs. (The crumbs are optional, but they help absorb some of the juice of the apple.)

5. Fill the center of the apples (where the cores used to be) with cinnamon sugar and raisins. Taste a small piece of apple for tartness, to help you judge how much sugar to use.

6. Brush the edges of the dough with water or egg wash. Draw up the four corners of the dough and overlap them at the top of the apple. Press the corners together to seal. Pinch the edges of the dough together to seal the seams.

7. Cut out 1-inch (2.5-cm) circles of dough. Moisten the top of each apple with egg wash and cap with a circle of dough. This covers the overlapping corners and makes the product more attractive.

8. Arrange the apples on parchment-lined pans. Brush with egg wash.

9. Bake at 400° F (200° C) until the pastry is browned and the apples are cooked through, but not too soft (or they will sag or flatten out). This will take 45 to 60 minutes, depending on the apples. Test for doneness by piercing one of the apples with a thin skewer. If the pastry browns too fast, cover lightly with a sheet of parchment or foil.

FIGURE 8.11 Gateau Pithiviers

Gateau Pithiviers (almond puff pastry cake)

1. Roll out puff pastry dough about ⅛ inch (3 mm) thick. Cut out two large circles of equal size (preferably a size that will fit your cardboard cake circles, if you use them).

2. Spread a thick layer of frangipane filling (p. 63) on one of the circles, leaving a 1-inch (2.5-cm) margin around the edges.

3. Moisten the margin with water or egg wash. Place the second circle of dough on top. Press the edges together to seal.

4. Refrigerate for at least 30 minutes.

5. Brush the top of the Pithiviers (pronounced "pee-tee-vyay") with egg wash.

6. With the tip of a knife, score the top of the pastry in a pinwheel pattern of arcs radiating from the center, as shown in Figure 8.11. If desired, you may also decorate the edge by pressing the back of a knife, held vertically, into the edge at 1-inch intervals.

7. Bake at 450° F (230° C) for 15 minutes. Reduce the heat to 350° F (175° C) and continue baking until browned and crisp, about 30 to 40 minutes, depending on size.

8. This cake is best served warm. It may be reheated to warm and crisp it before serving.

Fruit Tarts and Strips

Puff paste may be used instead of short dough to make fruit tarts. Fruit strips are fruit tarts made in the shape of long strips about 4 to 5 inches (10 to 12 cm) wide.

The procedure for assembling these desserts is the same as that for unbaked fruit tarts as described earlier in this chapter (p. 143), except that baked puff pastry bases are used instead of short dough bases. They should be assembled only at the last minute, because the pastry quickly becomes soggy.

The procedure for making the pastry shells is as follows. The shells can be made in any shape, but squares and rectangles are easiest.

1. Roll out puff pastry dough ⅛ inch (3 mm) thick.

2. Cut out squares or rectangles of desired size.

3. With remaining dough, cut strips about ¾ inch (2 cm) wide and long enough to make borders for the tarts.

4. Brush the rims of the dough squares with water; lay the strips in place on the moistened edges to make borders.

5. With a fork, knife tip, or roller docker, dock the inside of the shell (not the borders) to prevent blistering.

6. Rest in refrigerator 30 minutes before baking.

7. Bake at 400° F (200° C) until browned and crisp. Cool.

8. Assemble fruit tarts according to the procedure on p. 143.

Variation

Fruit Strips:

Follow the above procedure, but make the rectangles 4 to 5 inches wide and as long as your sheet pans. Put borders on the two long sides, but leave the ends open.

ECLAIR PASTE

Eclairs and cream puffs are made from a dough called éclair paste, or choux paste. The French name pâte à choux (pronounced "pot a shoo") means "cabbage paste," referring to the fact that cream puffs look like little cabbages.

Unlike puff pastry, éclair paste is extremely easy to make. The dough itself can be prepared in just a few minutes. This is fortunate, because for best baking results the dough should not be prepared ahead of time.

The exact procedure for making éclair paste is detailed in the formula that follows. In general, the method consists of these steps:

1. Bring the liquid, fat, salt, and sugar (if used) to a boil. The liquid must be boiling rapidly so that the fat is dispersed in the liquid, not just floating on top. If this is not done, the fat will not be as well incorporated into the paste, and some of it may run out during baking.

2. Add the flour all at once and stir until the paste forms a ball and pulls away from the sides of the pan.

3. Remove the paste from the heat and let it cool to 140° F (60° C). If the paste is not cooled slightly, it will cook the eggs when they are added.

4. Beat in the eggs a little at a time. Completely mix in each addition of eggs before adding more. If the eggs are added too quickly, it will be difficult to get a smooth batter.

5. The paste is now ready to use.

In principle, éclair paste is similar to popover batter (p. 96), even though the former is a thick dough and the latter a thin batter. Both products are leavened by steam, which expands the product rapidly and forms large holes in the center of the item. The heat of the oven then coagulates the gluten and egg proteins to set the structure and make a firm product. A strong flour is necessary in both for sufficient structure.

Eclair paste must be firm enough to hold its shape when piped from a pastry bag. You may occasionally find a formula that produces too slack a dough. Correct such a formula by reducing the water or milk slightly. On the other hand, éclair paste should not be too dry. It should look smooth and moist, not dry and rough. Paste that is too dry will not puff up well and will be thick and heavy.

Eclair paste for cream puffs and éclairs should be piped onto parchment-lined pans, not onto greased pans. Grease will cause the paste to spread and flatten when baked.

Proper baking temperatures are important. Start at a high temperature (425° F/220° C) for the first 15 minutes to develop steam. Then reduce the heat to 375° F(190° C) to finish baking and set the structure. The products must be firm and dry before being removed from the oven. If they are removed too soon or cooled too quickly, they may collapse. Some bakers like to leave them in a turned-off oven with the door ajar. However, if the oven must be heated again for other products, this may not be the best idea, especially in these times of high energy costs. It may be better to bake the products thoroughly, remove them carefully from the oven, and let them cool slowly in a warm place.

Note: French doughnuts or crullers, also made with eclair paste, are covered in Chapter 6, p. 104.

Eclair Paste

Ingredients	U.S.			Metric	%
Water, milk, or half water, half milk	1 lb			500 g	133
Butter or regular shortening		8	oz	250 g	67
Salt		0.18 oz (1 tsp)		5 g	1.5
Bread flour		12 oz		375 g	100
Eggs	1 lb	4	oz	625 g	167
Yield:	3 lb	8	oz	1755 g	468

Procedure:

1. Combine the liquid, butter, and salt in a heavy saucepan or kettle. Bring the mixture to a full, rolling boil.

2. Remove the pan from the heat and add the flour all at once. Stir quickly.

3. Return the pan to moderate heat and stir vigorously until the dough forms a ball and pulls away from the sides of the pan.

4. Transfer the dough to the bowl of a mixer. Or, if you wish to mix it by hand, leave it in the saucepan.

5. With the paddle attachment, mix at low speed until the dough has cooled slightly. It should be about 140° F (60° C), which is still very warm, but not too hot to touch.

6. At medium speed, beat in the eggs a little at a time. Add no more than a quarter of the eggs at once, and wait until they are completely absorbed before adding more. When all the eggs are absorbed, the paste is ready to use.

Note: If a sweeter product is desired, add ½ ounce (15 g) sugar in step 1.

Procedures for Making Eclair Paste Products

Cream Puffs

1. Line sheet pans with silicone paper.

2. Fit a large pastry bag with a plain tube. Fill the bag with the éclair paste.

3. Pipe out round mounds of dough about 1½ inches (4 cm) in diameter onto the lined baking sheets. Or, if preferred, drop the dough from a spoon.

4. Bake at 425° F(215° C) for 10 minutes. Lower heat to 375° F(190° C) until mounds are well browned and very crisp.

5. Remove them from the oven and let cool slowly in a warm place.

6. When cool, cut a slice from the top of each puff. Fill with whipped cream, pastry cream (p. 120), or other desired filling, using a pastry bag with a star tube.

7. Replace tops and dust with confectioners' sugar.

8. Fill as close to service time as possible. If cream-filled puffs must be held, keep refrigerated.

9. Unfilled and uncut puffs, if thoroughly dry, may be held in plastic bags in the refrigerator for a week. Recrisp in oven for a few minutes before use.

Eclairs

1. Proceed as for cream puffs, except pipe the dough out into strips about ¾ inch (2 cm) wide and 3–4 inches (8–10 cm) long. Bake as for cream puffs.

2. Fill baked, cooled eclair shells with pastry cream. Two methods may be used:

    a. Make a small hole in one end and fill with a pastry bag or a doughnut filling pump.

    b. Cut a slice lengthwise from the top and fill with a pastry bag.

3. Dip the tops of the eclairs in chocolate fondant (p. 124).

4. For service and holding, see cream puffs.

Variation

Frozen Eclairs or Profiteroles:

1. Fill éclairs or small cream puffs (profiteroles) with softened ice cream. Keep frozen until service.

2. At service time, top with chocolate syrup.

Paris-Brest

1. Line a sheet pan with silicone paper. Using a round cake pan of the desired size as a guide, draw a circle on the parchment. (An 8-inch (20-cm) circle is a popular size.)

2. Fit a large pastry bag with a plain tube. Pipe a ring of paste 1 inch (2.5 cm) thick just inside the drawn circle. Pipe a second ring inside the first one, just touching it. Then pipe a third ring on top of the other two.

3. Sprinkle the paste circles with sliced or chopped almonds.

4. Bake as for cream puffs and éclairs.

5. When cool, cut a slice off the top of the pastry. Fill with whipped cream, vanilla pastry cream (p. 120), pastry cream mousseline (p. 121), or crème St. Honoré (p. 121). Replace the top.

Gateau St. Honoré

1. Roll out short dough (p. 141) ⅛ inch thick. Cut out a circle of the desired size (such as 8 inches/20 cm). Place the circle on a baking sheet and dock the dough with a fork.

2. Fit a pastry bag with a large plain tube and fill with éclair paste.

3. Pipe a ring of éclair paste ¾ inch (2 cm) thick on the dough circle around the outer edge.

4. On a separate baking sheet, pipe out round mounds of paste about ½ inch (12 mm) across, as for making small cream puffs. You will need about 16 small puffs for an 8-inch (20-cm) cake, 20 for a 9-inch (23-cm) cake, 25 for a 10-inch (25-cm) cake.

5. Place both the large ring and the small puffs in an oven heated to 425° F (220° C). Bake 15 minutes. Lower the heat to 375° F (190° C) and continue baking until the pastry is crisp and brown. Note: The small puffs will be done first and should be removed when they are done. Cool.

6. Make a small hole in the bottom of each of the small puffs and fill each with vanilla pastry cream. Use a pastry bag with a very small plain tube.

7. Cook a sugar syrup to the light caramel stage (see p. 115). Keeping the caramel warm, dip the bottom of each puff in the caramel and immediately place it on the outer ring of pastry. Make a circle of filled puffs all around the ring (Figure 8.12).

8. Fill the center of the ring with crème St. Honoré (p. 121).

9. If desired, the cake may be decorated with fruit and whipped cream.

Variation

Individual pastries may be made by the same method. Each circle is 3 inches (7 cm) in diameter and is topped with three small puffs spaced evenly around it.

FIGURE 8.12   Gateau St. Honoré

STRUDEL AND PHYLLO

Puff pastry dough, you will remember, consists of over 1,000 layers of dough and fat. Starting with a single thick piece of dough, you fold in butter, and then continue to roll out and fold until you have a very flaky pastry of extremely thin layers.

Pastries made from strudel or phyllo doughs are even flakier than puff pastries. Unlike puff pastries, these desserts start out with paper-thin layers of dough that are brushed with fat and then stacked or rolled up to make many-layered creations.

Strudel is a Hungarian pastry that begins as a soft dough made of strong flour, eggs, and water. After mixing the dough well to develop the gluten, it is stretched by hand into a very thin, transparent sheet. This is a skilled operation that takes practice to do well.

Phyllo (pronounced "fee-lo," and sometimes spelled filo or fillo) is a Greek version of this type of paper-thin dough. Although not exactly the same as strudel dough, it is interchangeable with strudel dough for most of our purposes. Because it is available commercially, phyllo dough is widely used today for strudel-making. In fact, commercial phyllo is often labeled "phyllo/strudel dough."

Commercially made phyllo is almost always available frozen, and in some locations it can also be purchased fresh (refrigerated). The sheets usually measure about 11 or 12 inches × 17 inches (28 to 30 × 43 cm). A 1-pound package contains about 25 sheets.

The following recipes are for homemade strudel dough and for two popular strudel fillings, apple and cheese. Included with these are procedures for assembling and baking a strudel using both homemade dough and commercial phyllo leaves. Finally, we include a procedure for assembling and baking baklava, the popular Greek phyllo pastry filled with nuts and soaked with a honey syrup.

Handling Phyllo Dough

Commercially made phyllo is so thin and delicate that it must be handled very carefully. Two guidelines are important. First, thaw frozen phyllo completely *before opening the plastic package*. Do not try to handle frozen dough, or it will break.

Second, after opening the package and unfolding or unrolling the sheets of dough, keep the stack of leaves covered to prevent drying. Remove and work with one sheet at a time, while keeping the rest covered. (Note: Instructions often say to cover the dough with a damp cloth, but this is risky because the sheets will stick together if the dough becomes too damp.)

Strudel Dough

Ingredients	U.S.		Metric	%
Bread flour	2 lb		900 g	100
Water	1 lb 2	oz	500 g	56
Salt	0.5	oz	15 g	1.5
Eggs (3)	5	oz	140 g	15
Vegetable oil	2	oz	55 g	6
Yield:	3 lb 9	oz	1605 g	178

Enough for 3 sheets, each about 3 × 5 ft (1 × 1.6 m)

Mixing Procedure:

1. Mix all ingredients into a smooth dough. To develop the gluten well, mix at moderate speed for about 10 minutes. The dough will be very soft.

2. Divide the dough into three equal parts. Flatten each piece into a rectangle. Place the three pieces of dough on an oiled sheet pan. Oil the top of the dough lightly and cover it with plastic film.

3. Let the dough rest at least 1 hour at room temperature, or longer in the retarder.

Procedure for Stretching Strudel Dough:

1. Strudel dough stretches best if it is slightly warm, so place the dough in a warm place. Allow at least 1 to 2 hours if the dough has been refrigerated.

2. Cover a large table (at least 3 × 5 ft/1 × 1.6 m) with a cloth. Dust the cloth well with flour and rub the flour in lightly.

3. Using plenty of dusting flour, place one piece of dough in the center of the table and, with a rolling pin, roll it out roughly into an oval or rectangle. This step is meant only to start the stretching, so don't try to roll the dough too thin.

4. Put your hands under the dough with the backs of the hands up. Carefully begin stretching the dough from the center outward, using the backs of your hands, not your fingers, to avoid poking holes in the dough. Work your way around the table, gently stretching the dough little by little in all directions. Concentrate on the thickest parts of the dough, so that it is of even thickness all around.

5. Keep on stretching the dough until it is paper thin and nearly transparent. If small holes appear, you can ignore them; if large holes appear, patch them with pieces of dough from the edges after stretching is complete. Each piece of dough should make a sheet about 3 × 5 ft (1 × 1.6 m).

6. With scissors, cut off the heavy rim of dough all around the edge and discard it.

7. Let the dough dry for about 10 minutes, then fill it and roll it according to the following procedure.

Procedure for Filling, Rolling, and Baking Strudel

Method 1, using homemade dough:

1. Assemble the following ingredients:

1 sheet freshly made strudel dough	3 × 5 ft	1 × 1.6 m
Melted butter	8 oz	250 g
Cake crumbs, bread crumbs, finely chopped nuts, or a mixture of these	8 oz	250 g
Cinnamon	0.25 oz (1 tbsp)	7 g
Cheese filling	5–5½ lb	2300–2600 g
OR		
Apple filling	4–4½ lb	2000–2200 g

2. Sprinkle or brush the dough all over with the melted butter. If you brush the fat on, draw the brush very lightly over the dough to avoid tearing it.

3. Mix the crumbs, nuts, and cinnamon and sprinkle them evenly over the dough.

4. Arrange the filling in a 1½-inch (4-cm) thick band along one long side of the dough. Leave a margin of about 2 inches (5 cm) between the row of filling and the edge of the dough.

5. Standing on the side where the filling is, grasp the edge of the cloth and lift it upward and forward to start the strudel rolling. Using the cloth as an aid, roll up the strudel like a jelly roll.

6. Cut the strudel in lengths to fit on a greased or paper-lined sheet, or bend the strudel to fit it on in one piece. Pinch the ends closed.

7. Brush the top with butter or egg wash. Bake at 375° F (190°C) until browned, about 45 minutes.

8. When cool, dust butter-washed strudel with confectioners' sugar, or brush egg-washed strudel with a clear syrup glaze (p. 61).

Method 2, using phyllo leaves:

Each unit requires 4 phyllo leaves plus one-fourth of the filling ingredients needed in Method 1.

1. Assemble the following ingredients:

Phyllo leaves (11 × 17 inches)	4 sheets	4 sheets
Melted butter	2 oz	60 g
Cake crumbs, bread crumbs, finely chopped nuts, or a mixture of these	2 oz	60 g
Cinnamon	¾ tsp	2 g
Cheese filling	20–22 oz	575–625 g
OR		
Apple filling	16–18 oz	500–550 g

2. Mix together the crumbs, nuts, and cinnamon.

3. Lay a cloth or a sheet of parchment on the bench. Lay a sheet of phyllo on the cloth or paper. Brush it with butter and sprinkle it with one-fourth of the crumb mixture.

4. Lay a second sheet on top of the first one. Brush with butter and sprinkle with crumbs.

5. Repeat with the remaining two sheets.

6. Arrange the filling in a band along the wide side of the sheet, leaving a margin of about 2 inches (5 cm) between the filling and the edge.

7. Roll up and bake as in Method 1 (steps 5 to 7). Each unit will fit crosswise on a standard baking sheet, four to six units per sheet.

8. In the retail shop, it is customary to cut each of these baked units in half and display the halves with the cut edges toward the customer.

Cheese Filling for Strudel

Ingredients	U.S.			Metric	Cheese at 100% %
Baker's cheese	2 lb	8	oz	1200 g	100
Butter		10	oz	300 g	25
Sugar		12	oz	360 g	30
Cake flour		3	oz	90 g	7.5
Salt		0.5	oz	15 g	1.25
Vanilla		0.5	oz	15 g	1.25
Grated lemon zest		0.25	oz (1 tbsp)	8 g	0.6
Eggs		6	oz	180 g	15
Sour cream		8	oz	240 g	20
Raisins		8	oz	240 g	20
Yield:	5 lb	8	oz	2648 g	220

Enough for 4 strudels (16 inches/41 cm long each) or one 5–foot (1.6 m) strudel using homemade dough.

Procedure:

1. Combine the cheese and butter (at room temperature) and blend at low speed with the paddle attachment until smooth.

2. Add the sugar, flour, salt, vanilla, and lemon zest. Blend at low speed until just smooth and completely mixed. Do not cream too much air into the mixture or it will expand when baked and may burst the pastry.

3. Add the eggs a little at a time, and mix in at low speed. Mix in the milk.

4. Fold in the raisins.

Variation

Cream Cheese Filling for Strudel:

Use 3 lb (1440 g) cream cheese instead of the baker's cheese. Omit the butter. Mix as in basic recipe.

Note: Although the quantities of the other ingredients stay the same, the percentages change because the quantity of cheese is different, as follows:

Cream cheese	3 lb			1440 g	100
Sugar		12	oz	360 g	25
Cake flour		3	oz	90 g	6
Salt		0.5	oz	15 g	1
Vanilla		0.5	oz	15 g	1
Lemon zest		0.25	oz	8 g	0.5
Eggs		6	oz	180 g	12.5
Sour cream		8	oz	240 g	17
Raisins		8	oz	240 g	17

Apple Filling for Strudel

Yield: 4 lb (2000 g)

Ingredients	U.S.		Metric	Apples at 100% %
Apples, peeled and cored (see note)	3 lb		1500 g	100
Lemon juice	1	oz	30 g	2
Sugar	8	oz	250 g	17
Sugar	8	oz	250 g	17
Raisins	4	oz	125 g	8
Walnuts, chopped	4	oz	125 g	8
Cake crumbs	2	oz	60 g	4
Grated lemon zest	0.25	oz	8 g	0.5
Cinnamon	0.25	oz	8 g	0.5

Note: Canned sliced apples may be used. Weigh after draining. Omit the lemon juice and the first quantity of sugar. Omit steps 1 and 2 in the procedure

Procedure:

1.   Cut the apples into thin slices or into small dice. Mix with the lemon juice and the first quantity of sugar. Let stand for 30 minutes while preparing the pastry.

2.   Drain the apples well. The sugar will have drawn out juice that would otherwise run out of the strudel and make the bottom soggy.

3.   Mix the apples with the remaining ingredients.

Baklava

Yield: one 15 × 10-inch (38 × 25-cm) pan,
about 48 pieces

Ingredients	U.S.		Metric	
Pastry:				
Phyllo leaves	1 lb		500	g
Melted butter, or mixture of butter and oil	12	oz	375	g
Walnuts, chopped	1 lb		500	g
Sugar	2	oz	60	g
Cinnamon	0.06 oz (1 tsp)		2	g
Cloves, ground	0.04 oz (½ tsp)		0.5	g
Syrup				
Sugar:	1 lb		500	g
Water	12	oz	375	g
Honey	6	oz	190	g
Lemon peel	2 strips		2 strips	
Lemon juice	1	oz	30	g
Cinnamon stick	1		1	

Procedure:

1. Unfold the phyllo leaves and keep them covered.
2. Mix together the nuts, sugar, cinnamon, and cloves.
3. Butter the bottom and sides of a 15 × 10-inch (38 × 25-cm) baking pan.
4. Lay one of the phyllo sheets in the bottom of the pan, letting the ends of the dough fold upward at the sides of the pan. Brush the dough with butter.
5. Repeat until there are 10 buttered leaves in the pan.
6. Place one-third of the nut mixture in the pan in an even layer.
7. Put in two more phyllo leaves, buttering each one as it is placed in the pan.
8. Put in another third of the nuts, another two buttered phyllo leaves, and the rest of the nuts.
9. Finally, lay each of the remaining leaves in the pan and butter each leaf, including the top one.
10. There will be some excess dough sticking up around the edges of the pan. With a sharp knife, trim it off so that it is level with the top of the pastry.
11. Chill the pastry to congeal the butter. This will make cutting easier.
12. Cut the pastry into four rows of six squares, each about 2½ inches (6 cm) on a side. Then cut the squares diagonally to make triangles. (A traditional method is to cut baklava into diamond shapes, but this always leaves some small, odd-shaped pieces at the ends.)
13. Bake at 350° F (175° C) for 50–60 minutes, until golden brown.
14. While the baklava is baking, combine the syrup ingredients and bring to a boil. Simmer for 10 minutes, then cool to lukewarm. Remove the cinnamon stick and lemon peel. Skim off foam, if any.
15. When the pastry is baked, pour the warm syrup carefully over the hot baklava.
16. Let the baklava stand overnight so that the syrup can be absorbed.

BAKED MERINGUES

To refer to baked meringues as pastries may seem odd, since the term "pastry" usually refers to desserts made from flour goods such as puff pastry, short dough, or éclair paste. However, meringue that is bagged out into various shapes and baked until crisp is used in many of the same ways as flour pastry. It can be filled or iced with a variety of creams, icings, and fruits to make an interesting variety of attractive desserts.

Basic meringue mixtures are covered in Chapter 7, along with other creams, icings, and toppings. Common meringue and Swiss meringue are the types generally used to make crisp, baked shells. The basic procedure for baking meringue is presented in this section, followed by instructions for individual desserts. Also, a special meringue mixture containing nuts is introduced. This flavorful mixture is usually made into round, crisp layers that are used somewhat like cake layers. They may be filled and iced with buttercream, chocolate mousse, whipped cream, or similar light icings and creams.

Procedure for Making Crisp Baked Meringues

1. Following the recipes on pp. 117–118, prepare common meringue, chocolate meringue, or Swiss meringue.

2. Using a pastry bag, form the meringue into the desired shapes on baking sheets lined with silicone paper. Specific shapes are indicated in the procedures for specific desserts.

3. Bake at 200 to 225° F (100° C) until crisp but not browned. This will take 1 to 3 hours, depending on size.

4. Cool the meringues, then remove them from the parchment. Be careful, because they may be very fragile.

Procedures for Making Meringue Desserts

Meringue Chantilly

1. Shape the meringue into round mounds about 2 inches (5 cm) in diameter, using a ¾-inch (2-cm) plain tube in the pastry bag. Bake.

2. Optional step to allow more room for cream filling: When the shells are firm enough to handle but not completely crisp, remove them from the baking sheet; with your thumb, press a hollow in the base (the flat side). Return them to the oven to finish baking.

3. Cool shells and store them in a dry place until needed.

4. Just before serving, sandwich two shells together with vanilla-flavored whipped cream. Place the filled shells on their sides in paper cases.

5. Using a pastry bag with a star tube, decorate with additional whipped cream in the space between the shells.

6. If desired, the cream may be decorated with nuts or candied fruit.

Meringue Glacée

1. Prepare meringue shells as for meringue Chantilly.

2. Sandwich two shells together with ice cream instead of whipped cream.

3. Decorate with whipped cream.

Chocolate Heads

1. Using either plain meringue or chocolate meringue, make shells as for meringue Chantilly.

2. Sandwich two shells together with chocolate buttercream.

3. Refrigerate shells until firm.

4. Spread each meringue sandwich with more chocolate buttercream so that it is completely covered.

5. Roll in grated chocolate or chocolate sprinkles.

9. Fill the shells with sweetened whipped cream and fruit (such as strawberries or sliced peaches). Cubes of sponge cake moistened with a flavored syrup may be used in addition to fruit.

10. Using a pastry bag, decorate the top with more whipped cream. Also, arrange pieces of fresh or candied fruit in an attractive pattern on the top.

Vacherin

1. For large vacherin, draw 8-inch (20-cm) or 9-inch (23-cm) circles on sheets of parchment, using a cake pan as a guide. For individual vacherins, draw 2½-inch (6–7 cm) circles.

2. Using a pastry bag with a plain tube, make one meringue base for each vacherin. Do this by making a spiral starting in the center of a circle and continuing until the circle is filled in with a layer of meringue about ½ inch (12 mm) thick.

3. For the sides of the vacherin, make rings of meringue the same size as the bases. For each large vacherin, you will need four or five rings. For each individual vacherin, make two rings.

4. Bake as in the basic procedure.

5. Carefully remove the baked meringues from the parchment. Be especially careful with the rings, since they are very fragile.

6. Stack the rings on the bases, using additional unbaked meringue to stick the pieces together.

7. If the rings are neatly and uniformly made, you may leave the shell as is. If the sides are not attractive, you may spread the sides of the shell smoothly with fresh meringue, or you may later ice the sides of the finished shell with buttercream.

8. Bake the shells again to dry out the fresh meringue. Cool.

Meringue Mushrooms

These are used primarily for decorating Bûche de Noël (Christmas cake roll), p. 241.

1. Using a pastry bag with a small, plain tube, make small mounds of meringue in the shapes of mushroom caps. Make smaller, pointed mounds to use as stems.

2. If desired, sprinkle very lightly with cocoa.

3. Bake as in the basic procedure.

4. When baked, make a small hole in the bottoms of the caps. Attach the stems with meringue or royal icing.

Meringue Cream Cakes

1. For each cake, you will need two small 2½-inch (6 to 7-cm) japonaise meringues and about 2 oz (60 g) buttercream in any flavor.

2. Spread one japonaise circle with a thin layer of buttercream. Top with a second circle.

3. Ice the top and sides smoothly.

4. If desired, iced cakes may be coated with chopped nuts, grated chocolate, toasted coconut, etc.

Japonaise Meringues

Ingredients	U.S.	Egg whites at 100% Metric	%
Egg whites	1 lb	500 g	100
Sugar, fine granulated	1 lb	500 g	100
Confectioners' sugar, sifted	1 lb	500 g	100
Blanched hazelnuts or almonds, chopped very fine	1 lb	500 g	100
Yield:	4 lb	2000 g	400

Procedure:

1. Prepare baking sheets by lining them with silicone paper. Draw circles of the desired size on the paper, using cake pans or other round objects as guides.

2. With the whip attachment, beat the egg whites at medium speed until they form soft peaks.

3. Add the granulated sugar, a little at a time, with the machine running. Whip until the meringue forms stiff peaks.

4. Stop the machine. Mix together the confectioners' sugar and nuts. Fold this mixture into the meringue.

5. Using a pastry bag with a ½-inch (12-mm) plain tube, fill in the circles on the baking sheets by making spirals starting in the center of each circle. Each circle should be filled with a layer of meringue about ½ inch (12 mm) thick.

6. Bake at 250° F (120°C) until meringue is crisp and very lightly browned, about 1½ to 2 hours.

7. Use in place of or in addition to cake layers in assembling cakes and gateaux (Chapter 11).

TERMS FOR REVIEW

flaky pie dough
mealy pie dough
crumb crust
short dough
tart
Linzertorte
puff pastry
four-fold
blitz puff pastry
napoleon
éclair paste
pâte à choux
éclair
strudel dough
strudel
phyllo dough
baked meringue
japonaise
meringue glacée

QUESTIONS FOR DISCUSSION

1. Discuss the various factors that affect tenderness, toughness, and flakiness in pie dough. Why should emulsifier shortening not be used for pie dough?

2. What are some advantages and disadvantages of using butter in pie dough?

3. What would happen to a flaky pie dough if you mixed it too long before adding the water? After adding the water?

4. Describe the difference between mealy pie dough and flaky pie dough.

5. What is the purpose of docking tart shells before they are baked?

6. List four or five ingredients besides fruit and sugar that are sometimes used for filling baked fruit tarts.

7. Compare the mixing methods for puff pastry dough and blitz puff dough. Compare blitz puff dough and flaky pie dough.

8. What might happen to patty shells during baking, if the puff dough is not relaxed before cutting and baking? What might happen to them if they are cut out of soft dough with a dull cutter?

9. Why is it important to bake cream puffs and éclairs thoroughly and to cool them slowly?

10. What precautions must you take when handling frozen commercial phyllo/strudel dough?

11. In order to bake meringue shells until crisp, should you use a hot, moderate, or cool oven? Why?

CHAPTER 9

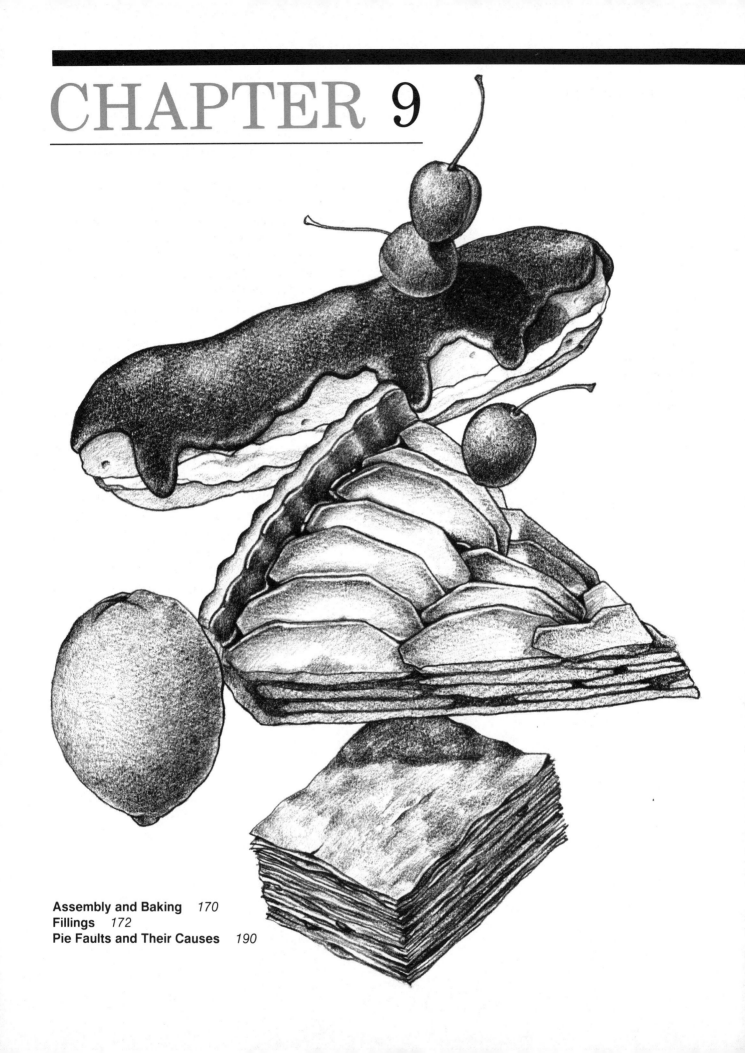

PIES

After studying this chapter, you should be able to:

1. Roll pie doughs and line pie pans.
2. Fill, assemble, and bake single-crust pies, double-crust pies, and lattice-topped pies.
3. Form and bake pie shells for unbaked pies.
4. Prepare fruit fillings.
5. Prepare soft or custard-type pie fillings.
6. Prepare cream fillings.
7. Prepare chiffon fillings.

On the early American frontier, it was not uncommon for the pioneer housewife to bake twenty-one pies each week — one for every meal. Pies were so important to the settlers that in winter, when fruits were unavailable, cooks would bake dessert pies out of whatever materials were available, such as potatoes, vinegar, and soda crackers.

Few of us today eat pie at every meal. Nevertheless, pies are still a favorite American dessert. Most customers will order and pay a higher price for a piece of chocolate cream pie than for chocolate pudding, even if the pie filling is the same as the pudding, and even if they leave the crust uneaten.

In the previous chapter, we discussed the mixing of various types of pie doughs, along with other pastries. In this chapter, we will study the preparation of pie fillings and the procedures for assembling and baking pies.

ASSEMBLY AND BAKING

Pies may be classified into two groups, based on method of assembling and baking.

Baked Pies

Raw pie shells are filled and then baked. *Fruit pies* contain fruit fillings and usually have a top crust. *Soft pies* are those with custard-type fillings, that is, liquid fillings that become firm when their egg content coagulates. They are usually baked as single-crust pies.

Unbaked Pies

Prebaked pie shells are filled with a prepared filling, chilled, and served when the filling is firm enough to slice. *Cream pies* are made with pudding or boiled custard-type fillings. *Chiffon pies* are made with fillings that are lightened by the addition of beaten egg whites and/or whipped cream. Gelatin or starch gives them their firm consistency.

The two main components of pies are the dough or pastry and the filling. The production of these two components are two quite separate and distinct operations. Once the pastry and fillings are made, rolling the dough and assembling and baking the pies can proceed rapidly.

Because these operations are separate and involve different kinds of problems and techniques, it is helpful to concentrate on them one at a time. The preparation of pie dough is discussed in the chapter on pastry, p. 138–140. This chapter begins with procedures for making pie pastry into pie shells and for filling and baking pies, followed by a discussion of pie fillings.

Procedure for Rolling Pie Dough and Lining Pans

1. *Select the best doughs for each purpose:*

   Mealy pie doughs are used whenever soaking is a problem, so they are mainly used for bottom crusts, especially bottom crusts for soft pie fillings such as custard and pumpkin. This is because mealy doughs resist soaking better than flaky dough does.

   Flaky pie doughs are best for top crusts. They can also be used for prebaked pie shells if the shells are filled with cooled filling just before serving. However, if the prebaked shells are filled with hot filling, it is safer to use mealy dough.

2. *Scale the dough:*

   8 oz (225 g) for 9-inch bottom crusts

   6 oz (170 g) for 9-inch top crusts

   6 oz (170 g) for 8-inch bottom crusts

   5 oz (140 g) for 8-inch top crusts

   Experienced bakers are able to use less dough when rolling out crusts, because they roll the dough to a perfect circle of the right size and need to trim away very little excess dough.

3. *Dust the bench and rolling pin lightly with flour.*

   Too much dusting flour toughens the dough, so use no more than needed to prevent sticking.

   Instead of rolling the dough directly on the bench, you may roll it out on flour-dusted canvas. Rolling on canvas does not require as much dusting flour.

4. *Roll out the dough.*

   Flatten the dough lightly and roll it out to a *uniform* ⅛ inch (3 mm) thickness. Use even strokes and roll from the center outward in all directions. Lift the dough frequently to make sure that it is not sticking. Finished dough should be a nearly perfect circle.

5. *Place the dough in pan.*

   To lift the dough without breaking it, roll it lightly around the rolling pin. A second method is to fold the dough in half, place the folded dough into the pan with the fold in the center, and unfold the dough.

   Allow the dough to drop into the pans; press it into the corners without stretching the dough. Stretched dough will shrink during baking.

   There should be no air bubbles between the dough and the pan.

6. For single-crust pies, flute or crimp the edges, if desired, and trim off excess dough. For double-crust pies, fill with cold filling, brush the edge of the crust with water, and top with the second crust, as explained in the procedure for preparing baked pies (p. 171). Seal edges; crimp or flute, if desired. Trim off excess dough.

   The simplest way to trim excess dough is to rotate the pie tin between the palms of the hands, while pressing with the palms against the edge of the rim. This pinches off the excess dough flush with the rim.

7. Some bakers feel that fluted edges add to the appearance of the product. Others feel that fluting takes too much time and only produces a rim of

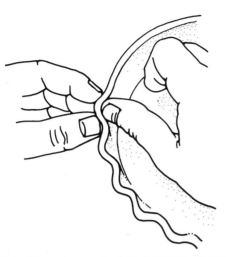

FIGURE 9.1 **To make a raised, fluted edge on a shell for soft-filled pies, leave an excess of dough on the top rim. Pinch this dough into a ridge, using the thumb and forefinger of one hand and the thumb or forefinger of the other. Pinching at 1-inch (2.5-cm) intervals makes a fluted edge.**

heavy dough that most customers leave on their plates. Follow your instructor's directions on this procedure. Whether you flute the edges or not, be sure that double-crust pies are well sealed. Many bakers like to make a raised, fluted rim of dough on pie shells for soft-filled pies such as custard or pumpkin. This raised edge enables them to fill the shell quite full, while reducing the chance of spill-over. See Figure 9.1 for the technique.

Instead of being given a top crust, fruit pies are sometimes topped with streusel (p. 61) or with a lattice crust (see the following procedure). Streusel is especially good on apple pies. Lattice crusts are best for pies with attractive, colorful fruit, such as cherry or blueberry.

Procedure for Making a Lattice Top Crust

1. Roll out fresh pie dough (not scraps) ⅛ inch (3 mm) thick.

2. Cut long strips about ⅜ inch (1 cm) wide and long enough to cross the center of the pie.

3. Egg wash the strips and the rim of the filled pie.

4. Place the strips across the pie about 1 inch (2.5 cm) apart. Be sure they are parallel and evenly spaced. Seal them well onto the rim of the pie shell and trim off excess.

5. Place additional strips across the pie at an angle to the first. They may be at a 45-degree angle to make a diamond pattern, or at a 90-degree angle to make a checkerboard pattern. Seal and trim excess.

   Note: Instead of laying the strips across each other, you may interweave them, but this is usually too time-consuming for a bakeshop and is generally done only in home kitchens.

Procedure for Preparing Baked Pies

Note: For pies without a top crust, omit steps 3 to 7.

1. Line pie pans with pie dough as in the basic procedure.

2. Fill with *cooled* fillings. See Table 9.1 for scaling instructions. Do not drop filling on the rims of the pie shells; this will make it harder to seal the rims to the top crusts, and leaking may result during baking.

   To avoid spilling custard fillings, place the empty shells on the racks in the ovens, then pour in the filling.

3. Roll out dough for the top crusts.

4. Cut perforations in the top crusts to allow steam to escape during baking.

5. Moisten the rim of the bottom crusts with water or egg wash to help seal them to the top crusts.

6. Fit the top crusts in place. Seal the edges together firmly and trim excess dough. The rims may be fluted or crimped if desired.

7. Brush tops with desired wash: milk, cream, egg wash, or melted butter. Sprinkle lightly with granulated sugar, if desired.

   Egg-washed tops will have a shiny appearance when baked. Tops brushed with fat, milk, or cream will not be shiny but will have a home-baked look.

8. Place pies on the lower level of an oven preheated to 425 to 450° F (210 to 220° C). The high initial heat helps set the bottom crust to avoid soaking. Fruit pies are baked at this high heat until done. For custard pies, reduce heat after 10 minutes to 325 to 350° F (165 to 175° C) to avoid overcooking and curdling the custard. Custard pies include all those containing large quantities of egg, such as pumpkin pie and pecan pie.

TABLE 9.1 **Scaling Instructions for Baked Pies**

	U.S.		Metric	
Pie size	Weight of filling	Pie size		Weight of filling
8 inch	26–30 oz	20 cm		750–850 g
9 inch	32–40 oz	23 cm		900–1150 g
10 inch	40–50 oz	25 cm		1150–1400 g

Note: Weights are guidelines only. Exact weights may vary, depending on the filling and the depth of the pans.

The Soggy Bottom

Underbaked bottom crusts or crusts that have soaked up moisture from the filling are common faults in pies. Soggy bottoms can be avoided in several ways:

1. Use mealy dough for bottom crusts. Mealy dough absorbs less liquid than flaky dough does.

2. Use high bottom heat, at least at the beginning of baking, to set the crust quickly. Bake the pies at the bottom of the oven.

3. Do not add hot fillings to unbaked crusts.

4. For fruit pies, line the bottom of the pie shell with a thin layer of cake crumbs before pouring in the filling. This helps absorb some juice that might otherwise soak into the crust.

5. Use dark metal pie tins, which absorb heat. (Since so many bakers use disposable aluminum pans, other methods must be relied on.)

Procedure for Preparing Unbaked Pies

1. Line pie pans with pie dough as in the basic procedure.

2. Dock the crust well with a fork to prevent blistering of the crust.

3. Place another pan inside the first one, so that the dough is between two pans.

4. Place the pans upside-down in a preheated oven at 450° F (230° C). Baking upside-down helps keep the dough from shrinking down into the pan.

   Some bakers like to chill the crusts before baking to relax the gluten and help reduce shrinkage.

5. Bake at 450° F (230° C) for 10 to 15 minutes. One pan may be removed during the last part of baking so that the crust can brown.

6. Cool the baked crust completely.

7. Fill with cream filling or chiffon filling. Fill as close as possible to service time to prevent soaking the crust.

8. Chill the pie until it is set enough to slice.

9. Most cream pies and chiffon pies are especially good topped with whipped cream. Some cream pies, especially lemon, are popular when topped with meringue and browned (procedure follows).

Procedure for Making Meringue Pie Topping

1. Make common meringue or Swiss meringue, using 1 pound of sugar per pound of egg whites. Whip until just stiff. See p. 117 for procedure.

2. Spread a generous amount of meringue on each pie. Mound it slightly and be sure to attach it to the edge of the crust all around. If this is not done, the meringue may slide around on the finished pie. Leave the meringue in ripples or peaks.

3. Bake at 400° F (200° C) until the surface is attractively browned. Do not use higher temperatures, since this will cause the surface of the meringue to shrink and toughen.

4. Remove from the oven and cool.

FILLINGS

Most pie fillings require thickeners of one sort or another. The two most important thickeners for pies are starches and eggs.

Starches for Fillings

Many kinds of pie fillings, especially fruit fillings and cream fillings, depend on starch for their thickness. Some egg-thickened fillings, such as pumpkin, also sometimes contain starch. The starch acts as a stabilizer and may also reduce the cost by allowing for a lower egg content.

Cornstarch is used for cream pies because it sets up into a firm gel that holds its shape when sliced. It may also be used for fruit pies.

Waxy maize or *modified starches* are best for fruit pies because they are very clear when set and make a soft paste rather than a firm gel. Waxy maize should be used for pies that are to be frozen, since this starch is not broken down by freezing.

Flour, tapioca, potato starch, rice starch, and other starches are used less frequently for fillings. Flour has less thickening power than other starches and makes fruit fillings cloudy.

Instant or *pregelatinized starch* needs no cooking because it has already been cooked. When used with certain fruit fillings, it eliminates the need to cook the filling before making up the pie. It loses this advantage, however, if the filling is made of raw fruit that must be cooked anyway. In the case of soft fillings such as pumpkin, instant starch can be used to eliminate a problem that often occurs with cornstarch: Cornstarch tends to settle out before gelatinizing. This creates a dense, starchy layer on the bottom and improperly thickened filling on top. Instant starches differ in thickening power, so follow the manufacturer's recommendations.

Cooking Starches

To avoid lumping, starches must be mixed with a cold liquid or with sugar before being added to a hot liquid.

Sugar and *strong acids,* such as lemon juice, reduce the thickening power of starch. When possible, all or part of the sugar and strong acids should be added *after the starch has thickened.*

Fruit Fillings

Fruit fillings consist of solid fruit pieces bound together by a gel. The gel consists of fruit juice, water, sugar, spices, and a starch thickener. As we have explained, modified starch such as waxy maize is the preferred thickener for fruit fillings, because it makes a clear, not cloudy, gel.

Of course, other starches, such as cornstarch, tapioca, or potato starch, may also be used. Cornstarch is frequently used in food service operations, in which baking is only part of the food preparation, making it inconvenient to have on hand all the specialty ingredients found in a bakery.

The functions of the gel are to bind the solid fruit pieces together, to help carry the flavors of the spices and the sweetness of the sugar, and to improve appearance by giving a shine or gloss to the fruit. However, the solid fruit is the most important part of the filling. To have a good-quality pie filling, you should have 2 to 3 pounds of drained fruit for each pound of liquid (juice plus water).

The two basic methods for making pie fillings are the *cooked juice method* and the *cooked fruit method.* In the cooked juice method, the gel is made separately by cooking fruit juice, water, and sugar with a starch. The gel is then mixed with the fruit. In the cooked fruit method, the fruit, water, and juices (if any) are all cooked together and then thickened with a starch.

Fruits for Pie Fillings

Fresh fruits are excellent in pies if they are at their seasonal peak. Fresh apples are used extensively for high-quality pies. But the quality of fresh fruits can vary considerably, and many fruits require a lot of labor.

Frozen fruits are widely used for pies because they are consistent in quality and readily available. Frozen fruits for quantity use are commonly packed with sugar in 30-pound tins. They may be defrosted in the refrigerator for 2 to 3 days, or in a water bath. A third method of thawing is to thaw the fruit just enough to free it from its container, add the water to be used in making it into a pie filling, and heat it to 185 to 195° F (85 to 90° C). Then drain the juice well and make the filling. Whatever method you use, be sure the fruit is completely thawed before preparing the filling. If it is partially frozen, you will not be able to drain the juice properly to make the gel. The frozen, undrained juice will then water down the filling later.

Some frozen fruits, especially berries, are packed without sugar. Naturally, the sugar content of any fruit must be taken into account when you are adding sugar to pie fillings.

Canned fruits, are packed in four basic styles: solid pack, heavy pack, water pack, and syrup pack. *Solid pack* means that no water is added, although you will be able to drain off a small quantity of juice. *Heavy pack* means that only a small quantity of water or juice is added. *Water pack* fruits are canned with the water that was used to process them. Sour cherries are usually packed this way. *Syrup pack* fruits are packed in a sugar syrup, which may be light, medium, heavy, or extra heavy. Heavy syrup means that there is more sugar in the syrup. In general, fruits packed in heavy syrup are firmer and less broken than fruits in light syrup.

With water-pack and syrup-pack fruits, it is important to know the *drained weight* (the weight of the solid fruit without the juice.) This information may be indicated on the label, or it is available from the processor.

The *net weight* is the weight of the total contents, including juice or syrup.

If the drained weight of a fruit is very low, you may need to add extra drained fruit to a batch of filling in order to get a good ratio of fruit to gel.

Dried fruits must be rehydrated by soaking and usually simmering before they are made into pie fillings.

Fruits must have sufficient acid (tartness) to make flavorful fillings. If they lack natural acid, you may need to add some lemon, orange, or pineapple juice to supply the acid.

Cooked Juice Method

The advantage of this method is that only the juice is cooked. The fruit retains better shape and flavor because it is subjected to less heat and handling. This method is used when the fruit requires little or no cooking before filling the pie. Most canned and frozen fruits are prepared this way. Fresh berries can also be prepared with this method: Part of the berries are cooked or puréed to provide juice, and the remaining berries are then mixed with the finished gel.

Procedure

1. Drain the juice from the fruit.
2. Measure the juice and, if necessary, add water or other fruit juice to bring to the desired volume.
3. Bring the juice to a boil.
4. Dissolve the starch in cold water and stir it into the boiling juice. Return to a boil and cook until clear and thickened.
5. Add sugar, salt, and flavorings. Stir until dissolved.
6. Pour the thickened juice over the drained fruit and mix gently. Be careful not to break or mash the fruit.
7. Cool.

Cooked Fruit Method

This method is used when the fruit requires cooking or when there is not enough liquid for the cooked juice method. Most fresh fruits (except berries) are prepared this way, as are dried fruits such as raisins and dried apricots. Canned fruits should not be prepared by this method because they have already been cooked and are likely to break up or turn to mush.

Procedure

1. Bring the fruit and juice or water to a boil. Some sugar may be added to the fruit to draw out juices.
2. Dissolve the starch in cold water and stir into the fruit. Return to a boil and cook until clear and thickened. Stir while cooking.
3. Add sugar, salt, flavorings, and other ingredients. Stir until dissolved.
4. Cool as quickly as possible.

Old-fashioned Method

This method is best suited for homemade pies made with fresh apples or peaches. It is not as widely used in food service operations as the other methods because the thickening of the juice is more difficult to control.

Procedure

1. Mix the starch and spices with the sugar until uniformly blended.
2. Mix the fruit with the sugar mixture.
3. Fill the unbaked pie shells with the fruit.
4. Place lumps of butter on top of the filling.
5. Cover with top crust or streusel and bake.

Apple Pie Filling (Canned Fruit)

Yield: About 9½ lb (4500 g)
Five 8-inch (20-cm) pies
Four 9-inch (23-cm) pies
Three 10-inch (25-cm) pies

Ingredients	U.S.			Metric

Canned apples,
  solid pack or heavy pack
  (one No. 10 can)
	6 lb	8	oz	3000 g

Drained juice plus water	1 pt	8	fl. oz	750 ml
Cold water		8	fl. oz	250 ml
Cornstarch OR		3	oz	90 g
Modified starch (waxy maize)		2.5	oz	75 g
Sugar	1 lb	4	oz	570 g
Salt		0.25	oz	7 g
Cinnamon		0.25	oz (4¼ tsp)	7 g
Nutmeg		0.08	oz (1 tsp)	2 g
Butter		3	oz	90 g

Procedure (Cooked Juice Method)

1. Drain the apples and save the juice. Add enough water to the juice to measure 1½ pt (750 ml).

2. Mix the cold water and starch.

3. Bring the juice mixture to a boil. Stir in the starch mixture and return to a boil.

4. Add the remaining ingredients, except the drained apples. Simmer until the sugar is dissolved.

5. Pour the syrup over the apples and mix gently. Cool completely.

6. Fill the pie shells. Bake at 425° F (220° C) about 30–40 minutes.

Variations

Dutch Apple Pie Filling:

Simmer 8 oz (250 g) raisins in water. Drain and add to apple pie filling.

Cherry Pie Filling:

Use one No. 10 can sour cherries instead of apples, and make the following ingredient adjustments:

Increase starch to 4 oz (125 g) cornstarch *or* 3 oz (90 g) waxy maize.

Increase sugar to 1 lb 12 oz (825 g).

Add 1.5 oz (45 ml) lemon juice in step 4.

Omit cinnamon and nutmeg. Add almond extract to taste (optional).

If desired, color with 2 to 3 drops red coloring.

Apple Pie Filling (Canned Fruit) Variations *(Continued)*

Peach Pie Filling:

Use one No. 10 can sliced peaches, preferably solid or heavy pack, instead of apples. Increase liquid in step 1 to 1 qt (1 l). Omit cinnamon and nutmeg.

Pineapple Pie Filling:

Use one No. 10 can crushed pineapple instead of apples. Gently press the fruit in a sieve to squeeze out the juice. Make the following ingredient adjustments:

Increase the liquid in step 1 to 1 qt (1 l).

Increase the starch to 4 oz (125 g) cornstarch or 3 oz (90 g) waxy maize.

Use 1 lb 8 oz (750 g) sugar and 8 oz (250 g) corn syrup.

Omit the cinnamon and nutmeg.

If desired, color with 2 to 3 drops yellow coloring.

Blueberry Pie Filling (Frozen Fruit)
Yield: About 15 lb (6750 g)
    Eight 8-inch (20-cm) pies
    Six 9-inch (23-cm) pies
    Five 10-inch (25-cm) pies

Ingredients	U.S.			Metric
Blueberries, frozen,				
unsweetened	10 lb			4500 g
Drained juice plus				
water	1 pt	8	oz	750 ml
Sugar		12	oz	350 g
Cold water		12	oz	375 ml
Cornstarch		6	oz	175 g
OR				
Modified starch				
(waxy maize)		4.5	oz	135 g
Sugar	1 lb	12	oz	825 g
Salt		0.5	oz	15 g
Cinnamon		0.25	oz (4¼ tsp)	7 g
Lemon juice		3	oz	90 ml

Procedure (Cooked Juice Method):

1. Thaw the berries in their unopened original container.

2. Drain the berries. Add enough water to the juice to measure 1½ pt (750 ml). Add the first quantity of sugar.

3. Mix the cold water and the starch.

4. Bring the juice mixture to a boil. Stir in the starch mixture. Return to a boil to thicken.

5. Add the remaining ingredients, except the drained berries. Stir over heat until the sugar is dissolved.

6. Pour the syrup over the drained berries. Mix gently. Cool completely.

7. Fill pie shells. Bake at 425° F (220° C) about 30 minutes.

Variations

Apple Pie Filling:

Use 10 lb (4.5 kg) frozen apples instead of blueberries. Make the following ingredient adjustments:

Reduce the starch to 3 oz (90 g) cornstarch or 2.5 oz (75 g) waxy maize.

Reduce the second quantity of sugar to 1 lb (450 g).

Add 1 tsp (2 g) nutmeg and 6 oz (175 g) butter in step 5.

Cherry Pie Filling:

Use 10 lb (4.5 kg) frozen cherries instead of blueberries. Make the following ingredient adjustments:

Increase the liquid in step 2 to 1 qt (1 l).

Reduce the starch to 5 oz (150 g) cornstarch or 4 oz (120 g) waxy maize.

Reduce the second quantity of sugar to 1 lb 4 oz (570 g).

Omit the cinnamon.

Reduce the lemon juice to 1.5 oz (45 ml).

Raisin Pie Filling

Yield: About 10½ lb (4.8 kg)
        Six 8-inch (20-cm) pies
        Five 9-inch (23-cm) pies
        Four 10-inch (25-cm) pies

Ingredients	U.S.		Metric
Raisins	4 lb		1800 g
Water	4 pt		2000 ml
Cold water	8	oz	250 ml
Cornstarch	2.5	oz	75 g
OR			
Modified starch			
(waxy maize)	2	oz	60 g
Sugar	1 lb 4	oz	570 g
Salt	0.33	oz (2 tsp)	10 g
Lemon juice	3	oz	90 ml
Grated lemon zest	0.1	oz (1 tbsp)	3 g
Cinnamon	0.06	oz (1 tsp)	2 g
Butter	3	oz	90 g

Procedure (Cooked Fruit Method):

1. Combine the raisins and water in a saucepan. Simmer 5 minutes.

2. Mix the water and starch. Stir into the raisins and simmer until thickened.

3. Add the remaining ingredients. Stir until the sugar is dissolved and the mixture is uniform.

4. Cool thoroughly.

5. Fill the pie shells. Bake at 425° F (220° C) about 30–40 minutes.

Rhubarb Pie Filling

Yield: About 11 lb (5 kg)

       Six 8-inch (20-cm) pies

       Five 9-inch (23-cm) pies

       Four 10-inch (25-cm) pies

Ingredients	U.S.		Metric
Fresh rhubarb	7 lb		3200 g
Water	1 pt		500 ml
Sugar	1 lb		450 g
Cold water	8	fl oz	250 ml
Cornstarch	5	oz	150 g
OR			
Modified starch			
(waxy maize)	4	oz	120 g
Sugar	1 lb		450 g
Salt	0.33 oz (2 tsp)		10 g
Butter	2	oz	60 g

Procedure (Cooked Fruit Method):

1. Cut the rhubarb into 1-inch (2.5 cm) pieces.

2. In a saucepan or kettle, combine the rhubarb and the first quantities of water and sugar. Bring to a boil and simmer 2 minutes.

3. Mix the second quantity of water and the starch. Stir into the rhubarb and boil until thick and clear. The rhubarb should be only partly cooked.

4. Remove from heat. Add the remaining ingredients. Stir gently until the sugar is dissolved and the butter is melted.

5. Cool completely.

6. Fill the pie shells. Bake at 425° F (220° C) about 30–40 minutes.

Variation

Fresh Apple Pie Filling:

Use 7 lb (3.2 kg) peeled, sliced fresh apples instead of rhubarb. Flavor with 1 tbsp (5 g) cinnamon, 1 tsp (2 g) nutmeg, and 1–2 oz (30–60 ml) lemon juice.

Fresh Strawberry Pie Filling

Yield: About 12 lb (5.5 kg)
       Six 8-inch (20-cm) pies
       Five 9-inch (23-cm) pies
       Four 10-inch (25-cm) pies

Ingredients	U.S.		Metric
Fresh whole strawberries	9 lb		4100 g
Cold water	1 pt		500 ml
Sugar	1 lb 12	oz	800 g
Cornstarch	4	oz	120 g
OR			
Modified starch (waxy maize)	3	oz	90 g
Salt	0.17 oz (1 tsp)		5 g
Lemon juice	2	oz	60 ml

Procedure (Cooked Juice Method):

1. Hull, wash, and drain the berries. Set aside 7 lb (3.2 kg) of the berries. These may be left whole if small, or cut in halves or quarters if large.

2. Mash or purée the remaining 2 lb (900 g) of the berries. Mix with the water. (If a clear filling is desired, this mixture may be strained.)

3. Mix together the sugar, starch, and salt. Stir into the berry-and-water mixture until no lumps remain.

4. Bring to a boil, stirring constantly. Cook until thickened.

5. Remove from the heat and stir in the lemon juice.

6. Cool to room temperature but do not chill.

7. Stir to eliminate lumps. Fold in the reserved berries.

8. Fill baked pie shells and chill (do not bake).

Old-Fashioned Apple Pie Filling

Yield: About 11 lb (5 kg)

        Six 8-inch (20-cm) pies

        Five 9-inch (23-cm) pies

        Four 10-inch (25-cm) pies

Ingredients	U.S.		Metric
Fresh peeled, sliced apples	9 lb		4100 g
Lemon juice	2	oz	60 ml
Sugar	2 lb		900 g
Cornstarch	3	oz	90 g
Salt	0.25	oz	7 g
Cinnamon	0.25	oz	7 g
Nutmeg	0.08	oz (1 tsp)	2 g
Butter	3	oz	90 g

Procedure (Old-Fashioned Method):

1. Select firm, tart apples. Scale *after* peeling and coring.

2. Combine the apple slices and lemon juice in a large mixing bowl. Toss to coat apples with the juice.

3. Mix together with sugar, starch, salt, and spices. Add to the apples and toss gently until well mixed.

4. Fill the pie shells. Dot the tops with pieces of butter before covering with top crusts. Bake at 400° F (200° C) about 45 minutes.

Custard or Soft Fillings

Custard, pumpkin, pecan, and similar pies are made with an uncooked liquid filling containing eggs. The eggs coagulate when the pie is baked, which sets the filling. For more information on custards, see p. 284.

Many soft fillings contain some starch in addition to eggs. Flour, cornstarch, and instant starch are frequently used. While starch is unnecessary if enough eggs are used, many bakers prefer to add a little starch because it allows them to reduce the egg content. Also, the use of starch helps bind the liquids and reduce the chance of separating, or "weeping," in the baked pie. If starch is used, be sure the mix is well stirred before filling the pies in order to reduce the danger of the starch settling out.

The greatest difficulty in cooking soft pies is to cook the crust completely, yet not overcook the filling. Start the pie at the bottom of a hot oven (425 to 450° F/220 to 230° C) for the first 10 to 15 minutes in order to set the crust. Then reduce the heat to 325 to 350° F (165 to 175° C) in order to cook the filling slowly.

To test for doneness:

1. Shake the pie very gently. If it is no longer liquid, it is done. The center will still be slightly soft, but its own heat will continue to cook the pie after it is removed from the oven.

2. Insert a thin knife an inch from the center. If it comes out clean, the pie is done.

Custard Pie Filling

Yield: 8 lb (3.7 kg)
   Five 8-inch (20-cm) pies
   Four 9-inch (23-cm) pies
   Three 10-inch (25-cm) pies

Ingredients	U.S.			Metric
Eggs	2 lb			900 g
Sugar	1 lb			450 g
Salt		0.17 oz (1 tsp)		5 g
Vanilla		1	oz	30 ml
Milk (see note)	5 pt			2400 ml
Nutmeg		1–2	tsp	2–3 g

Note: For a richer custard, use part milk and part cream.

Procedure:

1. Combine the eggs, sugar, salt, and vanilla and blend until smooth. Do not whip air into the mixture.

2. Stir in the milk. Skim off any foam.

3. Place the unbaked pie shells in preheated oven (425° F/220° C) and carefully ladle in the filling. Sprinkle tops with nutmeg.

4. Bake at 450° F (230° C) for 15 minutes. Reduce heat to 325° F (165° C) and bake until set, about 20–30 minutes more.

Variation

Coconut Custard Pie Filling:

Use 10 oz (280 g) unsweetened, flaked coconut. Sprinkle the coconut into pie shells before adding the custard mixture. The coconut may be lightly toasted in the oven before it is added to the pies. Omit the nutmeg.

Pumpkin Pie Filling

Yield: About 17 lb (8 kg)

Ten 8-inch (20-cm) pies

Eight 9-inch (23-cm) pies

Six 10-inch (25-cm) pies

Ingredients	U.S.			Metric
Pumpkin purée, one No. 10 can or four No. 2½ cans	6 lb 10		oz	3000 g
Pastry flour		4	oz	120 g
Cinnamon		0.5	oz	15 g
Nutmeg		0.08	oz (1 tsp)	2 g
Ginger		0.08	oz (1 tsp)	2 g
Cloves		0.04	oz (½ tsp)	1 g
Salt		0.5	oz	15 g
Brown sugar	2 lb 8		oz	1150 g
Eggs (see note)	1 lb 8		oz	700 g
Corn syrup, or half corn syrup and half molasses		8	oz	240 g
Milk	6 pt			3000 ml

Note: Pumpkin pie filling should be allowed to stand at least 30 minutes before being poured into the pie shells. This gives the pumpkin time to absorb the liquid and makes for a smoother filling that is less likely to separate after baking. If the filling is to stand for much more than an hour, do not add the eggs until the pies are to be filled. If the eggs are added earlier, the acidity of the pumpkin and brown sugar may cause the eggs to partially coagulate.

Procedure:

1. Place the pumpkin in the bowl of a mixer fitted with the whip attachment.
2. Sift together the flour, spices, and salt.
3. Add the flour mixture and sugar to the pumpkin. Mix at second speed until smooth and well blended.
4. Add the eggs and mix in. Scrape down the sides of the bowl.
5. Turn the machine to low speed. Gradually pour in the syrup, then the milk. Mix until evenly blended.
6. Let the filling stand for 30–60 minutes.
7. Stir the filling to remix. Fill the pie shells. Bake at 450° F (230° C) for 15 minutes. Lower heat to 350° F (175° C) and bake until set, about 30–40 minutes more.

Variations

Sweet Potato Pie Filling:

Substitute canned sweet potatoes, drained and puréed, for the pumpkin.

Squash Pie Filling:

Substitute puréed squash for the pumpkin.

Pecan Pie Filling
Yield: 8 lb (3.6 kg) filling plus 1 lb 4 oz (570 g) pecans
Five 8-inch (20)cm) pies
Four 9-inch (23-cm) pies
Three 10-inch (25)cm) pies

Ingredients	U.S.		Metric
Granulated sugar (see note)	2 lb		900 g
Butter		8 oz	230 g
Salt		0.25 oz	7 g
Eggs	2 lb		900 g
Dark corn syrup	3 lb 8 oz		1600 g
	(about 2½ pt)		
Vanilla		1 oz	30 g
Pecans	1 lb 4 oz		570 g

Note: Brown sugar may be used if a darker color and stronger flavor are desired.

Procedure:

1. Using the paddle attachment at low speed, blend the sugar, butter, and salt until evenly blended.

2. With the machine running, add the eggs a little at a time, until they are all absorbed.

3. Add the syrup and vanilla. Mix until well blended.

4. To assemble pies, distribute the pecans evenly in the pie shells and then fill with the syrup mixture.

5. Bake at 450° F (230° C) for 10 minutes. Reduce heat to 350° F (175° C). Bake about 40 minutes more, until set.

Cream Pie Fillings

Cream pie fillings are the same as puddings, which in turn are the same as basic pastry cream with added flavorings, such as vanilla, chocolate, or coconut. Lemon filling is made by the same method, using water and lemon juice instead of milk.

There is one difference between pastry cream and pie filling that you should note: *Cream pie fillings are made with cornstarch* so that slices will hold their shape when cut. Pastry cream may be made with flour, cornstarch, or other starches.

The basic principles and procedures for making pastry cream are included in Chapter 7. See pages 120–121 to review this information. For your convenience, the formula for vanilla pastry cream is repeated here under the name "vanilla cream pie filling." Popular flavor variations for cream pie fillings follow this basic recipe.

Opinions are divided as to whether pie shells should be filled with warm cream fillings, which are then cooled in the shell, or whether the filling should be cooled first and then added to the shell. For the best-looking slices, warm filling is best. The filling will cool to a smooth, uniform mass, and the slices will hold sharp, clean cuts. However, you must be sure to use a good, mealy pie dough that resists soaking, or you risk having soggy bottom crusts. Enriched pie pastry (p. 140) is good for this purpose. Many food service operations prefer to fill each pie shell with cold filling shortly before the pie is to be cut and served. The slice will not cut as cleanly, but the crusts will be crisp, and you can use flaky dough for the crusts. We use the warm filling method in this book, but you can, of course, modify the procedure to suit your needs.

Vanilla Cream Pie Filling

Yield: About 2¼ qt (2.25 l), or 6 lb 4 oz (3.1 kg)

Five 8-inch (20-cm) pies
Four 9-inch (23-cm) pies
Three 10-inch (25-cm) pies

Ingredients	U.S.		Metric
Milk	4 pt		2000 ml
Sugar		8 oz	250 g
Egg yolks (8)		5 oz	150 g
Whole eggs (4)		7 oz	220 g
Cornstarch		5 oz	150 g
Sugar		8 oz	250 g
Butter		4 oz	125 g
Vanilla		1 oz	30 ml

Procedure:

Before beginning production, review the discussion of pastry cream on p. 120.

1. In a heavy saucepan or kettle, dissolve the sugar in the milk and bring just to a boil.
2. With a whip, beat the egg yolks and whole eggs in a stainless steel bowl.
3. Sift the starch and sugar into the eggs. Beat with the whip until perfectly smooth.
4. Temper the egg mixture by slowly beating in the hot milk in a thin stream.
5. Return the mixture to the heat and bring it to a boil, stirring constantly.
6. When the mixture comes to a boil and thickens, remove it from the heat.
7. Stir in the butter and vanilla. Mix until the butter is melted and completely blended in.
8. Pour into baked, cooled pie shells. Cool, then keep chilled. Chilled pies may be decorated with whipped cream, using a pastry bag with a star tube.

Variations

Coconut Cream Pie Filling:

Add 8 oz (250 g) toasted, unsweetened coconut to the basic filling.

Banana Cream Pie Filling:

Using vanilla cream filling, pour half the filling into pie shells, cover with sliced bananas, and fill with remaining filling. (Bananas may be dipped in lemon juice to help prevent browning.)

Chocolate Cream Pie Filling I:

Melt together the following ingredients and mix into hot vanilla cream filling:

Unsweetened chocolate	4	oz	125 g
Sweet chocolate	4	oz	125 g

Chocolate Cream Pie Filling II:

This variation uses cocoa instead of chocolate. The cocoa is sifted with the starch. Some of the milk must be included with the eggs in order to provide enough liquid to make a paste with the starch and cocoa. Follow the procedure in the basic recipe, but use these ingredients:

Milk	3 lb 8	oz (3½ pt)	1750 ml
Sugar	8	oz	250 g
Egg yolks (8)	5	oz	150 g
Whole eggs (4)	7	oz	220 g
Cold milk	8	oz	250 g
Cornstarch	5	oz	150 g
Cocoa	3	oz	90 g
Sugar	8	oz	250 g
Butter	4	oz	125 g
Vanilla	1	oz	30 ml

Butterscotch Cream Pie Filling:

Combine in a saucepan:

Brown sugar	2 lb		1000 g
Butter		10 oz	300 g

Heat over low heat, stirring, until the butter is melted and the ingredients are blended. Prepare the basic vanilla cream filling recipe, but omit all the sugar and increase the starch to 6 oz (180 g). As the mixture comes to a boil in step 5, gradually stir in the brown sugar mixture. Finish as in the basic recipe.

Lemon Pie Filling:

Follow the procedure for vanilla cream filling, but use the following ingredients. Note that the lemon juice is added after the filling is thickened.

Water	4 pt		2000 ml
Sugar	1 lb		500 g
Egg yolks (8)	5	oz	150 g
Whole eggs (4)	7	oz	220 g
Cornstarch	6	oz	180 g
Sugar	8	oz	250 g
Grated lemon zest			
(2 lemons)	0.5	oz	15 g
Butter	4	oz	125 g
Lemon juice	8	oz	250 ml

Chiffon Pie Fillings

Chiffon fillings have a light, fluffy texture that is created by the addition of beaten egg whites and sometimes whipped cream. The egg whites and cream are folded into a cream or fruit base that is stabilized with gelatin. The folding in of the egg whites and the filling of the baked pie shells must be done before the gelatin sets. After the pie is chilled to set the gelatin, the filling should be firm enough to hold a clean slice.

When chiffon filling contains both egg whites and whipped cream, most chefs and bakers prefer to fold in the egg whites first, even though they may lose some volume. The reason is that if the cream is added first, there is more danger that it will be overbeaten and will turn to butter during the folding and mixing procedure.

For a review of the guidelines for beating egg whites, see p. 117. For the guidelines for whipping cream, see p. 115.

Bases for chiffons include the following three main types:

1. *Thickened with starch.* The procedure is the same as for fruit pie fillings made by the cooked juice method or cooked fruit method, except that the fruit is finely chopped or puréed. Most fruit chiffons are made this way.

2. *Thickened with egg.* The procedure is the same as for crème Anglaise (p. 119). Chocolate chiffons and pumpkin chiffons are sometimes made this way.

3. *Thickened with egg and starch.* The procedure is the same as for pastry cream or cream pie fillings. Lemon chiffon is usually made this way.

Guidelines for Using Gelatin

While some chiffons contain starch as their only stabilizer, most contain gelatin. Gelatin must be handled properly so that it is completely dissolved and mixed evenly throughout the filling. All references to gelatin in this book mean unflavored gelatin, not flavored, sweetened gelatin mixes.

1. Measure gelatin accurately. Too much gelatin makes a stiff, rubbery product. Too little will make a soft product that will not hold its shape.

2. Do not mix raw pineapple or papaya with gelatin. These fruits contain enzymes that dissolve gelatin. These fruits may be used if they are cooked or canned.

3. To dissolve unflavored gelatin, stir it into *cold* liquid to avoid lumping. Let it stand for 5 minutes to absorb water. Then heat it until it is dissolved, or combine it with a hot liquid and stir until dissolved.

4. After the gelatin is dissolved in the base, cool or chill it until it is slightly thickened, but not set. If the base starts to set, it will be difficult or impossible to fold in the egg whites uniformly.

5. Stir the base occasionally while it is cooling, so that it cools evenly. Otherwise the outside edges may start to set before the inside is sufficiently cooled, which will create lumps.

6. If the gelatin sets before you can add the egg whites, warm the base slightly by stirring it over hot water just until the gelatin is melted and there are no lumps. Cool again.

7. When folding in egg whites and whipped cream, work rapidly without pausing, or the gelatin might set before you are finished. Fill the pie shells immediately, before the filling sets.

8. Keep the pies refrigerated, especially in hot weather.

General Procedure for Making Chiffon Fillings

1. Prepare base.
2. Soften gelatin in cold liquid. Stir it into the hot base until dissolved. Chill until thickened, but not set.
3. Fold in beaten egg whites.
4. Fold in whipped cream, if used.
5. Immediately pour into pie shells and chill.

In addition to the following chiffons, you may also use bavarian creams as pie fillings (see p. 292). While bavarian creams contain gelatin and whipped cream, they are not, strictly speaking, chiffons, since they do not contain whipped egg whites. Nevertheless, their texture is similar to chiffons, due to the lightening effect of the whipped cream.

Strawberry Chiffon Pie Filling
Yield: 6 lb 8 oz (3 kg)
     Six 8-inch (20-cm) pies
     Five 9-inch (23-cm) pies
     Four 10-inch (25-cm) pies

Ingredients	U.S.		Metric
Frozen sweetened			
strawberries (see note)	4 lb		1800 g
Salt		0.16 oz (1 tsp)	5 g
Cornstarch	1	oz	30 g
Cold water	4	oz	120 ml
Gelatin	1	oz	30 g
Cold water	8	oz	240 ml
Lemon juice	1	oz	30 ml
Egg whites	1 lb		450 g
Sugar	12	oz	350 g

Note: To use fresh strawberries, slice or chop 3 lb (1.4 kg) fresh, hulled straw-berries and mix with 1 lb (450 g) sugar. Let stand in refrigerator for 2 hours. Drain and reserve juice and proceed as in basic recipe.

Procedure:

1. Thaw and drain the strawberries. Chop them coarsely.

2. Place the drained juice and salt in a saucepan. Bring to a boil.

3. Dissolve the cornstarch in the water and stir into the juice. Cook until thick. Remove from the heat.

4. Soften the gelatin in the second quantity of water. Add it to the hot, thickened juice and stir until completely dissolved.

5. Stir in the lemon juice and the drained strawberries.

6. Chill the mixture until thickened, but not set.

7. Beat the egg whites until they form soft peaks. Gradually add the sugar and continue to beat until a thick, glossy meringue is formed.

8. Fold the meringue into the fruit mixture.

9. Pour the meringue into baked pie shells. Chill until set.

Variations

Strawberry Cream Chiffon Pie Filling:

For a creamier filling, reduce the egg whites to 12 oz (350 g). Whip 1 pt (500 ml) heavy cream, and fold it in after the meringue.

Raspberry Chiffon Pie Filling:

Substitute raspberries for strawberries in the basic recipe.

Pineapple Chiffon Pie Filling:

Use 3 lb (1.4 kg) crushed pineapple. Mix the drained juice with an additional 1 pt (500 ml) pineapple juice, and add 8 oz (240 g) sugar.

Chocolate Chiffon Pie Filling

Yield: 7 lb (3.2 kg)
   Six 8-inch (20-cm) pies
   Five 9-inch (23-cm) pies
   Four 10-inch (25-cm) pies

Ingredients	U.S.	Metric
Unsweetened chocolate	10 oz	300 g
Water	1 pt 8 oz	750 ml
Egg yolks	1 lb	450 g
Sugar	1 lb	450 g
Gelatin	1 oz	30 g
Cold water	8 oz	240 ml
Egg whites	1 lb 4 oz	580 g
Sugar	1 lb 8 oz	700 g

Procedure:

1. Combine the chocolate and water in a heavy saucepan. Bring to a boil over moderate heat, stirring constantly until smooth.

2. With the whip attachment, beat the egg yolks and sugar together until thick and light.

3. With the mixer running, gradually pour in the chocolate mixture.

4. Return the mixture to the saucepan and stir over very low heat until thickened. Remove from heat.

5. Soften the gelatin in the water. Add it to the hot chocolate mixture and stir until the gelatin is completely dissolved.

6. Chill until thick, but not set.

7. Beat the egg whites until they form soft peaks. Gradually beat in the last quantity of sugar. Continue beating until a firm, glossy meringue is formed.

8. Fold meringue into the chocolate mixture.

9. Pour the mixture into baked pie shells. Chill until set.

Variation

Chocolate Cream Chiffon Pie Filling:

For a creamier filling, reduce the egg whites to 1 lb (450 g). Whip 1 pt (500 ml) heavy cream and fold it in after the meringue.

Lemon Chiffon Pie Filling

Yield: 7 lb (3.2 kg)

Six 8-inch (20-cm) pies
Five 9-inch (23-cm) pies
Four 10-inch (25-cm) pies

Ingredients	U.S.		Metric
Water	1 pt	8 oz	750 ml
Sugar		8 oz	240 g
Egg yolks		12 oz	350 g
Cold water		4 oz	120 ml
Cornstarch		3 oz	90 g
Sugar		8 oz	240 g
Grated lemon zest		1 oz	30 g
Gelatin		1 oz	30 g
Cold water		8 oz	250 ml
Lemon juice		12 oz	350 ml
Egg whites	1 lb		450 g
Sugar	1 lb		450 g

Procedure:

1. Dissolve the sugar in the water and bring to a boil.
2. Beat together the egg yolks, cold water, cornstarch, sugar, and grated lemon until smooth.
3. Gradually beat the boiling sugar syrup into the egg yolk mixture in a thin stream.
4. Return the mixture to the heat and bring it to a boil, beating constantly with a whip.
5. As soon as the mixture thickens and boils, remove it from the heat.
6. Soften the gelatin in the cold water.
7. Add the gelatin to the hot lemon mixture. Stir until it is dissolved.
8. Stir in the lemon juice.
9. Chill it until thick, but not set.
10. Beat the egg whites until they form soft peaks. Gradually add the sugar and continue to beat until a thick, glossy meringue is formed.
11. Fold the meringue into the lemon mixture.
12. Fill baked pie shells. Chill until set.

Variations

Lime Chiffon Pie Filling:

Substitute lime juice and zest for the lemon juice and zest.

Orange Chiffon Pie Filling:

Make the following ingredient adjustments.

Use orange juice instead of water in step 1.
Omit the first 8 oz (240 g) of sugar.
Substitute orange zest for the lemon zest.
Reduce the lemon juice to 4 oz (120 ml).

Pumpkin Chiffon Pie Filling

Yield: 7 lb 12 oz (3.4 kg)

      Six 8-inch (20-cm) pies
      Five 9-inch (23-cm) pies
      Four 10-inch (25-cm) pies

Ingredients	U.S.			Metric
Pumpkin purée	2 lb	8	oz	1200 g
Brown sugar	1 lb	4	oz	600 g
Milk		12	oz	350 g
Egg yolks, beaten		12	oz	350 g
Salt		0.17	oz (1 tsp)	5 g
Cinnamon		0.25	oz (4 tsp)	7 g
Nutmeg		0.16	oz (2 tsp)	4 g
Ginger		0.08	oz (1 tsp)	2 g
Gelatin		1	oz	30 g
Cold water		8	oz	240 ml
Egg whites	1 lb			450 g
Sugar	1 lb			450 g

Procedure:

1. Combine the pumpkin, sugar, milk, egg yolks, salt, and spices. Mix until smooth and uniform.

2. Place mixture in a double boiler. Cook, stirring frequently, until thickened, or until the temperature of the mix is 185° F (85° C). Remove from heat.

3. Soften the gelatin in the cold water. Add it to the hot pumpkin mixture and stir until dissolved.

4. Chill until very thick, but not set.

5. Beat the egg whites until they form soft peaks. Gradually add the sugar and continue to beat until a thick, glossy meringue is formed.

6. Fold the meringue into the pumpkin mixture.

7. Fill baked pie shells with mixture. Chill until set.

Variation

Pumpkin Cream Chiffon Pie Filling:

For a creamier filling, reduce the egg whites to 12 oz (350 g). Whip 1 pt (500 ml) heavy cream and fold it in after the meringue.

PIE FAULTS AND THEIR CAUSES

To remedy common pie faults, check the following trouble-shooting guide for possible causes and correct your procedures.

Fault	Causes
Crust	
Dough too stiff	Not enough shortening
	Not enough liquid
	Flour too strong
Tough	Overmixing
	Not enough short-ening

Fault	Causes
Tough *(Continued)*	Flour too strong
	Too much rolling, or too much scrap dough used
	Too much water
Crumbly	Not enough water
	Too much shortening
	Improper mixing
	Flour too weak
Not flaky	Not enough shortening
	Shortening blended in too much
	Overmixing or too much rolling
	Dough or ingredients too warm
Soggy or raw bottom crust	Oven temperature too low; not enough bottom heat
	Filling hot when put in shell
	Not baked long enough
	Use of wrong dough (use mealy dough for bottom crusts)
	Not enough starch in fruit fillings

Fault	Causes
Shrinkage	Dough overworked
	Not enough shortening
	Flour too strong
	Too much water
	Dough stretched when put in pans
	Dough not rested
Filling	
Filling boils out	No steam vents in top crust
	Top crust not sealed to bottom crust at edges
	Oven temperature too low
	Fruit too acidic
	Filling hot when put in shell
	Not enough starch in filling
	Too much sugar in filling
	Too much filling
Curdling of custard or soft fillings	Overbaked

TERMS FOR REVIEW

fruit pie
soft pie
cream pie
chiffon pie
lattice crust
instant starch
cooked juice method
cooked fruit method
solid pack
heavy pack
water pack
syrup pack
drained weight

QUESTIONS FOR DISCUSSION

1. What kind of crust would you use for a pumpkin pie? An apple pie? A banana cream pie?

2. How can you prevent shrinkage when baking empty pie shells?

3. How can you prevent soggy or undercooked bottom pie crusts?

4. What starch would you use to thicken apple pie filling? Chocolate cream pie filling? Lemon pie filling? Peach pie filling?

5. Why is lemon juice added to lemon pie filling after the starch has thickened the water? Wouldn't this thin out the filling?

6. Why is the cooked juice method usually used when making pie fillings from canned fruits?

7. What problem might you have if you make blueberry pie filling out of blueberries that are still partially frozen?

8. How can you test a custard pie for doneness?

CHAPTER 10

CAKE MIXING AND BAKING

After studying this chapter, you should be able to:
1. Perform basic cake mixing methods.
2. Produce high-fat or shortened cakes, including high-ratio cakes and cakes mixed by creaming.
3. Produce foam-type cakes, including sponge, angel food, and chiffon cakes.
4. Scale and bake cakes correctly.
5. Correct cake failures or defects.

akes are the richest and sweetest of all the baked products we have studied so far. From the baker's point of view, producing cakes requires as much precision as producing breads, but for completely opposite reasons. Breads are lean products that require strong gluten development and careful control of yeast action during the long fermentation and proofing periods.

Cakes, on the other hand, are high in both fat and sugar. The baker's job is to create a structure that will support these ingredients and yet keep it as light and delicate as possible. Fortunately, producing cakes in quantity is relatively easy if the baker has good, well-balanced formulas, scales ingredients accurately, and understands basic mixing methods well.

Cakes owe their popularity not only to their richness and sweetness, but also to their versatility. Cakes can be presented in many forms, from simple sheet cakes in cafeterias to elaborately decorated works of art for weddings and other important occasions. With only a few basic formulas and a variety of icings and fillings, the chef or baker can construct the perfect dessert for any occasion or purpose. In this chapter, we will focus on the procedures for mixing and baking the basic types of cakes. In Chapter 11, we will discuss how to assemble and decorate many kinds of desserts, using our baked cake layers and sheets in combination with icings, fillings, and other ingredients.

MIXING

The selection of high-quality ingredients is, of course, necessary to produce a cake of good quality. However, good ingredients alone will not guarantee a fine cake. A thorough understanding of mixing procedures is essential. Slight errors in mixing can result in cakes with poor texture and volume.

The mixing methods presented in this chapter are the basic ones used for most types of cakes prepared in the modern bakeshop. Each of these methods is used for particular types of formulas.

High-fat or shortened cakes:
Creaming method
Two-stage method
Flour-batter method

Low-fat or foam-type cakes:
Sponge method
Angel food method
Chiffon method

We discuss these methods and their variations in detail beginning on p. 195.

The three main goals of mixing cake batters are:

- To combine all ingredients into a smooth, uniform batter.

- To form and incorporate air cells in the batter.

- To develop the proper texture in the finished product.

These three goals are closely related. They may seem fairly obvious, especially the first one. But understanding these goals in more detail will help you to avoid many errors in mixing. For example, inexperienced bakers often become impatient and turn the mixer to high speed when creaming fat and sugar, thinking that high speed will do the same job faster. But air cells do not form as well at high speed, so the texture of the cake suffers.

Let's examine these three goals one at a time.

Combining Ingredients into a Homogeneous Mixture

Two of the major ingredients in cakes—fat and water (including the water in milk and eggs)—are by nature unmixable. Therefore, careful attention to mixing procedures is important if this goal is to be reached.

As you recall from Chapter 2 (p. 16), a uniform mixture of two unmixable substances is called an *emulsion*. Part of the purpose of mixing is to form such an emulsion. Properly mixed cake batters contain a water-in-fat emulsion; that is, the water is held in tiny droplets surrounded by fat and other ingredients. Curdling occurs when the fat can no longer hold the water in emulsion. The mixture then changes to a fat-in-water mixture, with small particles of fat surrounded by water and other ingredients.

The following factors can cause curdling:

1. *Using the wrong type of fat.*

   Different fats have different emulsifying abilities. High-ratio shortening contains emulsifiers that enable it to hold a large amount of water without curdling. You should not substitute regular shortening or butter in a formula that calls specifically for high-ratio, or emulsified, shortening.

   Butter has a desirable flavor but relatively poor emulsifying ability. Butter is, of course, used in many cake batters, but the formula should be specifically balanced so that it contains no more liquid than the batter can hold. Also, remember that butter already contains some water.

   Egg yolks, as you will recall, contain a natural emulsifier. When whole eggs or yolks are properly mixed into a batter, they help the batter hold the other liquids.

2. *Having the ingredients too cold.*

   Emulsions are best formed if the temperature of the ingredients is about 70° F (21° C).

3. *Mixing the first stage of the procedure too quickly.*

   If you do not cream the fat and sugar properly, for example, you will not form a good cell structure to hold the water.

4. *Adding the liquids too quickly.*

   In most cases the liquids, including the eggs, must be added in stages (that is, a little at a time). If they are added too quickly, they cannot be properly absorbed.

   In batters made by the creaming method (p. 195), the liquid is often added alternatively with the flour. The flour helps the batter absorb the liquid.

5. *Adding too much liquid.*

   This is not a problem if the formula is a good one. However, if you are using a formula that is not properly balanced, it might call for more liquid that the fat can hold in emulsion.

Forming Air Cells

Air cells in cake batters are important for texture and for leavening. A fine, smooth texture is the result of small, uniform air cells. Large or irregular air cells result in a coarse texture. Also, you will recall from p. 24 that air trapped in a mix helps to leaven a cake when the heat of the oven causes the air to expand. When no chemical leavener is used, this trapped air, in addition to steam, provides nearly all the leavening. Even when baking powder or soda is used, these air cells provide places to hold the gases released by the chemical leavener.

Correct ingredient temperature and mixing speed are necessary for good air cell formation. Cold fat (below 60° F/16° C) is too hard to form good air cells, while fat that is too warm (above 75° F/24° C) is too soft. Mixing speed should be moderate (medium speed). If mixing is done on high speed, friction will warm the ingredients too much. Not as many air cells are formed, and those that do form tend to be more coarse and irregular.

In the case of egg-foam cakes (sponge, angel food, chiffon), the air cells are formed by whipping eggs and sugar. For the best foaming, the egg and sugar mixture should be slightly warm (about 100° F/38° C). Whipping may be done at high speed at first, but the final stages of whipping should be at medium speed in order to retain air cells.

Developing Texture

Both the uniform mixing of ingredients and the formation of air cells are important to a cake's texture, as we have just discussed in the preceding sections. Another factor of mixing that affects texture is gluten development. For the most part, we want very little gluten development in cakes, so we use cake flour, which is low in gluten. Some sponge cake formulas call for cornstarch to replace part of the flour, so that there is even less gluten (the high percentage of eggs in sponge cakes provides much of the structure). On the other hand, some pound cake and fruit cake formulas need more gluten than other cakes, in order to give extra structure and to support the weight of the fruit. Thus, you will sometimes see such cake formulas calling for part cake flour and part bread flour.

As you recall from chapter one, the amount of mixing affects gluten development. In the creaming method, the sponge method, and the angel food method, the flour is added at or near the end of the mixing procedure, so that there is very little gluten development in properly mixed batters. If the batter is mixed too long after the flour is added, the cakes are likely to be tough.

In the two-stage method, the flour is added in the first step. But it is mixed with high-ratio shortening, which spreads well and coats the particles of flour with fat. This coating action limits gluten development. It is

important to mix the flour and fat thoroughly for the best results. Observe all mixing times closely. Also, high-ratio cakes contain a high percentage of sugar, which is also a tenderizer.

The Creaming Method

This method, also called the conventional method, was for a long time the standard method for mixing high-fat cakes. The development of emulsified, or high-ratio, shortenings has led to the development of simpler mixing methods for shortened cakes containing greater amounts of sugar and liquid. But the creaming method is still used for many types of butter cakes.

Procedure: Creaming Method

1. Scale ingredients accurately. Have all ingredients at room temperature (70° F/21° C).
2. Place the butter or shortening in the mixing bowl. With the paddle attachment, beat the fat slowly until it is smooth and creamy.
3. Add the sugar, and cream the mixture at moderate speed until the mixture is light and fluffy. This will take about 8 to 10 minutes.

   Some bakers prefer to add the salt and flavorings with the sugar to ensure uniform distribution.

   If melted chocolate is used, it is added during creaming.
4. Add the eggs a little at a time. After each addition, beat until the eggs are absorbed before adding more. After the eggs are beaten in, mix until light and fluffy. This step will take about 5 minutes.
5. Scrape down the sides of the bowl to ensure even mixing.
6. Add the sifted dry ingredients (including the spices if they were not added in Step 3) alternating with the liquids. This is done as follows:

   a. Add one-fourth of the dry ingredients. Mix just until blended in.

   b. Add one-third of the liquid. Mix just until blended in.

   c. Repeat until all ingredients are used. Scrape down the sides of the bowl occasionally for even mixing.

The reason for adding dry and liquid ingredients alternately is that the batter may not absorb all the liquid unless some of the flour is present to aid in absorption.

Variation

A few creaming-method cakes require an extra step: Egg whites whipped to a foam with some sugar are folded into the batter to provide additional leavening.

The fat specified in creaming-method formulas in this book is butter. Butter cakes are highly prized for their flavor; shortening adds no flavor to cakes. Butter also influences texture because it melts in the mouth, while shortening does not.

However, many bakers may prefer to substitute shortening for all or part of the butter in these formulas. Shortening has the advantage of being less expensive and easier to mix. In creaming recipes, use *regular shortening,* not emulsified shortening. Regular shortening has better creaming abilities.

It is usually a good idea not to substitute an equal weight of shortening for butter. Remember that butter is only 80% fat, so you will need less shortening. Also, butter contains about 15% water, so you should adjust the quantity of milk or water. The following procedures explain how to adjust formulas for these substitutions.

Procedures for Substituting Butter and Shortening in Creaming Method Batters

To substitute regular shortening for all or part of the butter:

1. Multiply the weight of the butter to be eliminated by 0.8. This gives the weight of regular shortening to use.
2. Multiply the weight of the eliminated butter by 0.15. This gives the weight of *additional* water or milk needed.

   Example: A formula calls for 3 lb butter and 3 lb milk. Adjust it so that you use 1 lb (16 oz) butter. How much shortening and milk will you need?

   Weight of butter to be eliminated = 2 lb
   0.8 × 2 lb = 0.8 × 32 oz
              = 26 oz shortening (rounded off)
   0.15 × 2 lb = 0.15 × 32 oz
              = 5 oz extra milk (rounded off)
   Total milk = 3 lb 5 oz

Procedure for Substituting Butter for All or Part of the Regular Shortening

1. Multiply the weight of the shortening to be eliminated by 1.25. This gives the weight of the butter to use.
2. Multiply the weight of the butter by 0.15. This gives the weight of water or milk to be *subtracted* from the formula.

   Example: A formula calls for 3 lb regular shortening and 3 lb milk. Adjust the formula so that you use 1 lb shortening. How much butter and milk will you need?

   Weight of shortening to be eliminated = 2 lb
   1.25 × 2 lb = 1.25 × 32 oz = 40 oz butter
   .15 × 40 oz = 6 oz milk to subtract
                       from the formula
   Total milk = 2 lb 10 oz

The Two-Stage Method

This mixing method was developed for use with modern high-ratio shortenings. High-ratio cakes contain a large percentage of sugar, more than 100% based on the weight of the flour. Also, they are made with more liquid than creaming method cakes, and the batter pours freely. The mixing method is a little simpler than the creaming method, and it produces a smooth batter that bakes up into a fine-grained, moist cake. It is called two-stage, because the liquids are added in two stages.

The first step in making high-ratio cakes is blending the flour and other dry ingredients with shortening. When this mixture is smooth, the liquids (including eggs) are added in stages. Throughout this procedure, it is important to follow two rules:

- Mix at low speed and observe correct mixing times. This is important to develop proper texture.
- Stop the machine and scrape down the sides of the bowl frequently during mixing. This is important to develop a smooth, well-mixed batter.

Note the variation following the basic procedure. Many bakers prefer this variation. It is somewhat simpler, because it combines steps 2 and 3.

Procedure: Two-Stage Method

1. Scale ingredients accurately. Have all ingredients at room temperature.

2. Sift the flour, baking powder, soda, and salt into the mixing bowl and add the shortening. With the paddle attachment, mix at low speed for 2 minutes. Stop the machine, scrape down the bowl and beater, and mix again for 2 minutes.

   If melted chocolate is used, blend it in during this step.

   If cocoa is used, sift it with the flour in this step or with the sugar in step 3.

3. Sift the remaining dry ingredients into the bowl and add part of the water or milk. Blend at low speed for 3 to 5 minutes. Scrape down the sides of the bowl and the beater several times to ensure even mixing.

4. Combine the remaining liquids and lightly beaten eggs. With the mixer running, add this mixture to the batter in three parts. After each part, turn off the machine and scrape down the bowl.

   Continue mixing for a total of 5 minutes in this stage.

   The finished batter will normally be quite liquid.

Variation

This variation combines steps 2 and 3 above into one step.

1. Scale ingredients as in basic method.
2. Sift all dry ingredients into the mixing bowl. Add the shortening and part of the liquid. Mix on low speed for 7 to 8 minutes. Scrape down the sides of the bowl and the beater several times.
3. Continue with step 4 in the basic procedure.

Flour-Batter Method

The following procedure is used only for a few specialty items. It produces a fine-textured cake, but there may be some toughening due to the development of gluten.

Flour-batter cakes include those made with either emulsified shortening or butter or both. There are no formulas in this book requiring this mixing method, although the batter for old-fashioned pound cake (p. 208) can be mixed by this method instead of the creaming method.

Procedure: Flour-Batter Method

1. Scale all ingredients accurately. Have all ingredients at room temperature.

2. Sift the flour and other dry ingredients *except sugar* into the mixing bowl. Add fat. Blend together until smooth and light.

3. Whip the sugar and eggs together until thick and light. Add liquid flavoring ingredients, such as vanilla.

4. Combine the flour-fat mixture and the sugar-egg mixture and mix until smooth.

5. Gradually add water or milk (if any) and mix smooth.

Egg-Foam Cakes

All egg-foam cakes are similar in that they contain little or no shortening and depend on the air trapped in beaten eggs for most or all of their leavening. We discuss three types of egg-foam cakes: sponge cakes, angel food cakes, and chiffon cakes.

Egg-foam cakes have a springy texture and are tougher than shortened cakes. This makes them valuable for many kinds of desserts that require much handling to assemble. For example, many European-style cakes or tortes are made by cutting sponge cake layers horizontally into thinner layers and stacking them with a variety of rich fillings, creams, icings, and fruits. In addition, sponge layers in this kind of cake are usually moistened with a flavored sugar syrup to compensate for their lack of moisture.

Sponge sheets for jelly rolls and other rolled cakes are often made without any shortening, so that they do not crack when rolled.

Flour for egg-foam cakes must be very weak in order to avoid making the cake tougher than necessary. Cornstarch is sometimes added to cake flour for these cakes to weaken the flour further.

Sponge Method

Although there are many types of sponge cakes, they all have one characteristic in common: They start with an egg foam that contains yolks. These are usually whole-egg foams, but in some cases the base foam is a yolk foam, and an egg white foam is folded in at the end of the procedure.

In its simplest form, sponge cake batter is made in two basic steps: (1) Eggs and sugar are whipped to a thick foam, and then (2) sifted flour is folded in. Additional ingredients, such as butter or liquid, complicate the procedure slightly. It would be too confusing to try to include all the variations in one procedure, so instead we describe four separate procedures.

Procedure: Plain Sponge Method

1. Scale ingredients accurately.

2. Combine the eggs, sugar, and salt and warm to about 110° F (43° C). This may be done in one of two ways.

   a. Stir the egg/sugar mixture over a hot water bath.

   b. Warm the sugar on a sheet pan in the oven (do not get it too hot) and gradually beat it into the eggs.

   The reason for this step is that the foam will attain greater volume if warm.

3. With the whip attachment, beat the eggs at high speed until they are very light and thick. This may take as long as 10 to 15 minutes.

4. If any liquid (water, milk, liquid flavoring) is included, add it now. Either whip it in in a steady stream, or stir it in, as indicated in the recipe.

5. Fold in the sifted flour, being careful not to deflate the foam. Many bakers do this by hand.

   If any other dry ingredients are used, such as cornstarch or baking powder, they should first be sifted with the flour.

6. Immediately pan and bake the batter. Delays will cause loss of volume.

Variation: Genoise or Butter Sponge

1. Follow the procedure for the Plain Sponge Method through step 5.

2. Carefully fold in the melted butter after the flour has been added. Fold in the butter completely, but be careful not to overmix, or the cake will be tough.

3. Immediately pan and bake.

Variation: Hot Milk and Butter Sponge

1. Scale ingredients accurately. Heat the milk and butter together until the butter is melted.

2. Whip the eggs into a foam as in the plain sponge method, steps 2 and 3.

3. Fold in the sifted dry ingredients (flour, leavening, cocoa, etc.) as in the basic procedure.

4. Carefully fold in the hot butter and milk in three stages. Fold in completely, but do not overmix.

5. Immediately pan and bake.

Variation: Separated Egg Sponge

1. Follow the basic plain sponge method, but use yolks for the basic foam (steps 2 and 3). Reserve the egg whites and part of the sugar for a separate step.

2. Whip the egg whites and sugar to firm, moist peaks. Fold into the batter. Fold in completely, but do not overmix.

3. Immediately pan and bake.

Angel Food Method

Angel food cakes are based on egg white foams and contain no fat. For success in beating egg whites, review the principles of egg white foams in Chapter 7, p. 117. Egg whites for angel food cakes should be whipped until they form soft, not stiff, peaks. Overwhipped whites lose their ability to expand and to leaven the cake.

Procedure: Angel Food Method

1. Scale ingredients accurately. Have all ingredients at room temperature. The egg whites may be slightly warmed in order to achieve better volume.

2. Sift the flour with half the sugar. This step helps the flour mix more evenly with the foam.

3. Using the whip attachment, beat the egg whites until they form soft peaks.

   Add salt and cream of tartar near the beginning of the beating process.

4. Gradually beat in the portion of the sugar that was not mixed with the flour. Continue to whip until the egg whites form soft, moist peaks. Do not beat until stiff.

5. Fold in the flour/sugar mixture just until it is thoroughly absorbed, but no longer.

6. Deposit the mix in ungreased pans and bake immediately.

Chiffon Method

Chiffon cakes and angel food cakes are both based on egg-white foams. But here the similarities in the mixing methods end. In angel food cakes, a dry flour-sugar mixture is folded into the egg whites. But in chiffon cakes, a batter containing flour, egg yolks, vegetable oil, and water is folded into the whites.

Egg whites for chiffon cakes should be whipped until they are a little firmer than those for angel food cakes, but do not overwhip then until they are dry. Chiffon cakes contain baking powder, so they do not depend on the egg foam for all their leavening.

Procedure: Chiffon Method

1. Scale all ingredients accurately. Have all ingredients at room temperature. Use a good-quality, flavorless vegetable oil.

2. Sift the dry ingredients, including part of the sugar, into the mixing bowl.

3. Mixing with the paddle attachment at second speed, gradually add the oil, then the egg yolks, water, and liquid flavorings, all in a slow, steady stream. While adding the liquids, stop the machine several times and scrape down the bowl and the beater. Mix until smooth, but do not overmix.

4. Whip the egg whites until they form soft peaks. Add the cream of tartar and sugar in a stream and whip to firm, moist peaks.

5. Fold the whipped egg whites into the flour-liquid mixture.

6. Immediately deposit batter in ungreased center-tube pans (like angel food cakes) or in layer pans that have had the bottoms greased and dusted, but not the sides (like sponge layers).

Prepared Mixes

Many mixes are available that contain all ingredients except water and sometimes eggs. These products also contain added emulsifiers to ensure even blending of ingredients. To use them, follow the package instructions exactly.

Most mixes produce cakes with excellent volume, texture, and tenderness. Whether or not they also taste good is a matter of opinion. On the other hand, cakes made "from scratch" are not necessarily better. They will be better only if they are carefully mixed and baked, and prepared from good, tested formulas, using quality ingredients.

CAKE FORMULA BALANCE

It is possible to change cake formulas, either to improve them or to reduce costs. However, ingredients and quantities can be changes only within certain limits. A cake formula in which the ingredients fall within these limits is said to be in balance. Knowing these limits helps you not only to modify recipes but also to judge untested recipes and to correct faults.

Keep in mind that new ingredients and procedures are frequently developed. Cake balancing rules that have worked well up until now may be changed as new developments come along that allow you to break the rules. A baker should be open to new ideas and be willing to try them out. For example, it was once a rule that the weight of sugar in a mix should not exceed the weight of flour. But the introduction of shortenings with emulsifiers led to formulas with higher proportions of sugar.

Ingredient Functions

For the purpose of balancing cake formulas, we can classify cake ingredients according to four functions: tougheners, tenderizers, driers, and moisteners. The idea of formula balancing is that tougheners should balance tenderizers, and driers should balance moisteners. In other words, if we increase the tougheners in a formula, for example, we must compensate by also increasing the tenderizers.

Many ingredients fill more than one function, sometimes even opposite functions. Egg yolks contain protein, which is a toughener, but they also contain fat, which is a tenderizer. The major cake ingredients are classified as follows:

Tougheners provide structure: flour, eggs (whites and yolks).

Tenderizers provide softness or shortening of protein fibers: sugar, fats (including butter, shortening, cocoa butter), chemical leaveners.

Moisteners provide moisture or water: water, liquid milk, syrups and liquid sugars, eggs.

Driers absorb moisture: flours and starches, cocoa, milk solids.

You can also use this table of ingredients as a trouble-shooting guide for cake failures. A cake that fails even if mixed and baked correctly may require formula balancing. For example, if a cake is too dry, you might increase one or more of the moisteners or decrease the driers.

This takes a certain amount of experience, however. Remember that most ingredients have more than one function. If you decide to increase the eggs in a dry cake, you may wind up with an even harder, tougher cake. While whole eggs do provide some moisture, they provide even more toughening power because of their strong protein content.

As a further complication, there are many successful cake formulas that apparently break the rules. For example, one rule for creaming-method cakes made with butter or regular shortening says that the weight of the sugar should not exceed the weight of the flour. But, in fact, there are successful recipes calling for more than 100% sugar. Many baking manuals insist on these balancing rules rather strongly. But it may be better to think of these rules not as ironclad laws, but as guidelines that give you a starting point for judging or correcting recipes.

In summary, it takes an experienced baker to be consistently successful at adjusting cake formulas. However, even beginning bakers should have some knowledge of formula balancing: It helps you to understand the formulas you are using and practicing, and it helps you to understand why you assemble and mix cakes in certain ways and what makes the mixtures work.

In the following discussions of balancing rules, it is helpful to think of ingredients in terms of baker's percentages (see p. 5) rather than as specific weights. This eliminates one variable: Flour is a constant 100%, so that other ingredients are increased or decreased with respect to flour.

Balancing Fat-type or Shortened Cakes

A normal starting point in discussing cake balancing is the old-fashioned pound cake (see p. 208). This cake is made of flour, sugar, butter, and eggs in equal parts. As bakers experimented with this basic recipe over the years, they reduced the quantities of sugar, fat, and eggs, and compensated by adding milk. This is the origin of the modern butter cake.

The general rules for balancing creaming-method cakes made with butter or regular shortening are as follows (all ingredients' quantities are, of course, by weight):

- The sugar is equal to or less than the flour.
- The fat equals the eggs.
- The eggs and liquids (milk and water) equal the flour.

With the development of emulsified shortenings, it became possible to increase the quantities of eggs and liquids. The general rules for balancing high-ratio cakes (using emulsified shortening) are as follows.

- The sugar is more than the flour (110 to 160%).
- The eggs are more than the shortening.
- The liquid (water, plus the water in the milk and eggs) is more than the sugar (see pp. 18 and 21 for the percentages of water in milk and eggs).

A common practice in balancing a formula is to decide upon the sugar-flour ratio, then to balance the rest of the ingredients against these. The following guidelines are helpful:

- If liquid (water or milk) is increased, reduce the eggs and shortening.
- If eggs are increased, increase the shortening.
- If extra milk solids are added as an enrichment, add an equal weight of water.
- If cocoa is added, add water equal in weight to 75 to 100% of the cocoa.
- If cocoa or bitter chocolate is added, the amount of sugar may be increased to as much as 180% of the weight of the flour in high-ratio cakes, and to over 100% of the weight of the flour in creaming-method cakes. This is because of the starch content of the cocoa and chocolate.
- In cakes to be baked in very large units, less liquid is needed, because less water will evaporate during baking.
- If a liquid sugar is added (honey, corn syrup, etc.), reduce other liquids slightly.
- If large quantities of moist ingredients, such as applesauce or mashed bananas, are added, reduce the liquid. Extra-large additions of moist ingredients may also require increasing the flour and eggs.
- Creamed batters need less baking powder than two-stage batters, because the creamed batters get more aeration in the creaming stage.

SCALING, PANNING, AND BAKING

Pan Preparation

Prepare pans before mixing cake batters, so that cakes can be baked without delay as soon as they are mixed.

1. For high-fat cakes, layer pans must be greased, preferably with a commercial pan greasing preparation. If this is not available, dust the greased pans with flour and tap out the excess.

2. For sheet cakes, line the pans with greased parchment. For thin layers, such as Swiss rolls, it is necessary to use level pans without dents or warps.

3. For angel food cakes and chiffon cakes baked in tube pans, do not grease the pan. The batter must be able to cling to the sides so that it won't sink back into the pan after rising.

4. For sponge cake layers with little or no fat, grease the bottoms but not the sides of the pans.

Procedure for Scaling Creaming-Method Batters

These batters are thick and do not pour easily.

1. Place a prepared cake pan on the left side of the balance scale. Balance the scale out by placing another pan on the right side.

2. Set the scale for desired weight.

3. Add batter to the left pan until the scale balances.

4. Remove the pan from the scale and spread the batter smooth with a spatula.

5. Repeat with remaining pans.

6. Give the pans several sharp raps on the bench to free large trapped air bubbles. Bake immediately.

Procedure for Scaling Two-Stage Batters

These batters are usually very liquid. They may be scaled like creamed batters, or for greater speed, they may be scaled as follows:

1. Place an empty volume measure on the left side of the balance scale. Balance the scale out to zero.

2. Set the scale for desired weight.

3. Pour batter into the measure until the scale balances.

4. Note the volume of batter in the measure.

5. Pour batter into the prepared pan, quickly scraping out the measure to get all the batter.

6. Scale remaining cakes with the volume measure, using the volume noted in Step 4.

7. Give the pans several sharp raps on the bench to free large trapped air bubbles. Bake immediately.

Procedure for Scaling Egg-Foam Cakes

Foam cake batters should be handled as little as possible and baked immediately, in order to avoid deflating the beaten eggs. While these cakes may be scaled like creamed batters, many bakers prefer to "eyeball" them in order to minimize handling.

1. Have all prepared pans lined up on the bench.

2. Scale the first pan as for creamed batters.

3. Quickly fill the remaining pans to the same level as the first pan, judging the level by eye.

4. Spread the batter smooth and bake immediately.

See Table 10.1 for average scaling weights, as well as baking temperatures and times.

TABLE 10.1 **Average Cake Scaling Weights, Baking Temperatures, and Times**

Pan Type and Size	Scaling Weight[a] U.S.	Metric	Baking Temperature U.S.	Metric	Approximate Baking Time in Minutes
High-fat cakes					
Round layers					
6 in (15 cm)	8–10 oz	230–285 g	375° F	190° C	18
8 in (20 cm)	14–18 oz	400–510 g	375° F	190° C	25
10 in (25 cm)	24–28 oz	680–800 g	360° F	180° C	35
12 in (30 cm)	32–40 oz	900–1100 g	360° F	180° C	35
Sheets and square pans					
18 × 26 in (46 × 66 cm)	7–8 lb	3.2–3.6 kg	360° F	180° C	35
18 × 13 in (46 × 33 cm)	3½–4 lb	1.6–1.8 kg	360° F	180° C	35
9 × 9 in (23 × 23 cm)	24 oz	680 g	360° F	180° C	30–35
Loaf (pound cake)					
2¼ × 3½ × 8 in					
(6 × 9 × 20 cm)	16–18 oz	450–500 g	350° F	175° C	50–60
2¾ × 4½ × 8½ in					
(7 × 11 × 22 cm)	24–27 oz	680–765 g	350° F	175° C	55–65
Cupcakes					
per dozen	18 oz	510 g	385° F	195° C	18–20
Foam-type cakes					
Round layers					
6 in (15 cm)	5–6 oz	140–170 g	375° F	190° C	20
8 in (20 cm)	10 oz	280 g	375° F	190° C	20
10 in (25 cm)	16 oz	450 g	360° F	180° C	25–30
12 in (30 cm)	24 oz	700 g	360° F	180° C	25–30
Sheets (for jelly roll or sponge roll)					
18 × 26 in, ½ in thick					
(46 × 66 cm, 12 mm thick)	2½ lb	1.2 kg	375° F	190° C	15–20
18 × 26 in, ¼ in thick					
(46 × 66 cm, 6 mm thick)	28 oz	800 g	400° F	200° C	7–10
Tube (angel food and chiffon)					
8 in (20 cm)	12–14 oz	340–400 g	360° F	180° C	30
10 in (25 cm)	24–32 oz	700–900 g	350° F	175° C	50
Cupcakes					
per dozen	10 oz	280 g	375° F	190° C	18–20

[a] The weights given are averages. Weights may be increased by 25% if thicker layers are desired. Baking times may then need to be increased slightly.

Baking and Cooling

Cake structure is very fragile, so proper baking conditions are essential for quality products. The following guidelines will help you avoid cake failures.

1. Preheat the ovens. But to conserve expensive energy, don't preheat longer than necessary.

2. Make sure ovens and shelves are level.

3. Do not let pans touch each other. If pans touch, air circulation is inhibited and the cakes rise unevenly.

4. Bake at correct temperature.

   Too hot an oven causes the cake to set unevenly with a humped center, or to set before it has fully risen. Crusts will be too dark.

   Too slow an oven causes poor volume and texture because the cake doesn't set fast enough and may fall.

5. If steam in the oven is available, use it for creamed and two-stage batters. These cakes bake with a flatter top if baked with steam because the steam delays the formation of the top crust.

6. Do not open the oven or disturb cakes until they have finished rising and are partially browned. Disturbing the cakes before they are set may cause them to fall.

Tests for Doneness

- Shortened cakes will shrink away slightly from sides of pan.
- Cake will be springy. Center of top of cake will spring back when pressed lightly.
- A cake tester or wooden pick inserted in center of cake will come out clean.

Cooling and Removing from Pans

- Cool layer cakes and sheet cakes 15 minutes in pans and turn out while slightly warm. Since they are fragile, they may break if turned out when hot.
- Turn out layer cakes onto racks to finish cooling.
- To turn out sheet cakes:

  1. Sprinkle top lightly with granulated sugar.
  2. Set an empty sheet pan on top, bottom-side down.
  3. Invert both pans.
  4. Remove top pan.
  5. Peel parchment off cake.

- Cool angel food cakes and chiffon cakes upside-down in pans, so that they do not fall back into the pans and lose volume. Support the edges of the pan so that the top of the cake is off the bench. When cool, loosen the cake from sides of the pan with a knife or spatula, and carefully pull out the cake.

Errors in mixing, scaling, baking, and cooling cakes cause many kinds of defects and failures. For easy reference, these various defects and their possible causes are summarized in the trouble-shooting guide in Table 10.2, p. 204.

ALTITUDE ADJUSTMENTS

At high altitudes, atmospheric pressure is much less than at sea level. This factor must be taken into account in cake baking. Formulas must be adjusted to suit baking conditions more than 2000 or 3000 feet above sea level.

While general guidelines can be given, the exact adjustments required will vary for different kinds of cakes. Many manufacturers of flour, shortening, and other bakery ingredients will supply detailed information and adjusted formulas for any given locality.

In general, the following adjustments must be made above 2000 or 3000 feet elevation. See Table 10.3, p. 205, for actual adjustments.

Leavening

Leavening gases expand more when air pressure is lower, so baking powder and baking soda must be *decreased*.

Creaming and foaming procedures should also be reduced so that less air is incorporated.

Tougheners: Flour and Eggs

Cakes require firmer structure at high altitudes. Both eggs and flour must be increased to supply adequate proteins for structure.

Tenderizers: Shortening and Sugar

For the same reasons, shortening and sugar must be decreased so that the structure will be firmer.

Liquids

As altitudes become higher, water boils at a lower temperature and evaporates more easily. Liquids must be increased to prevent excess drying both during and after baking. This also helps compensate for the decrease in moisturizers (sugar and fat) and the increase in flour, which absorbs moisture.

TABLE 10.2 **Common Cake Faults and Their Causes**

Fault	Causes
Volume and shape	
Poor volume	Too little flour
	Too much liquid
	Too little leavening
	Oven too hot
Uneven shape	Improper mixing
	Batter spread unevenly
	Uneven oven heat
	Oven racks not level
	Cake pans warped
Crust	
Too dark	Too much sugar
	Oven too hot
Too light	Too little sugar
	Oven not hot enough
Burst or cracked	Too much flour or flour too strong
	Too little liquid
	Improper mixing
	Oven too hot
Soggy	Underbaked
	Cooling in pans or with not enough ventilation
	Wrapping before cool
Texture	
Dense or heavy	Too little leavening
	Too much liquid
	Too much sugar
	Too much shortening
	Oven not hot enough
Coarse or irregular	Too much leavening
	Too little egg
	Improper mixing
Crumbly	Too much leavening
	Too much shortening
	Too much sugar
	Wrong kind of flour
	Improper mixing
Tough	Flour too strong
	Too much flour
	Too little sugar or shortening
	Overmixing
Poor flavor	Poor quality ingredients
	Poor storage or sanitation
	Unbalanced formula

TABLE 10.3 **Approximate Formula Adjustment in Shortened Cakes at High Altitudes**

Ingredient	Increase or Decrease	2500 ft.	5000 ft.	7500 ft.
Baking powder	decrease	20%	40%	60%
Flour	increase	—	4%	9%
Eggs	increase	2½%	9%	15%
Sugar	decrease	3%	6%	9%
Fat	decrease	—	—	9%
Liquid	increase	9%	15%	22%

To make adjustments, multiply the percentage indicated by the amount of ingredient and add or subtract this result as indicated.

Example: Adjust 1 lb (16 oz) eggs for 7500 ft.

$$.15 \times 16 \text{ oz} = 2.4 \text{ oz}$$
$$16 \text{ oz} + 2.4 \text{ oz} = 18.4 \text{ oz}$$

Baking Temperatures

Increase baking temperatures by about 25° F (14° C) above 3500 feet.

Pan Greasing

High-fat cakes tend to stick at high altitudes. Grease pans more heavily. Remove baked cakes from pans as soon as possible.

Storing

To prevent drying, wrap or ice cakes as soon as they are cool.

FORMULAS

The following cake mix formulas will give you practice with all major cake mixing methods. Many popular American cake types are included, sometimes in the form of variations on the basic cake types. These variations show that by making small changes in flavoring ingredients, you can make many different cakes from the same basic recipe. Adding new flavorings some-times requires making other ingredient changes. For example, in the case of the strawberry cake (p. 211), the flavoring ingredient is high in sugar, so the sugar in the formula is reduced.

Of course, many more variations are possible than there is room for here. As one example, we give a separate recipe for spice cake (made with brown sugar), but other spice cakes can be made by adding a similar spice mixture to a basic yellow cake.

The difference between chocolate cake and devil's-food cake is in the amount of baking soda used. As was explained in Chapter 2, an excess of soda will cause a reddish color in chocolate. By reducing the amount of soda (and increasing the baking powder to make up the lost leavening power), a devil's-food cake can be turned into a regular chocolate cake. Of course, both types of cake can be made with either cocoa powder or chocolate. See p. 27 for instructions on substituting one type of cocoa product for another.

Since we have already discussed the mixing procedures in detail, the procedures are not repeated for each formula. If necessary, review pp. 195–199 before beginning production.

Yellow Butter Cake

Ingredients	U.S.			Metric	%
Butter	2 lb	4	oz	1100 g	60
Sugar	3 lb			1450 g	80
Salt			0.5 oz	15 g	0.75
Eggs	1 lb	11	oz	810 g	45
Cake flour	3 lb	12	oz	1800 g	100
Baking powder			2.5 oz	72 g	4
Milk	2 lb	8	oz	1200 g	67
Vanilla		1	oz	30 g	1.5
Yield:	13 lb	7	oz	6477 g	358

Mixing: Creaming method

Scaling and baking: See Table 10.1.

Variation

Upside-Down Cake:

Increase the eggs to 50% (1 lb 14 oz/900 g). Decrease milk to 60% (2 lb 4 oz/1100 g). Add 0.75% (0.5 oz/15 g) lemon or orange flavor. Butter a sheet pan, spread with pan spread (below), and arrange desired fruit (pineapple rings, sliced peaches, etc.) on top of the pan spread. Scale batter at 7–8 lb (3200–3600 g) per sheet pan. Bake at 360° F (180° C). Immediately after baking, turn out of pan (see p. 203). Glaze with clear glaze (p. 61) or apricot glaze (p. 131).

Pan Spread (for one sheet pan)

Brown sugar	1 lb		450 g
Granulated sugar		6 oz	170 g
Corn syrup or honey		4 oz	120 g
Water (as needed)			

Cream together the first three ingredients. Add enough water to thin out to spreading consistency.

Chocolate Butter Cake

Ingredients	U.S.			Metric	%
Butter	2 lb			1000 g	67
Sugar	3 lb	8	oz	1725 g	115
Salt			0.75 oz	22 g	1.5
Unsweetened chocolate, melted	1 lb			500 g	33
Eggs	1 lb	8	oz	750 g	50
Cake flour	3 lb			1500 g	100
Baking powder		2	oz	60 g	4
Milk	1 lb	8	oz	750 g	50
Vanilla		1	oz	30	2
Yield:	13 lb	3	oz	6612 g	440

Mixing: Creaming method. Blend in the melted chocolate after the fat and sugar are well creamed.

Scaling and baking: See Table 10.1.

Brown Sugar Spice Cake

Ingredients	U.S.			Metric	%
Butter	1 lb	2	oz	600 g	60
Brown sugar	1 lb	14	oz	1000 g	100
Salt		0.5	oz	15 g	1.5
Eggs	1 lb	2	oz	600 g	60
Cake flour	1 lb	14	oz	1000 g	100
Baking powder		1	oz	30 g	3
Baking soda		0.1	oz (¾ tsp)	3 g	0.3
Cinnamon		0.16	oz (1 tbsp)	5 g	0.5
Cloves, ground		0.1	oz (1½ tsp)	3 g	0.3
Nutmeg		0.06	oz (¾ tsp)	2 g	0.2
Milk	1 lb	8	oz	800 g	80
Yield:	7 lb	9	oz	4058 g	405

Mixing: Creaming method

Scaling and baking: See Table 10.1.

Variations

Carrot Nut Cake:

Reduce the milk to 70% (1 lb 5 oz/700 g). Add 40% (12 oz/400 g) grated fresh carrots, 20% (6 oz/200 g) finely chopped walnuts, and 2 tsp (6 g) grated orange zest. Omit the cloves.

Banana Cake:

Omit the cinnamon and cloves. Reduce milk to 10% (3 oz/100 g). Add 125% (2 lb 6 oz/1250 g) ripe, puréed bananas. If desired, add 40% (12 oz/400 g) finely chopped pecans.

Applesauce Cake:

Reduce milk to 30% (9 oz/300 g) and add 90% (1 lb 11 oz/900 g) applesauce. Reduce baking powder to 2% (0.6 oz or 4 tsp/20 g). Increase baking soda to 1% (0.3 oz or 2 tsp/10 g).

Old-Fashioned Pound Cake

Ingredients	U.S.	Metric	%
Butter, or part butter and part shortening	2 lb	1000 g	100
Sugar	2 lb	1000 g	100
Vanilla	0.67 oz (4 tsp)	20 g	2
Eggs	2 lb	1000 g	100
Cake flour	2 lb	1000 g	100
Yield:	8 lb	4020 g	402

Mixing: Creaming method. After about half the eggs have been creamed in, add a little of the flour to avoid curdling.

Scaling and baking: See Table 10.1. Paper-lined loaf pans are often used for pound cakes.

Variations

Mace or grated lemon or orange zest may be used to flavor pound cake.

Raisin Pound Cake:

Add 25% (8 oz/250 g) raisins or currants, which have been soaked in boiling water and drained well.

Chocolate Pound Cake:

Sift 25% (8 oz/250 g) cocoa and 0.8% (¼ oz/8g) baking soda with the flour. Add 25% (8 oz/250 g) water to the batter.

Marble Pound Cake:

Fill loaf pans with alternating layers of regular and chocolate pound cake batters. Run a knife through the batter to marble the mixture.

Sheet Cake for Petits Fours and Fancy Pastries:

Increase eggs to 112% (2 lb 4 oz/1120 g). Bake on sheet pans lined with greased paper. Scale 4 lb (1800 g) for ¼-inch (6 mm) layers to make 3-layer petits fours. Scale 6 lb (2700 g) for ⅜-inch (9 mm) layers to make 2-layer petits fours.

Fruit Cake:

Use 50% cake flour and 50% bread flour in the basic recipe. Add 250–750% (5–15 lb/2.5–7.5 kg) mixed fruits and nuts to the batter. Procedure and suggested fruit mixtures follow.

1. Prepare fruits and nuts.

   a. Rinse and drain glazed fruits to remove excess syrup.

   b. Cut large fruits (such as whole dates) into smaller pieces.

   c. Mix all fruits and soak overnight in brandy, rum, or sherry.

   d. Drain well. (Reserve drained liquor for later batches or for other purposes.)

2. Mix batter as in basic procedure, using 80% of the flour. If spices are used, cream them with the butter and sugar.

3. Toss the fruits and nuts with the remaining flour. Fold them into the batter.

4. Baking: Use loaf, ring, or tube pans, preferably with paper liners. Bake at 350° F (175° C) for small cakes (1 – 1½ lb/450 – 700g), and 300° F (150° C) for large cakes (4 – 5 lb/1.8 – 2.3 kg). Baking time will range from about 1½ hours for small cakes to 3 to 4 hours or more for large cakes.

5. Cool. Glaze with clear glaze, decorate with fruits and nuts, if desired, and glaze again.

Percentages in the following fruit mixes are based on the flour in the basic pound cake recipe.

Fruit Mix I (Dark)

Dark raisins	2 lb		1000 g	100
Light raisins	2 lb		1000 g	100
Currants	1 lb		500 g	50
Dates	2 lb		1000 g	100
Figs	1 lb		500 g	50
Mixed glacé fruit	4 lb		2000 g	200
Glacé cherries		13 oz	400 g	40
Nuts (pecans, walnuts, filberts, brazil nuts)	1 lb	3 oz	600 g	60
Spices:				
Cinnamon		0.16 oz (1 tbsp)	5 g	0.5
Cloves		0.08 oz (1 tsp)	2.5 g	0.25
Nutmeg		0.08 oz (1 tsp)	2.5 g	0.25
Yield:	14 lb		7000 g	700

Fruit Mix II (Light)

Golden raisins	1 lb	8 oz	750 g	75
Currants	1 lb		500 g	50
Mixed glacé fruit	1 lb		500 g	50
Glacé pineapple		6 oz	200 g	20
Glacé orange peel		5 oz	150 g	15
Glacé lemon peel		5 oz	150 g	15
Glacé cherries		10 oz	300 g	30
Blanched almonds		8 oz	250 g	25
Spices:				
Grated lemon zest		0.125 oz (1 tsp)	4 g	0.4
Yield:	5 lb 10	oz	2800 g	280

Almond Cake for Petits Fours

Ingredients	U.S.		Metric	%
Almond paste	3 lb	6 oz	1500 g	300
Sugar	2 lb	8 oz	1150 g	225
Butter	2 lb	8 oz	1150 g	225
Eggs	3 lb	2 oz	1400 g	275
Cake flour		12 oz	340 g	67
Bread flour		6 oz	170 g	33
Yield:	12 lb	10 oz	5710 g	1125

Mixing: Creaming method. To soften the almond paste, blend it with a little of the egg until smooth, before adding the sugar. Proceed as for mixing pound cake.

Scaling and panning: 4 lb 3 oz (1900 g) per sheet pan. One recipe is enough for 3 pans. Pans must be level and without dents. Spread batter very smooth.

Baking: 400° F (200° C)

Sacher Mix

Ingredients	U.S.			Metric	%
Butter	1 lb	4	oz	500 g	100
Sugar	1 lb	4	oz	500 g	100
Sweet chocolate, melted	1 lb	9	oz	625 g	125
Egg yolks	1 lb	4	oz	500 g	100
Vanilla		0.67	oz (4 tsp)	15 g	3.3
Egg whites	1 lb	14	oz	750 g	150
Salt		0.17	oz (1 tsp)	4 g	0.8
Sugar		15	oz	375 g	75
Cake flour	1 lb	4	oz	500 g	100
Yield:	9 lb	11	oz	3769 g	750

Mixing: Modified creaming method.

1. Cream the butter and sugar; add the chocolate; add the egg yolks and vanilla, as in the basic creaming method.

2. Whip the egg whites with the salt. Add the sugar and whip to soft peaks.

3. Fold the egg whites into the batter alternately with the sifted flour.

Scaling: 10-inch (25-cm) cake: 36 oz (1020 g)
9-inch (23-cm) cake: 30 oz (850 g)
8-inch (20-cm) cake: 24 oz (680 g)
6-inch (15-cm) cake: 14 oz (400 g)

Baking: 325° F (165° C) for 45–60 minutes

See p. 238 for icing and decorating a sacher torte. Layers may be iced and decorated like any other chocolate cake, but then the cake should not be called sacher torte.

White Cake

Ingredients	U.S.			Metric	%
Cake flour	3 lb			1500 g	100
Baking powder		3	oz	90 g	6.25
Salt		1	oz	30 g	2
Emulsified shortening	1 lb	8	oz	750 g	50
Sugar	3 lb	12	oz	1875 g	125
Skim milk	1 lb	8	oz	750 g	50
Vanilla			0.75 oz (4½ tsp)	20 g	1.5
Almond extract			0.36 oz (2¼ tsp)	10 g	0.75
Skim milk	1 lb	8	oz	750 g	50
Egg whites	2 lb			1000 g	67
Yield:	13 lb	9	oz	6775 g	452

Mixing: Two-stage method

Scaling and baking: See Table 10.1.

Variations

Use water instead of milk, and add 10% (2.5 oz/70 g) non-fat dry milk to the dry ingredients.

Flavor with lemon extract or emulsion instead of vanilla and almond.

Yellow Cake:

Make the following ingredient adjustments:

Reduce shortening to 45% (1 lb 6 oz/675 g).

Substitute whole eggs for egg whites, using the same total weight (67%).

Use 2% (1 oz/30 g) vanilla and omit the almond extract.

Strawberry Cake:

Make the following ingredient adjustments:

Reduce the sugar to 100% (3 lb/1500 g).

Reduce the milk in *each stage* to 33% (1 lb/500 g).

Thaw and purée 67% (2 lb/1 kg) frozen, sweetened strawberries. Mix into the batter.

Cherry Cake:

Make the following ingredient adjustments:

Reduce the milk in *each stage* to 40% (1 lb 3 oz/600 g).

Add 30% (14 oz/450 g) ground maraschino cherries, with juice, to the batter.

Devil's Food Cake

Ingredients	U.S.			Metric	%
Cake flour	3 lb			1500 g	100
Cocoa		8	oz	250 g	17
Salt		1	oz	30 g	2
Baking powder		1.5	oz	45 g	3
Baking soda		1	oz	30 g	2
Emulsified shortening	1 lb 12		oz	870 g	58
Sugar	4 lb			2000 g	133
Skim milk	2 lb			1000 g	67
Vanilla		0.75 oz (4½ tsp)		20 g	1.5
Skim milk	1 lb 8		oz	750 g	50
Eggs	2 lb			1000 g	67
Yield:	15 lb			7495 g	500

Mixing: Two-stage method

Scaling and baking: See Table 10.1.

Angel Food Cake

Ingredients	U.S.		Metric	%
Egg whites	2 lb		1000 g	267
Cream of tartar		0.25 oz	8 g	2
Salt		0.17 oz (1 tsp)	5 g	1.5
Sugar	1 lb		500 g	133
Vanilla		0.33 oz (2 tsp)	10 g	2.5
Almond extract		0.17 oz (1 tsp)	5 g	1.25
Sugar	1 lb		500 g	133
Cake flour		12 oz	375 g	100
Yield:	4 lb 12	oz	2403 g	640

Mixing: Angel food method

Scaling and baking: See Table 10.1.

Variations

Chocolate Angel Food Cake:

Substitute 3 oz (90 g) cocoa for 3 oz (90 g) of the flour.

Coconut Macaroon Cupcakes:

Increase the first quantity of sugar to 167% (1 lb 4 oz/625 g). Mix 350% (2 lb 10 oz/1300 g) macaroon coconut with the flour/sugar mixture. Scale at 20 oz (575 g) per dozen cupcakes. Bake at 375° F (190° C) about 25 minutes.

Pound Cake (High-Ratio)

Ingredients	U.S.			Metric	%
Flour	2 lb	4	oz	1000 g	100
Salt		0.5	oz	15 g	2
Baking powder		0.5	oz	15 g	2
Emulsified shortening	1 lb	8	oz	670 g	67
Sugar	2 lb	10	oz	1170 g	117
Non-fat milk solids		2	oz	60 g	6
Water	1 lb			450 g	45
Eggs	1 lb	8	oz	670 g	67
Yield:	9 lb	1	oz	4050 g	405

Mixing: Two-stage method

Scaling and baking: See Table 10.1.

Variations

See variations following old-fashioned pound cake, p. 208.

Yellow Chiffon Cake

Ingredients	U.S.			Metric	%
Cake flour	1 lb	4	oz	500 g	100
Sugar	1 lb			400 g	80
Salt		0.5	oz	12 g	2.5
Baking powder		1	oz	25 g	5
Vegetable oil		10	oz	250 g	50
Egg yolks		10	oz	250 g	50
Water		15	oz	375 g	75
Vanilla		0.5	oz	12 g	2.5
Egg whites	1 lb	4	oz	500 g	100
Sugar		10	oz	250 g	50
Cream of tartar		0.1	oz (1¼ tsp)	2.5 g	0.5
Yield:	6 lb	7	oz	2576 g	515

Mixing: Chiffon method

Scaling and baking: See Table 10.1.

Variations

Chocolate Chiffon Cake:

Make the following ingredient adjustments:

Add 20% (4 oz/100 g) cocoa. Sift it with the flour.

Increase egg yolks to 60% (12 oz/300 g).

Increase the water to 90% (1 lb 2 oz/450 g).

(Continues)

Yellow Chiffon Cake Variations *(Continued)*

Orange Chiffon Cake:

Make the following ingredient adjustments:

Increase the egg yolks to 60% (12 oz/300 g).

Use 50% (10 oz/250 g) orange juice and 25% (5 oz/125 g) water.

Add 0.5 oz (2 tbsp/ 12 g) grated orange zest when adding the oil.

Sponge Roll I (Swiss Roll)

Ingredients	U.S.			Metric	%
Egg yolks		12	oz	350 g	100
Sugar		8	oz	235 g	67
Cake Flour		12	oz	350 g	100
Egg whites	1 lb	2	oz	525 g	150
Salt		0.25	oz	7 g	2
Sugar		6	oz	175 g	50
Yield:	3 lb	8	oz	1642 g	469

Mixing: Separated egg sponge method

Scaling: 1 lb 12 oz (820 g) per sheet pan. Line pans with greased paper.

Baking: 425° F (220° C), about 7 minutes

Variations

Chocolate Sponge Roll I (Chocolate Swiss Roll):

Sift 17% (2 oz/60 g) cocoa with the flour. Add 25% (3 oz/90 g) water to the whipped egg yolks.

Dobos Mix:

Blend 100% (12 oz/350 g) almond paste with the sugar. Add a little of the yolks and blend until smooth. Add the rest of the yolks and proceed as in the basic formula.

Scaling and panning: Seven layers are needed to make dobos torte (see p. 237 for assembly instructions). For a round dobos torte, spread a thin layer of mix onto the greased, floured bottoms of upside-down cake pans, or onto circles traced on parchment. One recipe makes about seven 12-inch (30-cm) circles, or fourteen 8- or 9-inch (20–22 cm) circles. For rectangular torten, spread a thin layer of mix on greased, paper-lined sheet pans. Four times the basic recipe will make seven full-size sheets. Or, to make only one strip, scale 20 oz (550 g) onto one sheet pan. When baked, cut into seven 3½-inch (9 cm) wide strips.

Baking: 400° F (200° C)

Genoise (Butter Sponge)

Ingredients	U.S.			Metric	%
Eggs	2 lb	4	oz	1125 g	150
Sugar	1 lb	8	oz	750 g	100
Cake flour	1 lb	8	oz	750 g	100
Butter, melted		8	oz	250 g	33
Vanilla (or lemon flavor)		0.5	oz	15 g	2
Yield:	5 lb	12	oz	2890 g	385

Mixing: Genoise or butter sponge method

Scaling and baking: See Table 10.1.

Variations

Chocolate Genoise:

Substitute 4 oz (125 g) cocoa powder for 4 oz (125 g) of the flour. Add 0.12 oz (¾ tsp/4 g) baking soda, dissolved in 1 oz (30 ml) water, to the egg foam.

Sponge for Seven-Layer Cake:

Add 50% (12 oz/375 g) egg yolks and 10% (2.5 oz/75 g) glucose to the first stage of mixing. Scale at 1 lb 12 oz (800 g) per sheet pan.

Almond Sponge I:

Make the following ingredients adjustments:

Add 50% (12 oz/375 g) yolks to the first mixing stage.

Increase the sugar to 150% (2 lb 4 oz/1125 g).

Add 117% (1 lb 12 oz/875 g) almond powder, mixed with the sifted flour.

(For other varieties, substitute other nuts for the almonds.)

Almond Sponge II:

Blend 125% (1 lb 14 oz/940 g) almond paste with 50% (12 oz/375 g) yolks and blend until smooth. Blend in the sugar (from the basic recipe) until smooth. Add the eggs and proceed as in the basic recipe. (Note: This mix does not develop as much volume as regular genoise, and it will make a layer ⅞-inch (22-mm) thick if scaled like genoise. If desired, scale 25% heavier to make a thicker layer.)

Sponge Roll II:

Omit butter from the basic recipe.

Chocolate Sponge Roll II:

Omit butter from chocolate genoise mix.

Jelly Roll Sponge

Ingredients	U.S.			Metric	%
Sugar	1 lb	6	oz	650 g	100
Eggs, whole	1 lb	4	oz	585 g	90
Egg yolks		4	oz	130 g	20
Salt		0.5	oz	15 g	2
Honey or corn syrup		3	oz	90 g	14
Water		2	oz	60 g	10
Vanilla		0.25	oz	7 g	1
Hot water		8	oz	235 g	36
Cake flour	1 lb	6	oz	650 g	100
Baking powder		0.33	oz	10 g	1.5
Yield:	5 lb	4	oz	2500 g	385

Mixing: Plain sponge method. Add the honey or syrup, the first quantity of water, and the vanilla to the sugar and eggs for the first mixing stage.

Scaling and baking: See Table 10.1. One recipe makes two sheet pans. Line the pans with *greased* paper. Immediately after baking, turn out of pan onto a sheet of parchment and remove the paper from the bottom of the cake. Spread with jelly and roll up tightly. When cool, dust with confectioners' sugar.

Milk and Butter Sponge

Ingredients	U.S.		Metric	%
Sugar	2 lb 8	oz	1250 g	125
Egg, whole	1 lb 8	oz	750 g	75
Egg yolks	8	oz	250 g	25
Salt	0.5	oz	15 g	1.5
Cake flour	2 lb		1000 g	100
Baking powder	1	oz	30 g	3
Skim milk	1 lb		500 g	50
Butter	8	oz	250 g	25
Vanilla	1	oz	30 g	3
Yield:	8 lb 2	oz	4075 g	407

Mixing: Hot milk and butter sponge method

Scaling and baking: Cake layers; see Table 10.1.

Variation

Instead of vanilla, add 1.5% (0.5 oz/15 g) lemon flavor.

TERMS FOR REVIEW

air cell
emulsion
creaming method
two-stage method
flour-batter method
high-fat cake
egg-foam cake
angel food method
chiffon method
sponge method
genoise
hot milk and butter sponge
pound cake
fruit cake
sponge roll

QUESTIONS FOR DISCUSSION

1. What are the three main goals of mixing cake batter?

2. How are the following concepts related to the goals in Question 1: Emulsion? Creaming of fat and sugar? Gluten development?

3. What are four precautions you should take to prevent a cake batter from curdling or separating?

4. List the steps in the creaming method of cake mixing.

5. List the steps in the two-stage, or high-ratio, mixing method.

6. List the steps in the sponge method. What extra steps are needed in the butter sponge or genoise method? In the hot milk and butter sponge method? In the separated egg sponge method?

7. What are the advantages and disadvantages of using butter in high-fat cakes?

8. Why is there a lot of emphasis on scraping down the sides of the bowl and the beater in both the creaming method and the two-stage method?

9. Which of the following cake ingredients are considered tougheners, which are tenderizers, which are driers, and which are moisteners?

   flour

   butter

   sugar

   egg whites

   egg yolks

   whole eggs

   milk (liquid)

   cocoa

   water

10. Why should angel food cake pans not be greased?

CHAPTER 11

ASSEMBLING AND DECORATING CAKES

uch of the appeal of cakes is due to their appearance. Cakes are a perfect medium with which a baker can express artistry and imagination. An undecorated cake is to a cake decorator what a blank canvas is to a painter. Decorated cakes range from the simple (such as an iced layer cake with a simple spiral pattern on top made with a bowl knife and a coating of chopped nuts on the sides) to the complex (such as a tiered wedding cake with garlands, lacework borders, and bouquets of icing flowers).

A cake need not be elaborate or complex to be pleasing. The most simple designs are often the most attractive, if they are done neatly and carefully. Certainly, a simple but neatly finished cake is better than a gaudy, overdecorated cake that is done carelessly or without any plan for a harmonious overall design.

There are of course many different styles of cake decorating, and within each style there are hundreds or thousands of different designs possible. This chapter is, in part, an introduction to some of the basic techniques for finishing cakes. The most important requirements for making effective desserts is hours and hours of practice with the pastry bag and paper cone—the decorator's chief tools. Even the simplest designs (such as straight lines) require a lot of practice and should be mastered well. Only then should you proceed to more advanced techniques, which are presented in various style manuals and cake decorating books.

A cake must, naturally, be assembled and iced before it can be decorated. In this chapter, we will discuss the procedures for assembling basic layer cakes, sheet cakes, and so forth. Then we proceed to a study of the slightly more elaborate European-style cakes, including procedures for a number of classic desserts.

After studying this chapter, you should be able to:
1. Assemble and ice simple layer cakes, sheet cakes, and cupcakes.
2. Make and use a paper decorating cone.
3. Use a pastry bag to make simple icing decorations.
4. Assemble a variety of European-style cakes, Swiss rolls, small cakes, and petits fours.

ASSEMBLING AND ICING SIMPLE CAKES

This section deals with simple, American-style cakes. Typical examples of this type are cupcakes, sheet cakes, and layer cakes made of two or three high-ratio or butter-cake layers. These are popular items in bakeshops and are standard desserts in many kinds of food-service operations. They may be iced but otherwise undecorated, or they may be given some decorative touches.

Selection of Icing

The flavor, texture, and color of the icing must be compatible with the cake.

In general, use heavy frostings with heavy cakes and light frostings with light cakes. For example, ice angle food cakes with a simple flat icing, fondant, or a light, fluffy, boiled icing. High-ratio cakes go well with buttercreams and fudge-type icings. Sponge layer cakes are often combined with fruits or fruit fillings, light French or meringue-type buttercreams, whipped cream, or flavored fondants.

Use the best-quality flavorings and use them sparingly. The flavor of the frosting should not be stronger than that of the cake. Fudge-type icings may be flavored most strongly, as long as the flavor is of good quality.

Use color sparingly. Light, pastel shades are more appetizing than loud colors. Paste colors give the best results. To use either paste or liquid colors, mix a little color with a small portion of the icing, then use this icing to color the rest.

Procedure for Assembling Layer Cakes

1. Cool cake layers completely before assembling and icing.

2. Trim layers if necessary.

    a. Remove any ragged edges.

    b. Slightly rounded tops are easily covered by icing, but excessively large bumps may have to be cut off.

    c. If desired, layers may be split in half horizontally. This makes the cake higher and increases the proportion of filling to cake, (Figure 11.1).

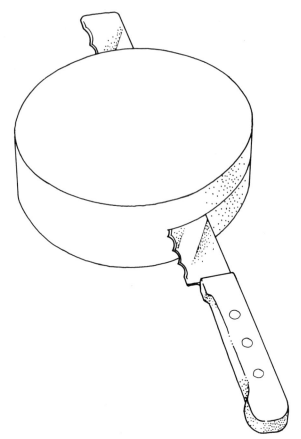

FIGURE 11.1 Cake layers may be split in half horizontally, using a long-bladed, serrated knife.

3. Brush all crumbs from cakes. Loose crumbs make icing difficult.

4. Place the bottom layer upside-down (to give a flat surface for the filling) on a cardboard cake circle of the same diameter. Place the cake in the center of a cake turntable. If a cake circle or turntable is not available, place the cake on a serving plate; slip sheets of wax paper or parchment under the edges of the cake to keep the plate clean.

5. Spread filling on bottom layer out to the edges. If the filling is different from the outside frosting, be careful not to spread the filling over the edges.

    Use the proper amount of filling. If applied too heavily, filling will ooze out when top layer is put in place.

6. Place top layer on bottom layer, right-side up.

7. Ice the cake:

    a. If a thin or light icing is used, pour or spread the icing onto the center of the cake. Then spread it to the edges and down the sides with a spatula.

b. If a heavy icing is used, it may be necessary to spread the sides first, then place a good quantity of icing in the center of the top and *push* it to the edges with the spatula.

Pushing the icing rather than pulling or dragging it with the spatula prevents pulling up crumbs and getting them mixed with the icing.

Use enough icing to cover the entire cake generously, but not excessively, with an even layer.

Smooth the icing with the spatula, or leave it textured or swirled, as desired.

The finished, iced cake should have a perfectly level top and perfectly straight, even sides.

Sheet Cakes

Sheet cakes are ideal for volume service because they require little labor to bake, ice, and decorate, and they keep well as long as they are uncut.

For special occasions, sheet cakes are sometimes decorated as a single unit with a design or picture in colored icing, and a "Happy Special Occasion" message. It is more common, however, to ice them for individual service as in the following procedure.

Procedure for Icing Sheet Cakes

1. Turn out the cake onto the bottom of another sheet pan or tray, as described on page 203. Cool the cake thoroughly.

2. Trim the edges evenly with a serrated knife.

3. Brush all crumbs from the cake.

4. Place a quantity of icing in the center of the cake and, with a spatula, push the icing to the edges. Smooth the top with the spatula, giving the entire cake an even layer of icing.

5. With a long knife or spatula, mark the entire cake off into portions, as in Figure 11.2, by pressing the back of the knife lightly into the icing. Do not cut the cake.

6. Using a paper cone or pastry bag fitted with a star tube, pipe a rosette or swirl onto the center of each marked-off portion. Or select another kind of decoration, as desired. Whatever decorations you use, keep them simple, and make them the same for every portion. The finished sheet cake will resemble that in Figure 11.3.

7. Cut portions as close as possible to service time to keep the cake from drying.

18 × 26 inch sheets

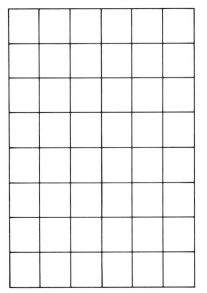
6 × 8 = 48 portions

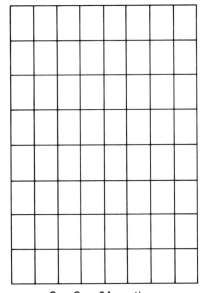
8 × 8 = 64 portions

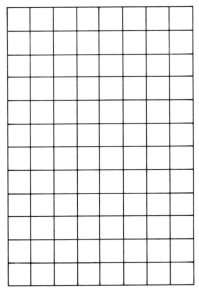
8 × 12 = 96 portions

FIGURE 11.2 Cake-cutting guides for sheet cakes and round layer cakes. For half-size sheets (13 × 18 in/33 × 46 cm), simply halve the above diagrams for full-size sheet cakes.

(*Continues*)

FIGURE 11.2   (Continued)

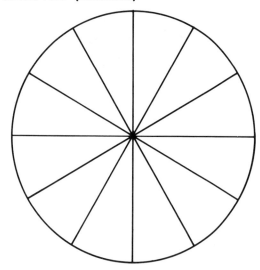

8–10 inch layers
12 portions

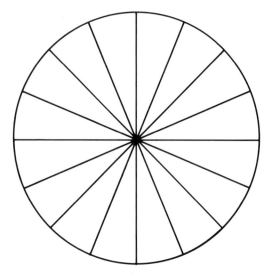

10–12 inch layers
16 portions

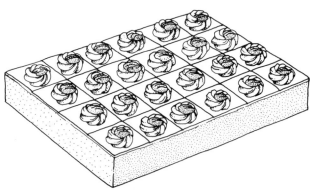

FIGURE 11.3   A finished sheet cake marked off into portions and decorated so that each portion is identical.

Cupcakes

There are three main methods for icing cupcakes. The first of these, dipping, is used for soft icings. The other methods are used when the icing is too stiff for dipping.

1. Dip the tops of the cupcakes in the icing. Do not dip them too deep; only the tops should touch the icing.

    If the icing is reasonably stiff, not flowing, twist the cakes slightly and pull them out quickly in one smooth motion.

    If the icing is flowing (such as flat icing or fondant), pull the cakes straight out of the icing. Hold them sideways for a moment so that the icing runs

to one edge. Then turn them upright and wipe the icing from the edge of the cakes with the finger. Do not let icing run down the sides.

2. Spread the icing with a spatula. Take enough icing for one cake on the tip of a bowl knife and cover the top of the cake in a smooth, neat motion, twisting the cake in one hand. Practice is necessary to develop speed and efficiency.

3. With a pastry bag fitted with a star tube, apply a swirl of icing to each cake.

Before the icing dries, cupcakes may be decorated with glazed fruit, coconut, nuts, colored sugar, chocolate sprinkles, etc.

Specialty items

A number of popular cake items don't fit in the above categories (layer cake, sheet cake, or cupcake). Among them are the following:

Boston Cream Pie

This is not a pie at all, but a simple layer cake. Bake sponge cake in standard layer pans or pie tins. When cool, split each cake into two layers. Fill with pastry cream (p. 120) and ice the tops with chocolate fondant or sprinkle with confectioners' sugar.

Cake Rolls

Besides the popular jelly rolls (p. 216), sponge rolls can be made with a variety of fillings, such as whipped cream, vanilla or chocolate boiled icing or marshmallow icing, or buttercream. Cake rolls are discussed in more detail in the section on European-style cakes (p. 240).

Ice Cream Cakes

Ice cream may be used in place of icing to fill layer cakes or cake rolls. If the bakeshop is cool, or if you have a walk-in refrigerator to work in, you can spread slightly softened ice cream on the layers or inside the rolls. If the temperature is warm, however, it is better to cut slices of hard-frozen ice cream to fill the cakes. Work quickly: Do not allow the ice cream to melt and drip out of the cake.

As soon as the layers are stacked or the rolls tightly rolled, return them to the freezer until they are firm. Then quickly frost the tops and sides with whipped cream. Store in the freezer until needed.

French Pastry

In this country, the term French pastry is used for a wide range of decorated pastry and cake products usually made in single-portion pieces. The simplest of the cake-based varieties are tiny, decorated layer cakes made in a variety of shapes. They are assembled as follows:

1. Using thin (½ to ¾ inch/1 to 2 cm) sheet cakes, stack two or three sheets with filling or icing between them. The filled cake layers together should be about 1½ to 2 inches (4 to 5 cm) thick.

   Buttercream is the most popular filling. Fruit jams and fudge icings may also be used.

2. Press the layers together firmly and chill briefly.

3. Using a sharp knife dipped in hot water before each cut, cut the sheet into desired shapes, such as squares, rectangles, or triangles. Circles may be cut out using large cutters. Pieces should be the size of a single portion.

4. Ice the sides and top of each piece with buttercream or fondant. After icing, sides may be coated with chopped nuts, coconut, chocolate sprinkles, etc.

5. Decorate the tops neatly.

French pastries are discussed further in the section on European-style cakes (pp. 242–243).

BASIC DECORATING TECHNIQUES

A number of simple decorating techniques are discussed in this section. Of these, perhaps the most difficult ones to learn are those using the pastry bag and paper cone. Some other techniques don't require so much practice, but instead rely simply on your steady hand and your sense of neatness and symmetry.

Tools

The following are needed for assembling and decorating cakes.

Bowl knife or steel spatula. A spatula with a long, flexible blade for spreading and smoothing icings and fillings.

Serrated knife. A scalloped-edge knife for cutting cakes and for splitting cake layers horizontally into thinner layers.

Icing screens or grates. Open-mesh screens for holding cakes that are being iced with a flow-type icing such as fondant. Excess icing drips off the cake and is collected on a tray under the rack.

Turntable. A pedestal with a flat, rotating top, that simplifies the job of icing cakes.

Icing comb. A plastic triangle with toothed or serrated edges. Used for applying a grooved or ridged pattern to the sides of iced cakes. The edge of the comb is held stationary in a vertical position against one side of the cake while the turntable is rotated.

Plastic or steel scraper. The flat edge can be easily used to make the icing on the sides of cake perfectly smooth. The technique is the same as the technique for using the icing comb (see above).

Brushes. Used to remove crumbs from a cake, to apply dessert syrups to sponge cake layers, and to glaze the surfaces of cakes with apricot glaze and other coatings.

Sugar dredger. Looks like a large metal salt shaker. Used to dust cakes with confectioners' sugar.

Cake circles and doilies. Layer cakes are placed on cardboard circles (same diameter as the cake) when being assembled. This makes them easy to ice and to move after icing. For easy, attractive display, place a paper doily 4 inches (10 cm) larger than the cake on a cake circle 2 inches (5 cm) larger than the cake. For example, to assemble, ice, and display a 10-inch cake, you will use a 10-inch circle, a 12-inch circle, and a 14-inch doily.

Parchment paper. For making paper cones.

Pastry bag and tubes. For making borders, inscriptions, designs, flowers, and other designs out of icing. The basic tubes are as follows (see Figure 11.4):

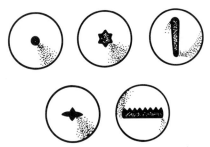

FIGURE 11.4 Basic cake decorating tubes, as seen from the end.
From left to right, top row: plain, star, rose.
Bottom row: leaf, basketweave.

Plain (round) tubes — for writing and for making lines, beads, dots, and so forth.

Star tubes — for making rosettes, shells, stars, and various borders.

Rose tube — for making flower petals. These tubes have a slit-shaped opening that is wider at one end than at the other.

Leaf tubes — for making leaves.

Ribbon or basketweave tubes — for making smooth or ridged stripes or ribbons. These have a slit opening that is ridged on one side.

Many other specialized tubes are used for unusual shapes. However, the plain and star tubes are by far the most important. It is probably best for the beginner to concentrate on these. They will make a wide variety of decorations. With the exception of roses and other flowers, the majority of cake decorations are made with the plain and star tubes.

The usual way of using a pastry tube is simply to fit it inside the pastry bag. When you need to use more than one tube with the same icing, you must use a separate bag for each tube, or you must empty out the bag to change the tube. However, special *couplers* are available that allow you to attach the tube to the outside of the bag. It is then a simple matter to change tubes even when the pastry bag is full of icing.

Using the Paper Cone

The paper cone is widely used in decorative work. It is inexpensive, easy to make, and it can simply be discarded after use. It is especially valuable if you are working with different colors; simply make a separate cone for each color icing. Figure 11.5 illustrates how to make a decorating cone from a triangle of parchment.

While it is possible to fit metal decorating tubes inside paper cones, the cones are usually used without metal tubes, for writing inscriptions and for making

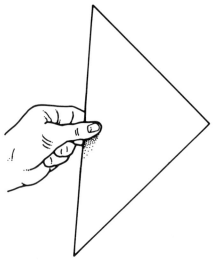

FIGURE 11.5 Making a paper cone.
(*a*) Hold the paper triangle as shown, grasping the center of the long side between the thumb and forefinger of the left hand.

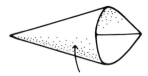

(*b*) With the right hand, roll the top corner down to the center of the triangle. Hold the paper in this position with the right hand.

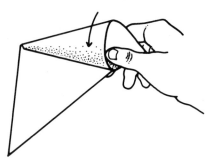

(*c*) With the left hand, roll the bottom corner up to complete the cone.

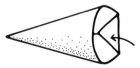

(*d*) Adjust the cone so that the point is completely closed and the point is sharp. Fold down the loose edges of the open end of the cone so that it will not unroll.

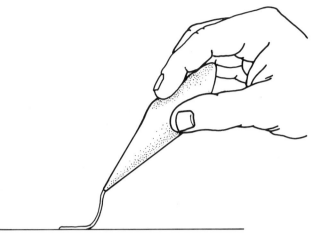

(e) Fill the cone and fold the open end several times so that it is tightly closed. Hold the cone between the thumb and fingers as shown.

line drawings and patterns. In other words, they are used the same way you would use a pastry bag fitted with a small plain tube. Since paper cones can be made rather small and are easy to control, pastry chefs generally prefer them to pastry bags when they are doing delicate work. For the most delicate work, a special type of plastic or cellophane is available that makes finer lines than paper because a smaller, cleaner opening can be cut on the tip.

Two factors are important if you are to be successful with both the paper cone and the pastry bag.

1. *Consistency of the icing.* Icing must be neither too thick nor too thin. With the paper cone or the writing tube, the icing must be thin enough to flow freely from the opening, but not too thin to form a solid thread. Stiff icing is very difficult to force through the opening and tends to break off. For flowers and large decorations, the icing must be stiffer, so that it holds its shape.

2. *Pressure on the cone or bag.* Pressure control is necessary for neat, exact decorations. As will be described below, sometimes you must keep the pressure steady and even. For other types of decorations, such as shell borders, you must vary the pressure from heavy to light, and then stop the pressure at the right time. Learning to control the pressure with which you squeeze the decorator's cone or pastry bag takes a lot of practice.

The following instructions for using the cone and pastry bag are written for right-handed people. If you are left-handed, simply reverse the hands in the instructions.

Procedure for Decorating with a Paper Cone

1. Make the paper cone as shown in Figure 11.5.

2. Fill the cone about half full of icing. If the cone is too full, it is hard to squeeze, and icing is likely to come out the top.

3. Fold down the top of the cone to close the open end.

4. With scissors, cut off a very small piece of the tip of the cone. It is better to make the opening too small rather than too large. Squeeze out a little of the icing to test the cone. If necessary, cut off a little more of the tip to enlarge the opening.

5. Hold the top end of the cone between the thumb and the first two fingers of the right hand (if you are right-handed). The fingers should be positioned so that they hold the folded end closed and at the same time apply pressure to squeeze the icing from the cone (see Figure 11.5).

6. The left hand does *not* squeeze the cone. Lightly hold the index finger of the left hand against the thumb of the right hand or against the cone in order to steady your right hand and help guide it.

7. Different types of decorations and inscriptions are made by the following two methods for using the cone.

The falling method is so called because the cone is held above the surface, and the icing is allowed to fall or drop from the tip of the cone onto the surface being decorated. This method is used to make lines of even thickness on horizontal surfaces. Much, if not most, paper-cone work is done this way, generally with royal icing, fondant, chocolate fondant, melted chocolate, or piping chocolate (p. 314).

Hold the cone vertically. Touch the tip of the cone to the surface to attach the icing to the point where you want the line to start. Then, as you begin to squeeze the cone, lift the tip of the cone from the surface and start your line. Hold the cone about an inch (2½ cm) from the surface as you trace your pattern. The thread of icing is suspended in air between the tip of the cone and the surface being decorated. Keep the pressure light and constant. To finish a line, lower the tip of the cone and touch the surface at the point where you want the line to end. At the same time, stop squeezing the cone.

This method allows you to make very fine, delicate lines and patterns while keeping the thickness of the line perfectly even. The opening in the tip of the cone should be cut quite small. At first, it may seem difficult to control the line while holding the

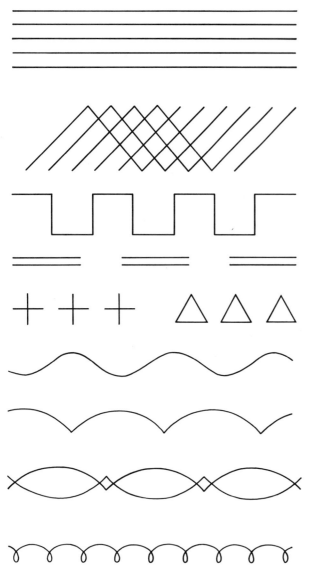

FIGURE 11.6 Simple patterns for practicing with the paper cone.

cone an inch above the surface. But with practice, you will be able to make very precise patterns.

The patterns illustrated in Figures 11.6, 11.7, and 11.8 are made with the falling method. Figure 11.6 shows simple patterns that the beginner should practice and master before proceeding to more complicated designs. Figure 11.7 shows a selection of designs that can be used to decorate cakes, while Figure 11.8 shows designs for petits fours. Any of these designs can be practiced by first drawing it in dark ink on a sheet of paper, then placing a sheet of translucent parchment or a plate of glass over the design. Pipe the icing onto the parchment, using the design as a guide.

The **contact method** is used in two cases: (1) When you want to vary the thickness of the line; (2) When you want to decorate a vertical surface, such as the side of a cake.

Hold the cone as you would hold a pen, with the tip in contact with the surface and at an angle of about 30 to 45 degrees. Draw lines as though you were drawing on paper with a pen. Control the thickness of the line by adjusting the pressure of your thumb. Squeezing harder will make a thicker line.

It takes a fair amount of practice to be able to control the thickness of the line. Normally, it is best to practice the falling method first, until you can make simple lines and patterns easily. Then, when you practice the contact method, you can concentrate on controlling pressure. The patterns in Figure 11.9 are made with the contact method. In addition to royal icing, fondant, and chocolate, buttercream is also used for decorating with the contact method.

FIGURE 11.7 Paper-cone designs for borders and other cake decorations.

FIGURE 11.8 Paper-cone designs for petits fours.

Using the Pastry Bag

An advantage of the pastry bag is that it makes it easy to use different metal tubes to create a wide variety of designs. Also, a pastry bag holds more than a paper cone. This is important when you are decorating with whipped cream or meringue. Buttercream flowers, shell borders, and many other decorations are made with the pastry bag.

Procedure for Using a Pastry Bag

1. Fit the desired metal tube into the pastry bag.

2. Turn down the top of the bag into a sort of collar. Slip your hand under this collar and hold the top open with your thumb and forefinger.

3. Fill the bag half to three-quarters full. Remember that stiff icings are relatively hard to force from the

FIGURE 11.9 Paper-cone designs made by the contact method.

bag, so the bag should be filled less. With meringue and whipped cream, the bag can be fuller.

4. Turn the top of the bag up again. Gather the loose top together and hold it shut with the thumb and forefinger of your right hand (if you are right-handed).

5. To force out the icing or cream, squeeze the top of the bag in the palm of your right hand.

6. The fingers of the left hand are used to lightly guide the tip of the bag, *not* to squeeze the bottom of the bag. The left hand is sometimes used to hold the item being filled or decorated.

7. The following illustrations show how to make several of the most commonly used decorations:

> Shells and shell borders: Figure 11.10
> Rosettes: Figure 11.11
> Scrolls and fleurs de-lis: Figure 11.12
> Bead border: Figure 11.13
> Basketweave: Figure 11.14
> Roses: Figure 11.15
> Leaves: Figure 11.16
> Drop string: Figure 11.17

(Text continued on p. 231.)

FIGURE 11.10 Shells and shell border.
Use a star tube. Hold the bag at a 45-degree angle with the tube just touching the surface. Squeeze the bag so that the icing swells out to make a broad base for the shell. As you pull the bag away from the base of the shell, relax the pressure so that the shell draws out to a narrow point. Stop the pressure and pull the bag away.

FIGURE 11.11 Rosettes.
Use a star tube. Hold the bag vertically or almost vertically. Squeeze the bag and at the same time move the tip in a tight circular motion, as if you are drawing a small letter "C." At the same time, lift the bag slightly. Stop the pressure and pull the bag away.

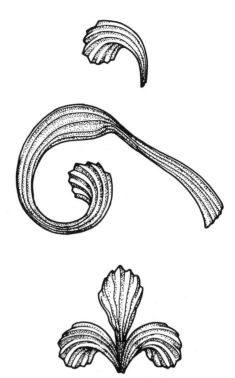

FIGURE 11.12 Scrolls and fleurs-de-lis.
Use a star tube. Scrolls are made like shells, but elongated into a sweeping, graceful curve. Two short scrolls on either side of a shell make a fleur-de-lis.

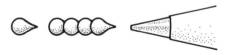

FIGURE 11.13 Bead border.
Use a small plain tube. Make a bead border exactly the same way you make a shell border.

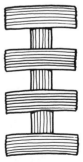

FIGURE 11.14 Basketweave.
(*a*) Use a basketweave tube or small star tube. Pipe a vertical line near the edge of the surface being decorated, or down the side of the cake. Pipe a series of horizontal bars across the vertical line, leaving a bar-width space between them. (*continues*)

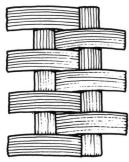

FIGURE 11.14 (continued)
(b) Pipe a second vertical line against the ends of the short bars, as shown. Again, pipe horizontal bars across this line, fitting them in between the first set of bars.

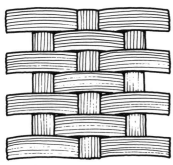

(c) Repeat, alternating vertical lines and horizontal bars, until the surface is covered with a basketweave pattern.

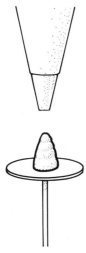

FIGURE 11.15 Roses.
(a) Hold the pastry bag in the right hand and the flower nail in the left hand so that you can spin the nail between the thumb and forefinger. Make a cone-shaped mound of icing in the center of the nail. This is easiest to do with a plain tube held vertically as shown, although with practice it is possible to do with the rose tube.

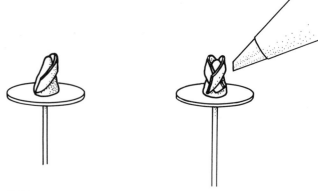

(b) Using the rose tube, hold the bag so that the narrow end of the opening in the tube is at the top. Place the tube so that the bottom of the opening is touching the icing cone about half-way up from the base. Squeezing with an even pressure, lift the tube up and then down again and turn the nail at the same time, so that you make a semicircular ribbon of icing that is wrapped halfway around the cone. This is the first petal. Make a second petal on the other side in the same way.

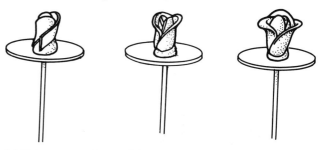

(c) Make a second row of three petals. Turn the tube at a slight angle away from the center cone so that the petals flare outward slightly. Also, start the base of the petals slightly lower on the cone base.

(d) Make a third row of four or five petals. Turn the tube outward even more, so that the petals flare outward and the top edges of the petals curl back. Stagger the petals so that they overlap the spaces between the petals in the second row.

(e) For larger flowers, continue making petals until the rose is built up to the desired size. Each row of petals should flare outward more than the preceding row.

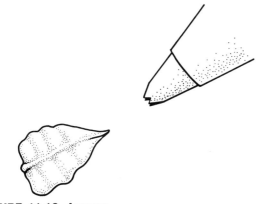

FIGURE 11.16 Leaves.
Use a leaf tube. Hold the end of the tube against the surface, with the bag at a 45-degree angle. Squeeze the bag while holding the tube in place for a moment so that the base of the leaf flares out. Relax the pressure as you pull the tube away so that the leaf becomes narrower. Stop the pressure and pull the tube away completely. (Note: If the leaf does not come to a point, the icing may be too stiff.)

FIGURE 11.17 Drop string.
(a) Use a small plain (writing) tube or a paper cone. Drop strings are applied to the sides of cakes, not the tops. This technique requires suspending a string of icing in air, as for the falling method used with the paper cone (p. 225). Touch the tube to the surface to attach the string. Pull the tube away while squeezing the bag, letting the string drop naturally into a semicircle. *Do not lower the tube.* Attach the string 1 inch (2.5 cm, or desired interval) from the beginning of the arc, but on the same level. Repeat at regular intervals.

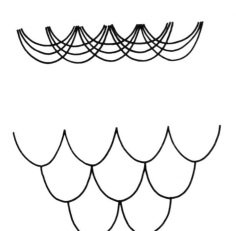

(b) For more elaborate string work, overlap strings or hang them from each other in various combinations.

Other Decorating Techniques

There are many dozens of techniques for decorating cakes. Below are some of the simpler, more commonly used techniques. In the last section of this book, on European-style cakes, and in the accompanying illustrations, you will see examples of these and other techniques.

A frequently used way of organizing the decoration of a cake is to divide the cake into portions by marking the icing on top with the back of a long knife. First mark the cake in quarters. Then divide each quarter in half, thirds, or fourths, depending on the size of the cake and the number of pieces desired.

Decorate the cake in a repetitive pattern so that each slice has the same decorations. For example, you might decorate a black forest cake (p. 236) with a rosette of cream at the wide end of each wedge, then place a cherry on each rosette. Examples of this method are illustrated in Figures 11.20 and 11.26.

The advantage of marking the cake into wedges is that it provides portion control. Thus, it is often used in restaurants and in retail shops that sell cakes by the slice. Each slice, when cut and served, still retains an attractive decoration.

Masking the Sides

Apply a coating of chopped or sliced nuts, coconut, chocolate sprinkles, chocolate shavings, cake crumbs, or another material to the sides of the cake. Hold the freshly iced cake (on a cardboard circle) in your left hand over the tray of nuts or other material. With your right hand, lightly press a handful of the material against the side of the cake, and let the excess fall back onto the tray. Turn the cake slightly and repeat until the coating is complete. You can coat the sides completely or just the bottom edge.

Stenciling

Designs can be made on a cake by masking part of the top with paper cutouts or paper doilies and then sprinkling the top of the cake with confectioners' sugar, ground nuts, shaved chocolate, cake crumbs, praline powder, or another fine material. Carefully remove the paper pattern to reveal the design. A very simple type of stenciling that is effective on chocolate icings is to place parallel strips of paper on the cake and dust with confectioners' sugar.

Marbling

This technique is most frequently used with fondant. Ice the top of the cake with one color fondant, then pipe lines or spirals in a contrasting color. Quickly, before the icing sets, draw the back of the knife through the icing to marble it. This is the same technique used to ice napoleons (Figure 8.10). Other patterns using this technique are shown in Figure 11.18.

Bowl Knife Patterns

Icing can be textured quickly and easily with a bowl knife as soon as the cake is iced. To make a spiral pattern, leave the cake on the turntable and press the rounded end of the blade lightly into the icing at the center of the cake. Slowly turn the turntable and at the same time gradually draw the tip of the bowl knife to the outer edge of the cake.

If you wish, this spiral can be "marbled" with the edge of the knife the same way you would marble the fondant stripes in Figure 11.18. Other patterns, such as

FIGURE 11.18 Marbled icing patterns are made by piping lines, circles, or spirals of a contrasting color fondant onto an iced cake top, then drawing the back of a knife or spatula across the lines before the icing sets.

straight, parallel ridges, can be made with the bowl knife and then "marbled."

Piping Jelly

Piping jelly is a transparent, sweet jelly used for decorating cakes. It is available in various colors and in a clear, colorless form that you can color yourself. Piping jelly can be piped directly onto a cake with a paper cone. For example, you can add a touch of color to petits fours by first decorating them with chocolate fondant, using some of the designs in Figure 11.4 and then filling in some of the small loops with colored piping jelly.

Another way to use piping jelly is to make jelly transfers. These are colored pictures that are made ahead of time and applied to cakes as needed. Their advantage is that they can be made during slack hours and stored until needed.

Procedure for Making Piping Jelly Transfers

1. Trace the desired drawing onto a sheet of tracing paper. Or, if you wish, draw a picture freehand.

2. Turn the drawing over so that the tracing is underneath and can be seen through the paper. (The paper is turned over so that the pen or pencil marks don't come off with the jelly.)

3. Outline the drawing with brown piping jelly.

4. Fill in the outlines with piping jelly of appropriate colors.

5. Let the jelly dry. This will take a day.

6. Turn the transfer over and place it, jelly-side down, on the iced cake.

7. Moisten the back of the paper lightly with a brushed dipped in water.

8. Let the cake and paper stand a few minutes. Then carefully peel off the paper, leaving the jelly picture on the cake.

Adding Fruits, Nuts, and Other Items

Arranging fruits, nuts, and other items on a cake in an attractive pattern is an easy and effective way to decorate a cake while at the same time adding to its flavor and its appeal to the customer. This technique is especially appropriate for cakes that are marked off into portions, as described at the beginning of this sec-

tion. Each portion can be topped with an appropriate item, as in the example of the cherries on the black forest cake.

Naturally, you should use items appropriate to the flavor of the cake. For example, you might place candy coffee beans on a mocha cake, or mandarin orange segments on an orange-flavored cake.

Following are some examples of items that can be arranged decoratively on cakes:

    whole strawberries
    sweet cherries
    mandarin orange segments
    pineapple wedges
    glacéed fruits
    candied chestnuts
    pecan halves
    walnut halves
    small, crisp meringues
    chocolates, such as chocolate truffles
    chocolate curls or other chocolate decorations
    small candies (except hard candies, as a customer
        might break a tooth)
    marzipan cutouts (cut from colored marzipan (p.
        315) rolled out in sheets) and marzipan figures

Decorating Sequence

While the order in which decorations are placed on the cake depends on the cake and on the baker's preferences, many pastry chefs prefer a sequence like the following:

1. The sides of the cake are coated with nuts, crumbs, etc., either before or after decorating. If the top decorations are delicate and might be damaged if the cake is handled, mask the sides first. However, if you are marbling the top of the cake or using some other technique that disturbs the icing on the sides of the cake, then mask the sides afterwards.

2. If the cake is to have any inscription or message, such as a person's name or a holiday or birthday greeting, put this on first.

3. Add borders and paper-cone designs.

4. Add flowers, leaves, and similar decorations made with a pastry bag.

5. Add any additional items, such as fruits, nuts, or candies.

The birthday cake in Figure 11.19, finished in a classic American style, was decorated using this basic sequence: first the inscription, then the bottom border, then the flowers and leaves.

FIGURE 11.19   Classic American birthday cake.
(Prepared by Vallette Pastry, Astoria, N.Y.)

EUROPEAN-STYLE CAKES

A typical American layer cake consists of two components—cake layers and icing. The cake has two or sometimes three fairly thick layers and is often a high-ratio or creaming-method cake. The iced cake may be 3 or 4 inches high or higher.

A typical European cake, on the other hand, can be described as follows: sponge cake, such as genoise, split into thin layers, moistened with a flavored syrup, filled and iced, and frequently set on a base of baked meringue, japonaise, or short dough. It is sometimes filled with fruit between the layers, and is almost always decorated on top. A European-style cake is usually less than 2½ inches high, and its broad, flat top provides an excellent medium for a pastry chef to display his decorating skills.

The above descriptions of American and European cakes are, of course, generalizations, so there are many exceptions to both descriptions. Nevertheless, they do give you some idea of the common differences and serve to introduce the subject of European-style cake assembly.

Gateaux and Torten

Two words you will see often in connection with European-style cakes are *gateau* and *torte*. Gateau is the French word for cake (the plural is gateaux; both singular and plural are pronounced "ga-toe"). It is nearly as general as our word "cake" and is used for a wide range of products. For example, in Chapter 8 you find gateau pithiviers, made of puff pastry and almond filling, and gateau St. Honoré, made of short dough and éclair paste and filled with a type of pastry cream. Gateaux can also refer to more conventional layer cakes.

The German word torte (torten, plural) is generally used for layer cakes. There are many definitions, which often contradict each other. According to a British definition, a torte is a sponge layer cake that is marked off into individual wedges, which are then individually decorated. Another entirely different definition says that a torte is a cake baked from a batter that contains nuts and/or crumbs and little or no flour. Yet there are classic tortes that fit within neither definition.

Rather than try to decide the issue or add to the confusion, we will simply use the words torte and gateau when they are parts of a generally accepted name of a classic dessert, such as sachertorte or gateau St. Honoré.

Popular Layer Cakes

As we have suggested several times in this book, much of a pastry cook's job is assembly work. That is, starting with a number of basic elements such as creams, fillings, and baked doughs and batters, the pastry cook builds a variety of desserts by putting these elements together in different and attractive ways. This is especially true of the construction of European-style cakes.

While the number of ingredients that can go into a cake is nearly limitless, the most commonly used components are listed below. Following this list is a general procedure for assembling a basic European-style cake. Following that, you will find procedures for making specific desserts, most of which are popular classics. However, once you are familiar with the general procedure, you should be able to go beyond those included here and put together your own cakes. Just make sure that the flavors of the cake layers, fillings, icings, and syrups that you choose go well together.

Basic Layer Cake Components

Optional bottom layer	Baked short dough circle (p. 141)
	Baked meringue or japonaise (p. 166)
Cake layers	Genoise, or butter sponge (p. 215)
	Almond sponge or other nut sponge (p. 215)
	Chocolate sponge (p. 215)
Additional specialty layers	Puff paste discs (p. 148)
	Japonaise or meringue discs (p. 164)

For moistening and flavoring cake layers	Dessert syrup (p. 115)
Fillings	Jam or jelly (especially apricot and raspberry) Buttercream (p. 125–127) Whipped cream (p. 115) Ganache (p. 122) Chocolate mousse (p. 123) Pastry cream and variations (p. 120) Bavarian cream (p. 293) Fruits (fresh, poached, canned, etc.)
Icings and coatings	Buttercream (p. 125) Fondant (p. 123) Whipped cream (p. 115) Melted chocolate Marzipan (p. 315)

General Procedure for Assembling European-style Layer Cakes

1. Assemble all ingredients and equipment.

2. Split sponge cake horizontally into two or three layers, depending on the thickness of the cake (see Figure 11.1).

3. If you are using a japonaise, meringue, or short-dough base, place it on a cardboard cake circle of the same size. Stick it down with a dab of icing or jam so that it doesn't slide off the cardboard.

4. Spread the base with a thin layer of desired filling. Raspberry or apricot jam is often used on short-dough bases.

5. Place one sponge layer on top of the base.

6. Brush the cake layer with dessert syrup. Use enough to moisten the cake well, but not so much that it is soggy.

7. Spread with desired filling.

8. If fruit pieces are being used, arrange them on top of the filling.

9. Top with another sponge layer and again brush with syrup.

10. If a third sponge layer is being used, repeat steps 7 and 9.

11. It is recommended that the top sponge layer be placed cut-side up, not crust-side up. This is especially helpful if a light, translucent icing such as fondant is being used. A dark crust will show through a thin fondant layer and detract from the appearance of the cake.

12. Ice the top and sides smoothly with desired icing.

13. Decorate.

Rectangular Cakes or Strips

Most popular cakes can also be made in a rectangular shape or strip about 2½ to 3½ inches (6 to 9 cm) wide and 16 to 18 inches (40 to 46 cm) long (the width of a sheet pan) or any fraction of that length. A cake baked in a standard sheet pan can be cut crosswise into seven pieces this size.

To produce one cake, cut strips of desired size from sheet cakes and layer with fillings as in basic procedure. Ice the top and sides. Ends may be iced, or they may be left uniced to show an attractive pattern of cake layers and fillings. Trim a thin slice off each end for a more attractive appearance. Use a sharp serrated knife, wiped clean and dipped in hot water before cutting each slice.

To produce rectangular or strip cakes in quantity, use full cake sheets and layer up as in basic procedure. Cut into strips of desired width, then ice the top and sides of each strip.

Strip cakes are divided into portions by cutting off rectangular slices about one inch (2.5 cm) wide. The tops may be marked off into portions and decorated in a regular pattern, just as round cakes are often marked off into wedges.

Special Icing Technique: Fondant

Fondant provides a thin, smooth, shiny coating for cakes and serves an excellent base for paper-cone decorations. Also, it is a good substitute for buttercream in hot weather, especially for cakes that, for one reason or another, may not be kept in a refrigerated case at all times.

When fondant is used to ice a cake, especially a sponge cake, it is a good idea to first brush the top and sides of the cake with hot apricot glaze. Let the glaze set before applying the fondant. This provides a moisture barrier between the fondant and the cake, and it reduces the chances of the fondant's drying out and losing its shine. Also, it cuts down the problem of loose crumbs that might spoil the smoothness of the icing layer.

Guidelines for using fondant are on p. 124. To ice a

cake with fondant, set it on an icing screen, then pour the warm fondant over the cake, using the bowl knife to guide the fondant evenly over the sides.

This same method can be used for coating products with melted chocolate.

Special Icing Technique: Marzipan

A thin layer of marzipan, a confection or paste made of almonds and sugar, can be used to coat cakes. It can be colored and used in place of icing, or it can be used under fondant or other icing. When used under fondant, marzipan, like apricot coating, serves as a moisture barrier to protect the fondant. The production of marzipan is explained in Chapter 14 (see p. 315).

The following are guidelines for using marzipan as a cake coating:

1. To make a sheet of marzipan, work marzipan in the hands to make it pliable, if necessary. Using confectioners' sugar to dust the bench and rolling pin, roll the marzipan out into a thin sheet as though you are rolling out pastry.

2. If the marzipan is to be on the outside of the cake (that is, not covered with icing), the sheet can be textured with a ridged rolling pin. Roll the ridged pin over the sheet of marzipan once to make a ridged texture. To make a checked or dimpled texture, roll the pin across the sheet a second time at a right angle to the first.

3. For a round layer cake, it is easiest to coat only the top with marzipan. Before putting the top layer on the cake, brush it with apricot coating so that the marzipan will stick. Place it upside-down on a sheet of marzipan and press it on lightly. Trim off the excess marzipan.

   The sides of the cake can then be iced in a conventional manner.

4. To coat the sides of a round layer cake after coating the top, first ice the sides so that the marzipan will stick. Roll out a strip of marzipan as wide as the cake is high and as long as three times the width of the cake. Roll the strip up loosely, then unroll it against the sides of the cake.

   The cake can now be coated with fondant or another light icing.

5. An alternative method for coating a cake is to roll out a sheet of marzipan large enough to cover the top and sides. Lift it with the rolling pin and drape it over the cake. With the hands, carefully mold the marzipan against the sides of the cake.

   This method produces a seamless coating for the cake, unlike the method above in Step 3. However, it is more difficult to do. The sides must be molded very carefully so that there are no ripples or folds in the marzipan.

6. To cover a strip cake or a sponge roll (Swiss roll) with marzipan, roll out a sheet of marzipan large enough to cover the strip or roll. Brush it with apricot glaze. Set the cake on the marzipan at one edge and roll it up in the sheet.

   As an alternative, you can first coat the cake with the apricot glaze, rather than brushing the glaze onto the marzipan.

Procedures for Assembling Various Gateaux and Torten

Note: The following procedures are for round cakes, but most may also be made as rectangles or strips. See the explanation on p. 235.

Black Forest Torte (Figure 11.20)

Chocolate sponge split into three layers

Dessert syrup flavored with kirsch

Whipped cream flavored with kirsch

Sweet dark pitted cherries, drained

Chocolate shavings

1. Moisten one chocolate sponge layer with syrup.

2. Spread with a thin layer of whipped cream.

3. With a pastry bag fitted with a large, plain tube, pipe a circle of cream in the center of the layer. Pipe a ring of cream around the edge. Then pipe another ring in the space between these two.

4. Fill the two spaces between these rings with well-drained cherries.

FIGURE 11.20 Black forest torte.
(Prepared by Vallette Pastry, Astoria, N.Y.)

5. Top with a second sponge layer. Moisten with syrup.

6. Spread with a layer of whipped cream.

7. Top with a third sponge layer, moistened with cream.

8. Ice the top and sides with whipped cream.

9. With the back of a knife, mark off the top of the cake into the desired number of wedges.

10. Mask the sides of the cake with chocolate shavings. Sprinkle chocolate shavings in the center of the cake.

11. With a star tube, pipe rosettes of whipped cream around the top edge of the cake so that there is one on each wedge. Place a cherry on each rosette.

Mocha Torte (Figure 11.21)

Genoise, split into three or four layers

Coffee-flavored buttercream

Dessert syrup, flavored with coffee or with coffee liqueur

1. Moisten the cake layers with syrup. Sandwich them together with buttercream.

2. Ice top and sides smoothly with buttercream.

3. Decorate as desired with a pastry bag filled with additional buttercream. Chocolate decorations are also appropriate. Sides may be masked with toasted, sliced almonds, if desired.

Variation

Use two thin layers of vanilla genoise alternating with two thin layers of chocolate genoise.

FIGURE 11.21 Mocha torte.
(Prepared by Vallette Pastry, Astoria, N.Y.)

FIGURE 11.22 Fruit torte.

Fruit Torte (Figure 11.22)

Short dough or almond short-dough circle

Genoise or almond sponge, split into two layers

Raspberry or apricot jam

Dessert syrup flavored with vanilla or kirsch

Buttercream flavored with vanilla or kirsch

Small fruits, preferable three or four kinds, in contrasting colors (such as mandarine orange slices, cherries, grapes, banana slices, strawberries, apricot halves, and pineapple wedges)

Apricot glaze

Almonds, sliced or chopped

1. Spread the short-dough base with jam.

2. Top with a sponge layer. Moisten with syrup.

3. Spread with a thin layer of buttercream.

4. Top with second sponge layer.

5. Moisten with syrup.

6. Ice top and sides with buttercream.

7. Arrange the fruits on the top of the cake in neat, concentric circles, as though you were making an unbaked fruit tart (p. 143).

8. Glaze the fruits with apricot glaze.

9. Mask the sides of the cake with almonds.

Variation

Instead of buttercream, used whipped cream or pastry cream.

Dobos Torte (Figure 11.23)

Seven dobos layers (p. 214)

Chocolate buttercream

FIGURE 11.23 Dobos torte.
(Prepared by Vallette Pastry, Astoria, N.Y.)

Chopped almonds

Sugar, cooked to the light caramel stage (p. 115)

1. Set aside the best dobos layer for the top.
2. Sandwich the other six layers together with chocolate buttercream.
3. Ice the top and sides completely. Mask the sides with chopped almonds.
4. Cook the sugar to the light caramel stage. Pour the hot caramel over the reserved dobos layer to coat the top completely with a thin layer.
5. With a heavy, buttered knife, immediately cut the caramel layer into portion-size wedges. This must be done before the caramel hardens.
6. Top the cake with the layer of caramel-covered wedges.

Seven-Layer Cake

Seven-layer cake is a variation of the dobos torte, except that it is generally made as a strip or rectangle (see p. 235 for an explanation) rather than as a round cake. Use dobos mix (p. 214), seven-layer mix (p. 215), or any thin sponge layers. Sandwich together seven layers of cake with chocolate buttercream. Coat the top and sides with chocolate buttercream, chocolate fondant, or melted chocolate.

Napoleon Gateau

Blitz puff paste or scrap puff paste

Pastry cream

White fondant

Chocolate fondant

Chopped almonds or puff paste crumbs

This is the same as a regular napoleon, but made in the shape of a cake.

1. Roll out puff dough ⅛ inch (3 mm) thick. Cut out three circles one inch (2.5 cm) larger in diameter than the desired cake (this allows for shrinkage during baking). Dock the pastry well. Let rest 30 minutes.
2. Bake the puff paste at 400° F (200° C) until browned and crisp. Cool. With a serrated knife, carefully trim the circles, if necessary, so that they are perfectly round and uniform.
3. Sandwich the three layers together with generous layers of pastry cream. Use the best pastry layer for the top and place it upside-down so that the top is flat and smooth.
4. Ice the top with white fondant and marble it with chocolate fondant (see p. 124).
5. Carefully smooth the sides, using additional pastry cream if necessary. Mask with almonds or pastry crumbs.

Kirsch Torte

Two baked meringue or japonaise discs

One baked genoise layer, about 1 inch (2.5 cm) thick

Dessert syrup flavored with kirsch

Buttercream flavored with kirsch

Confectioners' sugar

Chopped almonds or meringue crumbs

1. Moisten the genoise with enough kirsch syrup to saturate it well.
2. Place one meringue or japonaise layer upside-down (smooth-side up) on a cake circle.
3. Spread it with a layer of buttercream.
4. Place the genoise on top and spread it with buttercream.
5. Top with the second meringue layer, smooth-side up.
6. Spread the sides smoothly with buttercream and coat them with nuts or meringue crumbs.
7. Dust the top heavily with confectioners' sugar. With the back of a knife, mark the sugar in a diamond pattern.

Sachertorte

One baked sacher cake (p. 210)

Apricot jam

Chocolate fondant

1. Split the sacher cake into two layers.
2. Sandwich the layers together with hot apricot jam.
3. Coat the top and sides of the cake with hot, strained apricot jam. Let the glaze cool until set.
4. Ice the top and sides of the cake with chocolate fondant.
5. After the icing has set, write the word "Sacher" across the top of the cake with additional chocolate fondant.

Orange Cream Cake

Note: This procedure can be used with any appropriate fruit, such as strawberries, pineapple, apricots, and cherries. The flavor of the syrup and the cream should be appropriate to the fruit.

> One meringue disc
> Genoise split into two layers
> Orange-flavored dessert syrup
> Whipped cream lightly flavored with orange liqueur
> Mandarin orange segments

1. Spread the meringue layer with whipped cream.
2. Top with one sponge layer and brush it with syrup.
3. Spread with whipped cream.
4. Arrange a layer of orange segments, well drained, on the cream.
5. Top with a second genoise layer. Moisten with syrup.
6. Ice the top and sides of the cake with whipped cream.
7. Mark off the top of the cake into the desired number of wedges.
8. Decorate with rosettes of whipped cream around the top edge of the cake. Top each rosette with an orange segment.

Chocolate Ganache Torte (Figure 11.24)

> One plain or chocolate meringue disc (optional)
> Chocolate genoise, split into three layers
> Dessert syrup flavored with rum or vanilla
> Ganache
> Chocolate buttercream

1. Spread the meringue disc with ganache.
2. Top with a genoise layer. Moisten with syrup and spread with a layer of ganache.
3. Repeat with a second genoise layer and more syrup and ganache.

FIGURE 11.24 Chocolate ganache torte.
(Prepared by Vallette Pastry, Astoria, N.Y.)

4. Top with the remaining cake layer, moistened with syrup.
5. Ice the top and sides with chocolate buttercream.
6. Decorate as desired.

Chocolate Mousse Cake

> Three chocolate meringue discs
> Chocolate mousse (p. 123)
> Shaved chocolate

1. Sandwich together the meringue discs with chocolate mousse.
2. Ice the top and sides completely with chocolate mousse.
3. Coat the top and sides of the cake with shaved chocolate.

Almond Gateau (Figure 11.25)

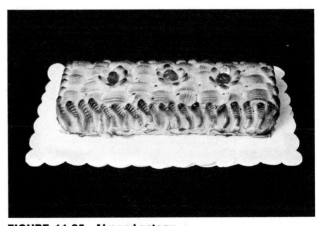

FIGURE 11.25 Almond gateau.
(Prepared by Vallette Pastry, Astoria, N.Y.)

Almond sponge split into two layers

Dessert syrup flavored with rum

Apricot jam and glaze

Almond macaroon mixture (p. 267)

1. Moisten the sponge layers with syrup and sandwich them together with apricot jam.

2. Coat the sides of the cake with the macaroon mixture. Using a star tube or basketweave tube, cover the top of the cake with macaroon mix in a basketweave pattern (p. 229).

3. Let stand for at least an hour.

4. Brown quickly in a hot oven (450° F/230° C), about 10 minutes.

5. While still warm, glaze with apricot glaze.

Bavarian Cream Torte (Figure 11.26)

Genoise or other sponge cut into three very thin (about ¼ inch/6 mm) layers

Bavarian cream in any flavor (pp. 294–298)

Whipped cream flavored to be compatible with the flavor of the Bavarian cream (use chocolate whipped cream with chocolate Bavarian torte)

Dessert syrup, flavored appropriately

1. Line the bottom of a cake pan or spring-form pan with a thin sponge layer. Moisten with syrup.

2. Prepare the Bavarian cream. Pour enough of the mixture into the cake pan to make a layer about ¾ inch (2 cm) thick.

3. Place a second layer of sponge cake on top of the cream. Moisten with syrup.

4. Fill with another layer of Bavarian cream.

5. Top with the remaining sponge layer.

FIGURE 11.26   Bavarian cream torte.
(Prepared by Vallette Pastry, Astoria, N.Y.)

6. Chill until set.

7. Unmold.

8. Ice the top and sides with whipped cream.

9. Decorate as desired.

Swiss Rolls

Swiss rolls are made up in much the same way as American jelly rolls, except that Swiss rolls are usually more delicate. They can be made with a great variety of fillings and are often iced and decorated on the outside.

General Procedure for Making Swiss Rolls

1. Bake Swiss roll sponge as directed in the recipe (p. 214 or 215). Turn out onto a sheet of parchment and carefully peel the paper off the back of the sponge. Cool it partially covered so that the cake retains moisture and does not dry out. (The cake may also be moistened with dessert syrup.)

2. Trim off the edges with a sharp knife. Crusty edges do not roll well.

3. Spread with desired filling, such as:
   Jam or jelly
   Buttercream
   Ganache
   Chocolate mousse
   Pastry cream variation
   Whipped cream
   Lemon filling
   Chopped fruits or nuts may be mixed with buttercream or pastry cream.

4. If any items — such as fruit pieces or a thin rope of marzipan — are to be rolled into the center of the roll, place these along one edge of the sheet on top of the filling. Begin rolling from this edge.

5. Roll up the cake tightly with the aid of the sheet of parchment under the sponge.

6. Ice or cover the outside of the roll as desired. For example:

   Brush with apricot glaze, then ice with fondant.

   Coat with melted chocolate.

   Coat with a sheet of marzipan (see p. 236), using apricot jam or glaze to make the marzipan stick.

   Spread with a thin layer of buttercream, then coat with marzipan.

Spread with buttercream, then roll in coconut or chopped nuts.

7. Swiss rolls may be sold as whole cakes or cut into individual slices.

Variation: Half Rolls

1. Before icing the outside of the roll, chill the roll to make it firmer.

2. Cut a sheet of baked short pastry or sponge cake into two strips, each as long and as wide as the sponge roll. Spread the strips with a thin layer of icing or jam.

3. With a sharp knife, carefully cut the chilled sponge roll in half lengthwise.

4. Mount each half cut-side down on one of the prepared sponge or short dough bases.

5. Ice and decorate as in the basic procedure.

Almond Swiss Rolls:

Spread plain Swiss roll sponge with apricot jam, then with almond pastry cream. Roll up. Brush with apricot glaze and ice with white fondant. While fondant is soft, place a row of toasted almonds along the top of the roll.

Black Forest Roll:

Fit a pastry bag with a plain tube and fill it with whipped cream fortified with gelatin (p. 116) and flavored with kirsch. Pipe strips of cream about ⅜ inch (1 cm) apart on a sheet of chocolate Swiss roll so that the strips run the length of the roll. Fill in the spaces between the strips with dark sweet cherries, well drained. Roll up. Coat with additional cream and then with chocolate shavings.

FIGURE 11.27 Bûche de Noël.
(Prepared by Vallette Pastry, Astoria, N.Y.)

FIGURE 11.28 Harlequin roll decorated with rose made of modeling chocolate (p. 314).

Bûche de Noël (Chocolate Christmas Roll):

Spread plain or chocolate Swiss roll sponge with chocolate buttercream. Roll up. Spread the ends with white buttercream and with a paper cone pipe on a spiral of chocolate icing to look like end grain of wood. Ice the rest of the roll with chocolate buttercream to resemble bark, either by using a pastry bag with a flattened star tube, or by spreading on the cream and then texturing it with an icing comb. Decorate with meringue mushrooms (p. 165). (See Figure 11.27.)

Harlequin Roll:

On a sheet of plain Swiss roll sponge, pipe alternating rows of vanilla and chocolate buttercream so that the roll is completely covered with stripes of buttercream running the length of the roll. Roll up and cover with melted chocolate, chocolate fondant, or marzipan colored with cocoa. (See Figure 11.28.)

Mocha Roll:

Spread plain Swiss roll sponge with coffee buttercream and sprinkle with chocolate shavings. Roll up and ice with more coffee buttercream. Decorate with chocolate drizzled over the icing.

Praline Ganache Roll:

Spread plain Swiss roll sponge with praline buttercream. Using a large plain tube, pipe a strip of ganache cream along one edge. Roll up so that the ganache is in the center. Cover with more buttercream. Roll in chopped or sliced hazelnuts.

Strawberry Cream Roll:

Spread plain Swiss roll sponge with pastry cream lightly flavored with orange flavor or orange liqueur.

Place a row of fresh strawberries along one edge. Roll up so that the strawberries are in the center. Dust with confectioners' sugar.

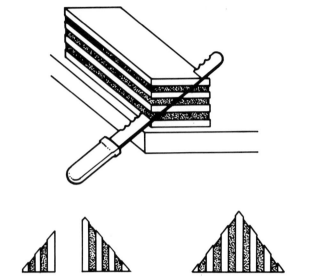

FIGURE 11.29 Procedure for cutting strip layer cake to make triangles.

Small Cakes

Small fancy cakes in individual-portion sizes can be made in many shapes and flavors. In some American bakeshops, these small cakes are known as French pastries. Using a variety of cakes, icings, fillings, and decorations, a baker can make an unlimited variety of small, attractive cakes. This section briefly discusses some of the more popular varieties.

Slices

These are simply portion-size slices of rectangular strip cakes (p. 235), Swiss rolls (p. 240), and half rolls (p. 241). An important part of the appearance of slices is the pattern of the icing and filling layers. Therefore, it is important to cut the slices carefully and neatly.

For best results, chill the rolls or strips before slicing, so that the fillings and icings are firm. Use a sharp knife. Wipe the knife clean and dip it in hot water before each cut.

Slices may be lined up on trays or placed in individual paper cases for display.

Triangles

Sandwich together four or five layers of ¼-inch (6-mm) thick sponge (such as Swiss roll sponge or seven-layer sponge) with buttercream in a contrasting color. Press the layers together firmly. Chill to solidify the cream. Cut the cake into strips 2 to 2½ inches (5 to 6 cm) wide.

Place a strip at the edge of the bench and, using a sharp knife, cut diagonally into triangles, as shown in Figure 11.29. Turn the triangles so that the layers are vertical. Attach them back to back with a layer of buttercream to form a larger triangle.

Coat with marzipan, melted chocolate, or icing. Cut into slices.

Squares

Layer two or three sheets of cake and icing or filling so that the assembled layers are 1½ to 1¾ inches (4 cm) high. Press the layers together firmly. Chill to make the filling firm.

Cut the cake into small squares, 2 inches (5 cm) across or less. Ice the sides, with buttercream, then the top. Decorate as desired.

Othellos

Othellos are small, round cakes made with a special sponge mixture. Prepare the mix for sponge roll I (p. 214), but reduce the first quantity of sugar to 25% (3 oz/90 g). Using a pastry bag with a plain tube, pipe 2 inch (5 cm) mounds onto silicone paper. Bake at 400° F (200° C). Cool. Scoop out a little of the cake from the flat side of each Othello base to make more room for the filling. Select half the cakes to be bottom halves and slice a little off the top of each to make a flat surface.

Sandwich two cakes together (one top and one bottom half) with appropriate filling (see below). Brush with apricot glaze. Set on screens and ice with fondant. To decorate, use a paper cone to pipe a spiral of fondant in the same color on the top of each Othello.

Although the term Othello is used for this whole category of pastries, it is traditional to use different names for cakes of different flavors as follows:

Othellos   Filling: chocolate pastry cream
                    Icing: chocolate fondant

Iagos	Filling: coffee-flavored pastry cream Icing: coffee fondant
Desdemonas	Filling: whipped cream flavored with vanilla Icing: white fondant flavored with kirsch
Rosilands	Filling: whipped cream flavored with rose water Icing: pink fondant flavored with rose water

Petits Fours

The term *petit four* can be used for almost any small cake or pastry item that is small enough to be eaten in one or two bites. "Petit" in French means "little," and "four" mean "oven." Most petits fours are small, baked items, although there are a few that are not baked.

Petits fours are divided into two categories. *Petits fours secs* ("sec" means "dry") include a variety of small, dainty cookies, baked meringues, macaroons, and puff pastry products. These will be discussed further in the next chapter.

Petits fours glacés are iced petits fours ("glacé" means, in this case, "iced"). This category includes such items as tiny éclairs, tartlets, filled meringues, and cakes. In fact, nearly any iced or creamed pastry or cake item can be called a petit four, as long as it is small enough to be eaten in one or two bites.

FIGURE 11.30 A selection of petits fours.
(Prepared by Vallette Pastry, Astoria, N.Y.)

In America, the usual type of petit four is a cake cutout iced with fondant. In fact, most people are probably not aware that there are any kinds of petit four other than this. Because of its popularity, the fondant-glazed petit four should be in the repertoire of every pastry cook. A general procedure is given here. Figure 11.30 shows a selection of this kind of petit four.

Procedure for Making Fondant-Iced Petits Fours

1. Select a firm, close-grained cake. Cake that is too coarse, soft, or crumbly is difficult to cut evenly into small shapes. Of the formulas in this book, almond cake (p. 210) is recommended. Other suitable choices are almond sponge II (p. 215) and pound cake (see the variation for petits fours on p. 208). For one sheet of petits fours you will need three sheets of cake, ¼ inch (6 mm) thick each. (The finished, iced petits fours should be no more than an inch high.)

2. Lay one sheet of cake on a sheet pan and spread with a *thin* layer of hot apricot jam or of buttercream. Top with the second sheet.

3. Repeat with the third sheet. Spread the top with a thin layer of jam or whatever filling is used between the layers.

4. Roll out a thin sheet of marzipan the same size as the cake sheet. Roll it up loosely on the rolling pin and unroll it to cover the cake. Run the rolling pin over the top to make sure that the layers are stuck together firmly, or press the layers together with a second sheet pan placed on top.

5. Chill the cake for an hour or more.

6. Cut out small squares, rectangles, diamonds, ovals, circles, or other shapes with a knife or cutter. Remember to keep them small, no more than an inch (2.5 cm) across.

   Note: The marzipan layer is sometimes difficult to cut through neatly. If this is the case, turn the cake upside-down before cutting.

7. Prepare some fondant for icing. The fondant should be thinned out with simple syrup so that it will coat the cakes with a very thin layer. Fondant may be colored *very lightly.*

8. Place the petits fours an inch apart on an icing grate over a tray. Pour the fondant over each one, making sure that the top and sides are completely covered.

   Alternatively, you may dip each cake in warm fondant. Push the cake upside-down into the fondant until the bottom is level with the icing. With a fork, invert the cake, lift it out, and set it on an icing grate to drain.

9. When the icing is set, use chocolate, piping gel, or colored fondant to decorate the tops of the petits fours, using the designs illustrated in Figure 11.8.

10. As an interesting variation, before icing the petits fours, pipe a small bulb of buttercream on top of each cake. Refrigerate to harden the buttercream. Then coat the petits fours with fondant.

TERMS FOR REVIEW

Boston cream pie
French pastry
icing screen
turntable
icing comb
paper cone
marbling (icing)
piping jelly
gateau
torte
Swiss roll
black forest torte
fruit torte
dobos torte
kirsch torte
sachertorte
Othello
petit four glacé

QUESTIONS FOR REVIEW

1. What are the steps for assembling and icing a two-layer cake?

2. What method would you use to ice cupcakes with fondant? With buttercream?

3. Why is the consistency of the icing important when you are decorating with a paper cone or pastry bag?

4. True or false: If you are right-handed, you should hold the top of the pastry bag shut with your right hand and squeeze the bag with your left hand. Explain your answer.

5. Name four techniques you can use for partially or completely decorating a cake without using a pastry bag or paper cone.

6. Briefly list the steps in assembling a typical, basic European-style torte.

7. Describe how to cut cake slices to achieve the neatest results.

CHAPTER 12

COOKIES

After studying this chapter, you should be able to:
1. Understand the causes of crispness, moistness, chewiness, and spread in cookies.
2. Prepare cookie doughs by the three basic mixing methods.
3. Prepare seven basic types of cookies: dropped, bagged, rolled, molded, icebox, bar, and sheet.
4. Bake and cool cookies properly.

he word "cookie" means "small cake," and that's more or less what a cookie is. In fact, some cookies are made from cake batter. For some products, such as certain kinds of brownies, it's difficult to know whether to classify them as cakes or cookies.

Most cookie formulas, however, call for less liquid than cake formulas do. Cookie doughs range from soft to very stiff, unlike the thinner batters for cakes. This difference in moisture content means some differences in mixing methods, though the basic procedures are much like those for cakes.

The most apparent differences between cakes and cookies are in makeup. Since most cookies are individually formed or shaped, there is a great deal of hand labor involved. Learning the correct methods and then practicing diligently are essential for efficiency.

COOKIE CHARACTERISTICS AND THEIR CAUSES

Cookies come in an infinite variety of shapes, sizes, flavors, and textures. Characteristics that are desirable in some types are not desirable in others. For example, we want some cookies to be crisp, and others to be soft. We want some to hold their shape, and others to spread during baking. In order to produce the characteristics we want and to correct faults, it is useful to know what causes these basic traits.

Crispness

Cookies are crisp if they are very low in moisture. The following factors contribute to crispness:

1. Low proportion of liquid in the mix. Most crisp cookies are made from a stiff dough.
2. High sugar and fat content. A large proportion of these ingredients make it possible to mix a workable dough with low moisture content.
3. Baking long enough to evaporate most of the moisture.
4. Small size or thin shape, so that the cookie dries faster during baking.
5. Proper storage. Crisp cookies can become soft if they absorb moisture.

Softness

Softness is the opposite of crispness, so it has the opposite causes, as follows:

1. High proportion of liquid in the mix.
2. Low sugar and fat.
3. Honey, molasses, or corn syrup included in the formulas. These sugars are hygroscopic, which means they readily absorb moisture from the air or from their surroundings.
4. Underbaking.
5. Large size or thick shape, so that they retain more moisture.
6. Proper storage. Soft cookies can become stale and dry if not tightly covered or wrapped.

Chewiness

Moisture is necessary for chewiness, but other factors are also important. In other words, all chewy cookies are soft, but not all soft cookies are chewy.

1. High sugar and liquid content, but low fat content.
2. High proportion of eggs.
3. Strong flour or gluten developed during mixing.

Spread

Spread is desirable in some cookies, while others must hold their shape. Several factors contribute to spread or the lack of it.

1. *Sugar*

   High sugar content increases spread. Coarse granulated sugar increases spread, while fine sugar or confectioners' sugar reduces spread.

2. *Leavening*

   High baking soda or baking ammonia content encourages spread.

3. *Creaming*

   The creaming together of fat and sugar contributes to leavening by incorporating air. Creaming a mixture until light increases spread. Blending fat and sugar just to a paste (without creaming in a lot of air) reduces spread.

4. *Temperature*

   Low oven temperature increases spread. High temperature decreases spread because the cookie sets up before it has a chance to spread too much.

5. *Liquid*

   A slack batter—that is, one with a high liquid content—spreads more than a stiff dough.

6. *Flour*

   Strong flour or activation of gluten decreases spread.

7. *Pan grease*

   Cookies spread more if baked on heavily greased pans.

MIXING METHODS

Cookie mixing methods are very much like cake mixing methods. The major difference is that less liquid is usually incorporated, so that mixing is somewhat easier. Less liquid means that gluten will become less developed by the mixing. Also, it is a little easier to get a smooth, uniform mix.

There are three basic cookie mixing methods:

One-stage

Creaming

Sponge

These methods are subject to many variations, due to differences in formulas. The general procedures are as follows, but always be sure to follow the exact instructions with each formula.

One-stage Method

This method is the counterpart of the two-stage cake mixing method, which was discussed in the last chapter. There is more liquid in cake batters, so it must be added in two or more stages in order to blend uniformly. Low-moisture cookies, on the other hand, can be mixed all in one stage.

Because all the ingredients are mixed at once, the baker has less control over the mixing with this method than with other methods. Therefore, the one-stage method is not frequently used. When overmixing is not a great problem, as with some chewy cookies, it can be used.

Procedure for One-Stage Method

1. Scale ingredients accurately. Have all ingredients at room temperature.
2. Place all ingredients in mixer. With the paddle attachment, mix these ingredients at low speed until uniformly blended. Scrape down the sides of the bowl as necessary.

Creaming Method

This is nearly identical to the creaming method for cakes. Since cookies require less liquid, it is not necessary to add the liquid alternately with the flour. It can be added all at once.

Note the importance of step 2, the creaming stage. The amount of creaming affects the texture of the cookie, the leavening, and the spread. Only a small amount of creaming is desired when the cookie must retain its shape and not spread too much. Also, if the cookie is very short (high in fat and low in gluten development), or if it is thin and delicate, too much creaming will make the cookie too crumbly.

Procedure for Creaming Method

1. Scale ingredients accurately. Have all ingredients at room temperature.
2. Place the fat, sugar, salt, and spices in the mixing bowl. With the paddle attachment, cream these ingredients at low speed.

   For light cookies, cream until the mix is light and fluffy, in order to incorporate more air for leavening. For denser cookies, blend to a smooth paste, but do not cream until light.
3. Add the eggs and liquid and blend in at low speed.
4. Sift in the flour and leavening. Mix until just combined. Do not overmix, or gluten will develop.

Sponge Method

This method is similar to the egg-foam methods for cakes. The procedure varies considerably, depending on the ingredients. Batches should be kept small because the batter is delicate.

Procedure for Sponge Method

1. Scale all ingredients accurately. Have all ingredients at room temperature, or warm the eggs slightly for greater volume, as for sponge cakes.
2. Following the procedure given in the formula used, whip the eggs (whole, yolks, or whites) and the sugar to the proper stage: soft peaks for whites, thick and light for whole eggs or yolks.
3. Fold in the remaining ingredients as specified in the recipe. Be careful not to overmix or to deflate the eggs.

TYPES AND MAKEUP METHODS

We can classify cookie types by their makeup methods as well as by their mixing methods. Grouping them by makeup method is perhaps more useful from the point of view of production, because their mixing methods are relatively simple, while their makeup procedures vary considerably. In this section, you will learn the basic procedures for producing seven cookie types:

Bagged

Dropped

Rolled

Molded

Icebox

Bar

Sheet

No matter what makeup method you use, follow one important rule: Make all cookies of uniform size and thickness. This is essential for even baking. Since baking times are so short, small cookies may burn before large ones are done.

If the tops of the cookies are to be garnished with fruits, nuts, or other items, place the garnishes on the cookies as soon as they are panned; press them on gently. If you wait until the surface of the dough begins to dry, the garnish may not stick and will fall off after baking.

Bagged

Bagged or pressed cookies are made from soft doughs. The dough must be soft enough to be forced through a pastry bag, but stiff enough to hold its shape.

1. Fit a pastry bag with a tip of the desired size and shape. Fill the bag with the cookie dough. Review p. 228 for tips on the use of the pastry bag.

2. Press out cookies of the desired shape and size directly onto prepared cookie sheets.

Dropped

Like bagged cookies, dropped cookies are made from a soft dough. Actually, this method can be considered the same as the bagged method, and many bakers use the term "drop" for both bagging out cookies and for depositing dough with a spoon or scoop. Usually, a pastry bag is faster, and it gives better control over the shape and size of the cookies. However, in the following situations, using a scoop to drop cookies may be preferred:

● When the dough contains pieces of fruit, nuts, or chocolate that would clog the pastry tube.

● When you want the cookies to have a rough, home-made look.

1. Select the proper size scoop for accurate portioning.

    A No. 30 scoop makes a large cookie, about 1 ounce.

    A No. 40 scoop makes a medium cookie.

    A No. 50, 60, or smaller scoop makes a small cookie.

2. Drop the cookies onto the prepared baking sheets. Allow enough space between cookies for spreading.

3. Rich cookies will spread by themselves. But if the formula requires it, flatten the mounds of batter slightly with a weight dipped in sugar.

Rolled

Cookies rolled and cut from a stiff dough are not made as often in bakeshops and food service operations as they are made in homes because they require excessive labor. Also, there are always scraps left over after cutting. When rerolled, these scraps make inferior, tough cookies.

The advantage of this method is that it allows you to make cookies in a great variety of shapes for different occasions.

1. Chill dough thoroughly.

2. Roll dough out ⅛ inch (3 mm) thick on a floured canvas. Use as little flour as possible for dusting, since this flour can toughen the cookies.

3. Cut out cookies with cookie cutters. Place cookies on prepared baking sheets. Cut as close together as possible to reduce the quantity of scraps. Roll scraps into fresh dough to minimize toughness.

4. Baked cutout cookies are often decorated with colored icing (royal icing, flat icing, or fondant) for holidays or special occasions.

Molded

The first part of this procedure (steps 1 and 2) is simply a fast and fairly accurate way of dividing the dough into equal portions. Each piece is then molded into the desired shape. This usually consists of simply flattening the pieces out with a weight. For some traditional cookies, special molds are used to flatten the dough and at the same time stamp a design onto the cookie.

The pieces may also be shaped by hand into crescents, fingers, or other shapes.

1. Refrigerate the dough if it is too soft to handle. Roll it out into long cylinders about 1 inch (2½ cm) thick, or whatever size is required.

2. With a knife or bench scraper, cut the roll into ½ ounce (15 g) pieces, or whatever size is required.

3. Place the pieces on prepared baking sheets, leaving 2 inches (5 cm) space between each.

4. Flatten the cookies with a weight, such as a can, dipped in granulated sugar before pressing each cookie.

   A fork is sometimes used for flattening the dough, as for peanut butter cookies.

5. Alternative method: After Step 2, shape the dough by hand into desired shapes.

Icebox

The icebox, or refrigerator, method is ideal for operations that wish to have freshly baked cookies on hand at all times. The rolls of dough may be made up in advance and stored. Cookies can easily be cut and baked as needed.

This method is also used to make multicolored cookies in various designs, such as checkerboard and pinwheel cookies. The procedures for making these designs are included with the recipes in this chapter (p. 254).

1. Scale the dough into pieces of uniform size, from 1½ lb (700 g) if you are making small cookies, to 3 lb (1400 g) for large cookies.

2. Form the dough into cylinders from 1 to 2 inches (2½ to 5 cm) in diameter, depending on the cookie size desired.

   For accurate portioning, it is important to make all the cylinders of dough the same thickness and length.

3. Wrap the cylinders in parchment or wax paper, place them on sheet pans, and refrigerate overnight.

4. Unwrap the dough and cut into slices of *uniform thickness*. The exact thickness required depends on the size of the cookie and how much the dough spreads during baking. The usual range is from ⅛ to ¼ in (3 to 6 mm).

   A slicing machine is recommended for ensuring even thickness. Doughs containing nuts or fruits, however, should be sliced by hand with a knife.

5. Place the slices on prepared baking sheets, allowing 2 in (5 cm) between cookies.

Bar

This procedure is called the bar method because the dough is baked in long, narrow strips, which are then cut crosswise into bars. It should not be confused with sheet cookies (see next procedure), which are sometimes called "bars" by home cooks.

1. Scale the dough into 1¾ lb (800 g) units. 1-lb (450-g) units may be used for smaller cookies.

2. Shape the pieces of dough into cylinders the length of the sheet pans. Place three strips on each greased pan, spacing them well apart.

3. Flatten the dough with the fingers into strips about 3 to 4 inches wide and about ¼ inch thick (8 to 10 cm wide, 6 mm thick).

4. If required, brush with egg wash.

5. Bake as directed in the formula.

6. After baking, while cookies are still warm, cut each strip into bars about 1¾ in (4½ cm) wide.

Sheet

Sheet cookies vary so much that it is nearly impossible to give a single procedure for all of them. Some of them are almost like sheet cakes, only denser and richer; they may even be iced like sheet cakes. Others consist of two or three layers added and baked in separate stages. The following procedure is only a general guide.

1. Spread cookie mixture into prepared sheet pans. Make sure the thickness is even.

2. If required, add topping or brush with an egg wash.

3. Bake as directed. Cool.

4. Cut into individual squares or rectangles.

PANNING, BAKING, AND COOLING

Preparing the Pans

1. Use clean, unwarped pans.

2. Lining the sheets with parchment or silicone paper is fast, and it eliminates the necessity of greasing the pans.

3. A heavily greased pan increases the spread of the cookie. A greased and floured pan decreases spread.

4. Some high-fat cookies can be baked on ungreased pans.

Baking

1. Most cookies are baked at a relatively high temperature for a short time.

2. Too low a temperature increases spreading and may produce hard, dry, pale cookies.

3. Too high a temperature decreases spreading and may burn the edges or bottoms.

4. Even a minute of overbaking can burn cookies, so watch them closely. Also, the heat of the pan continues to bake the cookies if they are left on it after being removed from the oven.

5. Doneness is indicated by color. The edges and bottoms should just be turning a light golden color.

6. Excessive browning is especially undesirable if the dough has been colored. The browning of the surface hides the color.

7. With some rich doughs, burnt bottoms may be a problem. In these cases, *double-pan* the cookies by placing the sheet pan on a second pan of the same size.

Cooling

1. For most cookies baked without silicone paper, remove them from the pans while they are still warm, or they may stick.

2. If cookies are very soft, do not remove them from the pans until they are cool enough and firm enough to handle.

   Some cookies are soft when hot, but become crisp when cool.

3. Do not cool too rapidly or in cold drafts, or cookies may crack.

4. Cool completely before storing.

PETITS FOURS SECS

In the preceding chapter, the subject of petits fours was introduced with a discussion of petits fours glacés, or iced petits fours (p. 243). Petits fours secs, or "dry" petits fours, are, by contrast, more properly discussed here with cookies than with cakes.

As you will recall, nearly any pastry or cake item that is small enough to be eaten in one or two bites can be considered as a petit four. The term "sec" or "dry" means that these pastries have no icing or cream filling, although they may be dipped in chocolate. In practice, small quantities of creams or jellies are sometimes used, for example, in sandwich-type cookies.

Petits fours secs are usually served with after-dinner coffee or as an accompaniment for such cold desserts as ice cream, mousses, and Bavarian creams.

The following items from this book may be served as petits fours secs, provided that they are quite small:

From Chapter 8:
   Sacristians
   Palmiers
   Allumettes
   Meringues

From this chapter:
   Butter tea cookies
   Almond macaroons
   Coconut macaroons (meringue type)
   Shortbread and short dough cookies
   Fancy icebox cookies
   Nut squares
   Spritz cookies
   Langues de chat
   Almond tuiles
   Florentines
   Almond slices

Formulas

Icebox Cookies

Ingredients	U.S.		Metric	%
Butter, or half butter and half shortening	2 lb		1000 g	67
Granulated sugar	1 lb		500 g	33
Confectioners sugar	1 lb		500 g	33
Salt		0.5 oz	15 g	1
Eggs	8	oz	250 g	17
Vanilla		0.5 oz	15 g	1
Pastry flour	3 lb		1500 g	100
Yield:	7 lb 9	oz	3780 g	252

Mixing: Creaming method

Makeup: Icebox method. Scale dough strips 1½ lb (750 g) each.
Slice cookies ¼ inch (6 mm) thick. Bake on ungreased pans.

Baking: 375° F (190° C) for 10–12 minutes

Variations

To reduce spread, use all confectioners' sugar.

Butterscotch Icebox Cookies:

Make the following ingredient adjustments:

In place of the sugars in the basic recipe, use 67% (2 lb/1 kg) brown sugar.
Use only butter, no shortening.
Increase the eggs to 20% (12 oz/375 g).
Add 1 tsp (5 g) baking soda with the flour.

Nut Icebox Cookies:

Add 25% (12 oz/375 g) finely chopped nuts to the sifted flour in the basic recipe or the butterscotch cookie recipe.

Chocolate Icebox Cookies:

Add 17% (8 oz/250 g) melted, unsweetened chocolate to the creamed butter and sugar.

(continues)

Icebox Cookies (*Continued*)

Fancy Icebox Cookies:

These are small cookies with designs in two colors. To make them, prepare white and chocolate icebox dough with only the 33% confectioners' sugar; omit the granulated sugar. This reduces the spread of the cookies and preserves the designs. Make the designs as follows:

Pinwheel Cookies:
Roll out a sheet of white dough about ⅛ inch (3 mm) thick. Roll out a sheet of chocolate dough the same size and thickness. Brush the white sheet lightly and evenly with egg wash, being careful not to leave any puddles. Lay the chocolate sheet on top and brush with egg wash. Roll up like a jelly roll until the roll is 1 inch (2.5 cm) thick. Cut off the dough evenly. Continue making rolls with the rest of the sheet. Refrigerate the rolls. Slice and bake as in the basic procedure.

Checkerboard Cookies:
Roll out one sheet of white dough and one sheet of chocolate dough ¼ inch (6 mm) thick. Egg-wash one sheet lightly and lay the second sheet on top. Cut the double sheet of dough in half. Eggwash one sheet and lay the second on top so that you have four alternating colors. Chill until firm. Roll out another sheet of white dough very thin (less than ⅛ inch) and brush with egg wash. From the chilled four-layer sheet, cut off four slices ¼ inch (6 mm) thick (Figure 12.1). Lay one of these strips on the rolled-out sheet of dough along one edge. Egg-wash the top. Lay a second strip on top with the colors reversed, so that chocolate dough is on top of white dough and white is on top of chocolate. Egg-wash the top. Repeat with the remaining two strips. Wrap in the thin sheet of dough. Chill, slice, and bake as in the basic procedure.

Bull's-eye Cookies:
Roll out a cylinder of dough ½ inch (12 mm) thick. Roll out a sheet of contrasting-color dough ¼ inch (6 mm) thick. Egg-wash the top. Wrap the cylinder in the sheet of dough. Chill, slice, and bake as in the basic procedure.

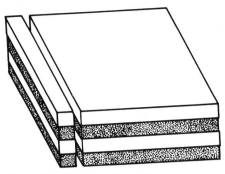

FIGURE 12.1   Checkerboard cookies.
(*a*) Assemble a four-layer sheet of cookie dough. Cut slices as shown, so that each color, when seen from the end, forms a square.

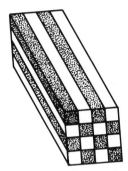

(*b*) Stack up four slices so that the colors alternate.

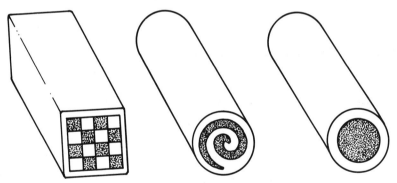

(c) Wrap each stack in a thin sheet of cookie dough. The wrapped dough is shown here before slicing, along with dough rolls for pinwheel and bull's-eye cookies.

Oatmeal Raisin Cookies

Ingredients	U.S.			Metric	%
Butter, or part butter and					
part shortening	1 lb			500 g	67
Brown sugar	2 lb			1000 g	133
Salt		0.33 oz (2 tsp)		10 g	1.5
Eggs		8	oz	250 g	33
Vanilla		0.67 oz (4 tsp)		20 g	3
Milk		2	oz	60 g	8
Pastry flour	1 lb	8	oz	750 g	100
Baking powder		1	oz	30 g	4
Baking soda		0.5	oz	15 g	2
Rolled oats (quick cooking)	1 lb	4	oz	625 g	83
Raisins (see note)	1 lb			500 g	67
Yield:	7 lb	8	oz	3760 g	500

Note: If raisins are hard and dry, soak them in hot water until soft, then drain them and dry them well before adding them to the cookie batter.

Mixing: Creaming method. Combine oats with other dry ingredients after they are sifted. Blend raisins in last.

Makeup: Drop method. Use greased or parchment-lined baking sheets.

Baking: 375° F (190° C) for 10–12 minutes, depending on size

Chocolate Chip Cookies

Ingredients	U.S.			Metric	%
Butter, or half butter and					
half shortening		12	oz	360 g	60
Granulated sugar		10	oz	300 g	50
Brown sugar		10	oz	300 g	50
Salt		0.25	oz	8 g	1.25
Eggs		6	oz	180 g	30
Vanilla		0.33 oz (2 tsp)		10 g	1.5
Water		2	oz	60 g	10
Pastry flour	1 lb	4	oz	600 g	100
Baking soda		0.25	oz	8 g	1.25
Chocolate chips	1 lb	4	oz	600 g	100
Chopped walnuts or pecans		8	oz	240 g	40
Yield:	5 lb	8	oz	2666 g	444

Mixing: Creaming method. Blend in chocolate chips and nuts last.

Makeup: Drop method. Use greased or parchment-lined baking sheets.

Baking: 375° F (190° C) for 8–12 minutes, depending on size

Chocolate Chip Cookies *(Continued)*

Variation

Brown Sugar Nut Cookies:

Make the following ingredient adjustments:

Omit the granulated sugar and use 100% (1 lb 4 oz/600 g) brown sugar.

Omit the chocolate chips and increase the nuts to 100% (1 lb 4 oz/600 g).

Sugar Cookies

Ingredients	U.S.		Metric	%
Butter and/or shortening	1 lb		500 g	40
Sugar	1 lb 4	oz	625 g	50
Salt		0.33 oz (2 tsp)	10 g	0.8
Eggs	4	oz	125 g	10
Milk	4	oz	125 g	10
Vanilla	0.5	oz	15 g	1.25
Cake flour	2 lb 8	oz	1250 g	100
Baking powder	1.25	oz	37 g	3
Yield:	5 lb 5	oz	2687 g	215

Mixing: Creaming method

Makeup: Rolled method. Before cutting the rolled-out dough, wash with milk and sprinkle with granulated sugar. Use greased or parchment-lined baking sheets.

Baking: 375° F (190° C) for 8–10 minutes

Variations

Lemon zest, extract, or emulsion may be used in place of vanilla.

Brown Sugar Rolled Cookies:

Make the following ingredient adjustments:

Increase butter to 50% (1 lb 4 oz/625 g).

Omit granulated sugar and use 60% (1 lb 8 oz/750 g) brown sugar.

Chocolate Rolled Cookies:

Substitute 4 oz (125 g) cocoa for 4 oz (125 g) of the flour.

Almond Slices

Ingredients	U.S.		Metric	%
Butter	12	oz	350 g	40
Brown sugar	1 lb 8	oz	700 g	80
Cinnamon	0.15 oz (2½ tsp)		4 g	0.5
Egg yolks	6	oz	175 g	20
Pastry flour	1 lb 14	oz	875 g	100
Slivered almonds	12	oz	350 g	40
Yield:	5 lb 4	oz	2454 g	280

Mixing: Creaming method. Blend each stage of mixing until smooth, but do not cream until light.

Makeup: Icebox method. Scale the dough into 12 oz (350 g) units. Roll into round strips about 1½ inches (4 cm) in diameter, or into rectangular strips about 1¼ × 1¾ inches (3.5 × 4.5 cm). Chill until very firm. Slice about ⅙ inch (4 mm) thick, using a sharp knife. Take care to slice through the almonds and not pull them out of the dough. Place slices on greased or paper-lined sheets.

Baking: 375° F (190° C)

Rich Shortbread

Ingredients	U.S.		Metric	%
Butter	1 lb 8	oz	750 g	75
Sugar	1 lb		500 g	50
Salt	0.25 oz (1½ tsp)		8 g	0.75
Egg yolks	8	oz	250 g	25
Optional flavoring (see note)				
Pastry flour	2 lb		1000 g	100
Yield:	5 lb		2508 g	250

Note: Traditional Scottish shortbread is made with butter, flour, and sugar, with no eggs, flavoring, or liquid. Because this dough is very crumbly, it is usually not rolled out but is pressed into pans or molds and baked. For the recipe given here, you may make the cookies without any added flavoring, or flavor to taste with vanilla, almond, or lemon.

Mixing: Creaming method

Makeup: Rolled method. Roll the dough ¼ inch (6 mm) thick (this is thicker than most rolled cookies). Use greased or parchment-lined pans.

Baking: 350° F (175° C) for about 15 minutes

Basic Short Dough for Cookies

Ingredients	U.S.		Metric	%
Butter, or half butter and half shortening	2 lb		1000 g	67
Sugar	1 lb		500 g	33
Salt		0.5 oz	15 g	1
Eggs		6 oz	190 g	12.5
Vanilla		0.5 oz	15 g	1
Pastry flour	3 lb		1500 g	100
Yield:	6 lb 7	oz	3220 g	214

Mixing: Creaming method

Makeup: Rolled method. Roll out ⅛ inch (3 mm) thick and cut out with cutters of various shapes. See variations below.

Baking: 375° F (190° C).

Variations

Short dough is a versatile mixture that can be made up in many ways to provide variety in the bakeshop. Some of the many possible variations are suggested here.

Flavoring the dough: During mixing, vary the dough by flavoring to taste with lemon, cinnamon, mace, maple, almond extract, or other flavoring. Fine coconut or chopped nuts may be mixed with the dough.

Garnishing before baking: Decorate the tops with chopped or whole nuts, colored sugar, chocolate sprinkles, coconut, glacéed fruits, or almond macaroon mixture. Tops may be egg-washed first to help the toppings stick.

Garnishing after baking: Some examples of materials for garnishing cookies are fondant, royal icing, pecan halves on dabs of fudge or fondant icing, and melted chocolate (to coat completely or to drizzle on with a paper cone).

Jam Tarts:

Cut out dough with large, round cutters. With a ½-inch (12-mm) cutter, cut out the centers of half the rounds. These will be the tops of the sandwiched cookies. When baked, cool completely. Dust the tops (the ones with the cutout centers) with confectioners' sugar. Sandwich tops and bottoms together with a small dab of jam, so that the jam shows through the hole on top.

Almond Crescents:

Cut out crescent shapes from rolled-out dough. Spread tops with a layer of almond macaroon mixture (p. 267). Dip tops in chopped almonds. Bake at 350° F (175° C). When cooled, dip the tips of the crescents in melted chocolate.

Peanut Butter Cookies

Ingredients	U.S.		Metric	%
Butter, or part butter				
and part shortening	1 lb 8	oz	750 g	75
Brown sugar	1 lb		500 g	50
Granulated sugar	1 lb		500 g	50
Salt	0.33 oz (2 tsp)		10 g	1
Peanut butter	1 lb 8	oz	750 g	75
Eggs	8	oz	250 g	25
Pastry flour	2 lb		1000 g	100
Baking soda	0.33 oz (2 tsp)		10 g	1
Yield:	7 lb 8	oz	3770 g	377

Mixing: Creaming method. Cream the peanut butter with the fat and sugar.

Makeup: Molded method. Use a fork instead of a weight to flatten the cookies. Use greased or parchment-lined pans.

Baking: 375° F (190° C) for 8 – 12 minutes, depending on size.

Cinnamon Cookies

Ingredients	U.S.		Metric	%
Butter, or part butter				
and part shortening	1 lb		500 g	80
Granulated sugar	8	oz	250 g	40
Brown sugar	8	oz	250 g	40
Salt	0.17 oz (1 tsp)		5 g	0.8
Cinnamon	0.33 oz (2 tbsp)		10 g	1.7
Eggs	3	oz	90 g	15
Milk	1	oz	30 g	5
Pastry flour	1 lb 4	oz	625 g	100
Yield:	3 lb 8	oz	1760 g	282

Mixing: Creaming method.

Makeup: Molded method. Roll cut pieces in cinnamon sugar before placing on greased baking sheets and pressing flat.

Baking: 375° F (190° C) for about 10 minutes

Variation

Chocolate Cinnamon Cookies:

Substitute 4 oz (125 g) cocoa for 4 oz (125 g) of the flour.

Nut Cookies

Ingredients	U.S.			Metric	%
Butter	1 lb 12	oz		875 g	87.5
Confectioners' sugar	10	oz		310 g	31
Brown sugar	4	oz		125 g	12.5
Salt	0.16	oz		5 g	0.5
Vanilla	0.67	oz		20 g	2
Bread flour	2 lb			1000 g	100
Ground nuts (hazelnuts, pecans, walnuts, almonds, etc.)	1 lb 8	oz		750 g	75
Yield:	6 lb 2	oz		3085 g	308

Mixing: Creaming method

Makeup: Molded method. Mold cookies by hand into desired shape, such as balls, fingers, or crescents.

Baking: 350° F (175° C) for about 25 minutes

Finish: Dust cooled cookies heavily with confectioners' sugar.

Speculaas

Ingredients	U.S.		Metric	%
Butter, or half butter and half shortening	2 lb		1000 g	67
Confectioners' sugar	1 lb 10	oz	825 g	55
Fine granulated sugar	8	oz	250 g	17
Grated lemon zest	0.33	oz (4 tsp)	10 g	0.7
Cinnamon	0.5	oz (8 tsp)	15 g	1
Cloves	0.1	oz (1½ tsp)	3 g	0.2
Cardamom	0.1	oz (1½ tsp)	3 g	0.2
Eggs	5	oz	150 g	10
Pastry flour	3 lb		1500 g	100
Yield:	7 lb 8	oz	3756 g	251

Mixing: Creaming method. Blend at each stage until smooth, but do not cream until light.

Makeup: The classic way to make these cookies is by the molded method. The dough is pressed into special wooden speculaas molds, then removed and placed on baking sheets. Or it is stamped with special tools to emboss a design in the dough.

   If these molds are not available, make up the cookies either as icebox cookies or as rolled cookies cut with cookie cutters. They can be made small or large as desired. Large cookies should be about ¼ inch (6 mm) thick.

   Optional: Press sliced or whole blanced almonds onto the cookies after makeup.

Baking: 375° F (190° C) for medium to large cookies; 400° F (200° C) for small, thin cookies

Pfeffernüsse

Ingredients	U.S.			Metric		%
Honey	1 lb	8	oz	750	g	50
Sugar		12	oz	375	g	25
Eggs		5	oz	150	g	10
Shortening		4	oz	125	g	8
Salt		0.5	oz	15	g	1
Cinnamon		0.25 oz (4 tsp)		8	g	0.5
Allspice		0.15 oz (2 tsp)		5	g	0.3
Cloves		0.15 oz (2 tsp)		5	g	0.3
Black or white pepper		0.07 oz (1 tsp)		2.5	g	0.15
Cardamom		0.07 oz (1 tsp)		2.5	g	0.15
Candied citron or citrus peel		8	oz	250	g	17
Baker's ammonia		0.25 oz		8	g	0.5
Baking soda		0.12 oz (¾ tsp)		4	g	0.25
Water		1	oz	30	g	2
Pastry flour	3 lb			1500	g	100
Yield:	6 lb	7	oz	3230	g	215

Mixing:

1. Blend together the honey, sugar, eggs, shortening, salt, spices, and candied peel.

2. Dissolve the ammonia and soda in the water. Blend into the honey mixture.

3. Blend in the flour.

Makeup: Molded method. Roll the dough into logs 1 inch in diameter. Cut off ½-inch (12-mm) pieces and roll into balls. Place on parchment-lined baking sheets.

Baking: 350° F (175° C) for about 10 minutes

Finishing: Cool. Dip in warm flat icing. Remove to racks to harden.

Butter Tea Cookies

Ingredients	U.S.			Metric	%
Butter, or half butter and half shortening	1 lb	8	oz	670 g	67
Granulated sugar		12	oz	330 g	33
Confectioners' sugar		6	oz	170 g	17
Eggs		9	oz	250 g	25
Vanilla		0.33 oz (2 tsp)		9 g	0.9
Cake flour	2 lb	4	oz	1000 g	100
Yield:	5 lb	7	oz	2429 g	242

Mixing: Creaming method

Makeup: Bagged method. Make small cookies about the size of a quarter, using a plain tube or star tube. Bag out onto ungreased or parchment-lined baking sheets.

Baking: 375° F (190° C), about 10 minutes

Butter Tea Cookies *(Continued)*

Variations

Flavor with almond extract instead of vanilla.

Fancy Tea Cookies:

Add 17% (6 oz/170 g) almond paste to the first mixing stage.

Sandwich-type Cookies:

Select cookies all of the same size and shape. Turn half of them over and dot the centers of the flat sides with a small amount of jam or fudge icing. Sandwich with the remaining cookies.

Chocolate Tea Cookies:

Substitute 6 oz (170 g) cocoa for 6 oz (170 g) of the flour.

Gingerbread Cookies

Ingredients	U.S.			Metric	%
Butter, or part butter					
and part shortening	1 lb	6	oz	675 g	45
Brown sugar	1 lb			500 g	33
Baking soda		0.33 oz (2 tsp)		10 g	0.7
Salt		0.25 oz (1½ tsp)		7 g	0.5
Ginger		0.33 oz (4½ tsp)		10 g	0.7
Cinnamon		0.12 oz (2 tsp)		4 g	0.25
Cloves		0.06 oz (1 tsp)		2 g	0.12
Eggs		7	oz	225 g	15
Molasses	1 lb	6	oz	675 g	45
Pastry flour	3 lb			1500 g	100
Yield:	7 lb	4	oz	3607 g	240

Mixing: Creaming method

Makeup: Rolled method
For small cookies, roll out ⅛ inch (3 mm) thick.
For large cookies, roll out ¼ inch (6 mm) thick.
Cut out cookies and place them on paper-lined or greased and floured baking sheets.

Baking: 375° F (190° C) for small, thin cookies
360° F (180° C) for larger, thicker cookies

Gingersnaps

Ingredients	U.S.			Metric	%
Shortening		12	oz	375 g	38
Sugar		12	oz	375 g	38
Salt		0.17	oz (2 tsp)	5 g	0.5
Ginger		0.5	oz (2 tbsp)	15 g	1.5
Molasses	1 lb	4	oz	625 g	63
Baking soda		0.5	oz (1 tbsp)	15 g	1.5
Water		4	oz	125 g	13
Pastry flour	2 lb			1000 g	100
Yield:	5 lb	1	oz	2540 g	256

Mixing: Creaming method. Blend the molasses into the creamed fat/sugar mixture first. Then dissolve the soda in the water and blend in. Add the flour last.

Makeup: Bagged method. With a plain tube, bag out the size of a quarter. Flatten lightly.
May also be chilled and made up by molded or rolled methods.
Use paper-lined or greased and floured pans.

Baking: 375° F (190° C) for about 12 minutes

Spritz Cookies

Ingredients	U.S.			Metric	%
Almond paste	1 lb	8	oz	750 g	100
Sugar		12	oz	375 g	50
Salt		0.25	oz (1½ tsp)	8 g	1
Butter	1 lb	8	oz	750 g	100
Eggs		9	oz	285 g	38
Vanilla		0.33	oz (2 tsp)	10 g	1.5
Cake flour		12	oz	375 g	50
Bread flour		12	oz	375 g	50
Yield:	5 lb	13	oz	2928 g	390

Mixing: Creaming method. Blend the almond paste to a smooth, soft paste with a little of the egg. Add the butter and sugar, and cream as in basic procedure.

Makeup: Bagged method. Bag out with star tube to desired shapes (small) on parchment-lined sheets. If desired, garnish tops with pieces of fruit or nuts.

Baking: 375° F (190° C)

Lemon Cookies

Ingredients	U.S.			Metric	%
Butter	1 lb			500 g	67
Sugar	1 lb	8	oz	750 g	100
Grated lemon zest		0.75 oz (3 tbsp)		25 g	3
Salt		0.25 oz (1½ tsp)		8 g	1
Baking soda		0.25 oz (1½ tsp)		8 g	1
Eggs		4	oz	125 g	17
Milk		2	oz	60 g	8
Lemon juice		1	oz	30 g	4
Pastry flour	1 lb	8	oz	750 g	100
Yield:	4 lb	8	oz	2256 g	301

Mixing: Creaming method. Cream at each stage just until smooth; do not cream until light.

Makeup: Bagged method. With a plain tube, bag out small mounds the size of a quarter on paper-lined pans. Flatten slightly.

Baking: 375° F (190° C)

Variation

Lime Cookies:

Substitute lime zest and juice for the lemon. This is an unusual and tasty cookie.

Langues-De-Chat

Ingredients	U.S.			Metric	%
Butter		14	oz	350 g	88
Sugar, extra-fine granulated		7	oz	175 g	44
Sugar, 4X		7	oz	175 g	44
Egg whites		10	oz	250 g	63
Vanilla		0.25 oz (1½ tsp)		6 g	1.6
Cake flour		12	oz	300 g	75
Bread flour		4	oz	100 g	25
Yield:	3 lb	6	oz	1356 g	340

Mixing: Creaming method

Makeup: Bagged method. Using a ¼ inch (6 mm) plain tube, bag out onto silicone paper in the shape of small fingers 2 inches (5 cm) long. Allow at least an inch between cookies to allow for spreading. Double-pan for more even baking.

Baking: 400° F (200° C) for about 10 minutes

Finishing: Langues-de-chat may be served plain as petits fours sec. They may be used as decorations for ice cream, Bavarian cream, or other desserts. Or they may be sandwiched together with ganache, buttercream, fudge, or jam. Sandwich cookies may be partially dipped in melted chocolate.

Ladyfingers

Ingredients	U.S.			Metric	%
Egg yolks	8	oz		240 g	80
Sugar	5	oz		150 g	50
Pastry flour	10	oz		300 g	100
Vanilla (optional)	0.25	oz (1½ tsp)		8 g	2.5
Egg whites	12	oz		360 g	120
Sugar	5	oz		150 g	50
Yield:	2 lb 8	oz		1208 g	402

Enough for about 8 dozen ladyfingers

Mixing: Sponge method

1. Whip egg yolks 1 minute at medium speed, using the whip attachment. With machine running, gradually add the first amount of sugar. Continue to whip until thick and light.

2. Sift the flour and fold about half of it into the yolks. If desired, add the vanilla. (Lemon flavor may be used instead.)

3. Whip the egg whites until they form soft peaks. Add the sugar and whip until stiff but still moist.

4. Fold the whites into the batter alternately with the remaining flour.

Makeup: Bagged method. Using a plain tube, bag out 3-inch long strips, ¾ inch wide (7.5 × 2 cm) onto sheets of parchment. Sprinkle lightly with extra-fine granulated sugar. Remove excess sugar by picking up the sheet of parchment by two corners and letting the sugar slide off. Carefully lay the sheets of parchment in baking pans.

Baking: 375° F (190° C) for about 10 minutes

Coconut Macaroons (Meringue-Type)

Ingredients	U.S.			Metric	Sugar at 100% %
Egg whites		8	oz	250 g	40
Cream of tartar		0.06	oz (1 tsp)	2 g	0.3
Sugar	1 lb	4	oz	625 g	100
Vanilla		0.5	oz	15 g	2.5
Macaroon coconut	1 lb			500 g	80
Yield:	2 lb 12		oz	1392 g	222

Mixing: Sponge method

1. Whip the egg whites with the cream of tartar until they form soft peaks. Gradually whip in the sugar. Continue to whip until stiff and glossy.

2. Fold in the coconut.

Makeup: Bagged method. Bag out with a star tube onto parchment-lined baking sheets.

Baking: 300° F (150° C) for about 30 minutes

Almond Macaroons

Ingredients	U.S.	Almond paste at 100% Metric	%
Almond paste and/or macaroon paste	2 lb	1000 g	100
Granulated sugar	2 lb	1000 g	100
Egg whites	12 oz	375 g	37.5
Yield:	4 lb 12 oz	2375 g	237

Enough for about 300 1½-inch (4-cm) cookies

Mixing: One-stage method. Blend the almond paste with a little of the egg whites to soften it, then blend together all ingredients. If the mixture is too stiff for a pastry bag, add a little extra egg white.

Makeup: Bagged method. Using a plain tube, deposit the mix on silicone paper in mounds the size of a quarter. Double-pan.

Baking: 350° F (175° C). Let cool before removing from the paper. To make it easier to remove the macaroons from the paper, turn the sheets over and brush the bottoms of the sheets with water.

Variation

Amaretti:

Make the following ingredient adjustments:

Use kernel paste instead of almond paste for a stronger flavor (optional).

Reduce the granulated sugar to 85% (1 lb 11 oz/850 g).

Add 85% (1 lb 11 oz/850 g) brown sugar.

Madeleines

Ingredients	U.S.	Metric	%
Eggs	8 oz	225 g	100
Sugar	8 oz	225 g	100
Salt	0.04 oz (¼ tsp)	1 g	0.5
Cake flour	8 oz	225 g	100
Melted butter	8 oz	225 g	100
Grated lemon zest	0.17 oz (2 tsp)	4 g	2
Yield:	2 lb	900 g	402

Enough for about sixty 2 × 3-inch (5 × 7½-cm) cookies

Mixing: Sponge method. Mix as for genoise or butter sponge (p. 198):

1. Combine the eggs, sugar, and salt. Stir over hot water to warm the mixture. Then whip until thick and light.

2. Fold in sifted flour.

3. Fold in butter and flavoring.

Panning: Deposit in well-greased madeleine molds (small, shell-shaped molds). Other small, shallow molds may be used if desired.

Baking: 375° F (190° C) for 12–15 minutes. Remove from pans immediately after baking.

Chocolate Macaroons

Ingredients	U.S.	Almond paste at 100%	
		Metric	%
Almond paste	12 oz	350 g	100
Sugar	1 lb 5 oz	600 g	175
Cocoa	2 oz	60 g	17
Macaroon coconut	3 oz	90 g	25
Egg whites	8 oz	225 g	67
Yield:	2 lb 14 oz	1325 g	284

Mixing: One-stage method. Blend the almond paste with a little of the egg whites until smooth. Mix in the remaining ingredients. If the mixture is still too stiff for a pastry bag, add a little extra egg white.

Makeup: Bagged method. Using a plain tube, deposit the mix on silicone paper in mounds the size of a quarter. Double-pan.

Baking: 350° F (175° C). Let cool before removing from the paper. To make it easier to remove the macaroons from the paper, turn the sheets over and brush the bottoms of the sheets with water.

Variation

Use ground nuts in place of the macaroon coconut.

Coconut Macaroons (Chewy Type)

Ingredients	U.S.	Sugar at 100%	
		Metric	%
Sugar	1 lb 8 oz	700 g	100
Macaroon coconut	1 lb 8 oz	700 g	100
Corn syrup	3 oz	90 g	13
Vanilla	0.33 oz (2 tsp)	10 g	1.5
Pastry flour	1.5 oz	42 g	6
Salt	0.12 oz (¾ tsp)	4 g	0.5
Egg whites	11 oz	315 g	45
Yield:	3 lb 15 oz	1861 g	268

Mixing: One-stage method. Blend all ingredients together. Place in a kettle or stainless-steel bowl and set over a hot water bath. Stir constantly until the mixture reaches 120° F (50° C).

Makeup: Using a star tube or plain tube, bag out onto paper-lined sheet pans. Make the cookies about 1 inch (2½ cm) across.

Baking: 375° F (190° C)

Variation

Chocolate Macaroons:

Add 1.5 oz (45 g) cocoa to the basic recipe. Thin out with an additional ½–1 oz (15–30 g) egg white, if necessary.

Almond Tuiles

Ingredients	U.S.	Metric	%
Sugar	1 lb	480 g	533
Sliced, blanched almonds	1 lb 2 oz	540 g	600
Bread flour	3 oz	90 g	100
Egg whites, lightly beaten	9 oz	270 g	300
Melted butter	3 oz	90 g	100
Yield:	3 lb 1 oz	1470 g	1633

Mixing:

1. Mix the sugar, almonds, and flour in a bowl.

2. Add the egg whites and melted butter. Stir until well mixed.

Makeup: Dropped method. Drop by the tablespoonful 2 inches apart onto a greased and floured baking sheet. Use about ⅓–½ oz (10–15 g) per cookie. Flatten with a fork dipped in water, spreading out the mixture so that it is very thin and flat. It will not spread during baking, and the cookies must be thin.

Baking: 375° F (190° C), until browned. Immediately remove one by one from the baking sheet with a spatula and drape them over a rolling pin to give them a curved shape. They will become crisp when cool. If they do not become crisp, they are underbaked; return them to the oven for a minute. If they become crisp before they can be curved, return them to the oven to soften them.

Nut Squares
Yield: 150–300 cookies, depending on size

Ingredients	U.S.	Metric
Old-fashioned pound cake batter	2 lb	900 g
Chopped pecans, chopped walnuts, or sliced almonds	8 oz	225 g
Cinnamon sugar	as needed	

Makeup: Sheet method

1. Spread batter evenly onto a greased and floured full-size sheet pan (18 × 26 in/ 46 × 66 cm).

2. Sprinkle with nuts, then with cinnamon sugar.

Baking: 375° F (190° C)
As soon as the sheet is baked, cut into small squares.

Swiss Leckerli

Ingredients	U.S.			Metric		%
Honey	10	oz		315	g	42
Sugar	6	oz		185	g	25
Baking soda	0.25	oz		8	g	1
Water	4	oz		125	g	17
Salt	0.17	oz (1 tsp)		5	g	0.7
Cinnamon	0.25	oz (4½ tsp)		8	g	1
Mace	0.06	oz (1 tsp)		1.5	g	0.2
Cloves	0.06	oz (1 tsp)		1.5	g	0.2
Candied lemon peel, finely chopped	2	oz		60	g	8
Candied orange peel, finely chopped	2	oz		60	g	8
Blanched almonds, chopped	4	oz		125	g	17
Bread flour	1 lb			500	g	67
Cake flour	8	oz		250	g	33
Yield:	3 lb 5	oz		1659	g	222

Mixing:

1. Heat the honey and sugar together until the sugar is dissolved. Cool.

2. Dissolve the baking soda in the water. Add to the honey mixture.

3. Add the remaining ingredients. Mix to a smooth dough.

Makeup: Sheet method. Roll out dough ¼ inch (6 mm) thick. Place on a well-greased baking sheet. Cut into small squares, but do not separate the squares until after they are baked.

Alternative method: Rolled method. Roll out ¼ inch (6 mm) thick and cut out with cutters, or cut into small squares. Place on greased, floured baking sheets.

Baking: 375° F (190° C) for 15 minutes or more. Immediately after baking, while still hot, brush tops with flat icing.

Brownies

Ingredients	U.S.		Metric	%
Unsweetened chocolate	1 lb		450 g	100
Butter	1 lb 8	oz	675 g	150
Eggs	1 lb 8	oz	675 g	150
Sugar	3 lb		1350 g	300
Salt	0.25 oz		7 g	1.5
Vanilla	1	oz	30 g	6
Cake flour	1 lb		450 g	100
Baking soda	0.25 oz		7g	1.5
Chopped walnuts or pecans	1 lb		450 g	100
Yield:	9 lb 1	oz	4312 g	907

Mixing: Sponge method

1. Melt the chocolate and butter together in a double boiler. Let the mixture cool to room temperature.

2. Whip the eggs, sugar, and salt together until very thick and light. Add the vanilla.

3. Blend in the chocolate mixture.

4. Sift the flour and soda together. Fold in.

5. Fold in the nuts.

Makeup: Sheet method. Grease and flour the pans or line them with parchment. One recipe will fill one full-size sheet pan (18 × 26 in/46 × 66 cm), two half-size sheet pans, four 9 × 13 in (23 × 33 cm) pans, or six 9-in (23-cm) square pans.

If desired, batter may be sprinkled with additional 50% (8 oz/225 g) chopped nuts after panning.

Baking: 325° F (190° C) for about 1 hour
For 2-in (5-cm) square brownies, cut sheet pan into eight rows of twelve to yield 96 pieces.

Florentines

Ingredients	U.S.	Metric	%
Butter	7 oz	210 g	350
Sugar	10 oz	300 g	500
Honey	3 oz	90 g	150
Heavy cream	3 oz	90 g	150
Sliced almonds	12 oz	360 g	600
Ground almonds or hazelnuts	2 oz	60 g	100
Chopped candied orange peel	4 oz	120 g	200
Bread flour	2 oz	60 g	100
Yield:	2 lb 11 oz	1236 g	2150

Mixing:

1. Combine the butter, sugar, honey, and cream in a heavy saucepan. Bring to a strong boil, stirring constantly. Cook, stirring, until the mixture reaches 240° F (115° C).

2. Mix together the remaining ingredients and add to the sugar mixture. Mix well.

Makeup: Dropped method. Drop while the mixture is hot; it will get very stiff when cool. Drop half-ounce (15-g) mounds on baking sheets lined with silicone paper or greased and floured. Allow at least 2 inches (5 cm) between cookies for spreading. Flatten the cookies with a fork.

Baking: 375° F (190° C), until browned. As soon as the pans are removed from the oven, use a round cookie cutter to pull the cookies back together into a round shape. Let cool.

Finishing: Spread the flat sides of the cookies with melted chocolate. Mark grooves in the chocolate with an icing comb.

Raisin Spice Bars

Ingredients	U.S.		Metric	%
Granulated sugar	1 lb 8	oz	700 g	100
Butter and/or shortening	8	oz	230 g	33
Eggs	8	oz	230 g	33
Molasses	4	oz	115 g	17
Pastry flour	1 lb 8	oz	700 g	100
Cinnamon	0.12 oz (2 tsp)		3 g	0.5
Cloves	0.04 oz (½ tsp)		1 g	0.16
Ginger	0.07 oz (1 tsp)		2 g	0.3
Baking soda	0.12 oz (¾ tsp)		3 g	0.5
Salt	0.17 oz		5 g	0.75
Raisins (see note)	1 lb		470 g	67
Yield:	5 lb 4	oz	2459 g	350

Note: If raisins are hard and dry, soak them in hot water until soft. Then drain them and dry them well before adding them to the cookie batter.

Mixing: One-stage method

Makeup: Bar method. Egg-wash strips with whole egg or egg whites.

Baking: 350° F (175° C) for about 15 minutes

TERMS FOR REVIEW

spread
one-stage method
creaming method
sponge method
dropped
bagged
rolled
molded
icebox
bar
sheet
double-panning

QUESTIONS FOR DISCUSSION

1. What makes cookies crisp? How can you keep them crisp after they are baked?

2. If you baked some cookies that were unintentionally chewy, how would you correct them in the next batch?

3. Describe briefly the difference between the creaming method and the one-stage method.

4. Besides cost control, why is accurate scaling and uniform sizing important when making up cookies?

CHAPTER 13

MISCELLANEOUS DESSERTS

This chapter discusses a variety of desserts not covered in earlier chapters. Although most of these items are not "baked goods" in the sense that breads, pastries, cakes, and cookies are, they are popular desserts that are important in food service. They include various fruit desserts, custards, puddings, creams, and frozen desserts.

Though this may seem like a catchall chapter, you will find that many of the items and techniques discussed are related to each other and to techniques discussed in earlier chapters. For example, many puddings, Bavarians, mousses, soufflés, and frozen desserts are based on two basic custards, crème anglaise and pastry cream, presented in Chapter 7. Also, the items in three of these sections — Bavarians, mousses, soufflés, and still-frozen desserts — depend on meringues (discussed in Chapter 7) and/or whipped cream for their texture.

As you now are fully aware, the art and science of baking and dessert preparation rely on a coherent set of principles and techniques that are applied over and over again to many kinds of products. The topics in this chapter are a further illustration of that fact.

After studying this chapter, you should be able to:
1. Prepare popular fruit desserts.
2. Prepare starch-thickened or boiled puddings.
3. Prepare baked custards and baked puddings.
4. Prepare steamed puddings.
5. Prepare Bavarian creams and mousses.
6. Prepare hot dessert soufflés.
7. Judge the quality of commercial ice creams.
8. Prepare ice cream desserts using commercial ice cream and sherbet.
9. Prepare still-frozen desserts, including bombes, frozen mousses, and frozen soufflés.

FRUIT DESSERTS

Fruits are important ingredients in many kinds of desserts. In earlier chapters, we have already discussed fruit pies, fritters, pastries, tarts, cakes, and sauces. There are many other types of fruit-based desserts, however, that do not fit neatly into these categories. A representative sampling of recipes is included here, although, of course, they are only a small fraction of the many hundreds of recipes to be found elsewhere. See also the ice cream and fruit combinations later in this chapter.

Traditional American favorites include cobblers, which are very much like fruit pies made in large baking pans, but without bottom crusts; crisps, which are like cobblers, but with brown sugar streusel topping instead of a pastry crust; and betties, which have alternating layers of rich cake crumbs and fruit.

A simple and versatile category of fruit dessert is the *compote*, which is simply fruit poached or simmered in a flavored syrup. Many variations are possible, depending on the selection of fruit and the flavoring of the syrup.

Finally, don't overlook fresh, uncooked fruits for dessert, served plain, with cream, or lightly sweetened with sugar, flavored syrup, or a sweet liqueur or wine.

Apple Crisp

Yield: One pan 12 × 20 in (30 × 50 cm)
48 portions, 4 oz (120 g) each

Ingredients	U.S.			Metric
Peeled, sliced apples	8 lb			4000 g
Sugar		4	oz	125 g
Lemon juice		2	oz	60 ml
Butter	1 lb			500 g
Brown sugar	1 lb 8		oz	750 g
Cinnamon		0.12 oz (2 tsp)		4 g
Pastry flour	1 lb 8		oz	750 g

Procedure:

1. Toss the sliced apples gently with the sugar and lemon juice. Spread evenly in a 12 × 20 in (30 × 50 cm) baking pan.

2. Rub the butter, sugar, cinnamon, and flour together until well blended and crumbly.

3. Sprinkle evenly over the apples.

4. Bake at 350° F (175° C) for about 45 minutes, until top is browned and apples are tender.

Variation

Peach, Cherry, or Rhubarb Crisp:

Substitute the indicated fruit for the apples. If rhubarb is used, increase the sugar in step 1 to 12 oz (375 g).

Fruit Cobbler

Yield: One-pan 12 × 20 in (30 × 50 cm)

48 portions, 5 oz (150g) each

Ingredients	U.S.	Metric
Fruit pie filling	12–15 lb	5.5–7 kg
Flaky pie dough	2 lb	1 kg

Procedure:

1. Place fruit filling in a 12 × 20 in (30 × 50 cm) baking pan.
2. Roll out the pastry to fit the top of the pan. Place on top of the filling and seal the edges to the pan. Pierce small holes in the pastry to allow steam to escape.
3. Bake at 425° F (220° C) for about 30 minutes, until top is browned.
4. Cut the dessert in six rows of eight, or forty-eight, portions. Serve warm or cold.

Variation

In place of the pie pastry, use biscuit dough. Roll out the dough ¼ inch (6 mm) thick and cut it into 1½ inch rounds. Place the rounds on top of the fruit filling.

Apple Betty

Yield: One pan 12 × 20 in (30 × 50 cm)

48 portions, 4 oz (120 g) each

Ingredients	U.S.		Metric
Peeled, sliced apples	8 lb		4000 g
Sugar	1 lb 8	oz	750 g
Salt	0.25 oz (1½ tsp)		7 g
Nutmeg	0.08 oz (1 tsp)		2 g
Grated lemon zest	0.12 oz (1½ tsp)		3 g
Lemon juice	2	oz	60 ml
Yellow or white cake crumbs	2 lb		1000 g
Melted butter	8	oz	250 g

Procedure:

1. Combine the apples, sugar, salt, nutmeg, lemon zest, and lemon juice in a bowl. Toss gently until well mixed.
2. Place one-third of the apple mixture in an even layer in a well-buttered 12 × 20-in (30 × 50-cm) baking pan.
3. Top with one-third of the cake crumbs.
4. Continue until all the apples and crumbs have been used. You will have three layers of fruit and three layers of crumbs.
5. Pour the melted butter evenly over the top.
6. Bake at 350° F (175° C) for about 1 hour, until fruit is tender.

Poached Fruit (Fruit Compote)
Yield: About 6 lb (3 kg), plus syrup

Ingredients	U.S.	Metric
Water	2 qt	2 l
Sugar (see note)	2–3 lb	1–1.5 kg
Vanilla (see note)	4 tsp	20 ml
Prepared fruit (see individual variations)	6 lb	3 kg

Note: The amount of sugar used depends on the desired sweetness of the dessert and the natural sweetness of the fruit. Other flavorings may be used in place of the vanilla. A popular alternative is to add 4 or 5 strips of lemon peel and 2 oz (60 ml) lemon juice to the syrup.

Procedure:

1. Combine the water and sugar in a saucepan. Bring to a boil, stirring until the sugar is dissolved.

2. Add the vanilla.

3. Add the prepared fruit to the syrup or, if using tender fruit, place the fruit in a shallow pan and pour the syrup over it.

4. Cook very slowly, just below a simmer, until the fruit is just tender.

5. Let the fruit cool in the syrup. When cool, refrigerate in the syrup until needed.

Variations

Poached Apples, Pears, or Pineapple:

Peel, quarter, and core the fruit. For pineapple, cut into small wedges. Poach as in basic recipe.

Pears in Wine:

Substitute red or white table wine for the water. Omit the vanilla. Add one sliced lemon to the syrup. Peel the pears but leave them whole.

Poached Peaches:

Peel the peaches by blanching them in boiling water for a few seconds and slipping off the skins. Cut in half and remove the stones. Poach as in the basic recipe.

Peaches in Wine:

Prepare the peaches as above. Poach as for pears in wine, flavoring the syrup with lemon.

Poached Apricots, Plums, or Nectarines:

Cut the fruits in half and remove the stones. (Nectarines may be peeled like peaches, if desired.) Poach as in the basic recipe.

Poached Cherries:

Pit the cherries with a cherry pitter. Poach as in the basic recipe.

Poached Dried Fruit:

Soak dried fruit in water overnight. Use the soaking liquid for making the syrup. Poach as in the basic recipe, adding 2 oz (60 ml) lemon juice to the syrup.

Fresh Fruit Salad:

This is an uncooked version of fruit compote. Prepare the syrup as in the basic recipe. Cool it completely. Prepare a mixture of fresh fruits; dice large fruits or cut them into bite-size pieces. Combine the fruits and cold syrup and let them stand several hours or overnight in the refrigerator.

Apple Charlotte

Yield: One 1-qt (1-l) mold

Ingredients	U.S.		Metric	
Tart cooking apples	2 lb		900	g
Butter	1	oz	30	g
Grated lemon zest	0.08	oz (1 tsp)	2	g
Cinnamon	0.01	oz (¼ tsp)	0.4	g
Puréed apricot jam	2	oz	60	g
Sugar	1–2	oz	30–60	g
Firm white bread, trimmed of crusts	12	slices	12	slices
Melted butter	4	oz	110	g

Note: Apple charlottes should normally not be made in sizes larger than 1 qt, or they are likely to collapse after unmolding. Also, to avoid collapse, the apple mixture must be cooked until it is quite thick. The bread should be firm, and the charlotte should be baked long enough to brown the bread well.

Procedure:

1. Peel, core, and slice the apples. Combine them with the butter, lemon zest, and cinnamon in a broad, shallow pan. Cook over moderate heat until soft. Mash the apples lightly with a spoon and continue to cook until they form a thick purée. Some lumps of apple are OK.

2. Stir in the apricot jam. Add sugar to taste, depending on the sweetness of the apples.

3. Line a 1-qt (1-l) charlotte mold, two 1-pt (5-dl) charlotte molds, or other straight-sided molds in the following manner: Dip bread slices in melted butter and line the mold with the buttered side against the inside of the mold. The bottom may be lined with one round slice or with wedges of bread cut to fit. Line the sides with half slices of bread overlapping each other shingle-fashion.

4. Fill with the apple purée and top with the remaining bread.

5. Bake at 400° F (200° C) for 30–40 minutes.

6. Cool for 20 minutes, then carefully unmold. Serve warm or cold.

Applesauce

Yield: About 1 qt (1 l)

Ingredients	U.S.	Metric
Apples	4 lb	2 kg
Sugar	as needed	as needed
Flavoring (see step 5)		
Lemon juice	to taste	to taste

Procedure:

1. Cut the apples into quarters and remove the cores. Skins may be left on because they will be strained out later. (Red peels will color the applesauce pink.) Coarsely dice the apples.

2. Place the apples in a heavy saucepan with about 2 oz (60 ml) water. Cover.

3. Set the pan over a low heat and cook the apples until very soft. Stir occasionally.

4. Remove the cover. Add sugar to taste. The amount depends on the desired sweetness of the sauce and the sweetness of the apples.

5. Add desired flavoring to taste; such as grated lemon zest, vanilla, or cinnamon. Add lemon juice to taste, especially if the apples lack tartness. Simmer for a few minutes to blend in flavors.

6. Pass the sauce through a food mill.

7. If the sauce is too thin or watery, let it simmer uncovered until thickened.

Cherry Clafouti

Yield: About 6 lb (3 kg), or 20–24 portions

Ingredients	U.S.		Metric
Pastry flour	4	oz	120 g
Sugar	8	oz	240 g
Salt	0.17 oz (1 tsp)		5 g
Milk	1 lb 4	oz	600 g
Eggs, beaten	8	oz	240 g
Vanilla	0.17 oz (1 tsp)		5 g
Butter	as needed		as needed
Pitted sweet cherries, well drained if canned	4 lb		2 kg

Procedure

1. Sift the flour, sugar, and salt into a mixing bowl.

2. Combine the milk, eggs, and vanilla. Gradually stir the liquid into the flour mixture to make a smooth batter.

3. Butter a half-size sheet pan well. Pour about half the batter into it.

4. Distribute the cherries evenly over the batter. Pour the remaining batter over the top.

5. Bake at 400° F (200° C) until set and lightly browned, about 30 minutes. (In order to avoid scorching the bottom of the dessert, it is advisable to double-pan it; that is, set the sheet pan on top of another one before placing it in the oven.)

6. Cut 4 × 5 or 4 × 6 into twenty to twenty-four rectangles. Serve warm or at room temperature, dusted lightly with confectioners' sugar.

Cherry Clafouti *(Continued)*

Variation

Apple Clafouti:

Substitute thinly sliced apples for the cherries. Before assembling the dessert, toss the apples with 4 oz (120 g) sugar and 1 oz (30 ml) lemon juice. Let stand for 30 minutes, then drain.

Raspberry or Cherry Gratin

Ingredients per portion	U.S.	Metric
Genoise layer (see step 2)		
Raspberries or sweet, pitted cherries	3 oz	90 g
Pastry cream	2 oz	60 g
Whipped cream	1 oz	30 g
Optional flavoring:		
kirsch, orange liqueur,		
or raspberry or cherry brandy	to taste	to taste
Sliced almonds	0.25 oz	7 g
Melted butter	0.25 oz	7 g
Confectioners' sugar		

Procedure:

1. Select a shallow gratin dish or other heat-proof dish large enough to hold the fruit in a shallow layer.

2. Cut a thin slice of genoise (about ⅜ inch/1 cm thick) to cover the bottom of the dish.

3. Arrange the fruit on top of the genoise. (If desired, marinate the fruit ahead of time in fruit brandy or liqueur and a little sugar. Drain and use the liquid in step 4.)

4. Combine the pastry cream, whipped cream, and flavoring. Spread the mixture over the fruit to cover completely.

5. Mix the almonds and butter and sprinkle over the pastry cream. Dredge the top heavily with confectioners' sugar.

6. Place under a broiler or in the top of a hot oven for a few minutes to brown the top.

7. Serve hot.

CUSTARDS AND PUDDINGS

It is very difficult to come up with a definition of pudding that includes everything called by that name. The term is used for such different dishes as chocolate pudding, blood sausages (blood puddings), and steak-and-kidney pudding. In this chapter, however, we are considering only popular American dessert puddings.

Two kinds of puddings, starch-thickened and baked, are the most frequently prepared in food service kitchens. A third type, steamed pudding, is less often served, and then only in cold weather, because it is usually rather heavy and filling.

Since custards are the basis of so many puddings, we will begin with a general discussion of this type of preparation. A **custard** is a liquid thickened or set by the coagulation of egg protein. There are two basic kinds of custards: *stirred custard,* which is stirred as it cooks and remains pourable when cooked: and *baked custard,* which is not stirred and which sets firm.

One basic rule governs the preparation of both types of custard: *Do not heat custards higher than an internal temperature of 185° F (85° C).* This temperature is the point at which egg-liquid mixtures coagulate. If they are heated beyond this, they tend to curdle. An over-baked custard will become watery, because the moisture will separate from the toughened protein.

Crème Anglaise, or vanilla custard sauce, discussed in detail in Chapter 7 (p. 118), is a stirred custard. It consists of milk, sugar, and egg yolks stirred over very low heat until lightly thickened.

Pastry cream, also discussed in Chapter 7 (p. 120), is stirred custard that contains starch thickeners as well as eggs, resulting in a much thicker and more stable product. Because of the stabilizing effect of the starch, pastry cream is an exception to the rule of not heating custards over 185° F. In addition to being used as a component of many pastries and cakes, pastry cream is also the basis for cream puddings.

Baked custard, like custard sauce, also consists of milk, sugar, and eggs, usually whole eggs for greater thickening power. Unlike the sauce, it is baked rather than stirred over heat, so that it sets and becomes firm. Baked custard is used as a pie filling, as a dessert by itself, and as a basis for many baked puddings.

Starch-Thickened Puddings

These are also called boiled pudding, because they are boiled in order to cook the starch that thickens them.

1. *Cornstarch pudding or blanc mange*

   Cornstarch pudding consists of milk, sugar, and flavorings, and is thickened with cornstarch (or sometimes another starch). If enough cornstarch is used, the hot mixture may be poured into molds, chilled, and unmolded for service.

2. *Cream puddings*

   Cream puddings, as we have suggested, are the same as pastry cream. Puddings are usually made with less starch, however, and may contain any of several flavoring ingredients, such as coconut or chocolate. Butterscotch pudding is given its flavor by using brown sugar instead of white sugar.

   If you will look again at the recipe for pastry cream (p. 120), you will see that the only difference between cornstarch puddings and cream puddings is that the latter contain eggs. In fact, cream puddings may be made by stirring hot cornstarch pudding into beaten eggs and then heating the entire mixture to just below a simmer. Care must be taken to avoid curdling the eggs if this method is used.

Since these puddings are basically the same as pastry cream, which in turn is used for cream pie fillings, it is not necessary to give separate recipes here. *To prepare any of the following puddings, simply prepare the corresponding cream pie filling (p. 183), but use only half the starch.* The following puddings can be made on that basis:

Vanilla pudding

Coconut cream pudding

Banana cream pudding (purée the bananas and mix with the pudding)

Chocolate pudding (two versions, using cocoa or melted chocolate)

Butterscotch pudding

Blanc Mange English Style
Yield: About 2½ qt (2.5 l)

Ingredients	U.S.	Metric	Milk at 100% %
Milk	4 lb (2 qt)	2000 ml	80
Sugar	12 oz	375 g	15
Salt	0.08 oz (½ tsp)	3 g	0.1
Cornstarch	8 oz	250 g	10
Milk, cold	1 lb (1 pt)	500 ml	20
Vanilla or almond extract	0.5 oz	15 ml	0.6

Procedure:

1. Combine the milk, sugar, and salt in a heavy saucepan and bring to a simmer.

2. Mix the cornstarch and cold milk until perfectly smooth.

3. Pouring it in a thin stream, add about 1 cup (2.5 dl) of the hot milk to the cornstarch mixture. Stir this mixture back into the hot milk.

4. Stir over low heat until the mixture thickens and comes to a boil.

5. Remove from the heat and add desired flavoring.

6. Pour into half-cup molds. Cool and then chill. Unmold for service.

Note: French blanc mange is very different from the English style. The French style is made from almonds or almond paste and gelatin.

Variations

Blanc mange or cornstarch pudding may be flavored in any way that cream puddings are. See the general discussion preceding this recipe.

For puddings that are to be served in dishes rather than unmolded, reduce the cornstarch to 4 oz (125 g).

Baked Puddings

Many, if not most, baked puddings are custards that contain additional ingredients, usually in large quantities. Bread pudding, for example, is made by pouring a custard mixture over slices or cubes of bread arranged in a baking pan and placing it in the oven to bake. Rice pudding, made of cooked rice and custard, is another popular item.

Baked custard, a mixture of eggs, milk, sugar, and flavorings, is baked until the eggs coagulate and the custard sets. A good custard holds a clean, sharp edge when cut.

The amount of egg in a custard determines its firmness. A custard to be unmolded requires more egg than one that is to be served in its baking dish. Also, egg yolks make a richer custard with a softer texture than do whole eggs.

When baking custards, note in particular these points:

1. Scald the milk before beating it slowly into the eggs. This reduces cooking time and helps the product cook more evenly.

2. Remove any foam that would mar the appearance of the finished product.

3. Bake at 325° F (165° C). High temperatures increase the risk of overcooking and curdling.

4. Bake in a water bath, so that the outside edges are not overcooked before the inside is set.

5. To test for doneness, insert a thin-bladed knife about an inch or two from the center. If it comes out clean, the custard is done. The center may not be completely set, but it will continue to cook in its own heat after removal from the oven.

The procedure for making many baked puddings, such as bread pudding, is the same as that for making plain baked custard. A water bath may not be necessary if the starch content of the pudding is high.

Soft pie fillings, such as pumpkin, can also be considered to be baked puddings and, in fact, can be served as such. These preparations are, strictly speaking, custards, because they are liquids or semi-liquids that are set by the coagulation of eggs. They may also contain small amounts of starch as a stabilizer.

It may surprise you to see recipes for cheesecake in this section. Technically, however, cheesecake is the same type of preparation as baked custard or pumpkin pie filling. It is a liquid mixture of milk, sugar, eggs, and cream cheese that becomes firm when the eggs coagulate. The fact that it happens to be called a "cake" has nothing to do with its composition. In fact, the same mixture is also used as a pie filling.

Baked Custard
Yield: 24 portions, 5 oz (150-g) each

Ingredients	U.S.		Metric	Milk at 100% %
Eggs	2 lb		900 g	40
Sugar	1 lb		450 g	20
Salt		0.17 oz (1 tsp)	5 g	0.2
Vanilla	1	oz	30 g	1.25
Milk	5 lb (2½ qt)		2500 ml	100

Procedure:

1. Combine the eggs, sugar, salt, and vanilla in a mixing bowl. Mix until thoroughly blended, but do not whip.
2. Scald the milk in a double boiler or in a saucepan over low heat.
3. Gradually pour the milk into the egg mixture, stirring constantly.
4. Skim off all foam from the surface of the liquid.
5. Arrange custard cups in a shallow baking pan. Butter the insides of the cups if the custards are to be unmolded.
6. Carefully pour the custard mixture into the cups. If bubbles form during this step, skim them off.
7. Set the baking pan on the oven shelf. Pour enough hot water into the pan around the cups so that the level of the water is about as high as the level of the custard mixture.
8. Bake at 325° F (165° C) until set, about 45 minutes.
9. Carefully remove the custard from the oven and cool. Store covered in the refrigerator.

Variations

Crème Caramel:

Cook 1½ lb (700 g) sugar with 4 oz (125 ml) water until it caramelizes (see the section on sugar cooking on p. 114). Line the bottoms of the custard cups with this hot caramel. (Be sure the cups are clean and dry.) Fill with custard and bake as in basic recipe.

Vanilla Pots de Crème:

Pots de crème (pronounced "poh duh krem") are rich cup custards. Substitute 2 pt (1 l) heavy cream for 2 pt (1 l) of the milk in the basic recipe. Use 1 lb (450 g) whole eggs plus 8 oz (225 g) egg yolks.

Chocolate Pots de Crème:

Follow the procedure for vanilla pots de crème above, but stir 1 lb 8 oz (675 g) chopped sweet chocolate into the hot milk until melted and evenly blended. Reduce the sugar to 8 oz (225 g).

Rice Pudding

Yield: About 9 lb (4.5 kg)

Ingredients	U.S.	Metric
Rice, medium or long grain	1 lb	500 g
Milk	6 lb (3 qt)	3 l
Vanilla	0.33 oz (2 tsp)	10 ml
Salt	0.08 oz (½ tsp)	3 g
Egg yolks	6 oz	190 g
Sugar	1 lb	500 g
Light cream	1 lb (1 pt)	500 ml
Cinnamon	as needed	as needed

Procedure:

1. Wash the rice well. Drain. (See note.)

2. Combine the rice, milk, vanilla, and salt in a heavy saucepan. Cover and simmer over low heat until the rice is tender, about 30 minutes. Stir occasionally to be sure the mixture doesn't scorch on the bottom. Remove from the heat when cooked.

3. Combine the egg yolks, sugar, and cream in a mixing bowl. Mix until evenly combined.

4. Ladle some of the hot milk from the cooked rice into this mixture and mix well. Then slowly stir the egg mixture back into the hot rice.

5. Pour into a buttered 12 × 20 in (30 × 50 cm) baking pan. Sprinkle the top with cinnamon.

6. Bake in a water bath at 350° F (175° C) for 30–40 minutes, until set. Serve warm or chilled.

Note: In order to remove even more loose starch, some cooks prefer to blanch the rice in boiling water for 2 minutes, then drain and rinse it.

Variations

Raisin Rice Pudding:

Add 8 oz (250 g) raisins to the cooked rice and milk mixture.

Rice Condé:

Make the following adjustments:

Increase the rice to 1 lb 5 oz (650 g).

Increase the egg yolks to 10 oz (300 g).

Omit the cinnamon.

As soon as the egg yolks have been incorporated, pour the rice mixture into shallow individual buttered molds. Bake as in basic recipe, then chill until firm. Unmold onto serving dishes.

Rice Condé can be served plain, served with whipped cream or fruit sauce, or used as a base for poached fruit. Arrange the fruit on top of the unmolded rice; brush with apricot glaze. Dishes made in this way are named after their fruit, such as apricot condé, pear condé, etc.

Tapioca Pudding:

This pudding is prepared like rice pudding up through step 4 in the procedure. However, it is not baked. Instead, whipped egg whites are folded in and the mixture is chilled. To prepare, make the following adjustments in the recipe:

1. Substitute 8 oz (250 g) of tapioca for the pound of rice. Do not wash the tapioca. Cook it in the milk until tender.

2. Reserve 4 oz (125 g) of the sugar (from step 3) for the meringue.

3. After the egg yolks are incorporated, return the pudding to low heat for a few minutes to cook the yolks. Stir constantly. Do not let the mixture boil.

4. Whip 8 oz (250 g) egg whites with the reserved 4 oz (125 g) sugar to a soft meringue. Fold into the hot pudding. Chill.

Bread and Butter Pudding

Yield: About 10 lb (5 kg)

Ingredients	U.S.		Metric	
White bread, in thin slices	2 lb		1	kg
Melted butter		12 oz	375	g
Eggs	2 lb		1	kg
Sugar	1 lb		500	g
Salt		0.17 oz (1 tsp)	5	g
Vanilla	1	oz	30	ml
Milk, scalded	5 lb (2½ qt)		2.5	l
Cinnamon	as needed		as needed	
Nutmeg	as needed		as needed	

Procedure:

1. Cut each slice of bread in half. Brush both sides of each piece with melted butter.

2. Arrange the bread so that it overlaps in a buttered 12 × 20-in (30 × 50-cm) baking pan.

3. Mix together the eggs, sugar, salt, and vanilla until thoroughly combined.

4. Gradually stir in the hot milk. (Note that this mixture is the same as the mixture for baked custard.)

5. Pour the custard mixture over the bread slices in the pan.

6. Sprinkle the top lightly with cinnamon and nutmeg.

7. Set the pan in a larger pan containing about an inch of hot water.

8. Place in the oven preheated to 350° F (175° C). Bake about 35–40 minutes, until set.

9. Cool. Serve with whipped cream or vanilla custard sauce, or dust with confectioners' sugar.

Variation

Cabinet Pudding:

Prepare in individual custard cups instead of a baking pan. Substitute diced sponge cake for the bread and omit the melted butter. Add about 1 tbsp (8 g) raisins to each cup before pouring in the custard mix.

Cream Cheesecake

Ingredients	U.S.		Metric
Cream cheese	10 lb		4500 g
Sugar	3 lb 8	oz	1575 g
Cornstarch	3	oz	90 g
Lemon zest, grated	0.5	oz	15 g
Vanilla	1	oz	30 g
Salt	1.5	oz	45 g
Eggs	2 lb		900 g
Egg yolks	12	oz	340 g
Heavy cream	1 lb		450 g
Milk	8	oz	225 g
Lemon juice	2	oz	60 g
Short dough or sponge cake for lining pans			
Yield:	18 lb 4	oz	8230 g

Enough for four 10-inch (25-cm) cakes
            five   9-inch (23-cm) cakes
            six   8-inch (20-cm) cakes

Procedure:

Cheesecake may be baked with or without a water bath. Baking in a water bath results in cakes with browned tops and unbrowned sides. Baking without a water bath results in browned sides and a lighter top. If you are not using a water bath, you may use either deep layer cake pans or springform pans (pans with removable sides). However, if you are using a water bath, you must use deep cake pans, not springform pans.

1. Prepare the pans by lining the bottoms with either a very thin layer of sponge cake or a thin layer of short dough. Prebake the short dough until it begins to turn golden.

2. Put the cream cheese in the mixing bowl and, with the paddle attachment, mix at low speed until smooth and lump-free.

3. Add the sugar, cornstarch, lemon zest, vanilla, and salt. Blend in until smooth and uniform, but do not whip. Scrape down the sides of the bowl and the beater.

4. Add the eggs and egg yolks, a little at a time, blending them in thoroughly after each addition. Scrape down the bowl again to make sure the mixture is well blended.

5. With the machine running at low speed, gradually add the cream, milk, and lemon juice.

6. Fill the prepared pans. Scale as follows:

   10-inch pans — 4½ lb   25-cm pans — 2050 g

   9-inch pans — 3½ lb   23-cm pans — 1600 g

   8-inch pans — 3   lb   20-cm pans — 1350 g

7. To bake without a water bath, place the filled pans on sheet pans and set them in an oven preheated to 400° F (200° C). After 10 minutes, turn the oven down to 225° F (105° C) and continue baking until the mixture is set, about 1 – 1½ hours, depending on the size of the cake.

8. To bake with a water bath, set the filled pans inside another, larger pan. Fill the outer pan with water and bake at 350° F (175° C) until set.

9. Cool the cakes completely before removing from pans. To unmold a cake from a pan without removable sides, sprinkle the top of the cake with granulated sugar. Invert the cake onto a cardboard cake circle, then immediately place another circle over the bottom and turn it right-side up.

Variations

Cheesecake with Baker's Cheese:

In place of the 10 lb of cream cheese, use 7½ lb (3400 g) baker's cheese plus either 3 lb (1350 g) butter or 2½ lb (1125 g) shortening. If desired, you may use all milk instead of part milk and part cream in step 5.

French Cheesecake:

This cheesecake has a lighter texture achieved by incorporating whipped egg whites into the batter of either the cream cheese version or the baker's cheese version. To make French cheesecake, make the following adjustments in either recipe above:

Increase the cornstarch to 5 oz (150 g).

Reserve 1 lb (450 g) of the sugar and whip it with 2 lb 4 oz (1040 g) egg whites to make a soft meringue.

Fold the meringue into the cheese batter before filling the pans.

Steamed Puddings

Steamed puddings are primarily cold-weather fare. Their heavy, dense texture and richness make them warming, comforting desserts on winter nights. These same characteristics, however, make them inappropriate for year-round use, so steamed puddings are not as popular as they were decades ago.

The most famous steamed pudding is the English Christmas pudding, known in the United States as plum pudding. A Christmas pudding, well made and with good ingredients, is an unforgetable combination of flavors. The long list of ingredients makes the recipe look difficult, but once the ingredients are assembled and scaled, the pudding is simple to produce.

In addition to Christmas pudding, recipes for less complex steamed puddings are included here to give you a little idea of the range of possibilities. Many steamed puddings could be baked in a water bath, but steaming is more energy-efficient and helps to keep the pudding moist during the long cooking time.

If a compartment steamer is available, simply set the filled covered pudding molds in steamer pans and place them in the steamer. To steam on top of the stove, set the covered molds in large, deep pans and pour in enough hot water to come halfway up the sides of the molds. Bring the water to a boil, lower the heat to a gentle simmer, and cover the pan. Check the pan periodically and add more hot water as needed.

Christmas Pudding

Ingredients	U.S.			Metric
Dark raisins	2 lb			1000 g
Light raisins	2 lb			1000 g
Currants	2 lb			1000 g
Dates, diced	1 lb			500 g
Chopped almonds		12	oz	375 g
Candied orange peel, finely chopped		8	oz	250 g
Candied lemon peel, finely chopped		8	oz	250 g
Brandy	1 pt	8	oz	750 ml
Bread flour	1 lb			500 g
Cinnamon		0.12 oz (2 tsp)		4 g
Nutmeg		0.03 oz (½ tsp)		1 g
Mace		0.03 oz (½ tsp)		1 g
Ginger		0.03 oz (½ tsp)		1 g
Cloves		0.03 oz (½ tsp)		1 g
Salt		0.5	oz	15 g
Beef suet, finely chopped	1 lb	8	oz	750 g
Brown sugar	1 lb			500 g
Eggs	1 lb			500 g
Fresh bread crumbs		8	oz	250 g
Molasses		2	oz	60 g
Yield:	15 lb	7	oz	7700 g

Procedure:

1. Soak the fruits and almonds in the brandy for 24 hours.

2. Sift the flour with the spices.

3. Combine the flour mixture, suet, sugar, eggs, crumbs, and molasses. Add the fruit and brandy and mix well.

4. Fill greased pudding molds, allowing a little room for expansion. Cover the pudding mixture with rounds of greased parchment cut to fit inside the molds. Then cover the molds with foil and tie it with string so that steam will not get inside.

5. Steam for 4–6 hours, depending on size.

6. For storage, cool the puddings until just warm, then unmold. Wrap in cheesecloth and cool completely, then wrap again in plastic. These will keep a year or more if sprinkled with brandy or rum from time to time.

7. Christmas pudding must be served warm. To reheat it, place it in molds and steam for 1–2 hours, until heated through. Serve with hard sauce (p. 134).

Steamed Blueberry Pudding

Ingredients	U.S.			Metric
Brown sugar	1 lb	4	oz	625 g
Butter		8	oz	250 g
Salt		0.08	oz (½ tsp)	3 g
Cinnamon		0.17	oz (1 tbsp)	5 g
Eggs		8	oz	250 g
Bread flour		4	oz	125 g
Baking powder		0.75	oz	22 g
Dry bread crumbs	1 lb	4	oz	625 g
Milk	1 lb			500 g
Blueberries, fresh or frozen, without sugar	1 lb			500 g
Yield:	5 lb	13	oz	2905 g

Procedure:

1. Cream together the sugar, butter, salt, and cinnamon.
2. Blend in the eggs, a little at a time. Cream until light.
3. Sift the flour with the baking powder, then mix with the bread crumbs.
4. Add the dry ingredients to the sugar mixture alternately with the milk. Blend to a smooth batter.
5. Carefully fold in the blueberries.
6. Fill well-greased molds about two-thirds full. Cover tightly and steam for 1½–2 hours, depending on the size of the molds.
7. Unmold and serve hot with hard sauce or vanilla custard sauce.

Variation

Steamed Raisin Spice Pudding:

Add 4 oz (125 g) molasses, 1 tsp (0.07 oz/2 g) ginger, and ½ tsp (0.04 oz/1 g) mace to the sugar mixture. In place of the blueberries, use 12 oz (375 g) raisins, soaked and drained, and 8 oz (250 g) chopped nuts. Serve hot with hard sauce, custard sauce, or lemon sauce.

Steamed Chocolate Almond Pudding

Ingredients	U.S.			Metric
Butter	8	oz		250 g
Sugar	10	oz		300 g
Salt	0.08	oz (½ tsp)		2 g
Unsweetened chocolate, melted	3	oz		90 g
Egg yolks	6	oz		190 g
Milk or dark rum	2	oz		60 g
Almond powder	12	oz		375 g
Dry bread crumbs	2	oz		60 g
Egg whites	10	oz		300 g
Sugar	3	oz		90 g
Yield:	3 lb 8	oz		1717 g

Procedure:

1. Cream the butter, sugar, and salt until light. Blend in the chocolate.

2. Add the egg yolks in two or three stages, then blend in the milk or rum. Scrape down the bowl to eliminate lumps.

3. Blend in the almond powder and bread crumbs.

4. Whip the egg whites and sugar to a soft meringue. Fold the meringue into the batter.

5. Butter the insides of molds and sprinkle with sugar. Fill three-fourths full with batter. Cover tightly and steam 1½ hours.

6. Unmold and serve hot with chocolate sauce or whipped cream.

BAVARIANS AND MOUSSES

Bavarians and mousses, along with soufflés, still-frozen desserts, and many other items discussed later in this chapter, have one thing in common: They all have a light, fluffy texture, which is created by the addition of whipped cream, beaten egg whites, or both.

Bavarian creams are classic gelatin desserts containing custard and whipped cream. Chiffon pie fillings, discussed in Chapter 9, are similar to Bavarians in that they are stabilized with gelatin and have a light, foamy texture. In the case of chiffons, however, this texture is due primarily to whipped egg whites; whipped cream may or may not be added. Chiffon pie fillings may also be served as puddings and chilled desserts.

Mousses have a softer texture than Bavarian creams. Many are made without gelatin, although a few may have a small amount. Their lightness is created by whipped cream, whipped egg whites, or both.

Bavarians

A Bavarian, also known as Bavarian cream, is made of three basic elements: custard sauce (flavored as desired), gelatin, and whipped cream. That's all there is to it. Gelatin is softened in cold liquid, stirred into the hot custard sauce until dissolved, and chilled until almost set. Whipped cream is then folded in, and the mixture is poured into a mold until set. It is unmolded for service.

Accurate measuring of the gelatin is important. If not enough gelatin is used, the dessert will be too soft to hold its shape. If too much is used, the cream will be too firm and rubbery. The use of gelatin is discussed in detail in the section of Chapter 9 pertaining to chiffon pie fillings. See p. 186 for guidelines.

Fruit Bavarians can be made like regular custard-baked Bavarian creams by adding fruit purées and flavorings to the custard base. But they can also be made without a custard base, by adding gelatin to a sweetened fruit purée and then folding in whipped cream. A separate recipe is included for this type of Bavarian cream.

Because they can be molded and decorated in many ways, Bavarian creams can be used to make more elaborate, elegant desserts. They are the basis for a variety of desserts called cold *charlottes,* which are molded Bavarian creams made in round, straight-sided molds lined with ladyfingers or other sponge products. Charlottes are usually decorated with whipped cream. Procedures for assembling various types of charlottes are included following the vanilla Bavarian recipe. In addition, Bavarian creams can be used as fillings for European-style cakes, as discussed on p. 240.

This section also includes two other desserts that are made with the same techniques. Rice impératrice or empress rice is an elegant, molded rice pudding. The base is made somewhat like custard sauce (which is the base for Bavarian cream), except that rice is cooked in the milk before the egg yolks and gelatin are added. Whipped cream is then folded in. (Another way of arriving at the same result is to combine equal parts rice condé mixture, found on p. 286, and vanilla Bavarian cream mixture, plus the candied fruit mixture indicated in the recipe on p. 296.) Cream cheese Bavarian is not made with a cooked custard base, but it contains gelatin and whipped cream. Thus it is similar in character and texture to other Bavarian creams.

To unmold a gelatin-based dessert, dip the mold into hot water for 1 or 2 seconds. Quickly wipe the bottom of the mold and turn it over onto the serving plate (or invert the plate over the mold and flip the plate and mold over together). If it doesn't unmold after a gentle shake, repeat the procedure. Do not hold in the hot water for more than a few seconds or the gelatin will begin to melt.

Procedure for Preparing Bavarian and Bavarian-type Creams

1. Prepare the base, either custard sauce (crème anglaise) or another base indicated in recipe.
2. Soften the gelatin in cold liquid and stir it into the hot base until dissolved. Or, if the base is not cooked, heat the gelatin and liquid until the gelatin is dissolved, then stir it into the base.
3. Cool the mixture until thick but not set.
4. Fold in the whipped cream.
5. Pour the mixture into prepared molds and chill until set.

Mousses

There are so many varieties of mousses that it is impossible to give a rule for all of them. In general, we could define a mousse as any soft or creamy dessert made light and fluffy by the addition of whipped cream, beaten egg whites, or both. Note that Bavarians and chiffons fit this description. In fact, they are often served as mousses, but with the gelatin reduced or left out so that the mousse is softer.

There are many kinds of bases for mousses. They may be nothing more than melted chocolate or puréed fresh fruit, or they may be more complex, like the bases for chiffons.

Some mousses contain both beaten egg whites and whipped cream. When this is the case, most chefs prefer to fold in the egg whites first, even though they may lose some volume. The reason is that if the cream is added first, there is more danger that it will be overbeaten and turn to butter during the folding and mixing procedure.

If egg whites are folded into a *hot* base, they will be cooked or coagulated, making the mousse firmer and more stable. Whipped cream should never be folded into hot mixtures, since it will melt and deflate.

In addition to the chocolate mousse recipe included in this section, you can also convert the chiffon pie filling recipes (p. 186) and the Bavarian cream recipes (p. 294) in this book to mousses. Just reduce the quantity of gelatin to one-third or one-half the amount indicated in the recipe. For creamier mousses made from the chiffon recipes, substitute whipped cream for part of the meringue. (Some of the variations following the main recipes indicate this substitution.) By making these recipe adjustments, you can make a number of popular mousses—including raspberry, strawberry, lemon, orange, and pumpkin mousses—without needing separate recipes.

Vanilla Bavarian Cream

Yield: About 3 qt (3 l)

Ingredients	U.S.			Metric
Gelatin		1.5 oz		45 g
Cold water		10 oz		300 ml
Crème anglaise:				
Egg yolks		8 oz		250 g
Sugar		8 oz		250 g
Milk	2 pt			1000 ml
Vanilla		0.5 oz		15 ml
Heavy cream	2 pt			1000 ml

Procedure:

1. Soak the gelatin in the cold water.

2. Prepare the custard sauce: Whip the egg yolks and sugar until thick and light. Scald the milk and slowly stir it into the egg yolk mixture, beating constantly. Cook over a hot water bath, stirring constantly, until it just thickens slightly. (Review p. 118 for detailed discussion of making crème anglaise.)

3. Stir the gelatin mixture into the hot custard sauce until it is dissolved.

4. Cool the custard sauce in the refrigerator or over crushed ice, stirring occasionally to keep the mixture smooth.

5. Whip the cream until it forms soft peaks. Do not overwhip.

6. When the custard is very thick but not yet set, fold in the whipped cream.

7. Pour the mixture into molds or serving dishes.

8. Chill until completely set. If prepared in molds, unmold for service.

Variations

Chocolate Bavarian Cream:

Add 12 oz (375 g) sweet chocolate, chopped or grated, to the hot custard sauce. Stir until completely melted and blended in.

Coffee Bavarian Cream:

Add 3 tbsp (12 g) instant coffee powder to the hot custard sauce.

Strawberry Bavarian Cream:

Reduce the milk to 1 pt (5 dl) and the sugar to 6 oz (190 g). Mash 1 lb (500 g) strawberries with 6 oz sugar (190 g), or use 1½ lb (750 g) frozen, sweetened strawberries. Stir this purée into the custard sauce before adding the whipped cream.

Raspberry Bavarian Cream:

Prepare like strawberry Bavarian cream, using raspberries.

Liqueur Bavarian Cream:

Flavor to taste with a liqueur or spirit, such as orange, kirsch, maraschino, amaretto, or rum.

Praline Bavarian Cream:

Mix 6 oz (190 g) praline paste with the hot custard sauce.

Diplomat Bavarian Cream

Moisten diced sponge cake (about 8 oz/250 g) and diced candied fruit (about 8 oz/250 g) with kirsch (about 3 oz/90 ml). Mix gently with vanilla Bavarian mixture.

Orange Bavarian Cream:

Proceed as in the basic recipe, except omit the vanilla and reduce the milk to 1 pt (5 dl). Flavor the custard sauce with the grated zest of 2 oranges or with orange flavor. Before adding the whipped cream, stir 1 pt (5 dl) orange juice into the cold custard mixture.

Charlotte Russe:

Line the bottom and sides of a charlotte mold with ladyfingers (p. 266). For the bottom, cut the ladyfingers into triangles and fit them in close together so that the points meet in the center. The ladyfingers must fit in tightly so that there is no space between them. Fill the mold with Bavarian cream mixture and chill until set. Before unmolding, trim the tops of the ladyfingers so that they are level with the cream, if necessary.

Another method for making Charlotte Russe, while not authentic, can make an attractive dessert. Mold some Bavarian cream mixture in an unlined charlotte mold. After unmolding, cover the top and sides with ladyfingers or langues de chat (p. 265), using a little melted Bavarian mixture to make them stick. Decorate with whipped cream.

Charlotte Royale:

Line a round mold with thin slices of a small jelly roll. Fit them close together so that there is no space between them. Fill the mold with Bavarian mixture and chill until set. If desired, the charlotte may be glazed with apricot glaze after unmolding.

Fruit Bavarian

Yield: About 5 pt (2.5 l)

Ingredients	U.S.		Metric
Fruit purée (see note)	1 lb		500 g
Sugar, extra fine granulated		8 oz	250 g
Lemon juice		2 oz	60 ml
Gelatin		1 oz	30 g
Cold water		10 oz	300 ml
Heavy cream	1 pt	8 oz	750 ml

Note: Use 1 lb unsweetened or lightly sweetened fresh, frozen, or canned fruit, such as strawberries, raspberries, apricots, pineapple, peaches, or bananas. To use heavily sweetened fruit, such as frozen, sweetened strawberries, use 1 lb 4 oz (625 g) fruit and reduce the sugar to 4 oz (125 g).

Procedure:

1. Force the fruit purée through a fine sieve. Mix it with the sugar and lemon juice. Stir the mixture or let it stand until the sugar is completely dissolved.

2. Soften the gelatin in the cold water for 5 minutes. Heat the mixture gently until the gelatin is dissolved.

3. Stir the gelatin mixture into the fruit purée.

4. Chill the mixture until thickened but not set. Note: If the fruit purée is cold when the gelatin is added, it will start to set very quickly, so that further chilling may not be needed.

5. Whip the cream until it forms soft peaks. Do not overwhip.

6. Fold the cream into the fruit mixture. Pour it into molds and chill.

Rice Impératrice

Yield: 2 qt (2 l)

Ingredients	U.S.		Metric
Rice, long grain		6 oz	190 g
Milk	2 pt		1 l
Vanilla		0.5 oz	15 ml
Egg yolks		4 oz	125 g
Sugar		6 oz	190 g
Gelatin		0.5 oz	15 g
Cold water		4 oz	125 ml
Diced candied fruits		6 oz	190 g
Kirsch		2 oz	60 ml
Heavy cream		12 oz	375 ml

Procedure:

1. Rinse and drain the rice. Simmer it slowly in the milk, covered, until tender. Add the vanilla.

2. Whip the egg yolks and sugar together. Stir in a little of the hot milk from the rice mixture. Then stir the egg yolk mixture into the rice mixture. Cook very slowly for a few minutes, stirring constantly, until it is lightly thickened.

3. Soften the gelatin in the cold water. Stir the gelatin mixture into the hot rice mixture until the gelatin is dissolved. (Note: For buffet service or in hot weather, increase the gelatin to 0.75 oz/22 g.)

4. Stir in the candied fruits, which have been soaked in the kirsch.

5. Chill the mixture until thick but not set.

6. Whip the heavy cream until it forms soft peaks. Fold it into the rice mixture.

7. Pour into molds (see note). Chill until set. Unmold onto serving plates. Decorate with candied fruits and whipped cream, if desired. Serve with melba sauce (p. 133).

Note: A traditional way of preparing this dish is to line the bottoms of the molds with about ¼ inch (6 mm) of red fruit gelatin. For the quantity in this recipe, you will need about ½ pt (250 ml) gelatin mixture. Use either 2 oz (60 g) flavored gelatin mix dissolved in 8 oz (250 ml) water, or ⅛ oz (1¼ tsp/4 g) plain gelatin dissolved in 8 oz (250 ml) sweetened red fruit juice. Pour it into molds and chill until set.

Chocolate Mousse

Ingredients	U.S.		Metric
Sweet chocolate	1 lb	4 oz	625 g
Water		5 oz	150 g
Egg yolks (9)		6 oz	180 g
Liqueur (see note)		2 oz	60 g
Egg whites (9)		9 oz	270 g
Sugar		4 oz	120 g
Heavy cream	1 pt		500 ml
Yield:	3 lb 14 oz		1905 g
	(about 4¼ pt)		(about 2.25 l)

Note: Any appropriate liqueur or spirit, such as orange liqueur, amaretto, rum, or brandy, may be used. If you don't wish to use a liqueur, use 2 oz (60 ml) strong coffee or 1 tbsp (15 ml) vanilla plus 3 tbsp (45 ml) water.

Procedure:

1. In a saucepan, add the chocolate to the water and melt it over low heat, stirring constantly so that the mixture is smooth.

2. Beat in the egg yolks. Whip the mixture over low heat for a few minutes until it thickens slightly.

3. Remove the mixture from the heat and stir in the liqueur or other liquid. Cool it completely.

4. Whip the egg whites with the sugar to form a firm meringue. Fold it into the chocolate mixture.

5. Whip the cream until it forms soft peaks. Fold it into the chocolate mixture.

6. Pour the mousse into serving bowls or individual dishes. Chill it for several hours before serving.

Cream Cheese Bavarian

Ingredients	U.S.			Metric	
Cream cheese	3 lb			1500	g
Sugar	1 lb			500	g
Salt		0.5	oz	15	g
Grated lemon zest		0.12	oz (1½ tsp)	4	g
Grated orange zest		0.08	oz (1 tsp)	2.5	g
Vanilla		0.25	oz (1½ tsp)	8	g
Lemon juice		4	oz	125	g
Gelatin		1	oz	30	g
Cold water		8	oz	250	g
Heavy cream	4 pt			2000	ml
Yield:	8 lb 13	oz		4434	g
	(about 6 qt)			(about 6.5 l)	

Procedure:

1. Place the cream cheese in the bowl of a mixer and mix at low speed to soften it. Add the sugar, salt, and flavorings and blend until smooth. Scrape down the sides of the bowl to eliminate lumps.

2. Blend in the lemon juice.

3. Soften the gelatin in the cold water, then heat the water gently until the gelatin is dissolved.

4. Whip the cream until it forms soft, not stiff, peaks. Do not overwhip.

5. Blend the warm gelatin mixture into the cream cheese mixture. Scrape down the bowl to make sure the gelatin is mixed in well.

6. Immediately fold in the cream. Do not let the cheese mixture stand after adding the gelatin, since it will set very quickly.

7. Pour the mixture into prepared molds or serving dishes. Chill until set.

Variation

Icebox Cheesecake:

Use one of the following methods:

1. Line the bottoms of cake pans or springform pans with thin sheets of sponge cake or with a crumb crust mixture (p. 139). Pour in the cream cheese Bavarian mixture and chill until set. Unmold.

2. Follow the procedure for Bavarian torte (p. 293), using the cream cheese Bavarian mixture.

One full recipe is enough for three 10-inch (25-cm) cakes, four 9-inch (23-cm) cakes, or five 8-inch (20-cm) cakes.

SOUFFLÉS

Soufflés are lightened with beaten egg whites and then baked. Baking causes the soufflé to rise like a cake because the air in the egg foam expands when heated. Toward the end of the baking time, the egg whites coag- ulate, or become firm. However, soufflés do not become as stable as cakes, and they will fall shortly after they are removed from the oven. For this reason, they should be served immediately.

A standard soufflé consists of three elements:

1. *Base.* There are many kinds of bases used for dessert soufflés, but most are heavy, starch-thickened preparations, such as pastry creams or sweetened white sauces. If egg yolks are used, they are added to the base.

2. *Flavoring ingredients.* These are added to the base and mixed in well. Popular flavorings include melted chocolate, lemon flavor, and liqueurs. Small quantities of solid ingredients such as dried candied fruits or finely chopped nuts may also be added.

The base and flavor mixture may be prepared ahead of time and kept refrigerated. Portions can then be scaled to order and mixed with egg whites.

3. *Egg whites.* Whenever possible, egg whites should be whipped with some of the sugar. This makes dessert soufflés more stable.

Butter soufflé dishes well and coat them with sugar. Fill dishes to about ½ in (1 cm) below the rim. When it is baked, the soufflé should rise 1 to 1½ inches above the rim.

Vanilla Soufflé
Yield: 10 to 12 portions

Ingredients	U.S.		Metric
Bread flour	3	oz	90 g
Butter	3	oz	90 g
Milk	1 pt		500 ml
Sugar	4	oz	120 g
Egg yolks (8-9)	6	oz	180 g
Vanilla	0.33 oz (2 tsp)		10 ml
Egg whites (10)	10	oz	300 g
Sugar	2	oz	60 g

Procedure:

1. Work the flour and butter together to form a smooth paste.

2. Dissolve the sugar in the milk and bring to a boil. Remove from the heat.

3. With a wire whip, beat in the flour paste. Beat vigorously to make sure there are no lumps.

4. Return the mixture to the heat and bring it to a boil, beating constantly. Simmer for several minutes until the mixture is very thick and no starchy taste remains.

5. Transfer the mixture to a mixing bowl. Cover and let cook for 5 to 10 minutes.

6. Beat in the egg yolks and vanilla.

7. Soufflés may be prepared ahead of time up to this point. Chill the mixture and scale portions of the base to order. Proceed with the following steps.

8. Prepare soufflé dishes by buttering the insides well and coating with granulated sugar. This recipe will fill ten to twelve single-portion dishes or two 7-inch (18-cm) dishes.

9. Whip the egg whites until they form soft peaks. Add the sugar and whip until the mixture forms firm, moist peaks.

10. Fold the egg whites into the soufflé base.

11. Pour the mixture into the prepared baking dishes and smooth the tops.

12. Bake at 375° F (190° C). Approximate baking times are 30 minutes for large dishes, 15 minutes for single-portion dishes.

13. Optional step: 3-4 minutes before soufflés are done, dust the tops generously with confectioners' sugar.

14. Serve as soon as removed from the oven.

Vanilla Soufflé *(Continued)*

Variations

Chocolate Soufflé:

Melt together 3 oz (90 g) unsweetened chocolate and 1 oz (30 g) sweet chocolate. Add to the base after step 5.

Lemon Soufflé:

Instead of vanilla, use the grated zest of 2 lemons for flavoring.

Liqueur Soufflé:

Flavor with 2–3 oz (60–90 ml) of desired liqueur, such as kirsch or orange liqueur, added after step 5.

Coffee Soufflé:

Flavor with 2 tbsp (15 g) instant coffee powder, or to taste, added to the milk in step 2.

Praline Soufflé:

Blend 4–5 oz (125–150 g) praline paste with the base after step 5.

FROZEN DESSERTS

The popularity of ice cream needs no explanation. Whether it is a plain scoop of vanilla ice cream in a dish or an elaborate assemblage of fruits, syrups, toppings, and numerous flavors of ice cream and sherbet, a frozen dessert appeals to everyone.

Churn-Frozen Desserts

Ice cream and sherbet are churn-frozen, meaning that they are mixed constantly while being frozen. If they were not churned, they would freeze into solid blocks of ice. The churning keeps the ice crystals small and incorporates air into the dessert.

Ice cream is a smooth, frozen mixture of milk, cream, sugar, flavorings, and sometimes eggs. *Philadelphia-style* ice cream contains no eggs, while *French-style* ice cream contains egg yolks. The eggs add richness and help make a smoother product because of the emulsifying properties of the yolks.

Ice milk is like ice cream, but with a lower butterfat content. *Frozen yogurt* contains yogurt in addition to the normal ingredients for ice cream or ice milk.

Sherbets and *ices* are made from fruit juices, water,

and sugar. American sherbets usually contain milk or cream and sometimes egg whites. The egg whites increase smoothness and volume. Ices, also called *water ices,* contain only fruit juice, water, sugar, and sometimes egg whites; they do not contain milk products. The French work *sorbet* (pronounced "sor-bay") is sometimes used for these products. *Granité* (pronounced "grah-nee-tay") is coarse, crystalline ice, made without egg whites.

Production and Quality

Very few establishments make their own ice cream because of the labor involved, the equipment required, and the convenience of commercially made products. Also, strict health codes in many states make it difficult for all but large producers to make ice cream.

If you have access to an ice cream freezer, you will be happy to know that you probably already know how to make basic ice cream mix. Simply make a custard sauce or crème anglaise (p. 119), add 1 to 2 parts heavy cream for every 4 parts milk used in the sauce, and flavor as desired, with vanilla, melted chocolate, instant coffee, sweetened crushed strawberries, and so on. Chill thoroughly, then freeze according to the instructions for your particular equipment.

When the mix has frozen, transfer it to containers and place these in a deep-freeze at below 0° F (−18° C) to harden. (Soft-frozen or soft-serve ice creams are served directly as they come from the churn freezer, without being hardened.)

Whether you make ice cream or buy it, you should be aware of several quality factors:

1. *Smoothness* is related to the size of the ice crystals in the product. Ice cream should be frozen rapidly and churned well during freezing so that large crystals don't have a chance to form.

    Rapid hardening helps keep crystals small. So do eggs and emulsifiers or stabilizers added to the mix.

    Large crystals may form if ice cream is not stored at a low enough temperature (below 0° F/ −18° C).

2. *Overrun* is the increase in volume due to incorporation of air when freezing ice cream. It is expressed as a percentage of the original volume of the mix. (For example, if it doubles in volume, then the amount of increase is equal to the original volume, and the overrun is 100%.)

    Some overrun is necessary to give a smooth, light texture. If ice cream has too much overrun, it will be airy and foamy and will lack flavor. It was once thought that ice cream should have from 80% to 100% overrun, and that less would make it heavy and pasty. This may be true for ice creams containing gums and other stabilizers. However, some quality manufacturers are producing rich (and expensive) ice cream with as little as 20% overrun.

3. *Mouth feel* or body depends in part on smoothness and overrun, as well as on other qualities. Good ice cream will melt in the mouth to a smooth, not too heavy liquid. Some ice creams have so many stabilizers that they never do melt to a liquid. Unfortunately, many people have become so accustomed to these products that an ice cream that actually does melt in the mouth strikes them as "not rich enough."

Storage and Service

1. Store ice creams and sherbets below 0° F (−18° C). This low temperature helps prevent the formation of large ice crystals.

2. To prepare for serving, temper frozen desserts at 8° to 15° F (−13° to −9° C) for 24 hours, so that they will be soft enough to serve.

3. When serving, avoid packing the ice cream. The best method is to draw the scoop across the surface of the product, so that the product rolls into a ball in the scoop.

4. Use standard scoops for portioning ice cream. Normal portions for popular desserts are as follows:

Parfait	3 No. 30 scoops
Banana split	3 No. 30 scoops
"A la mode" topping for pie or cake	1 No. 20 scoop
Sundae	2 No. 20 scoops
Plain dish of ice cream	1 No. 10, 12, or 16 scoop

5. Measure syrups, toppings, and garnishes for portion control. For syrups, use pumps that dispense measured quantities, or use standard ladles.

Popular Ice Cream Desserts

Parfaits are made by alternating layers of ice cream and fruit or syrup in tall, narrow glasses. They are usually named after the syrup or topping. For example, a chocolate parfait has three scoops of vanilla or chocolate ice cream alternating with layers of chocolate syrup and topped with whipped cream and shaved chocolate.

Sundaes or *coupes* consist of one or two scoops of ice cream or sherbet placed in a dish or glass and topped with any of a number of syrups, fruits, toppings, and garnishes. They are quick to prepare, unlimited in variety, and as simple or as elegant as you wish — served in an ordinary soda fountain glass or in a silver cup or crystal champagne glass.

Coupes are often elegant, attractively decorated desserts. Many types have been handed down to us from the classical cuisine of years ago. The following are some classic coupes and similar desserts that are still popular today.

Coupe Arlesienne. In the bottom of the cup, place a spoonful of diced candied fruits that have been soaked in kirsch. Add a scoop of vanilla ice cream, top with a poached pear half, and coat with apricot sauce.

Coupe Black Forest. Place a scoop of chocolate ice cream in the cup and add sweet, dark cherries flavored with a little cherry brandy. If desired, add a few chopped walnuts. Decorate with rosettes of whipped cream and shaved chocolate.

Coupe Edna May. Top vanilla ice cream with sweet cherries. Decorate with whipped cream mixed with enough raspberry purée to color it pink.

Coupe Gressac. Top vanilla ice cream with three small almond macroons that have been moistened with kirsch. Top with a small poached peach half, cut side up, and fill the center of the peach with red currant jelly. Decorate with a border of whipped cream.

Coupe Jacques. Place a scoop each of lemon sherbet and strawberry ice cream in a cup. Top with a mixture of diced, fresh fruit flavored with kirsch.

Coupe aux Marrons. Top vanilla ice cream with candied chestnuts (marrons glacés) and whipped cream.

Coupe Orientale. Place diced pineapple in the bottom of the cup and add pineapple sherbet. Top with apricot sauce and toasted almonds.

Peach Melba. Vanilla ice cream, topped with a poached peach half, covered with Melba sauce (p. 133), and topped with slivered almonds.

Pear Belle Hélène. Vanilla ice cream, topped with a poached pear half, covered with chocolate sauce, and garnished with toasted, sliced almonds.

Among other popular ice cream desserts mentioned earlier in this book are meringues glacés (p. 164) and frozen éclairs and profiteroles (p. 158). The popular festive dessert called baked Alaska is discussed in the following procedure.

Procedure for Making Baked Alaska

1. Pack softened ice cream into a dome-shaped mold of the desired size. Freeze solid.

2. Prepare a layer of sponge cake the same size as the flat side of the mold and about ½ inch (12 mm) thick.

3. Unmold the frozen ice cream onto the cake layer so that the cake forms the base for the ice cream.

4. With a spatula, cover the entire dessert with a thick layer of meringue. If desired, decorate with more meringue forced from a pastry bag.

5. Bake at 450° F (230° C) until the raised edges of the meringue decorations turn golden brown.

6. Serve immediately.

Still-Frozen Desserts

The air that is mixed into ice cream by churn-freezing is important to its texture. Without this air the ice cream would be hard and heavy, rather than smooth and creamy. Desserts that are still-frozen — that is, frozen in a container without mixing — also must have air mixed into them in order to be soft enough to eat. In this case, the air is incorporated before freezing by mixing in whipped cream, whipped egg whites, or both.

Thus, still-frozen desserts are closely related to many other products discussed in this chapter, such as Bavarians, mousses, and hot soufflés. These products are all given lightness and volume by adding whipped cream or an egg foam. In fact, many of the same mixtures used for these products are also used for frozen desserts. However, because freezing serves to stabilize or solidify frozen desserts, they don't depend as much on gelatin or other stabilizers.

Still-frozen desserts include bombes, frozen soufflés, and frozen mousses. In classical theory, each of these types is made with different mixes, but in actual practice today, many of these mixes are interchangeable.

A note on the use of alcohol in frozen desserts: Liqueurs and spirits are often used to flavor these items. However, even a small amount of alcohol lowers the freezing point considerably. If you find that liqueur-flavored parfaits, bombes, and mousses aren't freezing hard enough, you can add additional whipped cream. This will raise the freezing point. In future batches, you might try using less alcohol.

A high sugar concentration also inhibits freezing. It is important to avoid using too much sugar in these items so that they freeze properly.

Parfaits and Bombes

In this country, we think of a *parfait* as an ice cream dessert consisting of layers of ice cream and topping in a tall, thin glass. The original parfait, however, is a still-frozen dessert frozen in a tall, thin mold and unmolded for service. (No doubt the ice cream parfait is so named because the glass it is served in is similar in shape to a parfait mold.) The mixture for parfaits consists of three elements: a thick, sweet egg-yolk foam; an equal volume of whipped cream; and flavorings.

The parfait mixture is also called a bombe mixture, because it is used in the production of a dessert called a *bombe*. The bombe is one of the most elegant of frozen desserts, and it is often elaborately decorated with fruits, whipped cream, petits fours secs, and other items after unmolding. It is made by lining a chilled mold (usually spherical or dome-shaped) with a layer of ice cream or sherbet and freezing it hard. The center is then filled with a bombe mixture of compatible flavor, and then frozen again.

Mixtures for frozen mousses can also be used to fill bombes, as can regular ice cream or sherbet. But a special bombe mixture is most often used.

Two recipes are given below for bombe mixtures. The ingredients and final results are nearly the same, but the techniques differ. Note that the technique for the first mixture is the same as that used to make French buttercream (p. 126). The second recipe requires a sugar syrup of a specific strength; the recipe for this syrup is also provided.

A procedure for assembling bombes is given, followed by descriptions of a number of classic bombes that have been popular for many decades.

Basic Bombe Mixture I
Yield: 3 qt (3 l)

Ingredients	U.S.		Metric
Sugar	1 lb		500 g
Water		4 oz	125 g
Egg yolks (12)		8 oz	250 g
Flavoring (see variations following second recipe)			
Heavy cream	1 pt 8 oz		750 ml

Procedure:

1. Dissolve the sugar in the water over high heat and boil the mixture until it reaches 240° F (115° C). (See p. 114 for information on boiling sugar.)

2. While the syrup is boiling, whip the egg yolks (using the whip attachment of the mixing machine) until light and foamy.

3. With the machine running, slowly pour the hot syrup into the egg yolks. Continue whipping until the mixture is cool. It should be very thick and foamy.

4. This mixture will keep, covered and refrigerated, for up to a week. When you are ready to assemble a dessert, proceed with the next steps.

5. Stir the desired flavorings into the egg yolk mixture.

6. Whip the cream until it forms soft, not stiff, peaks. Do not overwhip.

7. Fold the cream into the base mixture. Pour the result into prepared molds or other containers and freeze it until firm.

Basic Bombe Mixture II
Yield: 3 qt (3 l)

Ingredients	U.S.	Metric
Egg yolks (18)	12 oz	375 g
Syrup for bombes (see recipe below)	1 pt	500 ml
Flavoring (see variations below)		
Heavy cream	1 pt 8 oz	750 ml

Procedure:

1. Whip the egg yolks lightly in a stainless steel bowl, then gradually beat in the syrup.
2. Set the bowl over hot water and whip the mixture with a wire whip until it is thick and creamy, about the consistency of a thick hollandaise sauce.
3. Remove it from the heat, set it over ice, and continue whipping the mixture until it is cold.
4. Add the desired flavoring.
5. Whip the cream until it forms soft peaks. Do not overwhip. Fold it into the egg yolk mixture.
6. Pour the mixture into molds or other containers. Freeze until firm.

Variations

To create bombes of different flavors, add the suggested flavorings to the egg yolk mixture before folding in the whipped cream.

Vanilla:

Add 1–1.5 oz (30–45 ml) vanilla extract.

Chocolate:

Melt 4 oz (125 g) unsweetened chocolate. Stir in a little stock syrup to make a thick sauce. Then fold this into the yolk mixture. (For a stronger chocolate flavor, melt 2–3 oz/60–90 g sweet chocolate with the 4 oz unsweetened chocolate.)

Liqueur:

Add 2–3 oz (60–90 ml), or to taste, of desired liqueur or spirit, such as orange liqueur, kirsch, or rum.

Coffee:

Add ½ oz (15 g) instant coffee dissolved in an ounce (30 ml) of water.

Praline:

Add 5 oz (150 g) praline paste, softened with a little water, to the yolk mixture.

Fruit (Raspberry, Strawberry, Apricot, Peach, etc.):

Add up to 1 lb (500 g) fruit purée.

Variations (Continued)

Bombe or Parfait with Fruit:

Instead of flavoring the bombe mixture with a fruit purée, add solid fruits cut in small dice to plain or liqueur-flavored bombe mixture.

Bombe or Parfait with Nuts, Sponge Cake, or Other Ingredients:

Other solid ingredients besides fruit may be mixed with plain or flavored bombe mixture, including chopped nuts, crumbled almond macaroons, marrons glacés (candied chestnuts), and diced sponge cake or ladyfingers moistened with liqueur.

Syrup for Bombes
Yield: about 3 qt (3 l)

Ingredients	U.S.	Metric
Sugar	6 lb	3 kg
Water	4 lb	2 kg

Procedure:

1. Combine the water and sugar in a saucepan. Bring the mixture to a boil, stirring until the sugar is completely dissolved.
2. Remove the syrup from the heat and let it cool. Store it in a covered container in the refrigerator.

Procedure for Making Bombes

1. Place the bombe mold in the freezer until very cold.
2. Line the mold with a layer of slightly softened ice cream, using your hand to press it against the sides and smooth it off. The ice cream layer should be about ¾ in (2 cm) thick for small molds, up to 1½ in (4 cm) for large molds.

   If the ice cream becomes too soft to stick to the sides, place it in the freezer to harden it, then try again.
3. Freeze the mold until the ice cream layer is hard.
4. Fill the mold, with bombe mixture, cover, and freeze until firm.
5. To unmold, dip the mold in warm water for a second, wipe off the water from the outside of the mold, and turn out the bombe onto a cold serving plate. (Note: To keep the bombe from sliding around on the plate, turn it out onto a thin sheet of genoise, which will act as a base.)
6. Decorate with whipped cream and appropriate fruits or other items.
7. Serve immediately. Cut into wedges or slices so that all portions are uniform.

A Selection of Popular Bombes

Bombe Africaine
Coating: chocolate ice cream
Filling: apricot bombe mixture

Bombe Aida
Coating: strawberry ice cream
Filling: kirsch-flavored bombe mixture

Bombe Bresilienne
Coating: pineapple sherbet
Filling: bombe mixture flavored with vanilla and rum and mixed with diced pineapple

Bombe Cardinale
Coating: raspberry sherbet
Filling: praline vanilla bombe mixture

Bombe Ceylon
Coating: coffee ice cream
Filling: rum-flavored bombe mixture

Bombe Coppelia
Coating: coffee ice cream
Filling: praline bombe mixture

Bombe Diplomat
Coating: vanilla ice cream
Filling: bombe mixture flavored with maraschino liqueur and mixed with candied fruit

Bombe Florentine
Coating: raspberry sherbet
Filling: praline bombe mixture

Bombe Formosa
Coating: vanilla ice cream
Filling: bombe mixture flavored with strawberry purée and mixed with whole strawberries

Bombe Moldave
Coating: pineapple sherbet
Filling: bombe mixture flavored with orange liqueur

Bombe Sultane
Coating: chocolate ice cream
Filling: praline bombe mixture

Bombe Tutti-Frutti
Coating: strawberry ice cream or sherbet
Filling: lemon bombe mixture mixed with candied fruits

Cassata Napoletana
Cassatas are Italian-style bombes lined with three layers of different ice creams and filled with Italian meringue mixed with various ingredients. The most popular, Cassata Napoletana, is made as follows. Line the mold first with vanilla, then with chocolate, and finally with strawberry ice cream. Fill with Italian meringue (p. 118) flavored with vanilla, kirsch, or maraschino, and mixed with an equal weight of diced candied fruits. A little whipped cream may be added to the meringue, if desired.

Frozen Mousses and Frozen Soufflés

Frozen mouses are light, frozen desserts containing whipped cream. Though they are all similar in charac-ter because of their whipped cream content, the bases for them are made in several ways. Three types of preparations are included here:

1. Mousse with Italian meringue base.
2. Mousse with syrup and fruit base.
3. Mousse with custard base.

The mixture for bombes and parfaits can also be used for mousses.

The simplest method for serving mousse is to pour the mixture into individual serving dishes and freezing them. The mixtures can also be poured into molds of various shapes. After unmolding, the mousse is cut into portions and decorated with whipped cream and appropriate fruits, cookies, or other items.

Frozen soufflés are simply mousse or bombe mixtures frozen in soufflé dishes or other straight-sided dishes. A band of heavy paper or foil is tied around the mold so that it extends 2 inches (5 cm) or more above the rim of the dish. The mousse or bombe mixture is poured in so that it comes within ½ inch (12 mm) of the top of this band. After the dessert is frozen, the band is removed. The dessert thus looks like a hot soufflé that has risen above its baking dish

Other items may be incorporated in the frozen soufflé, such as sponge cake, ladyfingers, baked meringue, fruits, and so forth. For example, you might pour one-third of the mousse mixture into the prepared dish, place a japonaise disc (p. 166) on top, pour in another layer of mousse, add a second japonaise, then fill with the mousse mixture. This same technique can also be used with thin sponge cake layers. For further variety, arrange a layer of fruit on top of each genoise layer before adding more mousse.

Frozen Mousse I (Meringue Base)
Yield: 3 qt (3 l)

Ingredients	U.S.	Metric
Italian meringue:		
Sugar	1 lb	500 g
Water	4 oz	125 ml
Egg whites	8 oz	250 g
Flavoring (see note)		
Heavy cream	1 pt 8 oz	750 ml

Note: Possible flavorings include fruit purées, liqueurs, and chocolate. Use up to 6 oz (190 ml) strong spirits (brandy, dark rum, etc.) or 8 oz (250 ml) sweet liqueur. Use 8 oz (250 g) melted unsweetened chocolate or up to 1 lb (500 g) thick fruit purée. Specific flavors are suggested in the variations following the basic procedure.

Procedure:

1. Make an Italian meringue (see p. 118): Dissolve the sugar in the water in a saucepan and boil the syrup until it reaches 250° F (120° C). Meanwhile, whip the egg whites until they form soft peaks. While whipping constantly, slowly pour the hot syrup into the egg whites. Continue to whip the meringue until it is completely cool (unless you are flavoring it with liqueur—see next step).

2. Stir or fold in flavoring ingredients. If you are using melted chocolate or a thick fruit purée, stir a little of the meringue into the flavoring, then fold this into the rest of the meringue. If you are using a liqueur or spirit, add it while the meringue is still warm, so that most of the alcohol will evaporate.

3. Whip the cream until it forms soft peaks. Fold it into the meringue mixture. Freeze.

Variations

The following are a few of many possible flavors for frozen mousse.

Liqueur Mousse:

Flavor with 6 oz (190 ml) brandy, dark rum, or calvados, or with 8 oz (250 ml) sweet liqueur.

Chocolate Mousse:

Melt 8 oz (250 g) unsweetened chocolate. Stir in a little syrup for bombes (p. 305) to make a thick sauce. Stir some of the meringue into this mixture, then fold the chocolate mixture into the rest of the meringue.

Apricot Mousse:

Soak 12 oz (375 g) dried apricots in water overnight, then simmer until tender. Drain and purée in a food mill. Fold into the meringue. If desired, add 1 oz (30 ml) rum or kirsch.

Banana Mousse:

Purée 1 lb (500 g) very ripe bananas with 1 oz (30 ml) lemon juice. Add them to meringue.

Lemon Mousse:

Add 6 oz (190 ml) lemon juice and the grated zest of two lemons to the meringue.

Chestnut Mousse:

Soften 14 oz (440 g) chestnut purée by blending it with 2 oz (60 ml) dark rum until smooth. Add it to the meringue.

Raspberry or Strawberry Mousse:

Force 1 lb (500 g) fresh or frozen (unsweetened) raspberries or strawberries through a sieve. Add them to the meringue.

Frozen Mousse II (Syrup and Fruit Base)

Yield: About 5 pt (2.5 l)

Ingredients	U.S.	Metric
Syrup for bombes (p. 305)	1 pt	500 ml
Fruit purée	1 pt	500 ml
Heavy cream	2 pt	1000 ml

Procedure:

1. Mix the syrup and fruit purée until uniformly blended.

2. Whip the cream until it forms soft peaks.

3. Fold the cream into the syrup mixture.

4. Pour the mixture into molds or dishes and freeze.

Frozen Mousse III (Custard Base)

Yield: About 3 qt (3 l)

Ingredients	U.S.	Metric
Egg yolks (15)	10 oz	300 g
Sugar	1 lb	500 g
Milk	1 pt	500 ml
Flavoring		
Heavy cream	2 pt	1 l

Procedure:

1. Whip the egg yolks with *half* the sugar until they are light and foamy.

2. Meanwhile, bring the milk to a boil with the rest of the sugar.

3. Pour the milk over the yolks, whipping constantly.

4. Set the milk and egg mixture over a hot water bath and cook, stirring constantly, until the mixture thickens like custard sauce (see p. 119). Do not overcook, or the custard will curdle.

5. Cool the mixture, then chill it in the refrigerator or over ice.

6. Add the desired flavoring. The same flavorings and quantities may be used as in Frozen Mousse I (p. 307).

7. Whip the cream and fold it into the custard mixture.

8. Pour the mousse into molds or dishes and freeze.

TERMS FOR REVIEW

compote
cobbler
custard
stirred custard
baked custard
cornstarch pudding
cream pudding
pot de crème
Christmas pudding
Bavarian cream
charlotte
rice impératrice
mousse
soufflé
ice cream
Philadelphia-style ice cream
French-style ice cream
ice milk
sherbet
ice
granité
overrun
coupe
parfait
baked Alaska
bombe
frozen mousse
frozen soufflé

QUESTIONS FOR DISCUSSION

1. What is the internal temperature at which the eggs in custard mixtures become cooked or coagulated? What happens to stirred custards and baked custards if they are cooked beyond this point?

2. The basic techniques used to make custard sauce (crème anglaise) and baked custard are also used for some of the following preparations. Identify which of the following desserts are made using a stirred custard (custard sauce) technique, which are made using a baked custard technique, and which are made without any custard.

Bread pudding	Apple cobbler
Christmas pudding	Charlotte Russe
Chocolate Bavarian	Chocolate pots de creme
Baked cheesecake	Apple charlotte

3. What is the main difference between cornstarch pudding and cream pudding?

4. In the production of Bavarian creams and other desserts that are stabilized with gelatin, why is it important to measure the gelatin carefully?

5. When making a Bavarian or chiffon pie filling, what difficulty would you encounter if you chilled the gelatin mixture too long before folding in the whipped cream or egg whites?

6. When making dessert soufflés, what is the advantage of adding part of the sugar to the whipped egg whites?

7. Why do ice cream and sherbet have to be frozen in a special freezer that mixes the product while it is being frozen? Why is it possible to freeze frozen mousses and similar desserts without this kind of freezer?

CHAPTER 14

DECORATIVE WORK AND DISPLAY PIECES

This final chapter is an introduction to the pastry chef's art of making decorative items out of sugar, chocolate, and other materials. Although all the ingredients used for these pieces are edible, and many of these items are used to decorate fancy cakes and other desserts, nevertheless many of them are not intended to be eaten. Rather, they are often made as show pieces, such as centerpieces for dessert buffet tables.

In hotels and other food service and retail operations, such show pieces can be useful and even profitable. They serve to draw the customers' attention to the skill and artistry of the pastry chef and, thus, indirectly lead to greater sales of desserts. Perhaps even more important from a pastry chef's point of view, they are an outlet for creative skills.

Some of the techniques discussed are comparatively easy. On the other hand, many, if not most, of the items introduced in this chapter are difficult to make. Materials such as pulled sugar require a great deal of practice before you can expect to achieve good results. Furthermore, they cannot usually be learned without live demonstrations from an instructor, followed by hands-on practice with the instructor's guidance. Consequently, a written discussion can be little more than an introduction. This chapter aims to provide such an introduction. It will also serve as a handy reference when you need to refresh your memory.

After studying this chapter, you should be able to:
1. Temper chocolate couverture.
2. Use tempered chocolate for dipping, molding, and decorating.
3. Make and handle marzipan, and mold decorative items from it.
4. Make pastillage and use it to create simple decorative items.
5. Make nougat and shape it into simple decorative items.
6. Boil sugar syrups correctly for spun and pulled sugar.
7. Make spun sugar, sugar cages, and cast sugar.
8. Pull sugar and use it to make simple decorative items.

CHOCOLATE

Chocolate is not only America's favorite sweet, but it is also a versatile medium that is useful for many types of decorative work, ranging from the simple to the elaborate. As you will recall from Chapter 2, plain, unsweetened chocolate consists of two components, cocoa solids and cocoa butter. This product is used as a flavoring ingredient in baked goods and desserts, but it is too bitter to be eaten as is. To make sweet chocolate, sugar is added. The addition of milk solids makes milk chocolate.

For many reasons, chocolate is difficult to work with. It is very sensitive to temperature and to moisture. Melting and cooling must be done with the utmost care. Unless a liquid is to be added for any reason, the chocolate must be carefully protected from moisture (including steam). A single drop of water will ruin its texture for dipping or molding.

Tempering

The process of preparing chocolate for dipping, molding, or similar purposes is called *tempering*. This process applies only to genuine chocolate containing only natural cocoa butter and no other fats. Such chocolate is known in Europe as *couverture,* meaning coating chocolate.

Do not confuse couverture with the chocolate product known in this country as cake coating, cookie coating, or cooking chocolate, which has had much of the cocoa butter replaced by other fats. It is easier to use than genuine chocolate couverture because it doesn't need tempering. It only has to be melted. On the other hand, it lacks the texture, shine, and flavor of properly tempered genuine chocolate.

The reason for tempering can be explained as follows. Cocoa butter consists of many different fats. Some of them melt at low temperatures, and others at high temperatures. The fats that melt at high temperatures are, of course, the first ones to solidify as the melted chocolate is cooled. These high-melt-point fats give high-quality chocolate its shine and its snap (a well-processed chocolate breaks with a clean, sharp snap). The objective of tempering is to create a very fine fat-crystal structure in the chocolate. In a melted, tempered chocolate, these high-melt-point fats have begun to solidify into very fine crystals that are distributed throughout the melted chocolate. When the chocolate is left to cool, the chocolate sets or solidifies quickly, because the fine crystals act as "seeds" around which the rest of the chocolate crystallizes.

The actual process of melting and tempering chocolate consists of three basic steps:

1. *Melting.* The chocolate is placed in a pan or bowl and set over hot water to melt. It should not be set over direct heat, since the chocolate is easily burned, which destroys both the texture and flavor. Stir constantly while the chocolate is melting.

   The chocolate must be brought to a temperature of about 115 to 118° F (46 to 48° C) in order to completely melt all the fats, including the high-melt-point fats. (Note: All the temperatures given here are averages. Every chocolate is different and requires different processing temperatures. The manufacturer or supplier should be able to provide recommended processing temperatures for each of its products. For example, a well-known Swiss manufacturer of premium-quality couvertures specifies a temperature of 122° F (50° C) for the first melting.)

2. *Tempering* (cooling or precrystalling). When the chocolate is melted, it is removed from the heat, set in a cool place, and stirred constantly until it is cooled to a temperature of about 78 to 79° F (26° C). At this point, fine fat crystals will have formed and the chocolate will be thick and pasty.

   Chocolate manufacturers recommend slow cooling with constant stirring in order to produce the best texture. However, many pastry chefs prefer to speed up the process, either by stirring the chocolate over cold water or by pouring it onto a marble slab and working it with a scraper until it is cool.

3. *Rewarming.* At this point, the chocolate is too thick for dipping, molding, or most other uses and must be warmed slightly before it is ready to be used. Set it over warm water and stir it until its temperature reaches 86 to 88° F (30 to 31° C). The chocolate is now ready to be used.

   This step must be done very carefully. Do not let the chocolate get warmer than the recommended temperature. If this happens, too many of the fat crystals melt and the chocolate is no longer tempered, making it necessary to repeat the whole process.

   If the chocolate is warmed too much and is no longer tempered, it will take a very long time to set. When it does finally set, its texture will not be as good. Also, some of the cocoa butter will separate and float to the surface, making a whitish coating known as "bloom."

   If the chocolate is still too thick, thin it out with a little melted cocoa butter. Do not try to thin it out by heating it more.

Now that this rather complicated explanation has been given, we can briefly summarize the process of tempering in the form of step-by-step procedures. Two procedures are given. The first is the standard procedure, as explained above. The second is a short-cut method that is often used in small shops. Instead of cooling the melted chocolate to form fat crystals as in the explanation just given, the liquid chocolate is "seeded" by adding chocolate shavings from a block of solid, tempered chocolate. Enough tempered shavings must be added so that they are just melted and will cool the liquid chocolate to the proper temperature.

Procedures for Tempering Chocolate

Method 1

1. In all stages of this procedure, do not let even a trace of moisture come in contact with the chocolate.

2. With a heavy knife, chop the chocolate into small pieces. Place the pieces in a *dry* saucepan or stainless steel bowl.

3. Set the pan or bowl in another pan of warm water. Stir the chocolate constantly so that it melts uniformly.

4. Continue stirring the chocolate until it is completely melted and reaches a temperature of 115 to 118° F (46 to 48° C).

5. Remove the bowl from the water bath. Set it in a cool place and stir the chocolate slowly but constantly (do not whip or beat air into it) until it is cool (78 to 79° F/26° C). It should be thick and pasty in texture.

6. Set the chocolate over the warm water again and stir it until it is warmed to 86 to 88° F (30 to 31° C). Be very careful, because this may happen very quickly. Do not let the chocolate get too warm.

7. The chocolate is now ready to use.

Method 2

1. Chop the chocolate to be melted into small pieces as in Method 1.

2. Cut fine shreds or shavings from a block of tempered chocolate and set them aside.

3. Melt the chopped chocolate as in Method 1.

4. Remove the melted chocolate from the water bath. Stir in some of the shaved chocolate.

5. When these shavings are nearly all melted, add a little more shavings. Continue adding chocolate

and stirring until the melted chocolate is cooled down to at least 86 to 88° F (30 to 31° C) and all the shavings are melted. Do not add the shavings too fast or they may not all melt.

6. If the temperature of the chocolate goes below 86 to 88° F (30 to 31° C), rewarm it carefully as in Method 1, but do not let it go over this temperature.

Dipping and Coating

The most important use of tempered chocolate for candy makers is, of course, for dipping candies. Bakers also use chocolate for dipping and coating various pastries, meringues, cookies, and even cakes. Also, hand-dipped nuts, marzipan, and other items make very elegant decorations for cakes and pastries, and they are always welcome on trays of petits fours.

The working area should be cool, preferably about 65 to 68° F (18 to 20° C). For best results, chocolate should not be force-cooled in the refrigerator. If the room is cool and the chocolate is tempered, setting will occur quickly without force-cooling.

To dip small items such as candies and nuts, place them one at a time on the surface of the tempered chocolate. With a fork, turn them over to cover them completely, then lift them out. Wipe off excess chocolate on the edge of the pan, then set the item on a sheet of parchment.

To half-dip items such as cookies, simply hold one end of the item and dip it in the chocolate part way. Set it on parchment to harden.

Tempered chocolate may also be applied with a palette knife, as when making sandwich cookies or coating the bottoms of Florentine cookies.

To coat large items, such as cakes, set them on an icing screen over a tray. Pour the chocolate over them like fondant.

Molding

Molding is made possible by the fact that chocolate contracts when it sets. Thus, it pulls away from the mold and can be easily removed. Molds are made of metal or plastic. They must be kept clean and dry, and the insides must be kept shiny and free from scratches. If they are scratched, chocolate will stick to them.

Small single-section molds are used to make solid or filled chocolates. To make solid chocolates, simply fill the molds with tempered chocolate and tap them with a wooden stick to release air bubbles. When the chocolate is completely set, tap the molds lightly to release the chocolates, then remove them.

To make filled chocolates, fill the molds as above. After a few moments, invert the molds to dump out the liquid chocolate, leaving a layer coating the inside of the mold. After the chocolate has set, fill three-fourths full with desired filling. Be careful not to get any filling on the top rim of chocolate. Pour tempered chocolate on top to completely enclose the filling, and let it set.

Two-part molds are used to make hollow chocolate items. There are two kinds: completely enclosed molds, and molds with open bottoms. To use the type with open bottoms, first clip the two parts together. Pour tempered chocolate into the opening until the mold is nearly full. Tap the mold with a wooden stick to release air bubbles. After a few moments, invert the mold over the chocolate pot and pour out the chocolate, leaving a layer of chocolate coating the mold. Set the mold, open-end down, on a sheet of parchment. Additional melted chocolate will run down the inside and seal the open end. Leave the filled mold in a cool place until set, then open it and remove the chocolate.

If you are using plastic molds, you can easily see when the chocolate has set and pulled away from the mold. With metal molds, however, you just have to let the molds stand long enough until you are certain the chocolate is set.

To use enclosed molds, pour enough tempered chocolate into one half of the mold to completely coat the inside of both halves. Place the second half of the mold on top and clip it in place. Turn the mold over and over so that the inside is completely coated with chocolate. Tap the mold several times while rotating it, in order to release air bubbles. Let the chocolate stand until set, then unmold.

Chocolate Decorations

Tempered chocolate can be used to make a variety of decorations for cakes, pastries, and other items. The most popular of these are described here briefly.

Chocolate Cutouts

Pour tempered chocolate onto a sheet of parchment and spread it to a thin, even layer with a spatula. When it is set but not yet hard and brittle, cut out desired shapes with cutters or a knife.

Chocolate Curls and Shavings

Spread tempered chocolate on a marble slab in a thin layer. Work the spatual back and forth until the choco-

late is nearly set. Holding the knife at a sharp angle, draw the knife across the chocolate as though you are shaving a layer off the surface. The chocolate should curl up into rolls.

This technique takes a fair amount of practice. Also, the chocolate should be in just the right condition. If it is too soft, it will just smear, rather than curl. If it is too hard, it will flake off without curling. Chocolate that has set too hard can often be softened slightly by rubbing the hand over it to warm it a little.

Smaller shavings for sprinkling on cakes can be made the same way, but let the chocolate set a little harder before drawing the knife across it. Alternatively, you can shave chocolate directly from the block with a knife or vegetable peeler.

Piping Chocolate

With the use of a paper cone as described in Chapter 11, melted chocolate can be used to make decorations for cakes, pastries, and other desserts. It can be piped directly onto the dessert, or piped onto parchment paper in small designs and left to harden. After they are set, the decorations can be removed from the paper and placed on the desserts. In this way, decorations can be made during slack hours and stored until needed.

Ordinary tempered chocolate is adequate for small, fine decorations, such as those for petits fours (see p. 228). But it is too thin for most other piped decorations. To make piping chocolate, add a very little warm simple syrup to the tempered chocolate. This will thicken the chocolate immediately. Stirring constantly, add more syrup very slowly until the chocolate is thinned out to piping consistency.

Modeling Chocolate

Modeling chocolate is a thick paste that can be molded by hand to make a variety of shapes, just as you might use marzipan. Simply combine melted chocolate with half its weight of glucose (corn syrup) that has been warmed to the temperature of the chocolate. Mix them together well. Place them in an airtight container and let stand for an hour or more. Knead the mixture until it forms a workable paste. Figure 11.27 shows a cake decorated with a flower made of modeling chocolate.

MARZIPAN

Marzipan is a paste made of almonds and sugar that is worked to a plastic consistency. Its texture allows it to be rolled out with a rolling pin like dough or to be modeled into the shapes of fruits, animals, flowers, and so forth.

Pastry chefs and confectioners once had to grind almonds in order to make marzipan, but today the ready availability of almond paste makes the job much easier. As you can see in the accompanying recipe, making marzipan involves moistening the almond paste and blending it with 10X sugar. Recipes may vary slightly, but the principle behind them is the same. Some recipes may call for more or less sugar or use different moistening agents, such as fondant or egg whites.

In order to preserve the color of the marzipan, be sure that all equipment, including bowls, mixer attachments, and work surfaces, is very clean. Use stainless steel rather than aluminum mixing bowls, since aluminum will discolor the marzipan.

Marzipan dries quickly when exposed to air and forms a crust on the surface. To avoid this when you are working with the product, keep unused portions in a bowl covered with a damp cloth. To store marzipan, keep it wrapped or covered in an airtight container. It will keep indefinitely if protected from air. If left uncovered, it will eventually become hard as a rock.

When marzipan is kneaded and worked, the oil content (from the almonds) comes to the surface and makes the marzipan sticky. To avoid this, dust the work surface lightly with confectioners' sugar. Keep a pan of confectioners' sugar handy for dusting as needed.

Marzipan Sheets and Cutouts

Marzipan can be rolled out into sheets with a rolling pin in the same way that you roll out short dough. Confectioners' sugar is used for dusting the workbench and rolling pin. Make sure that the bench and the pin are completely clean.

Marzipan sheets are useful for covering cakes and petits fours, as explained in Chapter 11. They may be left smooth or textured with a ribbed roller (see p. 236).

Colored patterns, such as stripes or polka dots, can be made on marzipan sheets as follows. Roll out a sheet of marzipan part way, so that it is about twice as thick as desired. Roll out another small piece of marzipan in a contrasting color until it is ⅛ in (3 mm) thick. Cut out small circles or strips and arrange them carefully on top of the thick sheet. Now continue to roll out this sheet to the desired thickness. Be very careful to roll it evenly in all directions in order to keep the design uniform.

Using round or fancy cutters, cut out small shapes from the marzipan sheets and use them to decorate cakes and desserts. For additional effect, spread the sheet of marzipan with tempered chocolate and texture it with an icing comb. Make cutouts before the chocolate hardens completely. Another variation is made by texturing the marzipan with ribbed rollers and then spinning fine lines of chocolate over the sheet, using a paper cone with a very small opening.

Marzipan petits fours can be made to look like fancy

Marzipan

Ingredients	U.S.	Metric
Almond paste	1 lb	500 g
Glucose (corn syrup)	3 oz	90 g
10X sugar, sifted	1 lb	500 g
Yield:	2 lb 3 oz	1090 g

Procedure:

1. In a clean stainless-steel bowl, blend the almond paste and glucose, using the paddle attachment, until smooth.

2. Add the sifted sugar, a little at a time, just as fast as it is absorbed. Stop adding sugar when the desired consistency is reached. It should be stiff but workable and not too dry.

3. If colored marzipan is desired, add a small amount of color and work it in.

icebox cookies. Using two colors of marzipan instead of icebox cookie dough, make checkerboard or pinwheel slices using the procedures for the icebox cookies (p. 255). (Do not bake the slices.)

Modeling with Marzipan

Small fruits, vegetables, animals, flowers, and many other shapes can be molded out of marzipan. Small marzipan fruits, served as petits fours or candies, are perhaps the most popular items.

Fruits

To make small fruits, first divide the paste into equal portions. For example, to make ¾-ounce (15 g) pieces, flatten 1½ lb (750 g) of marzipan into a fairly thick rectangle of uniform thickness. With a knife, carefully cut the rectangle into 4 rows of 8 to make 32 equal pieces.

Begin by rolling each piece between the palms of the hands into a round ball that is perfectly smooth and free of seams and cracks (bananas are an exception— begin by rolling the pieces into smooth sausage shapes.) Then start modeling the balls with the fingers into the shapes of pears, apples, and other fruits. The best way to make realistic looking fruits is to use real fruits as models. Imitate the shapes of the real fruits as closely as possible.

Special effects can be made with ordinary tools or with special modeling tools. For example, make the crease on the sides of peaches, apricots, plums, or cherries with the back of a knife. Texture the surfaces of strawberries by poking them lightly with a toothpick. Imitate the rough surface of lemons and oranges by rolling them lightly on a cheese grater.

Let the fruits dry overnight before coloring. Coloring can be done in two ways:

1. Start with tinted marzipan—green for apples and pears, yellow for bananas, peaches, and lemons, and so on. Apply food color with a brush to color in highlights and markings, such as the brown streaks and dots on bananas, the red blush on apples and peaches, and so on.

2. Or start with untinted marzipan. Color the finished fruits with background colors, using either a brush or a sprayer. Let the color dry, then color in the highlights.

Other Items

The variety of objects that can be modeled from marzipan is limited only by the imagination and talent of the pastry cook. Vegetables such as carrots, asparagus, potatoes, and peas in the pod can be made in the same way as fruits. Marzipan snowmen and holly leaves are often used to decorate the bûche de Noël (p. 241). Animals such as dogs, pigs, and frogs are popular subjects. Features such as eyes, nose, and tongue can be applied with royal icing, chocolate, or fondant.

Frames for chocolate paintings on pastillage (p. 318) are generally made of marzipan. Roll marzipan into long, round strips of perfectly uniform thickness and fasten them around the pastillage plaque. With assorted marzipan nippers and modeling tools, texture the marzipan to look like carved frames. The raised details can then be highlighted by very carefully browning them with a blowtorch.

Roses (Figure 14.1) are useful items to make because they can be used to decorate cakes as well as display pieces. Start by forming a cone-shaped piece for the center of the rose. Leave a large enough base on the cone so that it will stand up by itself; this base will be cut off when the rose is finished.

For each petal, shape a piece of marzipan into a flat disk. The edges of the disk must be tapered until they are almost paper-thin, while the center must be left thicker. This can be done by tapping the edges with a fingertip, or by running a smooth, round object, such as the top of a light bulb, around the edge. Dampen the center of the inside of the petal (so that it will stick) and wrap it around the cone-shaped center. Curl the top edge of the petal back slightly. Continue making and attaching petals in the same way. Petals should increase in size toward the outside of the rose, and their edges should be curled back more. Six to twelve petals are sufficient, depending on the size of the rose.

FIGURE 14.1 Making a marzipan rose.

PASTILLAGE

Pastillage (pronounced "pahss-tee-yahzh") is a paste made of sugar, which is used for modeling decorative items. Unlike marzipan and other modeling pastes, it is rarely if ever intended to be eaten. Although it is made entirely of edible items, pastillage is as hard and brittle as plaster of Paris when it dries, and nearly as tasteless. It is used primarily for making display pieces, such as centerpieces for dessert buffet tables, or small baskets or boxes to hold petits fours and candies. Pastillage is normally left pure white, although it may be colored various pastel shades.

The formula given here is a simple and popular one using readily available ingredients: confectioners' sugar, cornstarch (as a drying agent), water, cream of tartar (to help preserve whiteness), and gelatin (as a stiffening and stabilizing agent). Pastillage is sometimes called "gum paste," although that term is more correctly used when a vegetable gum (usually gum tragacanth) is used instead of gelatin.

Making and Handling Pastillage

Many of the same precautions must be taken in the production of pastillage as in the production of marzipan. Great care is essential to preserve the pure white color. Make sure all equipment is scrupulously clean, and use a stainless-steel bowl, not aluminum, for mixing (aluminum will impart a grayish color to the paste). Likewise, the work surface, rolling pin, and molds must be clean and dry.

Pastillage dries and crusts over even faster than marzipan, so it must be kept covered at all times. While working with pastillage, keep unused portions in a bowl covered with a damp cloth. Work quickly and without pause until your products are formed and ready for drying.

Most pastillage pieces are made of thin sheets of the paste that are cut to shape with the aid of paper patterns. The pieces are left flat or curved around molds and allowed to dry, then assembled by being glued together with royal icing. A marble slab is ideal for rolling out pastillage, because it gives the paste a very smooth surface. Use cornstarch to dust the work surface. Be careful not to use more starch than is necessary to keep the paste from sticking. Excessive starch will dry the surface of the paste very quickly and cause it to crust over and crack.

For the most attractive, delicate pieces, the pastillage sheets should be rolled thin (about ⅛ in/3 mm thick). Thick sheets make heavy, more clumsy-looking pieces. Have paper patterns ready, and as soon as the pastillage is rolled out, place the patterns on it and cut cleanly and accurately with a sharp knife or cutter.

For pieces to be molded, have the molds clean, dry, and dusted with cornstarch. For example, to make a pastillage bowl, you can use the outside of another bowl, placed upside-down on the workbench, as your

Pastillage

Ingredients	U.S.		Metric	Sugar at 100% %
Gelatin	1	oz	25 g	1.25
Cold water	11	oz	280 g	14
Confectioners' sugar (10X)	5 lb		2000 g	100
Cornstarch	10	oz	250 g	12.5
Cream of tartar	0.08 oz (1 tsp)		2 g	0.1
Yield:	6 lb 6	oz	2557 g	127

Procedure:

1. Stir the gelatin into the water. Let stand 5 minutes, then heat until the gelatin is dissolved.

2. Sift together the sugar, starch, and cream of tartar.

3. Place the gelatin and water mixture in a stainless-steel mixer bowl. Fit the mixing machine with the dough hook.

4. With the machine running at low speed, add the sugar mixture just as fast as it is absorbed. Mix to a smooth, pliable paste.

5. Keep the paste covered at all times.

FIGURE 14.2 A simple chocolate painting on pastillage, prepared by a student. The frame is made of marzipan.

mold. Carefully fit the sheet of paste outside or inside the mold, gently fitting it to the shape of the mold with your hands.

When the pastillage is partially dry and firm, turn it over to allow the bottom to dry. Continue turning it over from time to time so that it dries evenly. Pastillage that does not dry evenly has a tendency to curl or distort out of shape.

Dried pastillage may be lightly sanded with extra fine sandpaper until it is very smooth. This also helps to smooth down the cut edges, which may be rough or sharp. Finally, assemble the pieces using royal icing as cement. Use very little icing; any excess is likely to be squeezed out at the seams, which will spoil the appearance of the piece.

Because of its pure white, smooth surface, pastillage makes an ideal "canvas" for chocolate painting (Figure 14.2). Make a round, oval, or rectangular plaque of pastillage, let it dry, and sand it smooth. Using an artist's brush, draw a picture using melted, unsweetened chocolate as "paint." Create light and dark shades by diluting the chocolate with varying proportions of melted cocoa butter. For fine detail, etch lines in the chocolate with a sharp wooden pick. After the chocolate has set, the painting can be finished off with a marzipan frame (p. 316).

NOUGAT

Nougat is a candy made of caramelized sugar and almonds. It looks somewhat like peanut brittle but is more attractive because of the sliced almonds. Also, the caramelized sugar should be a clear amber, not cloudy.

Because the sugar is soft and pliable when it is hot, it can be cut and molded into various shapes to make decorative pieces.

Production and Shaping

As can be seen in the following recipe, the cooking of nougat involves two fairly simple steps: caramelizing the sugar, and adding the almonds. The lemon juice serves to invert some of the sugar (see p. 15), thus preventing unwanted crystallization. Cream of tartar or glucose is sometimes used in place of lemon juice.

When the nougat is ready, pour it out onto an oiled marble slab. It will cool quickly, so you have to work fast. When the sheet has begun to set, flip it over with a spatula so that it cools evenly. Have your paper pattern ready. Flatten the sheet with an oiled rolling pin to even out the thickness. Place the patterns on the sheet and quickly cut out shapes with a heavy, oiled knife. Because of the oiled surface, the patterns shouldn't stick, but don't press them down or leave them on the nougat too long.

Molds should be prepared ahead of time by oiling them lightly. For example, to make a nougat bowl, you can use the bottom of a stainless-steel bowl, placed upside-down on the bench and rubbed with oil. Place the soft, cut nougat over the bowl and carefully press it into shape.

If the nougat cools and hardens before you can shape it, place it on an oiled baking sheet and place it in a hot oven for a moment to soften it. You can even stick two sheets together by placing them next to each other and heating them. However, every time you reheat nougat it darkens a little more. Several shades of nougat in a display piece detract from its appearance.

When the molded nougat pieces have cooled and hardened, cement them together as necessary, using either royal icing or a hot sugar syrup boiled to 310° F (190° C). Nougat pieces can also be decorated with royal icing.

Other Uses of Nougat

Unlike some decorative materials, such as pastillage, nougat is a tasty confection. Thin nougat sheets can be cut into fancy shapes and used to decorate cakes and other desserts.

Hard nougat can be crushed and used like chopped nuts for masking the sides of cakes. Finely ground and sifted, or ground to a paste, it makes an excellent flavoring for creams and icings. This product is very similar to praline paste, except that praline paste generally contains hazelnuts.

Nougat

Ingredients	U.S.	Metric	Sugar at 100% %
Sugar	3 lb	1500 g	100
Lemon juice	2 oz	60 g	4
Sliced almonds	2 lb 4 oz	1125 g	75
Yield:	5 lb 6 oz	2685 g	179

Procedure:

1. Clean a marble slab and dry it well. Rub it lightly with oil.

2. Rub the sugar and lemon juice together in a heavy saucepan.

3. Set the pan over low heat. Stir until the sugar has completely melted and turned a light amber color.

4. While the sugar is melting, have the almonds ready in a warm place. They should be warmed so that they do not cool the sugar too much when they are added.

5. Stir the almonds into the melted sugar. When the mixture is golden, quickly pour it out onto the marble slab.

6. Let the mixture cool for a moment or two. When it has begun to set but is still hot, soft, and pliable, flip it over with a spatula so that it will cool evenly. Roll it out to an even thickness with a heavy, oiled rolling pin. Quickly, while the nougat is still soft, cut out desired shapes with a heavy, oiled knife, and mold them as desired.

BOILED SUGAR WORK

In Chapter 7 we discussed the boiling of sugar syrups for use in various desserts. If syrups are boiled until nearly all the water is evaporated, the sugar will become solid when it cools. This process enables us to make decorative pieces out of sugar that is boiled to 300° F (149° C) or more and shaped while still hot.

As you learned in Chapter 2 (p. 15), sugar that is boiled in a syrup undergoes a chemical change called *inversion,* in which a molecule of double sugar (sucrose) combines with a molecule of water and changes into two molecules of simple sugar (dextrose and levulose). Invert sugar, you remember, resists crystallization, while plain sucrose (granulated sugar) crystallizes easily. The amount of sugar that is inverted depends on the amount of acid that is present. This principle is used in the production of fondant icing (see p. 123): Just enough cream of tartar or glucose is added to the syrup to create a mass of extremely fine sugar crystals that gives fondant its pure white color.

This technique is also used for the sugar work discussed in this section, especially in pulled sugar. If too much cream of tartar or glucose is used, too much sugar is inverted, so that the sugar is too soft and sticky to work and doesn't harden enough when cool. If not enough cream of tartar or glucose is used, too little sugar is inverted, and the sugar is very hard, so that it is difficult to work and easily broken.

As long as it is kept within limits, the exact amount of tartar or glucose to be used depends largely on the preferences of the pastry chef or confectioner. Some artists prefer to work with a harder sugar, while some prefer a softer one. Consequently, you will see many different recipes. Your instructor may have his or her own favorite to substitute for those in this book.

Similarly, the temperature to which the syrup is boiled is important. The higher the temperature, the harder the sugar. The temperature used in this book for pulled sugar is 315° F (159° C), just a little below the upper limit. Above 320° F (160° C) the sugar begins to caramelize. Cooking to a lower temperature will make a softer sugar that is easier to work, but below 290° F (143° C) it is too soft and will not hold its shape or keep well.

Two more precautions are necessary, regarding temperature and the addition of cream of tartar or glucose. First, boiled invert sugar discolors more rapidly than pure sucrose. Therefore, cream of tartar or glucose should not be added to the syrup until it reaches a temperature of 220 to 230° F (104 to 110° C). Second, the syrup should be boiled rapidly over moderately high heat. Boiling slowly will give the syrup more time to discolor and it will not be clear white.

Procedure for Boiling Sugar

The following is a general procedure, applicable to spun sugar, pulled sugar, and so on. As soon as the syrup reaches the required temperature, follow the procedures for the specific product you are making.

1. Place the sugar and water in a clean, heavy pan. Place the mixture over low heat and stir it gently until the sugar is dissolved.

2. When the sugar is dissolved, raise the heat to moderately high, and *do not stir* any more. Place a sugar thermometer in the pan.

3. While boiling, keep the sides free of sugar crystals by washing them down with a brush dipped in water.

4. When the temperature reaches 220° to 230° F (104° to 110° C), add the cream of tartar, dissolved in a little water, or the glucose.

5. Boil rapidly until the desired temperature is reached.

Spun Sugar

Spun sugar is a mass of thin, threadlike or hairlike strands of sugar, used to decorate cakes and show pieces. Gateau St. Honoré (p. 158) is often decorated with spun sugar.

Spun sugar should be made just before it is needed, because it does not keep well. It gradually absorbs moisture from the atmosphere and becomes sticky. Eventually, this absorbed moisture causes the sugar to dissolve.

Prepare a work station by setting two long, lightly oiled wooden rods on the edge of a table so that they project horizontally beyond the edge of the table by 1 to 2 feet (30 to 60 cm). They should be parallel and be placed about a foot (30 cm) apart. Place plenty of paper on the floor under the rods to catch drippings. To spin the sugar, you will need a wire whip with the ends cut off. A fork can also be used, but it is not as efficient.

Using the basic sugar-boiling procedure described above, make a syrup with the following ingredients:

Sugar	2 lb	1 kg
Water	12 oz	375 ml
Cream of tartar	½ tsp	1 g

Boil the syrup to 300° F (149° C). As soon as this temperature is reached, remove the pan from the heat and plunge the bottom of the pan into cold water for a second to stop the cooking and cool the pan slightly.

Dip the end of the whip in the hot sugar and wave it rapidly over the wooden rods so that the sugar is thrown off in fine, long threads. Repeat until the desired amount of spun sugar is hanging from the rods. Carefully lift the sugar from the rods and shape it as needed.

If the sugar syrup cools too much to spin, simply rewarm it over low heat.

Sugar Cages

Sugar cages are delicate, lacework sugar domes made of caramelized sugar. Their decorative effect can be impressive and elegant. Sugar cages can be made large enough to cover whole cakes, bombes, bavarian creams, or other desserts, or small enough to cover individual portions.

Bowls of the desired size can be used as molds. Place the bowls upside down on the workbench and oil them lightly.

Prepare a sugar syrup as described above for spun sugar, but cook the syrup until it begins to caramelize. It should be a light golden brown.

Holding a mold in one hand, dip a spoon in the caramelized sugar and drizzle the sugar over the outside of the bowl in a random, lacy pattern. Turn the bowl so that the sides and bottom are drizzled evenly with the syrup. Let the sugar cool until it is hard, then carefully lift it off the bowl.

Cast Sugar

Cast sugar is clear, boiled sugar that is allowed to harden in various shapes. Usually, it is cast in flat sheets like glass, although it can, like nougat, also be shaped into bowls or other shapes. The syrup can also be colored before it is poured out.

To prepare a mold for cast sugar, bend a strip of metal into the desired shape (like a giant cookie cutter) and place it on a marble slab. For round shapes, simply use a flan ring. For small circles or other shapes, cookie cutters can be used. To keep the hot syrup from running out under the strip, fasten the strip down on the marble by sticking plasticene or another puttylike material (marzipan could be used, but it is costly) all around the outside of the metal strip. With a brush, lightly oil the inside of the strip and the marble slab.

Prepare a syrup exactly as you would for pulled sugar (see the next section, below). Pour it into the mold to the desired thickness. Let it cool for 5 minutes, then slide a palette knife under it to detach it from the marble. Let it cool completely, until it is hard and brittle.

To bend cast sugar around a mold, remove it from the marble while it is still soft enough to be pliable. If it gets too hard, simply place it on an oiled baking sheet and heat in an oven just until it is pliable. Then mold it exactly as you would mold nougat (p. 318).

Pulled Sugar and Blown Sugar

Pulled sugar and blown sugar are perhaps the most difficult of the pastry chef's decorative art forms. To be successful at making fine decorative pieces requires careful attention to demonstrations and a great deal of practice, with the guidance of an instructor. This section can not, of course, substitute for those demonstrations and guidance, but it can serve as an introduction and, later, as a reference to refresh your memory.

To work with pulled sugar, you will need the following tools:

A heat lamp or other warmer to keep the stock of sugar warm and soft.

A sieve or screen to hold the stock of pulled sugar while you are working with small pieces. An oiled pan can also be used, but the screen helps the sugar maintain a more uniform temperature.

A small fan to cool the shapes as they are made.

A base board and pegs for making baskets (described later).

Scissors and a knife for cutting pieces of sugar.

A bench scraper or spatula for turning the sugar before it is cool enough to pull.

A Bunsen burner, alcohol lamp, or another source of flame for melting the edges of shaped pieces so that they can be stuck together.

A metal tube for blowing sugar.

Procedure for Making Pulled Sugar

1. Following the basic procedure for boiling sugar (p. 320), make a syrup of the following ingredients:

Sugar	4 lb	2 kg
Water	1 lb	500 g
Cream of tartar	1 tsp	2 g

2. Boil the syrup to 315° F (157° C).

3. Immediately pour it out onto an oiled marble slab.

4. After it has cooled for a moment, fold the outside edges toward the inside with a spatula. It is necessary to continue to do this so that the sugar cools evenly. Otherwise the outside edges would cool faster and harden.

5. If different colors of sugar are required, divide the mass of sugar into portions. Rub each portion with a little paste color and fold it in well. It will get distributed more evenly during pulling.

6. When the sugar is cool enough to handle but still quite warm, start pulling the sugar by holding it on the marble with one hand and stretching it out with the other. Fold it over on itself. Continue to pull and fold the sugar until it begins to take on a glossy, silky appearance. (Note: The sugar is still quite hot, so handle it as lightly as possible. As a beginner, you will probably get some blisters.)

7. To get the proper silky appearance, you will need to pull and fold the sugar a total of 12 to 20 times. This silky effect is caused by the crystallization of the sugar. Do not pull the sugar more than necessary, or it will crystallize too much and lose its shine.

8. When the sugar is pulled and shiny, place the pieces on a sieve under a heat lamp or in front of a warmer to hold it while you are working on individual pieces. Turn the pieces over from time to time so they stay evenly heated.

Flowers and Leaves

To make petals for roses and other flowers, hold a piece of sugar between the thumb and forefinger of both hands. Pull apart with a twisting motion to stretch the sugar out into a thin fan-shaped petal. Pinch or snap the petal off the rest of the sugar. Roll it into a cone shape to form the center of the rose.

Make additional petals and curl them around the center cone, just as you would for a marzipan rose (p. 316). Make the outer petals a little larger, and curl back the edges to resemble the petals of a real rose.

An alternative method is to make all the petals first, without assembling them. Heat the bottom edges of the petals one at a time over a gas flame so that they will stick together, and assemble them to make the flower.

To make leaves, pull out a thin piece of sugar into a leaf shape and mark the veins with the back of a knife.

To make a stem that will support the weight of a flower, pull a strong piece of wire through warm pulled sugar so that it is completely coated. While the sugar is still soft, bend the covered wire to the desired shape.

Ribbons

A ribbon of a single color is made by simply pulling a piece of sugar out into a thin ribbon shape. This sounds easy, but making a thin, delicate ribbon of perfectly even thickness and width takes a great deal of practice and skill. Be sure that the piece of sugar is uniformly warm and that all parts of the strip stretch the same amount.

To make a two-colored ribbon, start with two pieces of sugar in contrasting colors. Shape them into strips of the same size and shape. Press them together side by side, then stretch them into a ribbon. For multiple stripes, cut the two-colored strip in half when it is partly stretched. Place the two pieces together side by side so that you have four alternating stripes. Finish stretching them out into a ribbon shape.

A ribbon of three or more colors can be made with the same technique.

To make a bow, cut off a length of ribbon with scissors and bend it into a loop. Cool the loop in front of a fan so that it holds its shape. Make as many loops as desired. Fasten them together into a bow by heating one end of each loop over a gas flame to soften the sugar and then pressing the heated ends together.

Simple Baskets

Roll out a piece of pulled sugar with a rolling pin into a thin sheet. Mold it over an oiled bowl or large tin can, just as you would mold nougat. A handle can also be attached.

Woven Baskets

A woven pulled-sugar basket filled with pulled-sugar flowers or fruit is one of the most impressive of all display pieces. To make the basket, you need a base board into which an uneven number of holes has been drilled. The holes should be evenly spaced and should form a circle, oval, or square. In addition, you need wooden pegs that fit loosely into these holes. The holes should be drilled at an angle so that the pegs tilt outward. This makes the basket wider at the top than at the bottom. Oil the pegs and board lightly before weaving the basket.

Take a ball of soft pulled sugar and start to pull a rope or cord of sugar from the ball. Starting at the inside edge of one of the pegs, weave the sugar cord in and out around the pegs, pulling out more of the sugar as you go. Be careful to keep the thickness of the cord uniform. Continue weaving the sugar around the pegs until the basket is as high as desired.

Make pulled sugar rods the same size and number as the wooden pegs. One by one, pull out the pegs and replace them with the pulled sugar rods. If necessary, trim the tops of the rods with a hot knife or scissors.

Make a base for the basket with cast sugar (p. 320) or with pulled sugar rolled out with a rolling pin. Attach it to the basket with hot boiled syrup.

To finish off the top and bottom edges, twist two cords of pulled sugar together to make a rope. Coil the rope around the top and bottom edges of the basket and seal the ends together. A handle for the basket can be made by shaping heavy wire and then weaving a rope of sugar around it.

Blown Sugar

Hollow sugar fruits and other items are blown from pulled sugar the same way glass is blown. Because sugar can be difficult to blow, many pastry chefs prefer to boil the syrup to a lower temperature, 290° to 300° F (143° to 149° C), so that the sugar will be a little softer. However, regular pulled sugar, which has been boiled to 318° F (159° C) makes harder finished pieces that keep a little better.

Form a piece of pulled sugar of appropriate size into a ball. Then make a deep impression in it with the end of an oiled wooden rod. Replace the rod with the end of a blow pipe, and press the sugar around it firmly. Begin to blow through the tube to expand and stretch the sugar. You will need to use short, strong puffs of air at first. As the sugar stretches and becomes thinner, blow more gently.

The shape of the sugar piece depends on how it is manipulated and supported with the hands and on how it is cooled or warmed. To make round objects, such as apples, hold the blow pipe and sugar upward at an angle, so that the weight of the sugar does not cause it to elongate. For long, thin objects such as bananas, stretch the sugar gently as you blow.

If the sugar on one side becomes too thin, cool that side slightly with a fan so that it hardens. By watching demonstrations and practicing, you can learn to control the temperature of the piece on all sides in order to shape it as you want. The best sugar pieces have a thin, delicate wall of sugar that is of even thickness all around.

When the sugar has hardened, paint the pieces with an artist's brush to add realistic color highlights and markings.

More complex pieces, such as animals, birds, and fish, can be made with practice. For example, make a long-necked bird by blowing the sugar into the shape of a vase and stretching out the neck to form the long neck of the bird. An animal's head and body may be blown separately and attached. Parts such as wings and fins are made separately from pulled sugar.

TERMS FOR REVIEW

tempering
couverture
bloom
modeling chocolate
marzipan
pastillage
gum paste
nougat
inversion
spun sugar
cast sugar
pulled sugar
blown sugar

QUESTIONS FOR DISCUSSION

1. Briefly explain how to temper chocolate and why tempering is important.

2. If tempered chocolate is too thick for dipping, how should you thin it out?

3. What precaution must you take when mixing marzipan in order to preserve its color?

4. Suppose you wanted to cover a strawberry-filled Swiss roll with white marzipan decorated with pink polka dots. How would you make the marzipan sheet?

5. What procedure is used to make sure that pastillage dries properly?

6. Describe briefly the procedure for making, cutting, and molding nougat.

7. What are some uses for leftover nougat trimmings?

8. When boiling sugar for pulled sugar, why is it important to boil it rapidly?

9. Starting with the boiling syrup, briefly describe the steps in making a clear white pulled-sugar ribbon.

APPENDIX 1
METRIC CONVERSION FACTORS

Weight

1 ounce equals 28.35 grams

1 gram equals 0.035 ounce

1 pound equals 454 grams

1 kilogram equals 2.2 pounds

Volume

1 fluid ounce equals 29.57 milliliters

1 milliliter equals 0.034 fluid ounce

1 cup equals 237 milliliters

1 quart equals 946 milliliters

1 liter equals 33.8 fluid ounces

Length

1 inch equals 25.4 millimeters

1 centimeter equals 0.39 inch

1 meter equals 39.4 inches

Temperature

To convert Fahrenheit to Celsius: Subtract 32, then multiply by $\frac{5}{9}$.

Example: Convert 140° F to Celsius.

$$140 - 32 = 108$$
$$108 \times \tfrac{5}{9} = 60° \text{ C}$$

To convert Celsius to Fahrenheit: Multiply by $\frac{9}{5}$, then add 32.

Example: Convert 150° C to Fahrenheit.

$$150 \times \tfrac{9}{5} = 270$$
$$270 + 32 = 302° \text{ F}$$

Note: The metric measurements in the recipes in this book are not equivalent to the corresponding U.S. measurements. See page 4 for a complete explanation.

APPENDIX 2

DECIMAL EQUIVALENTS OF COMMON FRACTIONS

Fraction	Rounded to 3 places	Rounded to 2 places
7/8	0.875	0.88
5/6	0.833	0.83
4/5	0.8	0.8
3/4	**0.75**	**0.75**
2/3	**0.667**	**0.67**
5/8	0.625	0.63
3/5	0.6	0.6
1/2	**0.5**	**0.5**
1/3	**0.333**	**0.33**
1/4	**0.25**	**0.25**
1/5	0.2	0.2
1/6	0.167	0.17
1/8	0.125	0.13
1/10	0.1	0.1
1/12	0.083	0.08
1/16	0.063	0.06
1/25	0.04	0.04

APPENDIX 3

APPROXIMATE VOLUME EQUIVALENTS OF DRY FOODS

The following equivalents are rough averages only. Actual weight will vary considerably. For accurate measurement, all ingredients should be weighed.

Following common practice, volume measures in this chart are represented as common fractions rather than as decimals.

Bread flour, sifted

    1 lb = 4 cups

    1 cup = 4 oz

Bread flour, unsifted

    1 lb = 3⅓ cups

    1 cup = 4.75 oz

Cake flour, sifted

    1 lb = 4¼ cups

    1 cup = 3.75 oz

Cake flour, unsifted

    1 lb = 3½ cups

    1 cup = 4.5 oz

Granulated sugar

    1 lb = 2¼ cups

    1 cup = 7 oz

Confectioners' sugar, sifted

    1 lb = 4 cups

    1 cup = 4 oz

Confectioners' sugar, unsifted

    1 lb = 3½ cups

    1 cup = 4.5 oz

Cornstarch, sifted

    1 lb = 4 cups

    1 cup = 4 oz

    1 oz = 4 tbsp = ¼ cup

    1 tbsp = 0.25 oz

Cornstarch, unsifted

    1 lb = 3½ cups

    1 cup = 4.5 oz

    1 oz = 3½ tbsp

    1 tbsp = 0.29 oz

Cocoa, unsifted

    1 lb = 5 cups

    1 cup = 3.2 oz

    1 oz = 5 tbsp

    1 tbsp = 0.2 oz

Gelatin, unflavored

    1 oz = 3 tbsp

    ¼ oz = 2¼ tsp

    1 tbsp = 0.33 oz

    1 tsp = 0.11 oz

Baking soda
Baking powder (phosphate type and sodium
    aluminum sulphate type)

    1 oz = 2 tbsp

    ¼ oz = 1½ tsp

    1 tbsp = 0.5 oz

    1 tsp = 0.17 oz

Cream of tartar

    1 oz = 4 tbsp

    ¼ oz = 1 tbsp

    1 tsp = 0.08 oz

Salt

    1 oz = 5 tsp

    ¼ oz = 1¼ tsp

    1 tsp = 0.2 oz

Cinnamon

    1 oz = 17 tsp

    ¼ oz = 4¼ tsp

    1 tsp = 0.06 oz

Ground spices (except cinnamon)

    1 oz = 14 tsp

    ¼ oz = 3½ tsp

    1 tsp = 0.07 oz

Grated lemon zest

    1 oz = 4 tbsp

    1 tsp = 0.08 oz

APPENDIX 4

TEMPERATURE CALCULATIONS FOR YEAST DOUGHS

In Chapter 3 (p. 39), a simple formula is presented to enable you to calculate what the water temperature should be in order to get a mixed dough of a specified temperature. This formula is sufficient for most straight doughs made in small batches. However, some other calculations may sometimes be required. These are detailed here.

Machine Friction

Machine friction depends on many factors, including the type of mixer, amount of dough, stiffness of dough, and mixing time. This friction may be determined for each dough prepared, assuming a constant batch size.

Procedure for Determining Machine Friction

1. Prepare a batch of dough, first measuring the room temperature, flour temperature, and water temperature. Add these three figures.
2. Measure the temperature of the dough as it comes from the mixer. Multiply this figure by 3.
3. Subtract the result of step 1 from the result of step 2. This is the machine friction.
4. Use this factor when calculating the water temperature required for subsequent batches of this particular dough, as explained on p. 39.

Example: Room temperature = 72° F
Flour temperature = 65° F
Water temperature = 75° F
Dough temperature = 77° F

1. $72 + 65 + 75 = 212$
2. $77 \times 3 = 231$
3. $231 - 212 = 19$
Machine friction = 19°

Ice Calculation

If your tap water is warmer than the water temperature you need for a batch of dough, you can cool the water with crushed ice. A simple formula can be used to calculate how much crushed ice to use.

This formula is based on the fact that it requires 144 BTUs of heat energy to melt 1 pound of ice. A BTU (British Thermal Unit) is the amount of heat needed to raise the temperature of 1 pound of water 1° F. Therefore it takes 144 BTUs to melt a pound of ice, but only one more BTU to heat that pound of melted ice from 32° F to 33° F.

You can, of course, use the following formula without having to understand how it is derived. However, if you wish to know where the formula comes from, an explanation follows the formula and sample calculation. Please note that this formula is more accurate than many of the formulas you will see elsewhere. Many other formulas allow for the heat energy needed to melt the ice, but they don't allow for the fact that the melted ice is also warmed up to the final water temperature.

Also, please remember that the ice counts as part of the water for the dough.

Procedure for Determining Ice Requirement

1. Measure the temperature of the tap water. Subtract the water temperature needed for your dough from the tap water temperature. This number is the temperature decrease needed.

    Tap water temperature
    − desired water temperature
    = temperature decrease

2. Calculate the weight of ice needed by using the following formula.

    $$\text{Ice weight} = \frac{\text{Total water} \times \text{temperature decrease}}{\text{Tap water temperature} + 112}$$

    "Total water" is the weight of water needed for the dough recipe.

3. Subtract the ice weight from the total water needed to get the weight of the tap water needed.

    Total water − ice = tap water

Example: For a batch of bread, you need 16 lb water at 58° F. Your tap water is 65° F. How much tap water and how much ice should you use?

$$\text{Ice} = \frac{16 \text{ lb} \times (65 - 58)}{65 + 112} = \frac{16 \text{ lb} \times 7}{177}$$

$$= \frac{112 \text{ lb}}{177} = 0.63 \text{ lb} = 10 \text{ oz}$$

Tap water = 16 lb − 10 oz = 15 lb 6 oz

You need 10 oz ice plus 15 lb 6 oz tap water.

The above formula is based on the fact that the number of BTUs needed to bring the ice up to the desired water temperature equals the number of BTUs lost by the tap water when it is cooled to the desired temperature. This can be expressed as follows:

BTUs to melt ice *plus*
BTUs to heat melted ice to desired temperature $\Big\}$ = BTUs lost by tap water

Remember, as explained earlier, that 144 BTUs are needed to melt a pound of ice, and that 1 BTU is needed to heat a pound of water 1° F. Therefore, the three BTU values in the above equation can each be expressed mathematically:

BTUs to melt ice = Ice weight (in pounds) *times* 144
BTUs to heat melted ice to temperature
     = Ice weight *times* degrees of temperature rise
          or
     Ice weight *times* (desired temperature *minus* 32° F)
BTUs lost by tap water = weight of tap water *times* degrees of temperature drop
          or
     (total water *minus* ice) *times* (tap water temperature *minus* desired temperature)

In order to make the calculations easier to read, we adopt the following abbreviations. Then we substitute them in our basic equation and proceed to simplify it mathematically.

I = ice weight
W = tap water weight
W + I = total water required in recipe
T = tap water temperature
D = desired temperature

BTUs to melt ice *plus*
BTUs to heat melted ice to desired temperature $\Big\}$ = BTUs lost by tap water

$$(I \times 144) + (I \times (D - 32)) = ((W + I) - I) \times (T - D)$$

$$I \times (144 + D - 32) = ((W + I) \times (T - D)) - (I \times (T - D))$$

$$(I \times (144 + D - 32)) + (I \times (T - D)) = (W + I) \times (T - D)$$

$$I \times (144 + D - 32 + T - D) = (W + I) \times (T - D)$$

$$I \times (112 + T) = (W + I) \times (T - D)$$

$$I = \frac{(W + I) \times (T - D)}{112 + T}$$

$$\text{Ice} = \frac{\text{Total water} \times \text{temperature decrease}}{\text{Tap water temperature} + 112}$$

APPENDIX 5

EQUIPMENT CHECKLIST

The following is a list of the basic equipment found in a small bakeshop. These items are used in preparing baked goods and desserts of the types discussed in this book. Most large, specialized equipment and automatic machinery used in large bakeries—such as dough molders, overhead proofers, and automatic droppers—are omitted.

STATIONARY EQUIPMENT AND OTHER LARGE EQUIPMENT

Cooking and Baking Equipment

Revolving ovens or reel ovens are large chambers containing many shelves or trays on a ferris-wheel type arrangement. These ovens eliminate the problem of hot spots or uneven baking because the mechanism rotates the foods throughout the oven.

Deck ovens are conventional ovens in which items are placed directly on the oven deck rather than on wire shelves. A supply of steam is important in such ovens for baking crisp-crusted breads and some other products.

Convection ovens contain fans that circulate the air and distribute the heat rapidly throughout the interior. The forced air may deform some soft items: Cake batters, for example, may develop ripples.

Cook stoves or cook tops are needed for cooking such items as syrups, sauces, stirred custards, and poached fruits.

Trunnion kettles are small, tilting, steam-jacketed kettles, which are convenient for cooking larger quantities of such items as pastry cream and pie fillings. These could also be cooked in saucepans on a cook top, but a trunnion kettle is easier to use for larger quantities.

Fryers are needed for doughnuts and other fried items. Small operations often use standard deep-fryers (or even stove-top kettles), but larger doughnut fryers are best if you make doughnuts in quantity. They should be used in conjunction with screens for lowering the doughnuts into the fat and for removing them when fried.

Mixers and Other Dough Equipment

Vertical mixers do most of the mixing work in small bakeshops. *Bench-model mixers* range from 5- to 20-qt capacity. *Floor models* are available as large as 140 qt. Adapter rings enable several sizes of bowls to be used on one machine. Most mixers have three, or sometimes four, operating speeds. (Large commercial bakeries use horizontal mixers for making bread doughs.)

Agitator attachments are of three major types. The *paddle* is a flat blade used for general mixing. The *wire whip* is used for whipping eggs, cream, and similar items. The *dough arm* is used for mixing and kneading yeast doughs. Additional specialized attachments, including wing whips, pastry knives, and sweet-dough arms, are also available.

Dough dividers cut scaled dough presses into small, equal units for rolls. See p. 66 for more information. *Divider-rounders* automatically round the small units after they are divided.

Dough rollers and sheeters are available in many models, each operating somewhat differently. Pairs of adjustable rollers sheet out dough to specifications. Dough is fed to the rollers by gravity from hoppers or by canvas belts. Some types also curl sheeted bread dough into loaves.

Dough fermentation troughs are used to hold mixed yeast doughs during fermentation. Small operations might simply use large *mixing bowls on stands* instead.

Proof boxes are enclosed boxes with controlled temperature and humidity, used to proof trays of made-up yeast goods. They come in all variations and sizes, are operated by steam or electricity, and have manual or automatic controls.

Storage, Holding, and Miscellaneous Large Equipment

Refrigerators, for ingredient storage, etc.

Retarders, for dough storage

Flour and ingredient bins

Tray racks

Work tables

Two- or three-compartment sink

Hand sink

Pan washer, for larger operations

PANS AND CONTAINERS

Sheet pans or baking sheets come in standard full size (18 × 26 inches/46 × 66 cm) and half size (18 × 13 inches/46 × 33 cm). For hearth-type breads and rolls, *perforated pans* allow better circulation of hot air.

Baking pans and molds come in an immense variety of shapes and sizes. Most commonly used are:

Round layer cake pans in various diameters and 1½, 2, and 3 inches deep

Loaf pans, for bread, pound cake, etc.

Center-tube pans, also called simply *tube pans,* for angel food cake and some sweet breads

Pie pans

Tart or quiche pans

Brioche tins

Muffin and cupcake tins

Stainless-steel *hotel pans or bake pans,* 12 × 20 × 2½ inches, sometimes used for such items as rice pudding, especially for counter service

Various other pans and fancy molds are used for specialty items, such as charlottes, Bavarians, gelatin-type desserts, individual baked custards, and soufflés.

Mixing bowls are usually round-bottomed, stainless-steel bowls in various sizes and are used for mixing various ingredients by hand and for holding ingredients, sauces, icings, etc. They are also used for items warmed or stirred over hot water.

Saucepans, double boilers, icing warmers, etc., are used for cooking and heating items on the cook stove.

Volume measures for liquids have lips for easy pouring. Sizes are pints, quarts, half gallons, and gallons. Each size is marked off into fourths by ridges on the sides.

HAND TOOLS AND OTHER SMALL TOOLS

Knives and Cutters

French knife (heavy)

Utility knife

Paring knife

Vienna knife or razor, for cutting tops of proofed breads

Long serrated slicer

Cookie cutters and biscuit cutters

Wheel knife

Roller cutters for biscuits, doughnuts, croissants, etc.

Roller docker, for docking sheets of puff pastry and other doughs

Decorating and Finishing Tools

Note: Many of the following are discussed on pp. 223–224.

Cake turntable

Pastry bag and tubes

Icing screens or grates

Icing comb

Sugar dredger

Jelly pump

Miscellaneous Tools

Rolling pins: *ball-bearing type* for puff pastry, Danish dough, etc.; *broom-handle type* for pie crusts and small items.

Pastry brushes, for glazing and applying washes

Bench brushes, for brushing flour

Bench scrapers, rectangular pieces of steel with a wooden handle on one edge, for scraping the workbench and dividing pieces of dough

Plastic **bowl scraper**

Bowl knife or metal spatula, used mostly for applying and spreading icings

Wire whips, for whipping and mixing by hand

Spoons, metal and wood

Sieves and strainers, for sifting flour and for straining and puréeing foods

Thermometers: dough thermometer, fat thermometer, and candy or sugar thermometer.

Peel, a broad, flat wooden shovel for inserting and removing hearth breads from the oven.

Balance scale, discussed on p. 4.

BIBLIOGRAPHY

Amendola, Joseph. *The Bakers' Manual for Quantity Baking and Pastry Making.* 3rd ed. Rochelle Park, N.J.: Hayden, 1972.

Amendola, Joseph, and Donald E. Lundberg. *Understanding Baking.* Boston: Cahners, 1970.

D'Ermo, Dominique. *The Modern Pastry Chef's Guide to Professional Baking.* New York: Harper & Row, 1962.

Escoffier, A. *The Escoffier Cook Book.* New York: Crown, 1969.

Fance, Wilfred J., ed. *The New International Confectioner.* 5th ed. London: Virtue & Co., 1981.

Hanneman, L. J. *Bakery: Bread and Fermented Goods.* London: Heinemann, 1980.

Hanneman, L. J. *Patisserie.* London: Heinemann, 1977.

Lenôtre, Gaston. *Lenôtre's Desserts and Pastries.* Woodbury, N.Y.: Barron's, 1977.

Lenôtre, Gaston. *Lenôtre's Ice Creams and Candies.* Woodbury, N.Y.: Barron's, 1979.

Matz, S. A. *Bakery Technology and Engineering.* 2nd ed. Westport, Connecticut: Avi, 1972.

Pyler, E. J. *Baking Science and Technology.* 2nd ed. 2 vols. Chicago: Siebel, 1973.

Sultan, William J. *Elementary Baking.* New York: McGraw-Hill, 1969.

Sultan, William J. *Practical Baking.* 3rd ed. Westport, Connecticut: Avi, 1976.

West, Bessie Brooks, Grace Severance Shugart, and Maxine Fay Wilson. *Food for Fifty.* 6th ed. New York: John Wiley, 1979.

GLOSSARY

Note: Many culinary terms in common use are taken from French. Phonetic guides for difficult words are included here, using English sounds. However, exact renderings are impossible in many cases because French has a number of sounds that don't exist in English.

Allumette: Any of various puff pastry items made in thin sticks or strips (French word for "matchstick").

Almond Paste: A mixture of finely ground almonds and sugar.

Angel Food Cake: A type of cake made of meringue (egg whites and sugar) and flour.

Angel Food Method: A cake mixing method involving folding a mixture of flour and sugar into a meringue.

Baba: A type of yeast bread or cake that is soaked in syrup.

Babka: A type of sweet yeast bread or coffee cake.

Baked Alaska: A dessert consisting of ice cream on a sponge-cake base, covered with meringue and browned in the oven.

Baking Ammonia: A leavening ingredient that releases ammonia gas and carbon dioxide.

Baklava: A Greek or Middle Eastern dessert made of nuts and phyllo dough and soaked with syrup.

Batter: A semiliquid mixture containing flour or other starch, used for the production of such products as cakes and breads, and for coating products to be deep-fried.

Bavarian Cream: A light, cold dessert made of gelatin, whipped cream, and custard sauce or fruit.

Beignet Soufflé *(ben yay soo flay):* A type of fritter made with eclair paste, which puffs up greatly when fried.

Black Forest Torte: A chocolate sponge layer cake filled with whipped cream and cherries.

Blanc Mange: (1) An English pudding made of milk, sugar, and cornstarch. (2) A French dessert made of milk, cream, almonds, and gelatin.

Bloom: A whitish coating on chocolate, caused by separated cocoa butter.

Blown Sugar: Pulled sugar that is made into thin-walled, hollow shapes by being blown up like a balloon.

Bombe: A type of frozen dessert made in a dome-shaped mold.

Boston Cream Pie: A sponge cake or other yellow cake filled with pastry cream and topped with chocolate fondant or confectioners' sugar.

Bran: The hard outer covering of kernels of wheat and other grains.

Bran Flour: Flour to which bran flakes have been added.

Bread Flour: Strong flour, such as patent flour, used for breads.

Brioche: Rich yeast dough containing large amounts of eggs and butter; or a product made from this dough.

Brown Sugar: Regular granulated sucrose containing various impurities that give it a distinctive flavor.

Buttercream: An icing made of butter and/or shortening blended with confectioners' sugar or sugar syrup and sometimes other ingredients.

Cabinet Pudding: A baked custard containing sponge cake and fruit.

Cake Flour: A fine, white flour made from soft wheat.

Caramelization: The browning of sugars caused by heat.

Cassata: An Italian-style bombe, usually with three layers of different ice creams, plus a filling of Italian meringue.

Cast Sugar: Sugar that is boiled to the hard crack stage and then poured into molds to harden.

Celsius Scale: The metric system of temperature measurement, with 0° C set at the freezing point of water and 100° C set at the boiling point of water.

Centi-: Prefix in the metric system meaning "one-hundredth."

Challah: A rich egg bread, often made as a braided loaf.

Charlotte: (1) A cold dessert made of Bavarian cream or other cream in a special mold, usually lined with ladyfingers or other sponge product. (2) A hot dessert made of cooked fruit and baked in a special mold lined with strips of bread.

Chemical Leavener: A leavener such as baking soda, baking powder, or baking ammonia, that releases gases produced by chemical reactions.

Chiffon Cake: A light cake made by the chiffon method.

Chiffon Method: A cake mixing method involving the folding of whipped egg whites into a batter made of flour, egg yolks, and oil.

Chiffon Pie: A pie with a light, fluffy filling containing egg whites and, usually, gelatin.

Chocolate Liquor: Unsweetened chocolate, consisting of cocoa solids and cocoa butter.

Christmas Pudding: A dark, heavy, steamed pudding made of dried and candied fruits, spices, beef suet, and crumbs.

Clear Flour: A tan-colored wheat flour made from the outer portion of the endosperm.

Coagulation: The process by which proteins become firm, usually when heated.

Cobbler: A fruit dessert similar to a pie but without a bottom crust.

Cocoa: The dry powder that remains after cocoa butter is pressed out of chocolate liquor.

Cocoa Butter: A white or yellowish fat found in natural chocolate.

Compote: Fruit cooked in a sugar syrup.

Confectioners' Sugar: Sucrose that is ground to a fine powder and mixed with a little cornstarch to prevent caking.

Coupe: A dessert consisting of one or two scoops of ice cream or sherbet placed in a dish or glass and topped with any of a number of syrups, fruits, toppings, and garnishes; a sundae.

Couverture: Natural, sweet chocolate containing no added fats other than natural cocoa butter; used for dipping, molding, coating, and similar purposes.

Creaming: The process of beating fat and sugar together to blend them uniformly and to incorporate air.

Creaming Method: A mixing method that begins with the blending of fat and sugar; used for cakes, cookies, and similar items.

Cream Pie: An unbaked pie containing a pastry-cream-type filling.

Cream Pudding: A boiled pudding made of milk, sugar, eggs, and starch.

Crème Anglaise *(krem awng glezz):* A light vanilla-flavored custard sauce made of milk, sugar, and egg yolks.

Crème Caramel: A custard baked in a mold lined with caramelized sugar, then unmolded.

Crêpe *(krepp):* A very thin French pancake, often served rolled around a filling.

Crêpes Suzette: French pancakes served in a sweet sauce flavored with orange.

Croissant *(krawh sawn):* A flaky, buttery yeast roll shaped like a crescent and made from a rolled-in dough.

Custard: A liquid that is thickened or set by the coagulation of egg protein.

Deci-: Prefix in the metric system meaning "one-tenth."

Dessert Syrup: A flavored sugar syrup used to flavor and moisten cakes and other desserts.

Devil's-Food Cake: A chocolate cake made with a high percentage of baking soda, which gives the cake a reddish color.

Diastase: Various enzymes, found in flour and in diastatic malt, that convert starch into sugar.

Disaccharide: A complex or "double" sugar such as sucrose.

Dobos Torte: A Hungarian cake made of seven thin layers filled with chocolate buttercream and topped with caramelized sugar.

Docking: Piercing or perforating pastry dough before baking in order to allow steam to escape and to avoid blistering.

Drained Weight: The weight of solid canned fruit after draining off the juice.

Dredge: To sprinkle thoroughly with sugar or another dry powder.

Drop Batter: A batter that is too thick to pour but will drop from a spoon in lumps.

Dutch Process Cocoa: Cocoa that has been processed with an alkali to reduce its acidity.

Eclair Paste: A paste or dough made of boiling water or milk, butter, flour, and eggs; used to make éclairs, cream puffs, and similar products.

Emulsion: A uniform mixture of two or more unmixable substances.

Endosperm: The starchy inner portion of grain kernels.

Extraction: The portion of the grain kernel that is separated into a particular grade of flour. Usually expressed as a percentage.

Fermentation: The process by which yeast changes carbohydrates into carbon dioxide gas and alcohol.

Foaming: The process of whipping eggs, with or without sugar, to incorporate air.

Fondant: A type of icing made of boiled sugar syrup that is agitated so that it crystallizes into a mass of extremely small, white crystals.

Frangipane: A type of almond-flavored cream.

French Pastry: A variety of small fancy cakes and other pastries, usually in single-portion sizes.

French-style Ice Cream: Ice cream containing egg yolks.

Fritter: A deep-fried item made of or coated with a batter or dough.

Frozen Mousse: A still-frozen dessert containing whipped cream.

Ganache: A rich cream made of sweet chocolate and heavy cream.

Gateau *(gah toe):* French word for "cake."

Gaufre *(go fr'):* French word for "waffle."

Gelatinization: The process by which starch granules absorb water and swell in size.

Genoise *(zhen wahz):* A sponge cake made with a batter containing melted butter.

Germ: The plant embryo portion of a grain kernel.

Glacé *(glah say):* (1) Glazed; coated with icing. (2) Frozen.

Glaze: (1) A shiny coating, such as a syrup, applied to a food. (2) To make a food shiny or glossy by coating it with a glaze or by browning it under a broiler or in a hot oven.

Gliadin: A protein in wheat flour that combines with another protein, glutenin, to form gluten.

Gluten: An elastic substance, formed from proteins present in wheat flours, that gives structure and strength to baked goods.

Glutenin: See **Gliadin.**

Gram: The basic unit of weight in the metric system; equal to about one-thirtieth of an ounce.

Granité *(grah nee tay):* A coarse, crystalline frozen dessert made of water, sugar, and fruit juice or another flavoring.

Gum Paste: A type of sugar paste or pastillage made with vegetable gum.

Hard Sauce: A flavored mixture of confectioners' sugar and butter; often served with steamed puddings.

Hard Wheat: Wheat high in protein.

Hearth Bread: A bread that is baked directly on the bottom of the oven, not in a pan.

Heavy Pack: A type of canned fruit or vegetable with very little added water or juice.

High-Ratio: (1) Term referring to cakes and cake formulas mixed by a special method and containing more sugar than flour. (2) The mixing method used for these cakes. (3) Term referring to certain specially formulated ingredients used in these cakes, such as shortening.

High-Ratio Method: See **Two-Stage Method.**

Homogenized Milk: Milk that has been processed so that the cream does not separate out.

Hydrogenation: A process that converts liquid oils to solid fats (shortenings) by chemically bonding hydrogen to the fat molecules.

Ice: A frozen dessert made of water, sugar, and fruit juice.

Ice Cream: A churn-frozen mixture of milk, cream, sugar, flavorings, and sometimes eggs.

Icing Comb: A plastic triangle with toothed or serrated edges; used for texturing icings.

Inversion: A chemical process in which a double sugar splits into two simple sugars.

Invert Sugar: A mixture of two simple sugars, dextrose and levulose, resulting from the breakdown of sucrose.

Italian Meringue: A meringue made by whipping a boiling syrup into egg whites.

Japonaise *(zhah po nez):* A baked meringue flavored with nuts.

Kernel Paste: A nut paste, similar to almond paste, made of apricot kernels and sugar.

Kilo-: Prefix in the metric system meaning "one thousand."

Kirsch: A clear alcoholic beverage distilled from cherries.

Kugelhopf: A type of rich, sweet bread or coffee cake usually made in a tube-type pan.

Ladyfinger: A small, dry, finger-shaped sponge cake or cookie.

Langue-de-Chat *(lahng duh shah):* A thin, crisp cookie. The French name means "cat's tongue," referring to the shape of the cookie.

Lean Dough: A dough that is low in fat and sugar.

Leavening: The production or incorporation of gases in a baked product to increase volume and to produce shape and texture.

Linzertorte: A tart made of raspberry jam and a short dough containing nuts and spices.

Liter: The basic unit of volume in the metric system; equal to slightly more than a quart.

Macaroon: A cookie made of eggs (usually whites) and almond paste or coconut.

Malt Syrup: A type of syrup containing maltose sugar, extracted from sprouted barley.

Marble: To partly mix two colors of cake batter or icing so that the colors are in decorative swirls.

Marron: French word for "chestnut."

Marshmallow: A light confection, icing, or filling made of meringue and gelatin (or other stabilizers).

Marzipan: A paste or confection made of almonds and sugar and often used for decorative work.

Meal: Coarsely ground grain.

Melba Sauce: A sweet sauce made of puréed raspberries and sometimes red currants.

Meringue: A thick, white foam made of whipped egg whites and sugar.

Meringue Chantilly *(shawn tee yee):* Baked meringue filled with whipped cream.

Meringue Glacée: Baked meringue filled with ice cream.

Meter: The basic unit of length in the metric system; slightly longer than one yard.

Milli-: Prefix in the metric system meaning "one-thousandth."

Modeling Chocolate: A thick paste made of chocolate and glucose, which can be molded by hand into decorative shapes.

Molasses: A heavy brown syrup made from sugar cane.

Monosaccharide: A simple or single sugar such as glucose and fructose.

Mousse: A soft or creamy dessert that is made light by the addition of whipped cream, egg whites, or both.

Napoleon: A dessert made of layers of puff pastry filled with pastry cream.

Net Weight: The weight of the total contents of a can or package.

No-Time Dough: A bread dough made with a large quantity of yeast and given no fermentation time except for a short rest after mixing.

Nougat: A mixture of caramelized sugar and almonds or other nuts, used in decorative work and as a confection and flavoring.

Old Dough: A dough that is overfermented.

One-Stage Method: A cookie mixing method in which all ingredients are added to the bowl at once.

Othello: A type of small (single-portion size), spherical sponge cake filled with cream and iced with fondant.

Oven Spring: The rapid rise of yeast goods in the oven due to the production and expansion of trapped gases caused by the oven heat.

Overrun: The increase in volume of ice cream or frozen desserts due to the incorporation of air while freezing.

Pain d'Epice *(pan day peece):* A type of gingerbread. French name means "spice bread."

Palmier *(palm yay):* A small pastry or petit four sec made of rolled, sugared puff pastry cut into slices and baked.

Parfait: (1) A type of sundae served in a tall, thin glass. (2) A still-frozen dessert made of egg yolks, syrup, and heavy cream.

Paris-Brest: A dessert consisting of a ring of baked éclair paste filled with cream.

Pasteurized: Heat-treated to kill bacteria that might cause disease or spoilage.

Pastillage: A sugar paste used for decorative work, which becomes very hard when dry.

Pastry Cream: A thick custard sauce containing eggs and starch.

Pastry Flour: A weak flour used for pastries and cookies.

Pâte à Choux *(pot ah shoo):* Eclair paste.

Pâte Feuilleté *(pot foo ya tay):* French name for puff pastry.

Peel: A flat wooden shovel used to place hearth breads in an oven and to remove them.

Petit Four: A delicate cake or pastry small enough to be eaten in one or two bites.

Petit Four Glacé: An iced or cream-filled petit four.

Petit Four Sec: An uniced or unfilled petit four ("sec" means "dry"), such as a small butter cookie or palmier.

Philadelphia-style Ice Cream: Ice cream containing no eggs.

Phyllo *(fee lo):* A paper-thin dough or pastry used to make strudels and various Middle Eastern and Greek desserts.

Piping Jelly: A transparent, sweet jelly used for decorating cakes.

Pithiviers *(pee tee vyay):* A cake made of puff pastry filled with almond cream.

Pot de Crème *(poh duh krem):* A rich baked custard.

Pour Batter: A batter that is liquid enough to pour.

Praline: A confection or flavoring made of nuts and caramelized sugar.

Press: A scaled piece of dough that is divided into small, equal units in a dough divider.

Profiterole: A small puff made of éclair paste. Often filled with ice cream and served with chocolate sauce.

Puff Pastry: A very light, flaky pastry made from a rolled-in dough and leavened by steam.

Pulled Sugar: Sugar that is boiled to the hard-crack stage, allowed to harden slightly, then pulled or stretched until it develops a pearly sheen.

Pullman Loaf: A long, rectangular loaf of bread.

Pumpernickel Flour: A coarse, flaky meal made from whole rye grains.

Punching: A method of expelling gases from fermented dough.

Purée: A food made into a smooth pulp, usually by being ground or forced through a sieve.

Retarding: Refrigerating a yeast dough to slow the fermentation.

Rice Condé: A thick, molded rice pudding, usually topped with fruit.

Rice Impératrice: A rich rice pudding containing whipped cream, candied fruits, and gelatin.

Rich Dough: A dough high in fat, sugar, and/or eggs.

Rolled-in Dough: Dough in which a fat has been incorporated in many layers by using a rolling and folding procedure.

Rounding: A method of molding a piece of dough into a round ball with a smooth surface or skin.

Royal Icing: A form of icing made of confectioners' sugar and egg whites; used for decorating.

Rye Blend: A mixture of rye flour and hard wheat flour.

Sabayon: A foamy dessert or sauce made of egg yolks whipped with wine or liqueur.

Sacristain *(sak ree stan):* A small pastry made of a twisted strip of puff paste coated with nuts and sugar.

St. Honoré: (1) A dessert made of a ring of cream puffs set on a short dough base and filled with a type of pastry cream. (2) The cream used to fill this dessert, made of pastry cream and whipped egg whites.

Savarin: A type of yeast bread or cake that is soaked in syrup.

Scaling: Weighing, usually of ingredients or of doughs or batters.

Scone: A type of biscuit or biscuitlike bread.

Scone Flour: A mixture of flour and baking powder that is used when very small quantities of baking powder are needed.

Sherbet: A frozen dessert made of water, sugar, fruit juice, and sometimes milk or cream.

Short: Having a high fat content, which makes the product (such as a cookie or pastry) very crumbly and tender.

Shortbread: A crisp cookie made of butter, sugar, and flour.

Shortening: (1) Any fat used in baking to tenderize the product by shortening gluten strands. (2) A white, tasteless, solid fat that has been formulated for baking or deep-frying.

Simple Syrup: A syrup consisting of sucrose and water in varying proportions.

Soft Wheat: Wheat low in protein.

Solid Pack: A type of canned fruit or vegetable with no water added.

Sorbet *(sor bay):* French word for "sherbet."

Soufflé: (1) A baked dish containing whipped egg whites, which cause the dish to rise during baking. (2) A still-frozen dessert made in a soufflé dish so that it resembles a baked soufflé.

Sourdough: (1) A yeast-type dough made with a sponge or starter that has fermented so long that it has become very sour or acidic. (2) A bread made with such a dough.

Sponge: A batter or dough of yeast, flour, and water that is allowed to ferment and is then mixed with more flour and other ingredients to make a bread dough.

Sponge Cake: A type of cake made by whipping eggs and sugar to a foam, then folding in flour.

Sponge Method: A cake mixing method based on whipped eggs and sugar.

Spun Sugar: Boiled sugar made into long, thin threads by dipping wires into the sugar syrup and waving them so that the sugar falls off in fine streams.

Staling: The change in texture and aroma of baked goods due to the loss of moisture by the starch granules.

Stollen: A type of sweet yeast bread with fruit.

Straight Flour: Flour made from the entire wheat kernel minus the bran and germ.

Streusel *(stroy sel):* A crumbly topping for baked goods, consisting of fat, sugar, and flour rubbed together.

Strong Flour: Flour with a high protein content.

Strudel: (1) A type of dough that is stretched until paper-thin. (2) A baked item consisting of a filling rolled up in a sheet of strudel dough or phyllo dough.

Sucrose: The chemical name for regular granulated sugar and confectioners' sugar.

Swiss Roll: A thin sponge cake layer spread with a filling and rolled up.

Syrup Pack: A type of canned fruit containing sugar syrup.

Tempering: The process of melting and cooling chocolate to specific temperatures in order to prepare it for dipping, coating, or molding.

Torte: German word for various types of cakes, usually layer cakes.

Tunneling: A condition of muffin products characterized by large, elongated holes; caused by overmixing.

Turntable: A pedestal with a flat, rotating top, used for holding cakes while they are being decorated.

Two-Stage Method: A cake mixing method, beginning with the blending of flour and high-ratio shortening, followed by the addition of liquids. Also called the high-ratio method.

Vacherin *(vah sher ran):* A crisp meringue shell filled with cream, fruits, or other items.

Wash: (1) A liquid brushed onto the surface of a product, usually before baking. (2) To apply such a liquid.

Water Pack: A type of canned fruit or vegetable containing the water used to process the item.

Weak Flour: Flour with a low protein content.

Whole Wheat Flour: Flour made by grinding the entire wheat kernel, including the bran and germ.

Young Dough: A dough that is underfermented.

Zabaglione: An Italian dessert or sauce made of whipped eggs yolks and Marsala wine.

Zest: The colored outer portion of the peel of citrus fruits.

INDEX